ISRAEL:
AS A PHOENIX ASCENDING

Touro University Press Books

Series Editor
MICHAEL A. SHMIDMAN, PhD (Touro College, New York)
SIMCHA FISHBANE, PhD (Touro College, New York)

ISRAEL:
AS A PHOENIX ASCENDING

Monty Noam Penkower

NEW YORK
2021

Copyright © Touro University Press, 2021
Library of Congress Cataloging-in-Publication Data

Names: Penkower, Monty Noam, 1942- author.
Title: Israel : as a phoenix ascending / Monty Noam Penkower.
Description: New York, NY : Touro University Press ; Brookline, MA : Academic Studies Press, 2021. | Series: Touro University Press books | Includes bibliographical references and index.
Identifiers: LCCN 2021016924 (print) | LCCN 2021016925 (ebook) | ISBN 9781644696743 (hardback) | ISBN 9781644696750 (paperback) | ISBN 9781644696767 (adobe pdf) | ISBN 9781644696774 (epub)
Subjects: LCSH: Zionism--History. | Israel--History. | Palestine--History.
Classification: LCC DS149 .P4236 2021 (print) | LCC DS149 (ebook) | DDC 956.9405--dc23
LC record available at https://lccn.loc.gov/2021016924
LC ebook record available at https://lccn.loc.gov/2021016925

Published by Touro University Press and Academic Studies Press.
Typeset, printed and distributed by Academic Studies Press.
ISBN 9781644696743 (hardback)
ISBN 9781644696750 (paperback)
ISBN 9781644696767 (adobe pdf)
ISBN 9781644696774 (epub)

Touro University Press
Michael A. Shmidman and Simcha Fishbane, Editors
320 West 31st Street, Fourth Floor,
New York, NY 10001, USA
tcpress@touro.edu

Book design by Kryon Publishing Services.
On the cover: Celebrating Yom Yerushalayim, the liberation of the Old City of Jerusalem by Israeli paratroopers on June 7, 1967, in front of the Western Wall.
Cover design by Ivan Grave.

Academic Studies Press
1577 Beacon Street
Brookline, MA 02446, USA
press@academicstudiespress.com
www.academicstudiespress.com

To Phyllis

Two are better off than one (*Ecclesiastes* 4:9)

Contents

Preface		vii
1	A Congress of Destiny	1
2	Jacob Robinson and the Rise of Israel	40
3	The Crusade to Save a Jewish State	81
4	Carl M. Eichelberger, Champion of the UN and of Israel's Rebirth	121
5	A Truce and Trusteeship for Palestine	169
6	Judah Leib Magnes: The Last Year	227
Index		271

Preface

Legend has it that the phoenix, a fabulous bird, which periodically regenerated itself, lived in Arabia. When it reached the end of its life at five hundred years, it burned itself on a pyre of flames, and from its ashes a new phoenix arose. As a sacred symbol in the Egyptian religion, beginning with the ancient *bennu* bird, the phoenix represented the sun, which dies each night and rises again each morning. According to Herodotus's account in the fifth century BCE, the residents of Heliopolis told a story that the bird, whose plumage was a brilliant scarlet and gold ("phoenix" is the Greek word for crimson, a deep purplish red) and which resembled an eagle came all the way from Arabia, bringing the ashes of the parent bird in a ball of myrrh to deposit them there in the Egyptian Temple of the Sun. The Persian *huma*, also known as the "bird of paradise," was similar to the Egyptian phoenix. The phoenix appeared on the coinage of the late Roman Empire as a symbol of the Eternal City; it also appealed to emergent Christianity and heraldry. Interpreted in Western literature as an allegory of death and resurrection, references to the phoenix surface, among other sources, in Ovid's *Metamorphoses*; Chaucer's *The Ploughman's Tale*; Shakespeare's *The Tempest*, *Timon of Athens*, and *Henry VI*; Byron's *English and Scotch Reviewers*; Shaw's *Cashel Byron's Profession*; and D.H. Lawrence's collection of posthumous writings, *Phoenix*. More recently, it appeared notably in Eudora Welty's short story "A Worn Path"; Edith Nesbit's *The Phoenix and the Carpet*; Ray Bradbury's *Fahrenheit 451*; and J. K. Rowling's *Harry Potter* series.[1]

The phoenix is present in Jewish sources as well. The book of *Job* includes the phrase "I shall multiply days as the *chol*" (29:18). A *midrash* on this biblical text speaks of a *chol* bird which lives for a thousand years, then dies a fiery red, and is later resurrected from its ashes. According to this *midrash*, Eve, upset after eating from the forbidden fruit in the

Garden of Eden and jealous of creatures still innocent, tempted all the other creatures of the garden to do the same. Only the *chol* (phoenix) resisted. As a reward, the phoenix was given eternal life, living in peace for a thousand years and then being reborn from an egg to continue to live in peace again, repeating the cycle eternally (*Bereishit Rabba* 19:5, with a similar version in *Midrash Shmuel* 12:2). Rabbi Shlomo Yitzhaki, better known as Rashi, commenting on the verse in the book of *Job*, declared that death has no power over the phoenix, "because it did not taste the fruit from the tree of knowledge." Rashi repeated this when the verse was cited in the Babylonian Talmud tractate *Sanhedrin* (108b) under the noun *avarshina* for *chol*. In another *midrash*, cited on that page in *Sanhedrin*, Noah found the *avarshina* sleeping in a hidden part of the ark. "Don't you want food?" he asked. The bird replied: "I saw that you were busy, and I decided not to burden you." Noah said: "May it be God's will that you will not die."[2]

Jacques Lipchitz, the first Cubist sculptor, placed a phoenix atop his last work of art. Toward the end of his life, he had been commissioned by the Hadassah Women's Zionist Organization of America to prepare a sculpture for the Hadassah Hospital on Mt. Scopus in Jerusalem. At his death in 1974, what Lipchitz called "The Tree of Life" had not been finished. Four years later, the statue was completed by Lipchitz's assistants, under the supervision of his widow. This towering artwork includes depictions of Noah, the sacrifice of Isaac with an angel restraining Abraham, the three Patriarchs, Moses and the burning bush, and a phoenix rising from the burning bush. Lipchitz's phoenix is holding the Ten Commandments. In the renowned artist's view, this sculpture represented the history of the Jewish people.[3]

Death and resurrection (*t'chiyat hameitim* in Hebrew), symbolized by the phoenix, is a core doctrine of traditional Jewish theology. Orthodox Jews believe that during the Messianic Age, the Holy Temple will be rebuilt in Jerusalem, the Jewish people ingathered from the far corners of the earth, and the bodies of the dead brought back to life and reunited with their souls. The rabbinic sages, simplifying the concept of bodily resurrection, posed this analogy: A tree, once alive with blossoms and fruit, full of the sap of life, stands cold and still in the winter. With the coming of spring, God resurrects nature, green leaves appear, and colorful fruits burst from their seed. The most dramatic portrayal of this bodily revival is depicted in the "Valley of Dry Bones" prophecy in chapter 37 of *Ezekiel*, where the "son of man" is told by the Lord God to say unto this "whole house of Israel": "Behold, I will open your graves, and cause you to come up out of your graves, O My people; and I will bring you into the Land of Israel."[4]

Arnold J. Toynbee, in his analysis of the rise and fall of twenty-six civilizations in the course of human history, did not think so. As early as 1934, in book one of the eventual twelve-volume *A Study of History* (1934–1961), his discussion of Jewish culture began with this sentence: "There remains the case where victims of religious discrimination represent an extinct society which only survives as a fossil. . . . By far the most notable is one of the fossil remnants of the Syriac Society, the Jews." A fossil, in scientific terms, retains its original shape and semblance without the breath of life; its very existence is an anachronism. Two years later, after meeting with Adolf Hitler, Toynbee told British Prime Minister Stanley Baldwin and the Foreign Office that he believed the German *Führer* was "sincere" in disclaiming any desire to conquer Europe. In the 1950s this erudite research professor of international history at the London School of Economics, a firm believer that history was shaped by spiritual forces, asserted that Jews and Judaism did not fit into any definition of nation, race, or religion. Jews were not a nation because they lived for centuries without a land and the Jewish people were scattered throughout the world. They were not a race because they accepted converts. Nor were they solely a religion, because Jews counted atheists among their numbers. According to Toynbee, the biblical Chosen People, following the spirit of their Hebrew God—provincial and exclusive—viewed its divine mission with arrogance, not as a burden of obligation to be carried with humility.[5]

The Jewish presence on earth for more than four thousand years notwithstanding, Toynbee was certain that the living Jewish historical drama had come to a halt with the rise of Christianity, when the Jewish people forfeited its political independence in the Land of Israel. With the Fifth and Twelfth Roman legions' crushing of the Bar Kokhba Revolt (132–135 CE), Jewish futurism died down, a people now relegated to the dustbin of history. Rather than what Joseph B. Soloveitchik, the prime rabbinic voice of Modern Orthodoxy, would later call "a developing, destiny-conscious Jewish nation," the British academic, whom many critics considered more of a Christian moralist than a historian, viewed the Jewish people as a mummified community that lived on in memories and thought in retrospective terms. Given Toynbee's conviction about the absence of continuity and creativity within that people, joined to his preference for some mystical, universal religious civilization rather than what he deemed "obsolete" national sovereignty, it is not surprising that he opposed the partition of Palestine into a Jewish and an Arab state.[6]

In Toynbee's view, delivered while addressing a Council on Foreign Relations select audience on April 20, 1948 in New York City, "a despotic government by a third party" in Palestine was "needed for an indefinite time to come," with the halting of Jewish immigration "at some definite time in the future." This air of pontification, coming but three weeks before the end of the British mandate for Palestine, rested upon Toynbee's belief that "the backgrounds of neither the Jews nor the Arabs contain the tradition of a national state." The Jews, "primarily a central or eastern European people," he described as "a penalized minority living in ghetto conditions," theirs "an autocratic tradition, and the political education they received was not therefore very good in gentile [sic] western terms." The Ottoman Empire's millet system, communities separated by religion while living side by side, had worked well for minorities in the Middle East, but the western institution of nationalism "poisoned the situation." The Balfour Declaration of 1917, when the British government pledged to facilitate "the establishment in Palestine of a national home for the Jewish people," "injected still another minority" into the area; Palestine was "sold twice over to two different peoples." Toynbee agreed on that occasion with the Jewish international banker Frank Altschul of Lazard Frères, who believed that "passionate Zionism might begin to fade in the United States" if the resettlement worldwide of Holocaust survivors were carried out on humanitarian grounds. Asked for a final comment, Toynbee replied that this was "certainly the first step in the solution of the problem and a realistic one."[7]

On January 18, 1955, Abba Eban, then Israel's ambassador to the United States, coined the phrase "The Toynbee Heresy" when addressing the Israel Institute at Yeshiva University. Toynbee's was the first broad, "vehement assault" by an historian on the entire Jewish historic process, he observed, commencing with the supersessionist theologian's belief that the birth of Christianity left the Jewish mission fulfilled and exhausted. Fanaticism was the one authentically Jewish idea, in Toynbee's eyes, not what Eban termed the "three circles" of Hebrew morality—individual conscience, social justice, and universal peace. For Toynbee, the reborn State of Israel, specifically the youth of its *kibbutzim*, was the abode of "a Janus figure, half American farmer-technician half Nazi sicarius." He portrayed Jewish survival (in the vein of many antisemites) as the result of an excessive ritualism and of financial astuteness, instead of an affirmative spiritual dedication. The tenacity with which world Jewry worked for the Restoration in Eretz Israel by mundane political and military means, usurping what Toynbee charged was the Divine Will to restore Israel to Palestine in the messianic era, invited the British professor's greatest indignation for its rejection of "political quietism." Omitting any thought of "international equity" allowing for Jewish independence and a far broader Arab emancipation, and neglecting the Zionist theme in the idealistic literature of Great Britain and the United States, Toynbee refused to accept that, alongside nine sovereign Arab states, it would be an "authentic tragedy" if the people which had suffered the Nazi onslaught most were not established in national freedom after the Holocaust. The State of Israel stands firm, Eban concluded, and "the pride of exaltation has come into the tents of Jacob everywhere."[8]

Toynbee's celebrity status, leading to an invitation to lecture at McGill University, in turn sparked a famous debate on January 31, 1961, with Israel's then Ambassador to Canada, the thirty-nine-year old Yaacov Herzog. Challenging the illustrious guest before a packed Hillel House and a live radio broadcast across the country on Toynbee's declaration in volume eight of his *A Study of History* that Israel's treatment of Arabs in its 1948 War of Independence was morally equivalent to, and actually an even greater tragedy than, the Nazis' "Final Solution of the Jewish Question," and on his repeated assertion that Judaism was a fossil, Herzog proudly defended his people's vitality and creativity over the centuries, and pressed the prominent intellectual to explain how Israel's actions during a war of self-defense against five invading Arab armies and the ensuing unfortunate uprooting of Arab communities could be compared to the Nazis' systematic slaughter of one people in Europe during World War II. Many nations had committed atrocities throughout history, including the massacres of Jewish civilians, Herzog noted, so why single out Israel's Jewish citizens—no more and no less guilty than any other modern state of crimes, and crimes that were condemned by wider Israeli society?

While declaring that "Israel has become defossilized as you can defrost a car," Toynbee continued to insist that, due to persecution and isolation, Jews had not played an influential role in much of history. Ultimately, after Toynbee acknowledged a continuous Jewish residence in the Land of Israel and "the continuous memory of the Jews for Palestine and for their return," Herzog invited the seventy-one-year-old guest to Israel, to witness its "defossilization" firsthand, Jewry's "passage through the Valley of Death down the ages" to where "we have come to life in our time." The leading Canadian dailies commended Herzog as the victor, Toynbee's wife overheard telling him afterwards, "I told you not to debate!"[9]

The "revival of the fossil remnant," eminent Hebrew University philosopher Natan Rotenstreich wrote one year after that Montreal stand-off, had in fact pitted traditional Jewish memory and self-understanding against the modern "return of the Jews to history" as conscious actors in the shaping of their own political destiny. European Jewry's quest for civil emancipation had witnessed over time a protracted struggle whose dialectic, in Rotenstreich's view, inevitably led to Zionism and the restoration of Jewish political sovereignty in the Land of Israel. Counter to Toynbee's "decreed petrification" of Zionism, a movement seen as the agent of a Syriac civilization and an "archaic" turning back to the past with the revival of the Hebrew language, Rotenstreich charged that this British historian ignored the special connection between the People of Israel and the Land of Israel. Writing in the spirit of an Arab nationalist, Toynbee's calumnious indictment equated Zionism with Nazi ideology as "naked Neo-Paganism," *Herrenvolk* racism, and a thirst for *Lebensraum*, "threatening the integrity and independence of the heart of the Arabic world." Nor did he mention the international background to Zionism's will and its triumph, most notably the UN decision on November 29, 1947, to partition Palestine into a Jewish and an Arab state. Jewish nationalism, Rotenstreich pointed out, aimed at not only liberation from political subjection, but the creation of the social basis for national life.[10]

Palestine's 600,000 Jews played the vital role in this denouement. Viewing Zionism as the legitimate movement of national return by an indigenous people intimately connected to that land for over three millennia and revolting against the litany of victimhood which had plagued Jewish history for centuries past, they had transformed the country from a primitive and corrupt Ottoman backwater into what they rightly called *hamedina baderekh* ("the state-in-the-making"). Its firm infrastructure already established in the 1930's, the *yishuv* (Palestinian Jewish community) continued to flourish economically during World War II, with impetus particularly given to industrial progress.[11] Its ongoing achievement thereafter under the aegis of the Jewish Agency for Palestine deeply impressed international investigatory committees and ultimately the required majority at the UN General Assembly, which endorsed a Jewish commonwealth in November 1947.

David Ben-Gurion carried the budding nation on the shoulders of his imagination and the wings of his vision. This phoenix rising on the shores of the Mediterranean due especially to his unwavering will to make the Jewish state a reality, the militant chairman of the Jewish Agency executive pressed forward with the feeling of *ein breira* ("we have no alternative"), a sense which captured the hearts of the collective entity whose back was to the wall in a war for national survival. Converted by the Holocaust, world Jewry, spearheaded by essential help from the five million Jews of America, embraced the Zionist thesis that their anomalous position as a homeless people had made the Jews expendable in the years of the *Shoah*, and that they, like all other peoples, had the right to national self-determination. A wave of support from non-Jews for realizing the Zionist dream mounted in these same three short years, dramatically confirmed by the fact that of the thirty-three countries which voted at the General Assembly for Jewish independence, a full thirteen were Latin American or Caribbean.

Compelled to fight and to win a war of liberation, the Jews of Palestine, with the heavy loss in battle of a full one percent of their population, proved to the Western world and a doubting Anglo-American military establishment that they were indeed a nation, not only a religious, or at best an ethnic, community as Prime Minister Clement Attlee, Foreign Secretary Ernest Bevin, and other mandarins, particularly in Britain, widely held at the time. Thus Ben-Gurion's last word to Richard Crossman, when the young, new Labourite MP for Coventry East and a member on the Anglo-American Committee of Inquiry on Palestine left that embattled country: "Remember we are not the Jews of the Bronx or Whitechapel. We are the ones who refused to live there. And if you want to get us right, imagine yourself out here, fighting for your national existence, and calculate that we shall behave as you would behave if you were in our situation."[12]

Preface

The chapters in this volume examine a few facets of the drama. I have briefly touched on them in the final part of my trilogy on the rise of the State of Israel between Hitler's coming to power in January 30, 1933, and Ben-Gurion's declaration of its independence on May 14, 1948, but remain convinced that they merit full exposition. Chapter 1 reviews the pivotal World Zionist Congress of December 1946, while Chapter 2 details the significant but overlooked input of Jacob Robinson in Israel's sovereign revival. One of American Jewry's crucial contributions in this saga, the raising of an incredible $50 million in early 1948 to save a Jewish state, is the subject of Chapter 3. The efforts of Carl Eichelberger, a forgotten champion of the UN and of Israel's rebirth, are discussed in Chapter 4. Chapter 5 investigates the efforts to create a truce and trusteeship for Palestine. Judah Leib Magnes's attempt in the last year of his life to create a federated state resting on Jewish-Arab community councils in Palestine (first published in *The American Jewish Archives* 71:11 [2019]), as well as the question of its relevance in today's Middle East, is analyzed in Chapter 6.

My late parents of cherished memory, Rabbi Murry S. Penkower and Lillian Stavisky Penkower, first taught me about what Yaacov Herzog called "the timeless identity of the Jew" over the generations. My family—children, grandchildren, siblings, and their spouses—is always a boundless joy. Professor Michael Popkin, former Touro College colleague and esteemed friend, again deserves my great thanks for reviewing the text for clarity. This volume of essays is dedicated to my dear wife, Phyllis Mayer. The new light of my life, she is a gifted listener and an exceptional companion. Her charm, her sensitivity, and her warmth make each day a wonder.

Some final thoughts: Having recently celebrated its seventy-second anniversary, Israel's population of 9.9 million (74.1 percent Jews and 21 percent Arabs) can justly point to its Jewish and democratic character, together with a record of extraordinary achievement in technology, the arts, and other fields. Biblical sources about the Lord's giving the Land of Canaan to Abraham and his descendants as an "everlasting holding" (*Genesis* 17:8), and the prophecies of Isaiah, Jeremiah, Ezekiel, and Amos concerning the Jewish revival there and the ingathering of the exiles, rang true for Truman, a devout Baptist, and still do for many, Jews and non-Jews alike. At the same time, the Jewish nation-state's right to exist, although having received 3.3 million immigrants from more than

150 countries since its establishment and sharing its advances for benefit worldwide, is yet denied by Toynbee's antisemitic successors, many of whom are also engaged in Holocaust denial, demonizing Jews and Israel as Nazis, employing modern guises of the Medieval blood libel and the *Protocols of the Elders of Zion*, and engaged in efforts to make the practice of Judaism in Europe impossible.[13]

Still, after two thousand years, the one people whose continuous historic memory—recalling the past but also identified with faith for the future—comprehends all the cycles of civilization which Toynbee recorded is reunited with its original inheritance. Indeed, Israel's remarkable victory in the Six-Day War of June 5–10, 1967, against the combined armed forces of Egypt, Jordan, and Syria, seemed to have changed even Toynbee. Coming twenty years after the famed historian had been featured on a *Time* magazine cover, he told Herzog that when he heard Israel's soldiers at the Western Wall on the British radio, "I began to grasp the nature of your bonds with this city of Jerusalem and this country." "How could you understand them?" asked Herzog, as the BBC broadcast in Hebrew the liberation of Judaism's holiest site and the soldiers did not speak English. "In such things, I have historical antennae," Toynbee replied. "I heard the voices and I understood."[14] Flaws are present, as would be the case with any living organism, but the State of Israel, the Third Jewish Commonwealth testimony to the greatest single collective affirmation of Jewish life in two millennia, remains committed to justice, compassion, and human dignity. Galvanizing Jews to renewed purpose, its message is crystalline clear: as a phoenix ascending of ancient legend, destruction can be followed by redemption, and even the Holocaust, the most unfathomable agony of all generations, by hope, renewal and national rebirth.

Jerusalem
Tish'a B'Av, 5780

Endnotes

1. W. Bridgwater and S. Kurtz, eds., "Phoenix," *The Columbia Encyclopedia*, 3rd ed. (New York, 1963), 1655; "Phoenix," *The Compact Edition of the Oxford English Dictionary*, vol. 2 (Oxford, 1971), 2156; Mary F. McDonald, "Phoenix Redivivus," *The Phoenix* 14:4 (Winter 1960): 187–206; R. van den Broek, *The Myth of the Phoenix According to Classical and Early Christian Sources*

(Leiden, 1972); *D. H. Lawrence Review* 5:3 (Fall 1972). It has been suggested that the name Phoenicia means "land of purple," since Tyrian purple (a dye derived from sea snails) may have been first used by the ancient Phoenicians of Tyre in today's Lebanon as early as 1570 BCE. On a related note, Phoenix, Arizona, was named such because it was a frontier station settled upon the ruins of a Native American site. The first European inhabitants decided to name their city in concurrence with the idea, recalling the legendary phoenix, that from the ruins of one city another was created.

2. Dan Pagis, "The Birth of Immortality: The Motif of the Phoenix in the Midrash and the Aggadah," in *The Hebrew Gymnasium in Jerusalem: Jubilee Book*, ed. Ch. Merchavia (Jerusalem, 1962), 74–90; M. R. Niehoff, "The Phoenix in Rabbinic Literature," *Harvard Theological Review* 89:3 (July 1996): 245–265; Nosson Slifkin, *Sacred Monsters: Mysterious and Mythical Creatures of Scripture, Talmud and Midrash* (Jerusalem, 2007), chap. 9. The equating of the *chol* and the phoenix is controversial, however, since the word *chol* has been translated as phoenix, sand, and palm tree in different versions. Other variants of the term cited in *Sanhedrin* 108b include *orshina*, *avrashina*, and *urshina*.

3. *Jewish Telegraphic Agency* (*JTA*), August 17, 1978. Rabbi Menachem Mendel Schneerson, the seventh Lubavitcher Rebbe, informed Lipchitz's widow that the *midrashic* commentary describes the *chol* as the phoenix—"hence the phoenix is a Jewish symbol." Dovid Zaklikowski, "How Jacques Lipchitz Found G-d: The Rabbi and the Sculptor," https://www.chabad.org/therebbe/article_cdo/aid/393257/jewish/How-Jacques-Lipchitz-Found-G-d.htm. Also see Zofja Ameisenowa and W. F. Mainland, "The Tree of Life in Jewish Iconography," Journal of the Warburg Institute 2:4 (April 1939): 326–345.

4. Maurice Lamm, *The Jewish Way in Death and Mourning* (New York, 1969). This spirit moved then Israeli Prime Minister Menahem Begin, when signing the Camp David Accords on September 17, 1978, with Egyptian President Anwar Sadat on the White House lawn, to recall learning as a young boy *Psalm 126*, with its divine promise of Zion's restoration, from his parents, who perished in the Holocaust along with the rest of his family from Brisk (Brest-Litovsk). Begin's father went to his death voicing his faith in God and singing the Zionist anthem *HaTikva*. And another example: Each year, the Jews of Rome keep the stubs of the candles that they use on Tish'a B'Av (the ninth day of Av), the annual fast day in the Jewish calendar marking the destruction of the two Holy Temples in Jerusalem (586 BCE. and 70 CE), as well as remembering other tragedies such as the martyrdom of the Rhineland Jewish communities during the First Crusade (1096), the burning of the Talmud in Paris (1242), the

expulsion of Jews from England (1290) and Spain (1492), and the Holocaust, in order to use them a few months later to light the menorah on Hanukah. Hanukah is the eight-day celebration, beginning on the twenty-fifth day of Kislev in the Jewish calendar, marking the rededication of the Holy Temple during the second century BCE, when the Jews had successfully risen against their Syrian-Greek oppressors of the Seleucid dynasty under Antiochus IV during the Maccabean Revolt. Herein lies the secret of Jewish endurance and Jewish eternity.

5. Arnold J. Toynbee, *A Study of History*, vol. 1 (Oxford, 1934), section 7, 135–139; William H. McNeill, *Arnold Toynbee: A Life* (Oxford, 1989), chap. 8; Francis Neilson, "Arnold Toynbee's 'Study of History,'" *The American Journal of Economics and Sociology* 14, supplement (April 1955): 1–77. In later printings, a footnote to the 1934 volume was appended which read "Mr. Toynbee wrote this part of the book before the Nazi persecution of the Jews opened a new and terrible chapter of the story. . . ." The subject was extensively debated, with input from critics, in his vol. 12, *Reconsiderations* (Oxford, 1961). After debates with Conservative rabbi Jacob B. Agus in particular, Toynbee changed his mind somewhat to declare that Judaism was a body of belief that had constantly reacted to philosophical challenges presented by Christianity and had continued to grow.

6. Joseph B. Soloveitchik, *Abraham's Journey* (New York, 2008), 5. Also see Franz Borkenau, "Toynbee's Judgment of the Jews: Where the Historian Misread History," Commentary 19 (May 1955): 421–427; Kenneth W. Thompson, "Toynbee's Approach to History Reviewed," Ethics 65:4 (July 1955): 287–303; Eliezer Berkovitz, *Judaism: Fossil or Ferment?* (New York, 1956); Maurice Samuel, *The Professor and the Fossil* (New York, 1956); Jacob L. Talmon, *The Nature of Jewish History—Its Universal Significance* (London, 1957); and Oskar K. Rabinowicz, *Arnold Toynbee on Judaism and Zionism: A Critique* (London, 1975). Also informative is the discussion between Toynbee and Solomon Zeitlin in the *Jewish Quarterly Review* 52:1 (July 1961): 1–34. For a recent critique of Toynbee's thought, see Jonathan Sacks, "On Creative Minorities," 2013 Erasmus Lecture, *First Things*, January 2014.

7. Discussion Group, April 20, 1948, Records of Groups, Box XV-B, Council on Foreign Relations Archives, New York City.

8. Abba Eban, "The Toynbee Heresy," in *Toynbee and History: Critical Essays and Reviews*, ed. Ashley Montagu (Boston, 1956), reprinted in *Israel Studies* 11:1 (Spring 2006): 91–107.

9. Yaacov Herzog, *A People That Dwells Alone*, ed. M. Louvish (London, 1975), 21–47; Yair Rosenberg, "When an Israeli Ambassador Debated a British

Historian on Israel's Legitimacy—and Won," *Tablet*, January 31, 2014. The equation of the Jewish State's treatment of Arabs in 1948 with the Nazi annihilation of European Jewry was first made in Arnold J. Toynbee, *A Study of History*, vol. 8 (London, 1954), 291n.304.

10. Nathan Rotenstreich, "The Revival of the Fossil Remnant: Or Toynbee and Jewish Nationalism," *Jewish Social Studies* 24:3 (July 1962): 131–143. Rotenstreich's last point had been articulated much earlier by Jean-Jacques Rousseau. In Book Four of *Emile* (1762), his treatise on the nature of education and on the nature of humankind, the great French philosophe of the Enlightenment wrote thus: "I shall never believe that I have seriously heard the arguments of the Jews until they have a free State, schools and universities, where they can speak and dispute without risk. Only then will we be able to know what they have to say." Israeli Prime Minister Binyamin Netanyahu cited Rousseau's observation when speaking at the Knesset special session in honor of the President of the French Republic, François Hollande, on November 18, 2013.

11. Monty Noam Penkower, *The Jews Were Expendable: Free World Diplomacy and the Holocaust* (Urbana, 1983); idem, *Palestine to Israel: Mandate to State, 1945–1948*, vol. 1, *Rebellion Launched, 1945–1946*, and vol. 2, *Into the International Arena, 1947–1948* (New York, 2019); Rafael Medoff, "'Hatikvah' in the Holocaust," *CT Jewish Ledger*, April 3, 2013.

12. Richard Crossman, *A Nation Reborn* (New York, 1960), 135n. On May 14, 1948, the day that Ben-Gurion declared Israel's independence, the British Dominions' Fortnightly Summary began: "The general feeling is that the British mandate on Palestine is ending on a note of exasperation, disappointment, and failure." Extract, May 14, 1948, RG 25, series A-12, vol. 2093, file AR35/1, pt. 6, Public Archives of Canada (PAC), Ottawa. One day later, Great Britain's Secretary of State for Commonwealth Relations informed Canada's foreign minister of the Attlee Cabinet's position that at the end of the mandate, and pending emergence of one or more states in Palestine to which international recognition could be accorded, Palestine would be a sort of *res nullius*. Noel-Baker to Pearson, May 15, 1948, MG 26, J4, vol. 397, PAC. The Latin term, from Roman law, signifies a thing which has no owner whether because never appropriated (as a wild animal), or because abandoned by its owner but acquirable by appropriation. His Majesty's Government delayed in granting *de facto* recognition of Israel until May 13, 1949, four months after the last of the Jews who had been detained in Cyprus camps for their attempting "illegal" immigration to Palestine reached the Land of Israel. London granted the Jewish State *de jure* recognition on April 28, 1950.

13. "Vital Statistics: Latest Population Statistics for Israel," (2020), https://www.jewishvirtuallibrary.org/latest-population-statistics-for-israel; Penkower, *Palestine to Israel: Mandate to State*, vol. 2, 725; Manfred Gerstenfeld, "Holocaust Inversion: The Portraying of Israel and Jews as Nazis," *Jerusalem Center for Public Affairs* 55 (April 2, 2007). Worthy of note is the German film *Phoenix* (2014), directed by Christian Petzold. It tells the story of a woman who, having survived Auschwitz with a reconstructed, disfigured face, returns to Berlin to seek out her gentile husband, a piano player who may or may not have betrayed her to the Nazis. While she naïvely wishes to return to a life or identity as it was before the war, her clear-eyed female friend looks to a future State of Israel as the hope for a haven for the Jewish people. Without recognizing his wife, the husband enlists her to play his wife in a bizarre hall-of-shattered-mirrors story that is as richly metaphorical as it is engrossing.

14. Herzog, *A People that Dwells Alone*, 53. It is telling that even Ben-Gurion, the supreme realist, had remarked in an interview with Edward R. Murrow on CBS-TV three weeks before his country's military victory in the 1956 Sinai Campaign against Egypt, "In Israel, in order to be a realist, you must believe in miracles." Ben-Gurion-Murrow interview, "Person to Person," CBS-TV, October 5, 1956.

1. A Congress of Destiny

The twenty-second World Zionist Congress, convening in Basle's Mustermesse convention hall, opened on December 9, 1946. Switzerland's largest exhibit center had witnessed the historic birth of political Zionism in 1897, when founder Theodor Herzl inaugurated the movement's official proceedings as a symbolic parliament in that same building. Seven years had elapsed since the last Congress, during which time an estimated six million Jews, more than one-third of world Jewry, had been systematically killed across the soil of Europe by Nazi Germany and collaborator nations in World War II.

The dais and the Zionist flag were draped in black. With 5,000 Jewish communities having been obliterated in what would be called the Holocaust, no longer were there substantial delegations from Germany, Hungary, Holland, Rumania, Czechoslovakia, or Belgium. Most notable of all was the absence of a delegation from Poland, the great center of Zionism during the period between the two World Wars.

The most tragic period in Jewish history had convinced many Jews to embrace the Zionist banner. No one could have foreseen that one nation would posit as the keystone of its worldview a murderous hatred of all Jews, nor that Christianity and the civilized world would abdicate their moral responsibility to aid a blameless people. Yet the basic tenet of Zionism had been rooted in the reality that the Jews' homelessness relegated this wandering community to the status of universal outsider, regular victim to exile and persecution because of the lack of national status. Jewish powerlessness had to undergo a radical transformation if Auschwitz-Birkenau were not to be repeated. In light of the *Shoah*'s ultimate confirmation of Zionist thought, it is not surprising that the proportion of Jews enrolled as subscribing Zionists had risen from

6.2 percent in 1939 to 19.6 percent in 1946, while world Zionist enrollment had more than doubled in absolute terms to well over two million.[1]

The United States had now replaced Poland as the chief Zionist hub, claiming almost half the world membership. The Americans' dynamic leader, fifty-three-year-old Rabbi Abba Hillel Silver of Cleveland's Reform Temple and president of the Zionist Organization of America (ZOA), championed a strong stand against the British mandatory power. The Palestinians, constituting the other major contingent at the Congress, found an equally forceful voice in sixty-year-old David Ben-Gurion, the doughty chairman of the Jewish Agency for Palestine Executive. Among the 385 delegates, these two groups would dominate the gathering.

The 68 American delegates, composed mostly of members from the ZOA and the women's Hadassah organization, were overwhelmingly committed to the General Zionist movement. (That movement came to the Congress with 123 delegates, the largest group, or 31.9 percent of the total.) Formally established a few months before the Congress, the World Confederation of General Zionists, not committed to a specific party, had divided earlier over accepting a British invitation to attend yet another round-table conference on Palestine and over a partition of that embattled country. Chaim Weizmann, president of the World Zionist Organization (WZO), favored both. Selig Brodetsky, Nahum Goldmann, Yitzhak Gruenbaum, Aliya Hadasha (the Palestinian association of Jewish immigrants from Germany and Central Europe), Barnett Janner, Louis E. Levinthal, Louis Lipsky, Stephen Wise, some Hadassah delegates led by Rose Halprin, and especially the British Zionist Federation all supported Weizmann's moderate stand. The more militant, anti-British element, led by Silver and his chief lieutenant and ZOA vice-president, Emanuel Neumann, along with World Confederation president Israel Goldstein, carried the day. Taken together, the US delegation offered a liberal-centrist viewpoint that commanded considerable weight.[2]

Party consciousness, by contrast, reflected the hotly contested political landscape of the *yishuv* (Palestinian Jewish community). Ben-Gurion's Mapai organization represented Socialist labor, weakened by the secession in 1944 of the more leftist Ahdut HaAvoda under Yitshak Tabenkin. HaShomer HaTsa'ir, generally pro-Weizmann but closer at the time to Soviet-inspired ideology, favored a binational Palestine. Mizrachi's program championed a state based on Orthodox Judaism.

The right-wing Revisionist Party, now rejoining the WZO after its secession in 1935, called for Jewish statehood on both sides of the Jordan River as first advocated by its late mentor, Vladimir Ze'ev Jabotinsky. In this embroiled arena of partisan allegiances, the General Zionist faction from Palestine was the weakest, having only four representatives present at the deliberations in Basle.[3]

A special status and place at the Congress was accorded delegates of the *Sh'eirit HaPleita*, "the surviving remnant" of European Jewry. Already on July 25, 1945, the first conference of the survivors of the Holocaust had demanded "the immediate establishment of a Jewish state in Palestine, the recognition of the Jewish people as an equal with all the Allied nations, and its inclusion in the peace conference." Led by David Trager, president of the Central Committee of Liberated Jews in the American zone of Germany and of the United Zionist Federation of Germany, a total of twelve survivors were chosen to attend this first World Zionist Congress after World War II. Accompanying them was Reuben Rubinstein, editor of the Central Committee's newspaper, *Unzer Veg* (Our Way). The Munich-based journalist expressed their overall stance when concluding a dispatch on December 8 thus:[4]

> To proclaim loudly, with pride and valor, the creation of a Jewish State is one task of the Congress. The second should be to put the proclamation into operation. This requires the election of leaders capable of mobilizing and activating all the folk forces and of fighting strongly for the upbuilding of the state.
>
> For us, the remnants of Israel in Europe, this convocation is a Congress of Destiny. The Sh'eirit HaPleita salutes the twenty-second Congress. From the depths of her limitless need and desolation, she sends to Basle the glowing words:
>
> May your hands be strengthened! We are waiting!

One of these survivors, listed as the single delegate of the General Zionist faction from Germany, was Kalman Sultanik. The thirty-year-old from Miechow, Poland, denied an immigration certificate to Palestine in the 1930's by the British mandatory power, had participated in underground activities against the Nazis as a member of HaNoar HaTsiyoni. After being transported to the Plaszów concentration camp and working for several months in Oskar Schindler's enamel factory outside Kraków, Sultanik was transferred to a labor camp working on tank production in Dresden. Following the Anglo-American bombing raids on that city in February 1945, he was sent with thousands of other prisoners on a lethal German "death march" to the Theresienstadt ghetto, where he was liberated by the Red Army on May 8, 1945. Active in Ihud, a Zionist organization seeking to prepare the remnant of Jews in Poland for *aliya* (immigration) to Eretz Israel by creating kibbutzim and then organizing clandestine passage (*bricha*) to American zones in Germany, Austria, and Italy, Sultanik set up the *kibbutz* (agricultural commune) in Kielce, and others subsequently in Katowice, Bytom, Zabrze, Giliwice, and different localities in Poland. By the end of that year, most of the kibbutzim youngsters had left for the US zone in Germany, and the Ihud executive sent him to head their kibbutzim there. Escaping possible arrest by the Polish and Soviet authorities for Ihud activities, Sultanik saw his efforts rewarded with election in August 1946 by Jews in the antiseptically named "Displaced Persons" (DP) camps as one of the younger delegates to the World Zionist Congress four months later.[5]

Well before the Congress, the American militant wing sought to strengthen Zionist opposition to British policy. After the mandatory authorities' arrest on Saturday morning, June 29, 1946, of more than 2,700 Palestine Jews and their extensive search for weapon caches in an effort to halt the united resistance movement (*tenuat hameri*) of the *yishuv*, what the latter termed "the Black Sabbath," Neumann received Silver's consent to invite Moshe Sneh to address the ZOA convention in October. The former head of the Hagana (the Jewish Agency's defense military organization), who was compelled to leave his post because of Weizmann's threat at resignation if resistance were not halted, Sneh had escaped the British dragnet, reached the like-minded Ben-Gurion in Paris, and would become director of the Jewish Agency's political department in Europe. Jacques Torczyner, sent by Neumann to confer with Sneh before the ZOA convention, reported home the impression that "politically he sees eye to eye with us" and "will try very hard to bring Silver and Ben-Gurion to the leadership of the movement." Sneh, like the Silverites, objected sharply to the Weizmann-Goldmann position, and, once in New York, advanced the idea of Weizmann retiring to the position of honorary president and the election of a presidium consisting of Silver, Ben-Gurion, and a third candidate, possibly Yehuda Leib Fishman (later Maimon) of the Mizrachi.[6]

Ben-Gurion maneuvered in his own fashion, seeking partners for a wide coalition of parties and opinions in the next Jewish Agency Executive. For the sake of Zionist unity, he had backed the Executive's readiness at meetings that August in Paris to discuss a proposal "for the establishment of a viable Jewish state in an adequate area of Palestine," a partition which the Silver camp denounced as a solution that would be regarded as the Zionist maximum demand and one that ran contrary to the May 1942 Biltmore Program calling for all of Western Palestine as a Jewish commonwealth. At the same time, Ben-Gurion sought to mollify the American Zionist chief, writing him on October 1 that eighty percent of Mapai favored an activist line that (unlike Weizmann) placed no faith in Britain's help towards the realization of Zionism. Shortly before the Congress, Ben-Gurion publicly declared what should be the program of "the Jewish state": the "chalutz [agricultural pioneer] spirit" for unimpeded immigration and development in Palestine, "a resistance . . . against every insult and act of discrimination," "the autonomous ordering of our lives," and "our equal membership in the family of nations."[7]

Ben-Gurion's rift with Weizmann surfaced in a closed meeting of Mapai, traditionally the single largest Zionist faction but now holding but 26.3 percent of the delegates, on the eve of the Congress. He reported that the Silverites' strength (with Silver refusing to serve in an Executive under Weizmann) mandated their inclusion in the Executive, and suggested an honorary presidency for the WZO avatar. He, Goldie Myerson (later Golda Meir), and the Palestinian activist majority sought to renew the *ma'avak* ("struggle") against Great Britain. Moderates, such as Palestinians Eliezer Kaplan and Yosef Sprinzak, thought this foolhardy, a position they, Pinhas Lubianiker (later Lavon), and a few others in Mapai had articulated before the Congress in a little pamphlet *L'Behinat HaDerekh* (Examining the Way). They urged that Weizmann was needed to lead the negotiations with London. Moshe Shertok (later Sharett), director of the Jewish Agency's political department, favored going to the proposed conference alongside a resumption of the *ma'avak* in Palestine. After Ben-Gurion threatened resignation, a compromise was finally achieved: support Weizmann at the Congress for the presidency;

confirm the Paris decision on partition; attend the London conference provided His Majesty's Government (HMG) would back partition or return to the pre-1937 Mandate; and let the movement's elected institutions decide the type of armed struggle to be undertaken.[8]

Weizmann's keynote speech to begin the Congress that afternoon, which he touched up in order to make a first draft by Isaiah Berlin and Aubrey (later Abba) Eban more pro-British, called for London to grant a Jewish state or return to the mandate years of generous immigration. Declaring that "six million graves testify to the consequences" of Jewry's homelessness and dispersion, with HMG guilty of maintaining the restrictive May 1939 White Paper on immigration and land purchase throughout the war, he thanked US President Harry S. Truman for urging the immediate admission of 100,000 Jews from Europe to Palestine. Zionism's impressive successes in the biblically covenanted Promised Land, he asserted, had brought "no injury" to the Arab peoples, who already possessed seven independent sovereignties. A Jewish state would offer the Arabs finality and the possibility of joint, beneficial economic ventures. Terrorism by dissident Jewish groups "contaminates our banner" and is "barren of all advantage." Absorbing 1.25 million survivors, the "overwhelming majority of whom are desperately pressing against the gates of Palestine," constituted our generation's first problem. The 600,000-strong *yishuv* stood as testimony to Zionist faith and achievement. He concluded with a prayer that the movement would achieve peace and freedom in Zion reborn.[9]

The packed hall of 2,000 gave these words a cold reception. Confidante Blanche Dugdale's diary recorded that Weizmann's ninety-minute speech in English, read with considerable difficulty by the half-blind leader of seventy-three years, had "no fire." He made the impression "of an aged and tired man," reported the local American consul general to Washington. Goldmann told Weizmann the same day that a vote taken that night would be against going to the London conference. Not attending, Weizmann retorted, would render Zionism "dead as a constructive political movement for a generation." Ben-Gurion's first speech the next evening, even longer, fared little better. The Executive chairman chose to gloss over their fundamental differences, his equivocation leaving listeners bewildered. While announcing that the Agency Executive still adhered to the Biltmore Program, he also stated that it would be amenable to discuss partition if proposed.

"This has put the cat among the pigeons with a vengeance," Dugdale observed.[10]

Silver, on the other hand, lost little time in throwing down the gauntlet. He extolled the wartime contribution of American Zionists in the face of Washington's "mere benevolent neutrality," beginning with the 1943 American Jewish Conference's open advocacy of a Jewish commonwealth in Palestine; the introduction in 1944 of pro-Zionist planks in the presidential election platforms of the two major parties; the adoption by forty state legislatures of resolutions favoring Jewish sovereignty in Palestine; and the role played in having the Truman administration's retreat from support of the July 1946 British cantonization plan for the country's future. Clearly opposing partition, Silver called on December 10 for "a forthright, aggressive and militant line of action," pledging that "a loyal and disciplined army of followers" was ready to give of themselves, their substance, their loyalty, and their devotion "to the cause of a free Israel in a free land of Israel."[11]

The general debate, with plenary sessions that would last for five days, began on December 11 with a scathing attack by Emanuel Neumann on the partition proposal suggested in August by the Jewish Agency Executive. That experimental plan was a "costly" failure, he opined, which the British did not accept even as the Arabs remained "inflexible." The proposed London conference, endorsed by the US State Department, should not be attended, inasmuch as Britain was currently "waging a war against the most vital interests of the Jewish people." The *yishuv* itself must determine the forms that resistance should take and the point to which it should be carried, and we would extend to "responsible elements" in the Palestinian Jewish community (notably the Hagana's effort to bring hundreds of thousands of Jews into the country "by all means") "every moral and material assistance." This decisive period demanded new leadership and methods, Neumann ended, which should be "inspired by the Dunkerque spirit" rather than "slide down the slippery road which leads to Vichy."[12]

All the while, the various delegations held special meetings to hammer out their particular stand. While the Canadian and American Poale Zion delegates voted to support the partition formula of the Executive, Mizrachi's Meir Berlin (an anti-Weizmannite then in

Palestine) urged, against Yehuda Fishman, an unmodified rejection of partition in any form. Moshe Shapiro of HaPo'el HaMizrachi (Mizrachi's labor wing) proposed a platform that returned to the Agency's 1937 demand for a Jewish state. The Revisionists stuck to their right-wing principles and resolved to fight for the election of a Jewish government-in-exile. In a meeting of all laborite delegates, Ben-Gurion pleaded for a united front, but HaShomer HaTsa'ir delegates emphasized that they could not join with Mapai unless he came out clearly against partition and pledge that he would not favor unconditional participation in the London talks. Others present criticized Goldmann's presentation of the partition proposal to the US Government in August, but Ben-Gurion pointed out that it was undertaken with the authorization of the Agency Executive, and he believed that that mission was a success. In an interview with the Yiddish New York newspaper *Der Tog*, Sneh stated that Ben-Gurion's abandoning the partition formula in his first speech had come round to Silver's viewpoint; laborite Berl Locker, the Agency's Palestinian representative in London, insisted *per contra* that Ben-Gurion still adhered to the Executive's partition plan.[13]

The sharp cleavages that rent the various factions surfaced on the first and second days of the general debate. Meir Grossman of the American United Revisionists urged the removal of the present Executive, and demanded "a Jewish state within the historic boundaries of Palestine, based on a Jewish majority." Ya'akov Hazan of HaShomer HaTsa'ir appealed for a binational state under the supervision of the United States, Great Britain, and the Soviet Union, claiming that a Jewish commonwealth could not be established with an Arab majority (currently more than 1.2 million) in the country. Countering that argument, Ahdut HaAvoda's Tabenkin attacked both partition and Britain, which he declared was opposed to a Jewish national homeland "because it wants to use Palestine as a military base for a third World War." Felix Rosenbleuth (later Pinhas Rosen) of Aliya Hadasha urged cooperation with England, fearing that resistance would bring British military retaliation which might spell the destruction of the *yishuv*; Shertok declared that the choice for the Jewish people lay between independence and integration into a sphere of influence.

Hadassah president Judith Epstein took issue with Weizmann's hope for a continuation of the mandate as indulging in "a false dream." Resistance in Palestine she considered necessary, along with "uncertified

Jewish immigration" into Palestine without qualification. Since, however, neither Weizmann nor Ben-Gurion prior to the general debate had elucidated the partition proposal or defended the action of the Executive meeting at Paris, she followed the Hadassah delegation's decision not to be the first speaker to openly champion that proposal.[14]

David Trager, the unchallenged spokesman for the survivors' delegation, had his moment in the spotlight on the last session of the morning of December 12. Speaking in Yiddish, he asserted that the *Sh'eirit HaPleita*, having passed through "the seven gates of hell of the bestial Nazi regime," resolved that world Jewry had no existence or right to existence without "a land of its own." Neighbors across Europe's blood-soaked landscape had aided in the murder process that constituted the Nazis' methodical "Final Solution of the Jewish Question" while an apathetic free world stood by. Only a Jewish state in Eretz Israel remains our sole hope, he averred, a sentiment confirmed by ninety-eight percent of the Jews in Displaced Persons camps when replying to questionnaires for the United Nations' Relief and Rehabilitation Administration.

Trager went on. Despite the progressive deterioration of conditions in the many months since liberation, which appeared "like a conspiracy to paralyze our will," the survivors were "alert and alive." The thriving of cultural, educational, and productive programs in their camps, along with the highest birth rate in the Western world, stood testimony to the vigor and tenacity of the more than 200,000 survivors in DP camps in Germany, Austria, and Italy. We have an unflinching faith, he pronounced, that the time of a mass exodus to our homeland will eventually come. Every road to Palestine is legal. No matter what happens, we will stand firm as long as it may be necessary, until the gates of Palestine are opened. "Having but one choice—*aliya* or *kelaya* [annihilation]," he concluded, "we have decided to live and create in an independent and free Jewish state in Eretz Israel." A thunderous ovation throughout the cavernous hall greeted Trager's forthright statement.[15]

Nahum Goldmann's address that afternoon, also in Yiddish, posed an able rebuttal to Neumann. Zionism must be ready for "tragic concessions," he began, to break the political deadlock, get rid of foreign rule, and open Palestine's gates to large immigration. The Executive sought from those assembled not blanket powers, but permission to negotiate at the London conference in order to ascertain what proposals could achieve success. The Biltmore Program had been drawn up on the assumption that millions of Jews would be transferred to Palestine after the war, and no one then had thought of partition. After the Holocaust, and at a time when HMG had rejected the entry of 100,000 survivors recommended in April by the Anglo-American Committee of Inquiry on Palestine, partition was the only way out. If no solution were found, Britain would place the issue before the United Nations, leading to further delay and deterioration of the situation of Jews both in Europe and in Palestine. Time worked for the Arabs in the meantime, he warned, and the belief that the United States might endanger its relations with Britain over Jewish rights was delusional.[16]

To attend the London conference or not, that issue found Shertok (who approved Goldmann's presentation) and Sneh on opposite sides of the fence. Participation offered a new opportunity "for putting up a fight for our future," the Agency's political director declared, the delegation to make it clear that any discussion of the July 1946 Morrison-Grady cantonization or federalization plan, giving the *yishuv* autonomy over only seventeen percent of Western Palestine, "was out of the question." Since England had "decided against Zionism," Sneh countered on December 13, the time had come to end the movement's "almost exclusive dependence," represented at its best by Weizmann for almost thirty years, on that imperial power; Sneh did not rule out cooperation with the United States, the Soviet Union, and even the Arabs. He favored "responsible resistance," the means of the Irgun and Stern group right-wing dissidents not justifying the end.[17]

Besides the outspoken Sneh, who saw no British and Arab adversary ready to accept either Goldmann's or Hazan's compromise solutions, the anti-partition camp found champions across the political spectrum. Aryeh Altman of the Palestine Revisionists charged that Weizmann symbolized "the defeat of Zionism, which has brought it to the present crisis." Yitzhak Riftin of HaShomer HaTsa'ir, supported by colleague Mordekhai Ben-Tov, stated that "peaceful life and development in Palestine is not possible without an agreement with the Arabs on the basis of bi-nationalism." Ya'akov Zerubavel of Poale Zion's left wing called for a Jewish commonwealth with a socialist orientation; Aharon Zisling of Ahdut HaAvoda stated that only an undivided Palestine could solve the Jewish problem. Bernard Joseph (later Dov Yosef), the Agency's legal advisor who had been imprisoned on the "Black Sabbath" for more than four months along with Shertok and others in Latrun prison, endorsed the Biltmore Program in light of HMG's rejection of the partition plan.[18]

In addition to members of the Executive who took part in the Paris meetings that August, partition had capable advocates as well. Yitshak Gruenbaum, against his former pupil Sneh, favored going to the London conference because "Britain must report on Palestine's future status to the United Nations." He insisted that more than 1,000,000 Jews had to be in Palestine as "a solid basis" for a Jewish state in the whole country. If given all of that territory now, the *yishuv* could not defend it. Hayim Greenberg, leader of the American Poale Zion and editor of *Jewish Frontier*, argued that partition offered the only practical solution. Two alternatives—the forced evacuation of the largest part of the Palestinian Arab population to another country or a Jewish state with Jews granted the status of a legislative majority—were obviously not feasible. The third, the immigration of at least one million Jews, required either assistance from London or the United Nations, but this would not be forthcoming. In some historical situations, Greenberg observed, the part is sometimes greater than the whole, and all Palestine without a Jewish majority was less than a partitioned Palestine under Jewish control. The Jews would have to put up a fight even to secure partition, he cautioned.[19]

As the general debate wound down, it became increasingly apparent that the questions of Weizmann's leadership, partition, and attendance at the London conference were inextricably entwined. Elected head of the sixteen-member presidium of the Congress by a vote of 191 to 48 (Mizrachi's delegates abstaining), Weizmann informed his inner circle that he could not work in a future Executive with either Silver or Ben-Gurion. Most of the American delegation, Louis Lipsky had informed Dugdale, was bound to Silver's policy of a break with Britain. In Mapai's ranks, a majority favored Weizmann's return as WZO president, but the party's public resolution on December 13 stated that the incoming Executive should participate in the London talks only on the basis of the Biltmore Program. Brodetsky, a member of the Agency Executive office in London's 77 Great Russell St. off Bloomsbury Square, announced that he favored Jewish resistance, strongly urged participation in the London talks, but disclaimed any preference for partition as an ideal solution of the Palestine problem.[20] Could these patent difficulties be resolved to the satisfaction of the twenty-second World Zionist Congress?

The last day of the debate on December 15 witnessed an impassioned if brief address by Lipsky, an American member of the Agency Executive and attendee at the Paris meetings, who declared that refusal to participate in the London conference "might set in motion forces which would jeopardize everything achieved by the Zionist movement in the last fifty years." Sharply disagreeing with William Ziff, American Revisionist leader, and especially Sneh, he insisted that joining the talks would help retain the support of the US government. Participation in the conference did not rule out continued Zionist efforts towards Palestine. Nor was it evident, as Sneh assumed, that London had decided "for all of time to liquidate its Zionist obligation." A cautious stance, Lipsky concluded, rather than Sneh's gamble that the *yishuv*'s armed strength and the political influence of the United States could force HMG to give the Jews the whole of Palestine, should be the Congress's approach vis-à-vis this last opportunity to test Britain's intentions.[21]

The same day, according to a *Jewish Telegraphic Agency (JTA)* report, the General Zionist delegation from the United States voted to support Weizmann for honorary president of the WZO, and called for a three-man presidium to replace him as president. Neumann found a receptive audience for the proposal in Mizrachi circles. The proposal had first been made to Silver by Sneh two months earlier and suggested by Ben-Gurion to the Mapai faction just prior to the Congress's opening. By now Ben-Gurion had come around to thinking this the best solution, and he sent his wife, Paula, to Dugdale, begging her to influence Weizmann to accept. "I would not wish my worst enemy a greater curse than responsibility without power," she responded. Mapai, Dugdale was told by a well-informed associate, would probably offer Weizmann the presidency, but on condition that he not conduct the London conference if Mapai participated. "It is an age of pygmies, and so much squalor, spite, folly and party hatreds seem to be devouring Zionist politics. I think the day is done for Zionists of the old school," she wrote in his diary just before leaving Basle for vacation in Dorset.[22]

Yet intrigue and rumors that would not down about these clandestine developments revived Weizmann, who refused the offer of honorary president and made a last, gallant attempt to win the Congress over. With Ben-Gurion declaring that he would no longer cooperate with Weizmann, setting in motion the Executive chairman's press behind the scenes (against his own party's support for Weizmann's election to the

WZO presidency) for an activist policy, the battle of ideology would be joined on December 16. At last the conferees would hear the two titans deliver clear, if contrasting, expositions of their views for the future of the movement.

Addresses by Silver and Wise, opponents during World War II for leadership of American Zionism, preceded this dramatic denouement. Reminding his listeners that, as chairman of the Political Commission at the world Zionist meeting in August 1945 in London, he had helped to draft the resolution which stated that Palestine, "undivided and undiminished," must be constituted as a Jewish state, Silver reiterated his objections to partition and to attendance at the London conference. "Sound and just proposals" will be made to us "sooner or later," he was certain, but in the meantime we must "strengthen the *yishuv*'s power of resistance." The seventy-two-year-old Wise challenged "what seems to be the ZOA's "dogmatic line." As one of the few surviving friends and disciples of Herzl, he urged attendance at the London conference, and through it to lay the foundations of a Jewish state in Palestine: "To do less is to repudiate Jewish history, to deny the hopes, the tears, the prayers of the Jewish People; and that we will not do."[23]

Ben-Gurion immediately followed in Yiddish with an unqualified declaration that he would only join an activist-oriented Executive, one committed to an armed conflict against the mandatory. A "Jewish state in Palestine," he stated, means the immigration to that country of the first 1,000,000 Jews in the shortest possible time. Aside from the Biltmore Program's call for the whole of Palestine, the Executive chairman suggested as a personal thought not a population transfer of Arabs and Jews, but giving Transjordan part of the thickly Arab-populated "triangle" of western Palestine, with the Jews obtaining the under-populated area in eastern Palestine round the Dead Sea stretching to the Gulf of Aqaba. Still another possibility would be negotiations in London to create a Jewish state in a diminished area on condition that it would be large enough "to give immigration and colonization adequate to solve the Jewish question." Whatever the options, the movement had to embrace the principle of resistance, he declared, but, unlike Silver and Neumann relying on the *yishuv* to decide, this was to be "the resistance of the whole Jewish people." Throughout history, Jews had always "stood up, weak against strong, few against many." "We have no choice," Ben-Gurion ended, "but a homeland and independence in Palestine."[24]

Speaking in Yiddish and without notes, interspersing in his unique fashion humor with gravitas, Weizmann quickly drew swords with Ben-Gurion. The true and only path, he declared, was not struggle against Britain, but—as the Executive had adopted in the past—an evolving stand of sustained negotiation. We chose not to "embark on adventures" but to go the way of building, "of laying brick upon brick and stone upon stone." The recent creation of eleven new settlements in the Negev will have greater significance than a hundred speeches about resistance, he insisted, "especially when the speeches are made in Washington and New York while the resistance shall take place in Jerusalem or Tel-Aviv. We must stop being intoxicated by our own words."

His voice now stronger than anyone remembered it in a long time, Weizmann pressed on. Our proposal for partition had not been rejected, he asserted; it took account of the large Arab population and the 10,000 square miles that made up Palestine's small area, reminding his enthralled audience with delicate scorn that "you can swim more easily in the sea than in a bath tub." There was no shame in failure, his grandfather having said that "he never made any mistakes in the letters that he did not write." Speaking as a professional chemist, Weizmann insisted that "we must go on experimenting," until "trial and error" brought success. Resistance, championed by Ben-Gurion, is "indivisible. You may know where you begin, but you cannot know where it will end." A great and important leader of American Jewry said that that community would provide moral, financial, and political support to the solidarity with the *yishuv*'s determination struggle, he continued, but that is "precious little when you send others to the barricades, if you send others to pit themselves against British guns and tanks."

"This is demagoguery," Neumann shouted, refusing to accept the bitter allusion to Silver, who (like Neumann) had merely expressed his moral solidarity with the yishuv's determination to resist Great Britain's anti-Zionist policy. Stung, incorrectly hearing it as "demagogue!," and unable to see who had hurled such a challenge that had never happened to him in any Congress, Weizmann interrupted his speech. Removing his glasses, he launched with a passionate fury into a defense of his decades-long contribution in having gone through all the "agonies of Zionist work": "The person who hurled that epithet at me should know that every farm-house and stable in Nahalal, and every building down to the tiniest workshop in Tel-Aviv or Haifa, contains a drop of my life's blood."

At this point the assembly rose almost to a man (Silver and Neumann, the Revisionists, and Mizrachi did not) in a spontaneous burst of cheering. Stirred, Weizmann went on:

> It is for this reason that I have the right, I feel, to speak as I do now, and no impolite interjections will put me off: for I believe that what I tell you is the truth. That sometimes makes painful hearing but you will listen to me. I warn you once again against taking short cuts, against following false prophets and will-o-the-wisp generalizations, and against the falsification of historical facts.

Recalling that his misfortune had always been to point out the movement's weaknesses and lay emphasis on its "sober side," Weizmann pointed out that the British understandably responded with the "Black Sabbath" two weeks after the Hagana had blown up ten of the eleven bridges connecting Palestine to its neighbors. Sneh's assumption that Zionists had to look for "new orientations" because they could expect nothing from Britain was not a certainty. Weizmann feared that terrorism would become the "dominating feature of Jewish life," and he warned the movement of the urgent need to "check the growth of this cancer." Referencing the cultural Zionist philosopher Ahad Ha'Am (Asher Ginsberg), his ideological mentor, Weizmann characterized Sneh's arguments as "this is not the way"; they lead us "along false paths."

Concluding the most eloquent speech of his long Congress career, the frail tribune exhorted his rapt audience not to rely on miracles, resembling his grandmother, who, having two sons with different vocations requiring rain and frost, prayed that the Almighty send down a "warm frost." They had to continue with Zionist work. The securing of redemption through means which did not accord with "Jewish morale, ethics, or history" meant the worshiping of "false gods" and endangering everything that the Zionist enterprise had built up over a few decades. Reread the prophets Isaiah, Jeremiah, and Ezekiel, he urged. They knew that "Zion will be redeemed through righteousness"—and not by any other means.[25]

Rows of applauding delegates stood "in awe and contrition" as Weizmann painfully groped his way to the street, Eban recalled years later, but the half-hour address may have cost him the WZO presidency. Many, elated by his soaring words and appreciative of his singular half-century contribution to the successes of Zionism in the past, thought his consistent stance too moderate for the future of the movement. Shertok privately deemed Weizmann's delivery "exceptional," but already the day afterwards Dugdale heard some criticisms: "too flippant—much too pro-British, etc.," Ben-Gurion suggesting that his rival almost seemed to excuse the arrests of "Black Sabbath." With the battle in full sway, a very calm Weizmann determined to have his own policy "or pull right out." Reporting for the *New York Times*, Julian Meltzer quoted a reliable source that Weizmann was "not inclined to be a figurehead for anyone else's policy." On December 18, Dugdale still thought that on the fundamental issue of attending the London conference (which also meant backing Weizmann for the presidency) the delegates "will not commit suicide."[26]

The same day, Ben-Gurion addressed the Congress's closed political committee. Speaking freely, he warned of the dangers that the *yishuv* would face in the not distant future from the armies of surrounding Arab states, aided by England and other countries. To this end, a city in the southern Negev region had to be established as soon as possible, to become a center of Jewish strength. Resistance meant opposition to the White Paper, and to do as much as possible to frustrate its implementation. That included far larger, safer boats for "illegal" immigration (*aliya bet*), since that effort (termed *ha'apala*, or "ascent" to Eretz Israel) by *ma'apilim* Holocaust survivors constituted the primary battle in the struggle for the Jewish right to reach Eretz Israel. Murder of innocents by dissident groups was forbidden in all circumstances, and this principle demanded strict national discipline. Attending the London conference was not morally possible if we knew that the British and the Arabs would object even to partition. There were fewer reasons to rely on HMG than in the past, Ben-Gurion observed, consequently requiring the movement to broaden its efforts in the Arab world and at the United Nations, including the Soviet Union, and to strive at strengthening the *yishuv* in order that it achieve independence.[27]

Appearing before the Congress's steering committee one day later, Ben-Gurion made it clear that, while having great esteem for Weizmann, he could not serve in an Executive governed by the elder statesman and his basic political stance. That line, as Weizmann had made clear in his final address, ruled out *ma'avak*. The *yishuv* and the survivors represented the "dynamic factor" in Zionism, in Ben-Gurion's view, with *aliya*—never to cease as part of the struggle against Great Britian—and defense at the center of the *yishuv*'s survival. He would serve in a wide coalition, in which the Americans would occupy a prominent place, that embraced this program. If Weizmann did not become honorary president, then the presidency itself, a symbolic position, should be left vacant. The chairmanship of the Executive, which he would again accept if offered, would speak for Zionism in the future. As late as December 20, with the Congress still not having chosen a new Executive, Ben-Gurion pressed steering committee head Zalman Rubashov (later Shazar) to decide conclusively and without delay if Weizmann had a majority or not to form an Executive. Otherwise, he warned, the movement faced "ruin."[28]

A peaceful end to the riven Congress appeared nowhere in sight. The majority in Mapai did not wish to yield on either Weizmann or Ben-Gurion, but the latter insisted that his faction first decide on its political stand. The *JTA* reported on a party compromise whereby a temporary truce in the *ma'avak* would be in effect during the London conference, whereas the labor newspaper *Davar* quoted Weizmann telling the General Zionists that his presidency rested on partition, an end to armed resistance, and unconditional participation at the London talks. He did not budge from this stance when speaking to the Political Committee, reported both the *JTA* and prominent journalist Azriel Carlebach in *Yediot Acharonot*. On that occasion, as described in the Yiddish *Morning Journal*, Weizmann exclaimed "I am no Petain and will not accept [an] honorary presidency to cover up things with which I do not agree." Once having proposed partition, a Hadassah delegate recalled, he asserted that the movement could not go back to the Biltmore Program, "which ended in Latrun." A three-day session of the World Union of Po'alei Zion voted 90 to 30 to support Weizmann for the presidency if he agreed to their resolution that the Executive would attend the London conference on the basis of a British pledge that HMG would implement the terms of the mandate or agree to the principle of a Jewish state. Shertok and Kaplan presented this to Weizmann, who replied that he would need time to consider the ramifications of the resolution, and would also have to take into consideration the composition of the Executive to be elected by the Congress.

Seeking the support of Hazan's party, Weizmann had confidant Meyer Weisgal offer a new proposal that the Congress decide to appoint a temporary Executive for three months, a broad coalition ranging from the Revisionists to HaShomer HaTsa'ir. That body would participate in the London conference. If the talks failed, a new Congress would take up the issue afresh. In Weizmann's view, given the current "no exit" situation, this offered some "last opening of hope." Ben-Gurion, Weisgal added, had not yet given an answer to this suggestion. Hazan immediately responded that his people would not sit in an Executive with Revisionists. Secondly, he asked, would each political faction in that Executive be free to express its stance at the conference? Weisgal assumed that to be the case, but Hazan was not certain that this intermediary would determine the matter.

Ultimately, Ben-Gurion's call in the Mapai party meeting for the immediate end to the White Paper, together with the "assurance of the creation of the Jewish State" or no going to London, triumphed against Kaplan's pro-Weizmann stance by a vote of 77 to 55. At the same time, a vote of 89 to 30 (with many laborite members anxious about Silver's coming to power) supported Weizmann for the WZO presidency. Even as Ben-Gurion walked out in protest, the pro-Silver group within the General Zionist camp worked assiduously against Weizmann's return as president. Sneh, for his part, continued pushing for the bestowal of an honorary presidency upon the Anglophile Weizmann.[29]

Silver's appointment as head of the Political Committee, in recognition of his status and the strong following which he had at the Congress, proved crucial to the outcome. Neumann, chosen by him to chair the subcommittee on resolutions, intended to follow the precedent set by the most recent ZOA convention. Its resolution, which he had drafted, had demanded a Jewish state in Palestine, and stated that any project (no mention was made of partition) offered by HMG or any other government leading to that objective would be seriously considered. The General Zionists, aided by Mizrachi and the Revisionists, secured a narrow majority of 21:16 not to attend the London conference "under present conditions"; if the situation improved, the resolution added, the Va'ad HaPo'el HaTsiyoni (Zionist Actions Committee) would decide on participation. The minority resolution, brought by Mapai and strengthened by Hadassah's Marian Greenberg, allowed the Executive to participate in the London talks with the understanding that its negotiations would be based on the consideration of the early establishment of a Jewish state. Now it was up to the Congress delegates.[30]

At a late hour on December 23, Weizmann appeared before the full Congress and apologized that it would be difficult for him to participate this time in the lengthy deliberations that would undoubtedly follow. "If I have said harsh things to anyone," said he in a short farewell, "I did not intend to hurt." He thanked his supporters, and wished his opponents that if they assumed responsibility they would succeed "to open a new era of great activity." "The Jewish people, especially those waiting in the camps," he told the assembled, "look to you to open the gates. I thank you all." This time, all the delegates without exception stood. They escorted him out of the hall with resounding ovations and the singing of the Zionist anthem, *HaTikva*. If the Congress decided against going to the London talks, Weizmann told his political advisors that same evening, he would not seek the WZO presidency. From there, Weizmann traveled to London and the quiet of his apartment in the city's Dorchester Hotel.[31]

Shortly after midnight, Silver began reading out the political resolutions. These continued into the next day, and lasted for almost fourteen hours. Resolution No. 1 reasserting the Biltmore Program was adopted. Terrorism, as opposed to resistance that sought to avoid the shedding of innocent blood (Shertok's formulation), was condemned with a fair degree of unanimity; the Revisionists' attempt to water down the resolution was badly defeated. A move by Weizmann's supporters in Mapai to vote first on the presidency before the London Conference resolution, assuming that the majority which would vote for Weizmann would then agree to participate at those talks, was defeated by a coalition composed of Ahdut HaAvoda, General Zionists, Mizrachi, and the Revisionists. Hearing the crucial resolution about the London conference, Myerson then proposed that the decision be left to the new Executive. This last-minute motion failed by a vote of 167 to 158, and with a vote at 3 a.m. of 171 (the group fashioned by the Silverites, Ben-Gurion, and Sneh plus Ahdut HaAvoda-Poale Zion) to 154 (Mapai, General Zionists who supported Weizmann, and Aliya Hadasha) the Congress chose not to go to the conference under "the present circumstances."[32]

A few factors explain why Mapai and Weizmann failed at this decisive juncture. Only 350 out of 585 delegates voted. In addition, some of the Mizrachi delegates, under Ben-Gurion''s influence, had shifted from their declared support of Mapai's position. The Revisionists's compact bloc of 45 votes was thrown into the balance against every attempt to steer a moderate course. Finally, although supporting Weizmann for the presidency, HaShomer HaTsa'ir voted separately for its own resolution against participation in the London Conference "as this would inevitably lead to being caught in the trap of partition." Paradoxically, the 25 votes cast as a bloc for their separate resolution by these firm advocates of a binational state in Palestine denied Weizmann triumph.[33]

Hearing the bitter news in London, Weizmann understandably saw this as tantamount to a vote of no confidence in him, and he announced the removal of his candidacy for the WZO presidency. Realizing that the majority which voted against the London talks would vote against a new proposal for Weizmann as president, to be joined by many within their own party, Mapai leaders decided not to bring that question to the full Congress. At 4:30 in the afternoon of December 24, party member David Remez announced as chairman of the proceedings that the conditions of time, place, and the absence of a list of candidates for the new Executive meant that elections to that body could not take place before the Congress finished its deliberations. Instead, he advised that the Va'ad HaPo'el be given full authority to establish the Executive. By a vote of 116 to 37, with 65 abstentions, this was passed.[34]

To extended applause, Ben-Gurion closed the twenty-second World Zionist Congress a half hour later by suggesting that the failure to complete its work regarding an Executive might well symbolize the fracture of world Jewry. The *Shoah* also shattered the Zionist movement, he observed, for the void created by the annihilation of European Jewry, Zionism's prime reservoir of support, was not filled. After sending the Congress's greetings to "the great Jew of our generation"—Dr. Chaim Weizmann, Ben-Gurion declared that the movement's first obligation was to bring the survivors to the *moledet* (homeland). Its second was to redeem the land, and then to augment the *yishuv*'s strength. Finally, its supporters had to fight for world Jewry's rights as a sovereign nation. We all hope, he concluded, that we will be privileged to meet at the next Congress in "Zion liberated." Expressing a personal feeling that this was "the Congress of the difficult birth pangs of the Messiah, of the Jewish state in Eretz Israel," Remez then uttered the prayer chanted at the close of the Yom Kippur and Passover services: "Next Year in Jerusalem!" With that traditional cry, the Congress came to an end.[35]

Even as the Va'ad HaPo'el began its sessions on December 25, with Wise the "senior member" (rather than chairman) of a special fifteen-member presidium to decide whether to attend the London conference, the majority in Mapai and the General Zionists under Silver each sought behind the scenes to achieve an Executive of their political persuasion. Sneh acted as a mediator between Ben-Gurion and Silver, while the pro-Weizmann camp sought (unsuccessfully) an alliance with HaShomer HaTsa'ir, some anti-Silver General Zionists, and Mizrachi to bring Weizmann back as president. Two days later, *Yediot Acharonot* editor-in-chief Carlebach reported that the former group had arrived at a compromise: Ben-Gurion would return as Executive Chairman in Jerusalem, Silver head the Jewish Agency in the United States, and Shertok direct the Agency's political delegation in Washington, D.C. HaShomer HaTsa'ir's newspaper, *Mishmar*, added the same day that the Mapai majority still called for Weizmann's inclusion in the new Executive unconditionally, while Mizrachi and the General Zionists also raised the possibility that the two parties would set up a narrow-based coalition for the Executive.[36]

When Remez began the Va'ad HaPo'el's last meeting on December 28 by declaring that its members had to decide on the WZO presidency, Sneh proposed that no president be elected this time. Otherwise, he explained, difficult efforts that had been made to form a new Executive would fail. To strengthen this suggestion, Silver announced that he and his faction could not serve in a coalition if Weizmann were chosen president. Ben-Gurion quickly followed with a proposal that the presidency be left vacant for the next two years, then surprised all with the assertion that he would only be part of an Executive with "an activist majority" which had to include the General Zionists. The hope of Kaplan, whom Ben-Gurion attacked in thunderous terms, shouting "It is I who am the head of the Party," and seventy percent of his Mapai colleagues to split the General Zionists in order to attain support for Weizmann's candidacy met with failure. Sneh's maneuver forced Va'ad HaPo'el chairman Sprinzak to bring the far-reaching proposal to a vote as the first order of business. Since that received approval by 47 to 32, the question of Weizmann's election to the presidency never even came up for discussion. Supporting Sneh's motion were the General Zionists minus Brodetsky and Goldmann, Mizrachi, the Revisionists, and Ahdut Ha'Avoda. Opposed were Mapai, HaShomer HaTsa'ir, and Aliya Hadasha. Immediately thereafter, Silver announced that the new Executive would be composed of General Zionists, Mapai, and Mizrachi.[37]

The very next day, meeting in the Three Kings Hotel with the strength of a nineteen-member coalition that was chosen by the Va'ad

HaPo'el, Ben-Gurion was reelected chairman of the Jewish Agency Executive and took on the crucial security portfolio. The General Zionists included Silver, Neumann, Sneh, Brodetsky, Goldmann, Gruenbaum (vice-chairman), Halprin, and the Palestinian Peretz Bernstein, editor of the party's newspaper, *HaBoker*. Mapai had seven members: Ben-Gurion, Greenberg, Locker, Myerson (the new director of the Political Department), Kaplan, Shertok, and past immigration director Eliyahu Dobkin. Mizrachi-Poale Mizrachi was represented by Fishman, Ze'ev Gold, Moshe Shapira, and S. Z. Shragai. This represented the same party distribution as in the outgoing Executive, with largely the same personnel. Moreover, with fourteen of the Executive in favor of participating in the London conference and in favor of partition, Hadassah's Epstein thought this a "Pyrrhic victory" that went counter to the American Zionists' opposition on both issues. To satisfy Silver's demand, the independently minded Goldmann would be transferred from activity in Washington to Europe.

Ben-Gurion urged his colleagues to focus on three issues. These included pursuing relations with Great Britain, encouraging immigration, and exploring the status of the *yishuv*'s security. After assigning portfolios and declaring that we will ask Weizmann's help because "he is the first man in Zionism," Ben-Gurion urged that his associates bring to the movement not the Congress's "bitter" elements, but the same "inner strength" that existed in Zionism. If the situation did not improve, he concluded, "we will know to stand in the battle."[38]

As the year 1946 drew to its close, Ben-Gurion issued a manifesto for *Davar*'s readers which surveyed the proceedings of the Congress and projected Zionism's urgent needs. The destruction of European Jewry; the split in labor's ranks; the division in American Zionist circles between Wise and Silver—all made their mark in the difficult weeks that had just passed in Basle. Despite these manifestations, however, the "eternity" of the Zionist *chalutz* spirit in Eretz Israel had overcome "the bitter and at times depressing" deliberations. As a result, the overall results of the Congress were "positive and welcome," both internally and even more so externally. His desire for a wide coalition, to include HaShomer HaTsa'ir and Ahdut Ha'Avoda, did not materialize, but the new Executive insured our three principles: *chalutziyut*, *ma'avak*, and *medina* (statehood). Burdened with heavy responsibility, the movement and the Executive had to unite for more *ha'apala*, settlement, and security; reinforce our self-sufficiency; increase efforts to gain world sympathy; renew cooperation with England; seek mutual understanding and treaty with the Arab world; and work towards "the speedy establishment of *medinat haYehudim*" (the State of the Jews). On that note, Ben-Gurion left for a brief trip to London and then flew on to Palestine.[39]

Having lost the reins, Weizmann fell into what Eban characterized as "an aggrieved solitude," venting his depression and bitterness in private letters. Although telling US Associate Supreme Court Justice Felix Frankfurter that he had "emerged from the slime of the Basle Congress on to firm ground," and now could focus on scientific work at his newly inaugurated Institute in Rehovot, Weizmann thought of creating a progressive moderate group so as not to "leave the filibustering Rabbi of Cleveland as the sole representative of our Movement." In reply to another correspondent, he found "deplorable" that the Congress, "standing as it did by the graves of six million of our people, was not yet inspired to forget or rise above petty intrigue and personal ambition." Ben-Gurion, who "behaved liked a real contortionist," he classed as one of the unclean animals in the "Noah's Ark" that housed the new coalition. He could not accept Kaplan, Locker, and Goldmann remaining in the Executive, and broke with Shertok upon hearing that the long-time favored disciple had abstained in the critical vote to attend the London conference.[40]

Weizmann's defenders pilloried the outcome. Richard Crossman, leftist Labour Party spokesman who, as a member of the Anglo-American Committee, fell under the spell of his charismatic charm and embraced the cause of partition, feared that "Silver Imperialism" would lead to the "complete ruin" of Zionist aspirations. "I saw with dismay the evil machinations of Silver at Basle and the ungenerous decision of the Americans there," leading Labourite theoretician Harold Laski wrote privately to Weizmann. "Not a single speech, with the notable exception of Dr. Weizmann's, revealed any greatness of personality or of moral and intellectual understanding," declared former *Jüdische Rundschau* editor Robert Weltsch, who bemoaned the fact that the Congress, "still upholding the tradition of a messianism living in a world of dreams," did not like Weizmann's facts. The proceedings, opined Britain's Harold Nicholson, "have not been such as to fill the British friends of Jewry with either satisfaction or hope." Speaking at the Free Synagogue in New York City, Wise, to Weizmann's satisfaction, characterized the

Congress as "a disaster," "unworthy," "tragic in its inadequacy in relation to a great hour," and he withdrew from all office in the "present imperiling regime" of the ZOA.[41]

What took place at the Congress was not "an American maneuver or an American achievement," Silver properly countered in his report to fellow congregants in Cleveland. A "widespread feeling" did exist, he observed, that Weizmann, symbol of a line and policy which failed and which had to be abandoned, should not be re-elected WZO president. Some seventy percent of the General Zionists, joined by Revisionists, Mizrachi, and almost all of Ahdut Ha'Avoda, voted accordingly. The Congress, as evident in the final resolutions, disagreed with Weizmann's stand against all forms of resistance and his insistence on going to the London talks without conditions. The movement, Silver averred, is determined "that there should be no more retreat," and the Congress repudiated the leadership "which did not represent this dynamic and militant mood." In the heart of those assembled, including the delegation of Holocaust survivors present at the Congress, he concluded, there is "a determined resolve finally and at long last" that there should be established "a Jewish state in the land of Israel for all Jews who want to or who have to go there."[42]

The British Colonial and Foreign Office Secretaries quickly grasped this seismic shift in Zionist orientation. In a memorandum dated December 31, 1946, Arthur Creech Jones summarized for Ernest Bevin their agreement that the Congress results underscored the victory of "the extremist group headed by Dr. Silver": Weizmann's overthrow and "the collapse of the moderate leaders"; the refusal of the Jews to attend the Palestine Conference "in existing circumstances"; and the fact that Zionists would accept no arrangement in Palestine, "which involves further trusteeship or tutelage of any kind." HMG had failed to avert these results, and could now anticipate "a recrudescence of terrorism and an increase of violence and disorder"; an increase in illegal immigration, as well as in Arab disturbances; more resentment on the part of the British forces in Palestine facing various forms of "violence and humiliation" without being able to take "adequate countermeasures"; and the "heavy strain," under which the Civil Administration in Palestine was already laboring, "reaching a breaking point." HMG could either impose a policy on Palestine or refer the whole question to the United Nations. With the first option riddled with difficulties, the second—"no easy course particularly if Palestine is the scene of violence and civil conflict"—appeared the only alternative.[43]

Ben-Gurion confirmed this overall assessment, telling Creech Jones two days later that Weizmann had been defeated because of his "one-sided cooperation" with HMG and his "blind trust" in Britain. The *yishuv* as a whole, he went on, considered itself a nation and wanted to be allies, not subjects. Their requirements included free immigration, cultivation of all Palestinian soil excluding that actually cultivated by the Arabs, and the ability to "shape their own life as freely as any other free people." The recent resolution adopted at Basle did not bar informal, exploratory talks in London, and the Agency Executive was not bound to any formula. The Jews felt they had no choice in approving illegal immigration, which he did not regard as illegal. Almost all sections at the Congress took the view that as long as HMG ruled Palestine it was bound by the mandate. If for any reason, he ended, the government could not carry it out, "there must be a Jewish state."[44]

While also informing Palestine's Chief Secretary that the Congress sought some conciliatory move on Britain's part to "end the tension," Myerson expressed to the Mapai secretariat her disappointment with the Basle deliberations. European Jewry was absent and the American delegates acted with a heavy hand, with Hadassah falling under Silver's dominating influence, at a time when the labor movement had suffered a serious division. Mapai lacked unity, unlike the other parties. With Weizmann not criticizing the "Black Sabbath" or championing *aliya*, proving that he could not head the WZO any longer, his accepting the honorary presidency and agreeing to head the delegation to the London Conference would have "saved" the Congress. Aside from Mapai, the "decisive majority" of delegates clearly did not want him as president. Mapai saw no point in seeking an endorsement for the partition resolution of the August meetings in Paris because the British had not given us a positive reply; Ben-Gurion's endorsement of the Biltmore Program, its major principle subsequently reaffirmed in the ultimate resolution "that Palestine be established as a Jewish Commonwealth integrated in the structure of the democratic world," at the same time that the Paris resolution on partition was an "open secret," did not add "strength and grace." In sum, Shertok's successor as the new director of the Agency's Political Department felt that there was "not much good" that could be said about the Congress just past.[45]

The reaction of the *yishuv* press to the Congress varied, but skepticism as to its effectiveness was fairly general. While regretting that Weizmann was not reelected, *Davar* felt that the next Executive assured "a large measure for action," and Mizrachi's *HaTzofeh* declared that the decision not to choose a president was aimed against Weizmann's political system. On the other hand, the Revisionist party's *HaMashkif*, whose Congress delegates were furious not to have been included in the new Executive, assumed that that body would strive for partition, a surrender that might lead to "a Jewish civil war." Declaring that the increase of the rightists' strength signaled that "progressive Zionism has been betrayed," *Mishmar* of HaShomer HaTsa'ir agreed that the Executive would "plunge full steam ahead towards partition." The most moderate *Ha'Aretz* warned that the creation of a "new quasi-independent center of gravity in Washington increases inordinately the obstacles in the path of concentrated and united policy." The rightist *HaBoker* doubted that the Executive could achieve unity on a specific political program, and expressed disappointment at the fact that the most important posts in the Executive were retained by the Laborites.[46]

In point of fact, the discussions and the outcome of those tumultuous weeks in Basle marked a watershed in Zionist history. The *London Times*' leading editorial gloomily headlined "disturbing new phase Zionist movement," while a review in the *Nation* spoke of "the crisis of Zionism." Yet by 1946, in Michael Cohen's phrase, Weizmann had become "a political anachronism," unable to sever the British connection. Look at the result of Weizmann's favoring a policy of negotiation with HMG over the past thirty years, penned confidant Richard Meinertzhagen in his diary after dinner with Weizmann at the Dorchester Hotel: "Sabotage, broken promises and exasperation." Girding for inevitable war, the *yishuv* needed the militancy of Ben-Gurion, his hand strengthened by the equally determined Silver. Weizmann never recovered from the loss of leadership, although he would play a significant role when later called upon by the movement to intervene on its behalf.[47]

The divided labor parties of the *yishuv*, limited to 153 delegates at the Congress, lost crucial ground to the 222 delegates who composed the right-wing factions of the General Zionists, Mizrachi, and the Revisionists. The collapse of the British Empire; the victory of the Zionist militant camp; the failure of informal talks in London with the Zionist delegation headed by Ben-Gurion; ongoing attacks against the mandatory authorities by the Irgun and Stern group in Palestine; Arab intransigence; increased pro-Zionist sentiment in the United States and elsewhere—all, taken together, ultimately persuaded Bevin and his cabinet colleagues in February 1947 to turn the conundrum over to the United Nations. The new WZO Executive, the real differences in ideology between laborite Ben-Gurion and anti-socialist Silver notwithstanding, ably shepherded the Zionist case until victory with the rebirth of the State of Israel. What transpired in the international arena until May 14, 1948 gave validity, in retrospect, to the appellation coined by *Unzer Weg*'s editor on behalf of the survivors on the eve of the Congress—"a Congress of Destiny."

The contribution of the *Sh'eirit HaPleita* to the unfolding drama proved to be of seminal importance. Other than Trager's impassioned address on behalf of European Jewry after the Holocaust, many speakers at the Congress made reference to the survivors' plight as conclusive proof of the urgent need for a Jewish commonwealth. Their singular travail in World War II triggered Truman's repeated request of Prime Minister Clement Attlee to admit 100,000 survivors to Palestine. The US President's personal envoy, Earl Harrison, had come to a similar conclusion in August 1945 when meeting with survivors in Germany and Austria. Britain's refusal to depart significantly from the 1939 White Paper, granting as of October 1945 the entry of but 1,500 Jewish refugees a month, brought the *yishuv*'s three underground movements to launch a united resistance campaign against the mandatory. The Anglo-American Committee on Inquiry came to better appreciate the pull of Palestine after visiting DP camps a few months later. HMG's decision in August 1946 to deport *aliya bet* passengers to Cyprus, followed by media coverage of the armed seizure of these rickety vessels crammed with more than 70,000 men, women, and children, brought the sympathy and support of world public opinion to the Zionist cause, and demonstrated the resolve of the Jewish people to pursue independence.

Ben-Gurion, in particular, understood early on the significance of the determined *ma'apilim* in the struggle against British domination. After visiting Zeilsheim "displaced persons" camp in October 1945, where ecstatic hundreds greeted him with singing *HaTikva* and received his assurance that Palestine's Jewish community would bring them home to a warm welcome, the Jewish Agency Executive chairman wrote in his diary that the *yishuv* and its strength, America, and the DP camps in Germany constituted Zionism's three major forces. He repeated this theme often, most notably at the Congress in Basle. Under Ben-Gurion's leadership, the survivors would be forged into a "political factor" of prime importance.[48]

The *Sh'eirit HaPleita*'s "decisive leadership groups," to use Ze'ev Mankowitz's characterization, were fully wedded to the call of Jewish sovereignty in Eretz Israel as the only hope for European Jewry's rescue and rehabilitation. Philip Bernstein, advisor on Jewish affairs to US military forces in postwar Europe, had reported to the World Zionist Congress that 192,000 "displaced" Jews in the American zones of Germany and Austria, of whom he estimated that eighty to ninety percent were sustained by the hope of emigration to Eretz Israel, faced a breakdown in morale unless a quick decision concerning their future was made. *Yishuv* emissaries in Europe then present at the Congress made the same point at a meeting with Mapai's delegation in insisting on increased *aliya bet* activity. Kalman Sultanik and the eleven other delegates from the DP camps returned there with renewed vigor, determined to wield the "surviving remnant" into a cohesive unit committed to *aliya* by all means without delay. The success in doing so of the Central Committee of Liberated Jews in Germany, to which Sultanik was elected not long after the Congress ended, made a great impression on the United Nations Special Committee on Palestine (UNSCOP).[49]

In August 1947, during a meeting of the General Zionist Council in Zurich, the WZO Executive invited the presidium of the Central Committee to meet with the leaders of the Jewish Agency. Those who came, provided with travel documents by the Hagana, included Trager, Sultanik, Abrasha Blumovicz, Leon Retter, and their colleagues Piekarz and Yaffe. Shertok lavished praise on the Committee's political achievements, particularly in connection with the UNSCOP members' visits to the DP camps and the struggle of *Exodus 1947* the previous July. The British Royal Navy's boarding outside of Palestine's territorial waters of that dilapidated Hagana ship, crammed with 4,554 survivors, and the ensuing fierce battle in which three Jews were killed and 100 wounded, had gained the Zionists' widespread sympathy worldwide; "this is the best testimony of all" commented the Yugoslav UNSCOP member when witnessing the survivors' arrival at the port of Haifa. Bevin's subsequent decision to have the refugees forcibly returned to their port of embarkation in Germany, hoping thereby to stem the tide of "illegal" immigration, after they refused France's offer of hospitality, gained Zionists an invaluable public relations victory.

Years later, Sultanik recalled vividly Ben-Gurion's words to the Central Committee members at their meeting in Zurich:

> Nothing in the world can stop our people to go forward by the thousands, by sea and by air, both above and underground, to reach their goal—their homeland in Israel. I want you, the leaders of *Sh'eirit HaPleita*, to make sure when the United Nations deliberates about the partition resolution, our people by the hundreds of thousands should proceed towards their destination—to Israel.

Pointing with his finger, Ben-Gurion went on to proclaim before his visitors: "We will see the creation of a reborn Jewish State."[50] A half year later, his prediction came true, and a scattered, shattered people re-entered history.

Once the State of Israel came into being, Kalman Sultanik, one of the participants in the 1946 World Zionist Congress, entered a life of service to the cause of Zionist fulfillment. With the support of his wife for sixty-five years, Bronia neé Burganski, a Kovno-born survivor of the Nazi "death march" of Jews from the Stutthof concentration camp to Chinov near Danzig (Gdańsk), he shifted his energies to become an organization executive.[51] In 1948, Sultanik assumed the position of secretary general of the World Confederation of General Zionists, and then of director four years later when he moved with his family from Israel to New York at the invitation of Confederation president Israel Goldstein, chairing it for more than half a century. In that capacity, he served as steward for the ongoing partnership between the World Confederation and Hadassah. In 1956 Sultanik was elected a member of the Zionist General Council. He joined the WZO Executive in 1972, and continued to serve for four decades, representing the World Confederation of United Zionists. In 1975, he succeeded Emanuel Neumann as chairman of the Theodor Herzl Foundation in New York, publisher of the *Herzl Yearbook* and the monthly *Midstream* magazine. Twenty years later, due to the efforts of Aryeh Dulzin, then chairing the WZO Executive, and under Sultanik's chairmanship of the Herzl Press, the *New Encyclopedia of Zionism and Israel* appeared in two volumes.

In 1984, thanks to Sultanik's initiative, the Confederation House opened its doors as a center for ethnic music and poetry. Overlooking the Old City walls of Jerusalem, the restored historic three-story building on Emile Botta Street brings together the multifarious communities that live in the capital of the State of Israel, using the universal languages of music and art as a bridge connecting different peoples. Some of those showcased include Jewish, Arabic, Ethiopian, Ashkenazi, and Sephardi cultural heritages. A venue for theatre shows, poetry recitations, and concerts, the house also sponsors the national Poets Festival every year in Metula and hosts the Jerusalem International Oud Festival and On the Wings of the Raga Indian Music Days. Groups from across the world are invited to perform as well. The Confederation House also has its own theatre ensemble, Hullegeb (Amharic for "open to all"), whose work draws from both the Ethiopian, Israeli, and Western traditions. Appreciating Sultanik's vision of celebrating diversity, tolerance, and dialogue through varied cultures, the Confederation House executive board resolved in 2004 to name the historic building in his honor.

Sultanik's activities and interests broadened in the same decades to embrace the needs of the Jewish people-at-large. In 1977, he was elected vice-president of the World Jewish Congress, where he would take an active role for many years to come. In 1983, President Jimmy Carter appointed Sultanik a member of the United States Holocaust Memorial Council, on which he served for a decade. Since 1988, at the request of the Polish government, he vigorously took part in the efforts of the International Council of the Auschwitz Museum, first assuming office as deputy chairman. As chairman of the Budget and Finance Committee of the Auschwitz Museum, he raised some $30 million from European governments for the upkeep of that site. In recognition of his tireless services, in 1995 Sultanik was awarded by Polish President Lech Walesa the Commander's Cross of the Order of Poland Reborn, that government's second highest civilian honor after the Order of the White Eagle. In the 1990s Sultanik became chairman of the WZO's American Section and vice-chairman of the United Israel Appeal. He also served for many years as president of the Federation of Polish Jews and a board member of the Jewish Telegraphic Agency.[52]

In these various executive capacities, Sultanik remained a passionate activist. Aware from visits abroad that Arab-sponsored propaganda was making great inroads, he warned fellow Zionists in 1975 against overconfidence in the Sinai Pact between Egypt and Israel. The same year, he called for an end to Zionist parties in the Diaspora, claiming that no distinction existed between Jews and Zionists. Thousands of Nazi war criminals would enjoy immunity, he cautioned in 1979, if the West German government failed to abolish the statute of limitations for persecution of these criminals. When drawing a line between the enemies of Israel and antisemites, he charged, well-meaning Jews ignored the "irrevocable bond" that existed between Israel and the Jewish people. The UN General Assembly's resolution on November 10, 1975, stating that Zionism "is a form of racism and racial discrimination," drew his ire for demonstrating that the "blatantly biased majority of Arab petrodollars and Soviet dominated delegates" sought to delegitimize the State of Israel. Sultanik worked assiduously to improve Polish-Israeli relations, and supported Jewish activists in Riga in their calling on the Soviet Congress to study the problem of antisemitism and to register all Jewish organizations. "Too little and too late" was his official response to Polish minimal gestures at offering restitution to Jewish victims of the Holocaust.[53]

In an exchange of letters with Ronald Reagan in 1989 that became public two years later, Sultanik insisted that German hosts had "shamefully duped" the former US President into thinking that some of the forty-nine SS men buried in the Bitburg military cemetery had been executed for trying to shield Jewish concentration camp inmates "from the ovens." When Reagan had remained steadfast in the spring of 1985 not to cancel his visit to lay a wreath there in the company of Chancellor Helmut Kohl "in a spirit of reconciliation," then, after mounting criticism, announced that he would precede this with a stop at the Bergen-Belsen concentration camp, Elie Wiesel, eminent survivor-author and founding chairman of the US Holocaust Memorial Museum, wished his Council associates to resign in protest. Sultanik, persuading the great majority not to take this step, participated in a demonstration at Bergen-Belsen that Menahem Rosensaft, first chairman of the International Network of Children of Jewish Holocaust Survivors, spearheaded minutes after Reagan and Kohl left for Bitburg. That October, Sultanik vented his rage in *Midstream*, charging that by visiting Bergen-Belsen at the same time as Bitburg, the President "was desecrating the memory of the martyrs," and that Reagan's explicitly comparing the victims of the Holocaust with their killers "is simply immoral."[54]

During a memorial service in Poland to mark fifty years after the July 1946 pogrom in Kielce that murdered 42 Holocaust survivors, Sultanik asserted that from 1945 to 1946, more than 1,000 (*sic*) Jews were killed by Poles, a fate he had escaped by hiding his face when traveling on a train from Kielce to Ostrowiec. He lobbied successfully against the creation of a mini-mall across from Auschwitz and for the removal of crosses (and Stars of David) from that largest killing site in history. Deeming the Auschwitz-Birkenau death camp "a sacred zone of inviolability," he persuaded Steven Spielberg not to film there for "Schindler's List." He spoke out against on-going antisemitic manifestations in Poland, Switzerland's military aid to Germany during World War II, and Pope Benedict XVI for not decrying Jew-hatred when visiting Auschwitz in May 2006 as "a son of the German people" making a plea for reconciliation and world peace. "The new antisemitism," Sultanik warned in a prescient *Midstream* essay, joining the *jihad* cries of Muslim fundamentalists with terrorist acts to target Israel as its murderous objective, posed a far more dangerous threat to Jews everywhere, to Christian Arabs, to women, and to the world as a whole. In his view, Muslim antisemitism, buttressed by "a devil's alliance with the Left," constituted tomorrow's problem. "We remain silent," he concluded, "in the face of either at our peril."[55]

On October 19, 2014, Kalman Sultanik died at the venerable age of ninety-eight in New York City, his final resting place the Westchester Hills Cemetery. In an obituary published in the *New York Times*, Hadassah national president Marcie Natan called him "the quintessential Zionist idealist and leader, working for pluralistic, non-partisan Zionism." The World Jewish Congress's notice declared that the deceased "believed in the preservation of historical memory to educate future generations and tirelessly taught the lessons of the Holocaust in the battle against antisemitism." On its website, the Euro-Asian Jewish Congress averred that he was "verily a legendary figure in the international Jewish movement. The memory of this remarkable Man and Jew will remain forever in the hearts of those who knew him." Speaking on behalf of the Polish government, eminent World War II underground activist and Auschwitz survivor Władyzław Bartoszewski, chairman of the International Auschwitz Council and Secretary of State in the Chancellery of the Prime Minister, officially announced the death of "Kalman Sultanik [of] blessed memory, Polish tested friend and well-deserved builder of bridges between people."[56]

Four years earlier, Sultanik was given the honor of delivering the opening speech of the thirty-sixth World Zionist Congress in Jerusalem. As the last surviving delegate at the 1946 WZO Congress, he recalled being in awe of some of the illustrious leaders present, the "very dramatic and frequently very stormy" sessions, Weizmann's eloquent farewell address, and Ben-Gurion's speech foretelling the emergent Jewish state, the Arab violence that would precede it, and the "total war" that would be imposed upon Israel. "Mine was the generation of the *Shoah* and the subsequent *techiya* [rebirth] that was achieved by blood and heroism," he reminded the audience. After recalling Ben-Gurion's charge in 1947 to him and other members of the Central Committee of Liberated Jews, Sultanik declared that Herzl's goals proposed at the first Congress "are still valid and vigorous." "My generation that witnessed the creation of the State of Israel must see to it that the following generation preserve and fulfill his vision," he proclaimed, lest we betray the "glorious work" of thirty-five past Congresses and all the Passover seders that have always ended with "Next year in a rebuilt Jerusalem." Loyally following the spirit of political Zionism's founder, he concluded by enjoining those assembled to enthusiastically cite Herzl's words: "If we will it, This too shall not be a fairytale."[57]

Kalman Sultanik, like the other delegates who convened in Basle for the twenty-second World Zionist Congress, never abandoned his faith in Zionism and in his people's future. The persistent weight of the Holocaust, in which both his parents and his two sisters were murdered after being sent to the Belzec death camp, remained. Rather than be burdened with grief, however, Sultanik chose to focus on life, to help bring his fellow survivors to their biblical Promised Land. Zionism, as he put it upon the naming of Confederation House in his honor, represented the "beacon of light" after the darkness of the *Shoah*. Thereafter, he dedicated himself to serve as a voice of memory, viewing the task of witness as "a sacred obligation" and an ethical imperative, and to insure that Israel continue to thrive, in his words, as "a robust democratic state and model of human rights."[58] For many, his message resonates still.

Endnotes

I dedicate this chapter to the memory of Kalman Sultanik (1916–2014).
1. Monty Noam Penkower, *The Jews Were Expendable: Free World Diplomacy and the Holocaust* (Urbana, 1983); idem, *The Holocaust and Israel Reborn: From Catastrophe to Sovereignty* (Urbana, 1994); Conor Cruise O'Brien, *The Siege, The Saga of Israel and Zionism* (New York, 1986), 270.
2. Israel Goldstein, *My World as a Jew: The Memoirs of Israel Goldstein*, vol. 2 (New York, 1984), 230.
3. The official record of the Congress delegates gave the following breakdown: General Zionists—123; Ihud Ha'Olami of Po'alei Zion-Hitahdut—101; Mizrachi—58; Revisionists—41; HaShomer HaTsa'ir—26; Ahdut HaAvoda-Po'alei Zion—26; HaAliya HaHadasha—5; non-allied—5. In addition, 58 members from the Va'ad HaPo'el and 10 with advisory status took part. *HaKongress HaTsiyoni HaKhaf-Bet* (Jerusalem, 1947), 15–19.
4. Monty Noam Penkower, *Decision on Palestine Deferred: America, Britain and Wartime Diplomacy, 1939–1945* (London, 2002), 354; Leo W. Schwarz, *The Redeemers, A Saga of the Years 1945–1952* (New York, 1953), 193. A pioneering analysis in this regard is Zeev Mankowitz, "The Formation of *She'erit Hapleita*: November 1944–July 1945," *Yad Vashem Studies* 20 (1990): 337–370.
5. Bronia Sultanik interview with Leslie Fass, May 16, 1996 (video courtesy of Aaron Sultanik); Sultanik address, January 16, 2000, The US Holocaust Memorial Museum, Washington, DC.
6. Neumann to Sneh, September 9, 1946; Neumann to Torczyner, September 10, 1946; Torczyner to Neumann, September 11, 1946, and September 24, 1946; Neumann to Torczyner, October 14, 1946; all in P18-019, Jacques Torczyner MSS., Menahem Begin Center Archives, Jerusalem; Neumann to Silver, November 4, 1946, Silver correspondence, Emanuel Neumann MSS., New York City (courtesy of the late Emanuel Neumann).
7. Michael Cohen, *Palestine and the Great Powers, 1945–1948* (Princeton, 1982), chap. 8; Torczyner to Neumann, October 1946, Torczyner MSS.; Ben-Gurion to Silver, October 1, 1946, Z6/2306, Central Zionist Archives (hereafter CZA), Jerusalem; David Ben-Gurion, "What Are Our Objectives?," *Zionist Review*, November 29, 1946. For a thorough biography of Sneh in this respect, see Eli Shaltiel, *Tamid B'Meri, Moshe Sneh, Biografiya: 1909–1948* (Tel Aviv, 2000).
8. Yosef Gorni, *Shutfut U'Ma'avak* (Tel Aviv, 1976), 176–186; *L'Behinat HaDerekh* (Tel Aviv, 1947). Shimon Peres, attending the Congress as a Mapai youth delegate together with Moshe Dayan, subsequently wrote that a despairing

Ben-Gurion had at one point thought to leave the Congress and form a new Zionist movement. Shimon Peres, *From These Men: Seven Founders of the State of Israel* (New York, 1979), 49–53.

9. *HaKongress*, 7–16. For British action during the Holocaust, see Bernard Wasserstein, *Britain and the Jews of Europe, 1939–1945* (London, 1979); Penkower, *Decision on Palestine Deferred*.

10. Baffy, *The Diaries of Blanche Dugdale, 1936–1947*, ed. N. A. Rose (London, 1973), 242–243; Scholes to State, December 17, 1946, 867N.01/12-1746, State Department MSS., National Archives (NA), Suitland, MD; *HaKongress*, pp. 59-74.

11. *HaKongress*, 45–54.

12. *HaKongress*, 77–90. For the endorsement of the US State Department, see Byrnes's statement, December 2, 1946, S25/10488, CZA. As the Allies were losing the Battle of France to German armed forces on the Western Front, the Battle of Dunkirk was the defense and evacuation to Britain of British and other Allied forces in Europe from May 26 to June 4, 1940, by private and commercial vessels. While more than 330,000 Allied troops were rescued from this coastal city in northern France, the British and French military nonetheless sustained heavy casualties and were forced to abandon nearly all their equipment. The British Expeditionary Force (BEF) alone lost some 68,000 soldiers during the French campaign. The term "Dunkirk Spirit" refers to the solidarity of the British people in times of adversity. Marshal Philippe Pétain's authoritarian government, the so-called French State, relocated to the town of Vichy after France's decisive defeat by the *Wehrmacht* in June 1940. It aided in the rounding up of Jews to be delivered to Nazi death camps, and collaborated in other ways with Nazi Germany. Pétain's government remained there until late 1944, when it lost its *de facto* authority due to the Allied invasion of France. After the war, Pétain was tried and convicted for treason. He was originally sentenced to death, but due to his age and World War I service his sentence was commuted to life in prison. He died in 1951.

13. *ZOA Bulletin* 2 (December 13, 1946), Zionist Archives (ZA), New York (subsequently transferred to the Central Zionist Archives, Jerusalem); Berlin to Mizrachi delegates, December 18, 1946, box 31, Meir Bar-Ilan MSS., Bar-Ilan University, Ramat Gan, Israel. For a brief analysis of Goldmann's mission in Washington, see Cohen, *Palestine and the Great Powers*, 147–150.

14. *HaKongress*, 97–120, 129–135; Epstein and Greenberg reports, January 8, 1947, National Board minutes, Hadassah Archives, New York City. For the

Aliya Hadasha manifesto issued prior to the Congress, see "Statement of Policy," n.d. J18/82, CZA.
15. *HaKongress*, 125–128.
16. *HaKongress*, 142–151. For an early study of the Anglo-American Committee, see Allen Howard Podet, *The Success and Failure of the Anglo-American Committee of Inquiry, 1945–1946* (Lewiston, 1986). Also see Monty Noam Penkower, *Palestine to Israel: Mandate to State, 1945–1948*, vol. 1, *Rebellion Launched, 1945–1946* (New York, 2019), chap. 3.
17. *HaKongress*, 154–163, 190–199. For the Morrison-Grady Plan, see Cohen, *Palestine and the Great Powers*, chap. 7.
18. *HaKongress*, 174–183, 255–262, 225–229, 252–255, 211–217. For Shertok's letters, smuggled out to colleagues, while in Latrun, see Moshe Sharett, *Yerahim B'Emek Ayalon*, ed. Pinhas Ofer (Tel Aviv, 2011).
19. *HaKongress*, 202–208, 230–236.
20. *Baffy*, 243; *ZOA Bulletin* 3 (December 16, 1946), ZA; *HaKongress*, 184–190.
21. *HaKongress*, 241–252.
22. *ZOA Bulletin* 3 (December 16, 1946); December 15, 1946, Mizrachi faction meeting, World Mizrachi Archives, Beit Meir, Jerusalem; *Baffy*, 244–245.
23. *HaKongress*, 322–331. For the increasing altercation between Wise and Silver during World War II, see Penkower, *Decision on Palestine Deferred*, passim.
24. *HaKongress*, 331–338.
25. *HaKongress*, 339–345. The final quotation was from *Isaiah* 1:27. The only copy of the English version of Weizmann's speech (incorrectly dated December 18) is to be found in file Z4/30987, CZA.
26. Abba Eban, "Tragedy and Triumph," in *Chaim Weizmann, A Biography by Several Hands*, ed. M. W. Weisgal and J. Carmichael (London, 1962), 293; Shertok to Ben-Zvi, December 17, 1946, A116/85I, CZA; *New York Times*, December 16, 1946; *Baffy*, 244.
27. David Ben-Gurion, *Likrat Ketz HaMandat*, ed. M. Avizohar (Tel Aviv, 1993), 266–278.
28. Ibid., 278–288.
29. Ibid., 289–290; *JTA*, December 22 (Basle, December 20), 1946; *Yediot Acharonot*, December 19–20, 1946; *JTA*, December 23 (Basle, December 22), 1946; Greenberg report, January 8, 1947, National Board meeting, Hadassah Archives; HaShomer HaTsa'ir faction meeting, December 20, 1946, file (7) 7.10.95, HaShomer HaTsa'ir Archives, Givat Haviva, Israel; *ZOA Bulletin* 4 (December 19, 1946), ZA.

30. Emanuel Neumann, *In the Arena, An Autobiographical Memoir* (New York, 1976), 229–230; Epstein report, January 8, 1947, National Board minutes, Hadassah Archives.
31. Eban, "Tragedy and Triumph," 293; Ben-Gurion, *Likrat Ketz HaMandat*, 291.
32. *HaKongress*, 491–498. For an analysis of Sneh's significant role at the Congress, see Shaltiel, *Tamid B'Meri*, chap. 17.
33. Gorny, *Shutfut U'Ma'avak*, 193–194.
34. Ben-Gurion, *Likrat Ketz HaMandat*, 291; Gorny, *Shutfut U'Ma'avak*, 194; *HaKongress*, 538–539. For HaShomer HaTsa'ir's stance, see ? to Bernard, December 22, 1946, file (7)7.10.95, HaShomer HaTsa'ir Archives; Ze'ev Tsahor, *Chazzan—Tenuat Chayim* (Jerusalem, 1997), 174–176.
35. *HaKongress*, 540–542.
36. Gorny, *Shutfut U'Ma'avak*, 195–196; Ben-Gurion, *Likrat Ketz HaMandat*, 293–294; Va'ad HaPo'el meeting, December 28, 1946, S5/2584, CZA.
37. S5/2584, CZA; Neumann, *In the Arena*, 234; *Ha'Aretz*, December 29, 1946. For a fuller exposition of these negotiations, see Epstein report, January 8, 1947, National Board minutes, Hadassah Archives.
38. Ben-Gurion, *Likrat Ketz HaMandat*, 297–300; Epstein report, January 8, 1947, National Board minutes, Hadassah Archives.
39. Ben-Gurion, *Likrat Ketz HaMandat*, 300–301.
40. Eban, "Tragedy and Triumph," 294; Weizmann to Frankfurter, January 7, 1947; Weizmann to Dreyfus, January 10, 1947; Weizmann to Jarblum, January 13, 1947; Weizmann to Laski, January 13, 1947; all in Weizmann Archives (WA), Rehovot, Israel. His published memoirs, completed that spring with the help of Maurice Samuel, took a softer tone: "Perhaps it was in the nature of things that the Congress should be what it was; for not only were the old giants of the movement gone—Shmarya Levin and Ussishkin and Bialik, among others—but the in-between generation had been simply wiped out; the great fountains of European Jewry had been dried up. We seemed to be standing at the nadir of our fortunes." Chaim Weizmann, *Trial and Error, The Autobiography of Chaim Weizmann* (New York, 1949), 443. Goldmann defended his staying in the Executive by claiming that he was "one of the few" in whom Bevin and others "will have some confidence and with whom they will be ready to negotiate." Goldmann to Wise, December 31, 1946, box 109, Stephen Wise MSS., American Jewish Historical Society Archives, Waltham (now at the Center for Jewish History, New York City).
41. Richard Crossman, "Silver Imperialism," *New Statesman and Nation*, January 4, 1947; Laski to Weizmann, January 10, 1947, WA; Robert Weltsch, "The End

of the Biltmore Road," *Commentary* 3 (February 1947): 101–108; Harold Nicholson, "Marginal Comment," *The Spectator*, January 3, 1947; Stephen Wise, "My Report on the World Zionist Congress," January 3, 1947, Wise MSS.; Weizmann to Wise, January 6, 1947, WA.

42. Abba Hillel Silver, "Report of the World Zionist Congress," Sermon 682, Abba Hillel Silver Archives, The Temple, Cleveland.
43. Creech-Jones to Bevin, December 31, 1946, Foreign Office (FO) records 371/61762, Public Record Office (PRO), Kew, England.
44. Ben-Gurion interview at the Colonial Office, January 2, 1947, FO 371/61762, PRO.
45. Meyerson-Remez interview with the Chief Secretary, January 7, 1947, S25/28, CZA; Meyerson remarks, January 9, 1947, file 811/8P, Israel State Archives, Jerusalem. For the evaluation by some other Mapai delegates after the Congress, see Mazkirut Mapai, January 1, 1947, David Ben-Gurion Archives, Sdeh Boker, Israel.
46. Sidney Hertzberg, "The Month in History," *Commentary* 3 (February 1947), 161.
47. Gallman to State, December 27, 1946, 867N.01/12-2746, State Department MSS., NA; Joel Carmichael, "The Crisis of Zionism," *Nation*, January 25, 1947, 90–92; Cohen, *Palestine and the Great Powers*, 182; Richard Meinertzhagen, *Middle East Diary, 1917–1956* (London, 1959), 218; Gorny, *Shutfut U'Ma'avak*, 200–206; Norman Rose, *Chaim Weizmann, A Biography* ((New York, 1989), chap. 20.
48. Judah Nadich, *Eisenhower and the Jews* (New York, 1953), pp. 230-232; Joseph Heller, *The Birth of Israel, 1945-1949: Ben-Gurion and His Critics* (Gainesville, 2000), pp. 114-115; Shabtai Teveth, *Ben-Gurion, The Burning Ground, 1886-1948* (Boston, 1987), p. 873.
49. Zeev W. Mankowitz, *Life between Memory and Hope, The Survivors of the Holocaust in Occupied Germany* (Cambridge, 2002); *HaKongress*, 208–211; Idelson remarks, Mazkirut Mapai, January 1, 1947, Ben-Gurion Archives; Kalman Sultanik speech, January 16, 2000. For subsequent developments leading to the State of Israel's establishment, see Monty Noam Penkower, *Palestine to Israel: Mandate to State, 1945–1948*, vol. 2, *Into the International Arena, 1947-1948* (New York, 2019).
50. Sultanik speech, January 16, 2000; Kalman Sultanik, "Text of the Speech Opening the 36th Zionist Congress of the World Zionist Organization (June 15–17, 2010) in Jerusalem," *Midstream*, Fall 2010, 4. For a thorough study, see Aviva Halamish, *The Exodus Affair: Holocaust Survivors and the Struggle for Palestine* (Syracuse, 1998).

51. Sultanik interview with Fass, May 16, 1996 (video courtesy of Aaron Sultanik). Kalman's two (younger) brothers survived the Holocaust; none of Bronia's family survived. The couple had two sons, Aaron and Samuel, named after Bronia's father and Kalman's father.
52. *Ha'Aretz*, October 21, 2014.
53. *JTA*, September 9, 1975; June 5, 1975; April 11, 1979; December 18, 1980; February 14, 1980; March 26, 1987; April 22, 1988; June 1, 1989; January 22, 1991. For the limitations of Poland's stance vis-à-vis such restitution, see Monica Krawczyk, "The Effect of the Legal Status of Jewish Property in Post-War Poland on Polish-Jewish Relations," in *Jewish Presence in Absence, The Aftermath of the Holocaust in Poland, 1944-2010*, ed. F. Tych and M. Abramczyk-Garbowska, trans. G. Dąbkowski and J. Taylor-Kucia (Jerusalem, 2014), 791–821.
54. *JTA*, April 29, 1991; Elie Wiesel, *And the Sea is Never Full, Memoirs, 1969–*, trans. M. Wiesel (New York, 2000), 227–250; Sultanik interview with Fass, May 16, 1996; Kalman Sultanik, "An Overview of 'Bitburg.'" *Midstream* 31:8 (October 1985): 11–14; Ilya Levkov, ed., *Bitburg and Beyond: Encounters in America, German and Jewish History* (New York, 1986).
55. *JTA*, July 1, 1995; April 2, 1996; July 9, 1996; June 6, 1997; December 9, 1997; February 17, 1999; June 2, 1999; May 16, 2006; May 30, 2006; Sultanik interview with Fass, May 16, 1996; Kalman Sultanik, "Remembering the Victims of the Holocaust is a Sacred Obligation," in idem, *Preserving for the Future*, trans. W. Brand (Krakow, 2004), 81–85; Kalman Sultanik, "The New Antisemitism," *Midstream* 50:7 (November–December 2004): 15–17. A history sponsored by the Israeli Defense Ministry states that 311 Jews were murdered in Poland during the eleven months after the end of World War II. Hani Zvi and Yoav Gelber, *Bnei Keshet* (Tel Aviv, 1998), 119.
56. *New York Times*, October 21–22, 2014; http://eajc.org/page84/news47758.html; wyborcza.pl/NEKROLOGI, October 23, 2014.
57. Kalman Sultanik, "Text of the Speech," *Midstream*, Fall 2010, 4.
58. Sultanik address at Confederation House, 2004 (video courtesy of Aaron Suiltanik); Sultanik, "Remembering the Victims of the Holocaust," 81–85; Sultanik, "The New Antisemitism," 17.

2. Jacob Robinson and the Rise of Israel

San Francisco's leap into the global limelight occurred on April 25, 1945, when that city, whose harbor looks far into the Pacific, opened its doors to the conference that founded the United Nations. Some 5,000 people, along with an additional 1,000 journalists and broadcasters, convened over the next two months in its stately War Memorial Opera House and adjacent War Memorial Veteran's Building on the western side of Van Ness Avenue for the historic conclave. While the federal government provided printing stations, translators, transportation, taping equipment, private quarters, coatrooms, and mini-libraries, hundreds of military personnel were detailed to help out with sedans, jeeps, naval buses, and private limousines carrying around town secretariat officials and delegates from fifty nations. The ultimate UN Charter in five languages, signed by 153 diplomats at a huge round blue table in the Veterans' Building auditorium hall on June 26 and to become effective four months later, reflected the determination of the 850 representatives present from over eighty percent of the world's population to set up an organization in the new postwar order which would preserve peace and help build a better world.

Hopes for success were high at that moment. President Harry S. Truman declared to the final session that "with this Charter the world can begin to look forward to the time when all worthy human beings may be permitted to live decently as free people." Anne O'Hare McCormick well captured the sense of euphoria, the famed *New York Times* foreign news correspondent writing at the time: "San Francisco is a lusty city, with youth in every line of its uplifted profile and vigor in every breath of its brisk trade winds. . . . More than any other city, it is a sign of the promise of resurrection."[1]

The City of the Golden Gate offered little such promise to Hitler's primary victims, however. Although witness to the Charter's statement of high purposes for humanity, all Jewish organizations were denied official status at the conference. Having suffered during World War II the darkest era in its bimillennial history of expulsion and persecution, world Jewry's anomalous position as a homeless and stateless people continued after the Holocaust. What David Ben-Gurion, executive chairman of the Jewish Agency for Palestine, called "the Jewish problem" did not appear on the agenda. Yet the last-minute entry into the Allied camp alongside Iraq of Saudi Arabia, Egypt, Syria, and Lebanon before Germany's defeat, the pro-Nazi wartime record of three of these countries notwithstanding, gave five Arab states full representation.

Since the five major powers had resolved beforehand that no specific territorial issue could be considered, Jewish Agency spokesmen focused on safeguarding the rights of the *yishuv* (Palestinian Jewish community) under the League of Nations mandate accorded in 1922 to Great Britain. Thanks particularly to the firm hand of Peter Fraser, New Zealand's prime minister and chairman of the Trusteeship Territories Commission, the final clause (bearing the phrase all "peoples," rather than the Arab formulation of all "people" in accordance with the principle of national self-determination by the current majority of a country's population) affirmed in effect the unique nature of the Palestine Mandate in its pledge to Jews worldwide. With the expert legal advice of the World Jewish Congress's fifty-six-year-old Lithuanian-born Jacob Robinson, the Jewish Agency helped secure paragraph 1 of Article 80 of the UN Charter, which maintained the prior obligations of mandatories. As Robinson would later observe on various occasions, the only people specifically cited by name in the entire mandates system was the Jewish people, and that article, expressly recognizing the right of the Jewish people to have its national home in Palestine, thus constituted part of the legal charter of the United Nations.[2]

Long acknowledged as an articulate and learned champion of minority rights, first as a Jewish member of the Second Lithuanian Parliament (1923–1926) and counsel for Jewish minorities at the European Nationalities Congress in Geneva (1925–1933), the Warsaw University law graduate who had spent more than two years in a German Prisoner of War camp in World War I had successfully defended Lithuania against charges regarding the autonomous Memel Territory's

German minority before the Permanent Court of International Justice at the Hague (1932). He also came up with the successful idea of the Bernheim Petition (1933) to the League, which called for the grant to Jews in German Upper Silesia of equal civil and political rights under the German-Polish Convention of May 1922. Author in 1928 of a two-volume annotated bibliography covering twenty languages (!) on the legal protections for minorities under the League of Nations, he gained recognition in academic circles around the world.

Driven by a form of Jewish national self-perception that was particularly pronounced in Eastern Europe, Robinson strongly advocated Zionism as essential for the future of world Jewry. Zionists alone, he insisted, truly believed in "the principle of world-wide Jewish solidarity," and Hebrew was "the key to freeing ourselves from the [spirit of] Exile and to "building our own political life." After the August 1929 Arab massacre of Jews in Palestine, he led a protest demonstration of 5,000 Jews in Kovno, and sent an urgent telegram to Geneva demanding League emergency intervention against the British mandatory's "hypocritical and criminal actions" which had created "a situation where our elementary rights and interests . . . are scorned in the most brutal way." This stance dovetailed with his clarion call, one that made Robinson an international celebrity four years earlier at the first Congress of European National Minorities, for each "national group" to be permitted "to conserve and develop its national individuality in corporations of public law."

With the outbreak of World War II, Robinson returned from vacation in France to Vilna (Vilnius), where he helped stabilize the situation of local Jews and Polish refugees with the Lithuanian authorities. Just before the Soviet occupation in June 1940, he traveled first to Moscow, Rumania, and Yugoslavia, then, reunited with his family in southern France, boarded a ship in Lisbon for New York with a US visa that November. Two months later, Robinson founded the Institute of Jewish Affairs (IJA) as a joint project of the American Jewish Congress and the World Jewish Congress (WJC). In his view, it was designed to advance the diaspora nationalist political agenda which organizations such as the Comité des Délégations Juives and later the World Jewish Congress had promoted between the two world wars, seeking a return once World War II ended to the League of Nations' system of Jewish minority rights in Europe.[3]

Together with his brother Nehemiah, also a lawyer, and a few other scholars on Jewish matters, Jacob began focusing on the basic legal issues of restitution and reparation and on the fortification of Jewish life in postwar Europe and the punishment of the criminals. By late 1943, however, with the grim reality of Jewish annihilation across Nazi-occupied Europe increasingly known and what he termed "the current process of the homogenization of the European state units," including population transfers, Robison had concluded radically that there was no future for minority rights on that Continent. The nine governments-in-exile which in 1942 had quietly convened the St. James Conference in London (Jews purposely not invited) denied that Hitler's first and primary victims died as Jews; global justice, he insisted, "must begin with an acknowledgment of Jewish nationhood." The "conspiracy of silence" had "condemned our people to live and to suffer in the shadow of anonymity"; recognizing "the gravity of this crime against the Jews for all humanity" would advance the cause of international law. No publication achieved more significance than the Institute's *Hitler's Ten Year War against the Jews* (1943), the first meticulously documented, comprehensive study of the systematic murder of European Jewry, where Robinson's summary noted that "some 3,000,000 Jews of Europe have perished since the war began four years ago."

Given the small number of Jews who would be left in postwar Europe, Robinson urged the WJC's Peace Planning Committee that the Congress's exclusive demand should be "a Jewish commonwealth in Palestine which would absorb the remaining Jews in Europe after the war." The following year, he played a prominent role in the WJC's War Emergency Conference in Atlantic City, which adopted an eleven-point program for war crimes accountability and another, which he drafted, on reparations. The unparalleled atrocities against the Jews, the conference stressed, had to be seen as a planned crime against a collectivity—the Jewish people, which merited official representation at future trials of the criminals.[4]

With the end of the Second World War, Robinson's life became devoted almost exclusively to two major aims—the establishment and continued well-being of a Jewish commonwealth in Palestine, which would absorb the Jewish refugee remnant after the war, and the liquidation as far as possible of the effects of that global conflict on the survivors of the Holocaust. At San Francisco, while the Agency focused on protecting Jewish interests under the Covenant of the League of Nations and the Palestine Mandate, the WJC and the American Jewish Conference mainly concentrated their efforts on what has since become known as "human rights," their definition and protection, which were introduced in place of the League Minorities Treaties of 1919. Robinson's services were available to all three delegations, and won high praise for what was his initial effort at Jewish diplomacy directly on the inter-governmental level.[5]

Prior to the conference, Robinson and WJC colleague Maurice Perlzweig had learned in Washington that, since the inclusion of "inner political criteria" would harm consideration of their application, they should seek admission for such organizations whose principal focus was equality and liberty. Accordingly, their preparatory work was limited to the request to "strengthen the demand for Human Rights in the future charter." This "very modest undertaking," he reported to the WJC's office committee on June 7, 1945, was possibly what led to some success. As the entire question of the League of Nations was not to be discussed in San Francisco, the Congress's memorandum, astutely circulated in the official languages (save Chinese) spoken by the delegates, eliminated its original demand that Minority Treaties should remain valid, thus not antagonizing some of the nations (Yugoslavia and Czechoslovakia) in attendance.

"Specific Jewish demands" could not be brought forth, Robinson observed, "because we are not a state, because we are a *sui generis*, a unique nation." Consequently, the WJC had to deal for the time being only with the question of human rights and watching that the conference did not become "a source of attacks against us." One of the signs of our decline, he continued, was the lack of Jews among the various delegations. Almost no disunity existed among the Jewish groups, but these were impermanent, and a greater staff of experts with experience in diplomatic negotiations was needed. "Only the man who is aware of the disproportion between effort and result can be active in Jewish politics," he concluded. Easy and quick results were "not to be expected" in the future. The UN Charter's declaration of principles relating to human rights, lacking concrete obligations on the part of states whose compliance could be legally enforced before a supervisory body, disappointed him greatly.[6]

Five days later, Robinson, accompanied by New York State Judge Nathan Perlman and Dr. Alexander Kohanski, met United States

Supreme Court Associate Justice Robert Jackson, one month after the latter had been appointed by President Truman to serve as Chief of Counsel to the US prosecution team for the prospective Nuremberg War Crimes Tribunal. In their confidential encounter at New York City's Federal Court House, the tireless crusader began by noting that the Institute had been "working in this field for four and a half years." The IJA's accumulation of invaluable documentation on the Holocaust, he asserted, made it clear that "the Jewish people is the greatest sufferer of this war.... It therefore has a case of its own against the master Nazi criminals and their accomplices."

The core of the Nazi "master plan" and its horrific consequence, leading to the murder of an estimated six million Jews, reflected "a well-conceived, deliberately plotted and meticulously carried out conspiracy" directed against all Jews, Robinson continued that morning. A novel charge of criminal conspiracy should be included in the indictment, encompassing each German collaborator engaged in the murder of European Jewry. As Europe remained "infested ... with anti-Jewish feeling," a "specific indictment for the crime committed against our people will clear the atmosphere in Europe and make it easier for the survivors to reestablish themselves there." Jewish survivors, he stressed, were "entitled to have someone represent them at the trials." Jackson listened intently and asked for supportive documentation. Yet, while explaining that it was intended to have "one military trial embracing the whole conspiracy of the Nazis against the world, in which the Jewish count should have its place," the Justice noted that the International Military Tribunal (IMT) "might not be well disposed" to more general representation: other groups "might also ask for some consideration, which would complicate matters."[7]

From then on, Robinson and his lobby worked assiduously at providing a great deal of material to Jackson on both legal and substantive matters, including problems associated with defining aggressive war. He urged Jackson to include Adolf Eichmann (Robinson the first to identify him as the architect of the Nazis' "Final Solution of the Jewish Question") alongside the Grand Mufti of Jerusalem, Haj Amin al-Husseini, among the defendants. As one of what he called the "competent outsiders," Robinson was summoned to Nuremberg that autumn to give evidence to support some of the indictment regarding the Jewish victims and to assist the American presentation of what was euphemistically called "the

Persecution of the Jews," including in the interrogation of at least one of the key German witnesses, SS Captain and Adolf Eichmann deputy Dieter Wisliceny. He also prepared an affidavit on the Jewish death toll of 5.7 million. As a result of Robinson's suggestions, much of the "Jewish Brief" was rewritten.

Robinson would remain critical of various aspects of the IMT proceedings. These included the insufficient attention on Jewish matters in the indictment; the momentous tribunal decision not to include crimes against the Jews before World War II within what constituted crimes against humanity; its conclusion that there was no conspiracy on the part of the defendants to commit War Crimes and Crimes Against Humanity; and perhaps most significantly that the Holocaust, its total geographical scope, was never singled out as a specific crime. At the same time, he praised the United States, which had captured twenty of the twenty-four top Nazi criminals and obtained the incriminating Nazi documents now being used as evidence against them, for driving home the case for "Crimes against Humanity," however limited these were, to be punishable only if committed in connection with, or in the execution of, the crimes of aggressive war or violations of laws and customs of war.[8]

In a fifteen-page review for the WJC in December 1945, Robinson unreservedly praised Jackson's six-hour opening speech as a *tour de force* when describing the goal of the Holocaust. In the Justice's words: "It is my purpose to show a plan and design, to which all Nazis were fanatically committed, to annihilate all Jewish people.... The persecution of the Jews was a continuous and deliberate policy." A year later, Robinson proclaimed, in reviewing the 283 legal-size page judgment at Nuremberg, that it is "important to emphasize that time and again the Court underlines the connection between the initial stage of persecution and the so-called 'final solution.'" Practically all of those who were actively engaged in commission of crimes against humanity were sentenced to death, whether or not they were active in other criminal activities. This leads to the conclusion, he ended, that the Court "was consistently aware of the importance of the Jewish element in the trial." Robinson's evaluation in 1972 for the *Israel Law Review* averred that the evidence submitted to the tribunal in the Jewish case, "juridically the strongest of all the counts," was "overwhelming."

As Jackson wrote to Zionist avatar Chaim Weizmann, to call a Jew to testify would have been an "anti-climax." The Justice explained: "The

Nazi documents are so coldly cruel and so complete as to the purpose to exterminate the Jews and so detailed as to their accomplishment of this object that nothing could be added." In the end, practically all of those who had been actively involved in committing crimes against humanity received the death penalty when the tribunal announced its judgment on October 1, 1946.This illustrated, Robinson ended his review, how the IMT was "consistently aware of the Jewish element in the trial." The extensive documentation led "inexorably" to the conclusion of the existence of a conspiracy to destroy the Jewish people, and its "ruthless implementation," resulting in the "death of some six million Jews, which constituted 75 percent of the Jewish population of Europe."[9]

Upon completing his duties at Nuremberg, Jackson acknowledged with appreciation on September 1, 1946, the IJA's contribution to the case presented by the American prosecution before the tribunal at Nuremberg. The Institute's planning and research work, "carefully sifted and selected," relating to the persecution of the Jews by the Nazis and the compilation of this material was a product of "prodigious labor and careful research," and it "generously" made these documents available for the prosecution's preparation of evidence. Jackson also wished to record his appreciation to the director, Dr. Jacob Robinson, who "so promptly acceded" to the request of the Board of Review of the US Chief of Counsel to come to Nuremberg, where he lent his "scholarly counsel and advice, his untiring efforts and critical judgment to the task." The Nazi persecution of the Jews, concluded the Justice, was one of the "major phases" of the Prosecution's case, and the successful presentation of that aspect of the case was "greatly aided" by the IJA's contribution. He warmly commended the Institute and its Director for "the initiative, devotion, industry and service rendered to the cause of justice to war criminals."[10]

Robinson did not forego his commitment to the cause of human rights. That May, the Institute of Jewish Affairs published his study *Human Rights and Fundamental Freedoms in the Charter of the United Nations*. Its flaws notwithstanding, he praised the Charter's effecting the "first breach in the formerly inaccessible citadel of domestic jurisdiction," the rightful authority of international law remaining an open question to be properly pursued. Towards the end of November, Robinson accepted an appointment as United Nations Social Affairs officer, serving until February 1947 as an expert consultant to the team creating and establishing the UN Commission on Human Rights. Power politics frustrating his hopes for the equal and consistent application of international law to individual states, Robinson found his worst fears confirmed, and left him dismayed regarding the attainment of a global consensus about the protection of human rights and a binding legal mechanism for enforcement. Still, Canadian law professor John P. Humphrey, Director of the Division of Human Rights, thanked him for his "very great assistance," noting that a large part of the credit for the success of the meetings "certainly belongs to you." At the same time, Robinson's overriding mission—that the identity of the Jewish people be recognized, both as "the victim of the Nazi fury" and as meriting its sovereign national home in the biblical Eretz Israel—remained to be fulfilled.[11]

As early as January 1946, Robinson had linked the terrible plight of the "destitute and uprooted masses" of the surviving Jews in Eastern Europe and the "displaced Jews everywhere" with the necessity for their rehabilitation in "the sole country where this is humanly possible—in the land of hope of the Jewish people—Palestine." Authoring under the IJA's auspices a summary of the current situation of European Jewry in January 1946, he estimated the annihilation of European Jewry in thirteen countries minus the USSR. at 5,266,000 and the present number of "displaced Jews" (those outside their home country) at 415,000. The situation in the first category of countries (France, Belgium, Holland, Italy, and the Czech regions) was far better than in the second (Poland, Hungary, Romania, and Slovakia), where antisemitism and utter destitution were rampant, while in the third (Bulgaria, Yugoslavia, and Greece) there was "hardly a Jewish question at all" other than extreme poverty. The seeds of antisemitism were "deeply rooted" in Germany and Austria, where the reintegration of the survivors into the life of these countries had not shown any appreciable progress.

Most of the refugees and deportees were idle and not welcome, Robinson charged, while none could or wished to return to "the horrible scenes of martyrdom" or to remain in the midst of a population which "tortured and murdered them." They could be again made useful members of society only in surroundings where their Jewishness "is not a crime or a shame, but a natural thing." That is why the "overwhelming majority" wished to go and insisted on going to Palestine, why they could go only there, and why they should be brought there. It would be a tragedy, he closed, should the Allies not recognize their terrible plight and their need to emigrate to that ultimate destination.[12]

Truman's public statement the next month to a delegation from the United Jewish Appeal provided some comfort. Although not openly endorsing Palestine as the haven for Holocaust survivors, the President acknowledged that the Nuremberg war trials had established the fact that 5,700,000 Jews "perished under the murderous reign of Hitlerism," and that crime "will be answered in justice." There were left in Europe 1,500,000 Jews whom the "ordeal" has left homeless, hungry, sick, and without assistance. These, too, were victims of the crime "for which retribution will be visited upon the guilty." But neither the dictates of justice nor that "love of our fellowman which we are bidden to practice," Truman ended, would be satisfied "until the needs of these sufferers are met."[13]

On the eve of the Paris Peace Conference that July, Robinson reiterated that "the most outstanding feature of Jewish life in the former satellite countries" was the insufficient measures taken by governments to restore to Jews their properties, right and interests, as well as the positions they were robbed of. Despite unity among the Jewish delegations present to restore Jewish collective rights, these "non-state actors" did not even get a chance to officially voice their demands. Absent was any reference in the final amendments to the protection of collective rights of minorities. "Not only is the word 'Jew' taboo," he observed while at the conference, but "the general dislike of a renewal of the experiment of the protection of minorities . . . has been carried to its most radical consequences." The sentiment of disdain toward minority protection was voiced at the same time as Poland, Czechoslovakia, Hungary, and Yugoslavia were expelling millions of members of minority groups, primarily ethnic Germans, to their purposed ethnic "homelands" with Allied support.

After he attended the Paris Peace Conference, Robinson's conclusion was clear. The era of Jewish diaspora nationalism, as famously advocated by the Jewish historian Simon Dubnow, had come to an end. The Jews of postwar Europe, Robinson had already noted one year earlier, had become "dwarf communities" who now inhabited regimes "which leave no place for autonomous public law bodies for religious or national groups." The frustrated, even humiliated, Jewish groups at the conference could do no more than send a letter of protestation to the

Allies, expressing their hope that "the statesmen assembled in Paris . . . are not indifferent to the great tragedy that has overwhelmed the Jews in Europe and of the need for a solution to the problems confronting them." The Jews remained in a most uncertain state, his short pamphlet *Unfinished Victory* declared, stymied by "the failure, or sheer unwillingness, of governments to see . . . Jews as Jews." The vast majority of Holocaust survivors in Europe looked "to emigration as their one hope for survival," with Palestine as their destination. Jewish rights depended above all on Jewish sovereignty. The traditional view, articulated by modern conservatism founder Edmund Burke's positing a "law of nations" whereby "humanity" must be the "protector and ally" of the powerless Jews, had to undergo a radical transformation. An independent place in the international order, Robinson concluded, was essential to complete their triumphant survival in the harsh world of realpolitik.[14]

April 2, 1947, offered Robinson the special opportunity to play a vital role in his personal quest. When His Majesty's Government (HMG) formally requested of the United Nations on that date that a special session as soon as possible of the General Assembly (GA) discuss "the future government of Palestine," implicitly recognizing the UN's authority in the matter of mandates and the continued validity of the Palestine Mandate, the Jewish Agency urgently needed legal expertise. Both Nahum Goldmann and Eliyahu Epstein (later Elath), representing the Jewish Agency at the San Francisco Conference, had been much impressed with, and paid "special tribute" to, Robinson's formulating the most important Zionist and WJC memoranda at that gathering as "of the greatest value." While in London that fall, he had advised Ben-Gurion how to receive immediate funds from America for the *yishuv*'s revolt against British rule. In June 1946 Goldmann continued negotiating with Robinson about coming in as an advisor on international law to the Jewish Agency.

Now, one day after HMG's request for a GA special session, to confine itself to appointing a special committee to investigate and make recommendations for solution of the Palestine issue, Moshe Shertok (later Sharett) cabled Executive Committee colleague Goldie Myerson (later Golda Meir) in Jerusalem. In the view of the Agency's political director, the discussion by the Executive in New York about the special committee's terms of reference would have to be deferred pending Robinson's return from Nuremberg. The only Jewish expert at the time regarding the UN, he would be asked to prepare the legal ground for the Zionist case.[15]

At this point, Robinson had no doubts as to British intentions. In his opinion, having "dillydallied" for twenty years between the Arab and the Jews and getting no friendship from either, and with public opinion against continued mandates, HMG saw no solution but to turn to the UN. He had no faith in Ernest Bevin, whom he first met by chance in a Prague hotel dining room in the early 1930s, whose first question to the Lithuanian intellectual was "Why don't Jews want to work?" The British Foreign Secretary objected to Truman's call for the immediate transfer of a hundred thousand Holocaust survivors to Palestine, and he certainly did not want a Jewish State. With what Robinson would characterize as "repeated monotony," Prime Minister Clement Attlee's Labour Government had adopted the anti-Zionist stance of its Conservative predecessor. Robinson consequently proceeded on the assumption that the British meant what they said. Once appointed by Shertok Legal Counsel for the Agency, he turned to prepare a first draft of a memorandum on the Mandate and Britain's restrictive 1939 White Paper. Within days, he was coopted to the Agency's office in Washington.[16]

In tackling the possible terms of reference for the UN investigatory committee (known as the United Nations Special Committee on Palestine, UNSCOP), Robinson's memo on April 16, 1947 urged that the Jewish Agency endeavor to be involved in the work of the committee, and that that body visit both Palestine and the camps in Europe for the Jewish survivors, officially designated with other postwar refugees "Displaced Persons" (DPs). A basic dilemma arose, he pointed out the next day to the American Section of the Jewish Agency Executive: The committee might reject the Agency's basic idea that the solution had to comply with its rights under the Palestine Mandate and that any alteration required the Agency's agreement, a rejection which could also occur if the Agency did not insist on forcing such limitations regarding the reference terms. On the other hand, it could be argued that the terms were limited anyway by existing international instruments whose "provisional permanency" had been proclaimed in Article 80 of the UN Charter. Obviously, Robinson declared, each case would have to be thoroughly sounded out with friendly delegations before the Agency Executive definitely made up its mind as to proceeding. Distinguishing between the unwritten law of nations and the written UN Charter, Robinson recalled years later, he sought to integrate the two.[17]

The Jewish Agency's "Grand Strategy" in its action with the UN, Robinson observed on April 17 to the Executive in New York, required facing two problems. First: could the Agency avoid taking sides in this "iron age" of power politics? Neutrality had in its favor Palestine's being the country of the Holy Places for the three religions and its geographic position as dividing certain important strategic areas. At the same time, the idea of "obsoleteness of the whole notion" might be invoked, and a neutral country could not be a UN member. Second: should the Agency pursue an independent policy in regard to Palestine or seek the help of as many states as possible for an Anglo-American compromise? By implication, pursuing the first path would lead to a two-front war against HMG and the Arab League, which had been formed on March 22, 1945, while the second would require that the Agency's whole attitude toward Great Britain would have to be "mitigated." Realistically, one or more of the great powers could be charged with carrying out the UN's decision, in which case they might then have a greater say than the "mechanical application" of the principle—one state, one vote—would involve. Robinson was not prepared at this stage to give answers to these questions, but to state them and to indicate the possible implications of decisions that might be taken.[18]

The Agency Executive's Aide-Memoire to the UN on April 18, reflecting Robinson's great influence, was circulated among the delegates although not recognized as an official document. Rooted in his determination that the Jewish case was first and foremost a juridical matter and should be based on HMG's Balfour Declaration of 1917 and the text of the Palestine Mandate, it began by emphasizing one "absolute basic principle": no solution would meet the Palestine issue unless the rights of the Jews "enshrined in the Mandate are respected, preserved and safeguarded." The Agency should be accorded a special status enabling it to be represented, although without possessing a vote, in the Assembly proceedings. As five Arab member states were identified with the "intransigent leadership" of the Palestine Arab Higher Committee, it would be "advantageous to all who seek a fully rounded picture" of the situation that the Jewish Agency be able to take part as well.[19]

Further, the memo continued, the UN would not wish the "present unhappy state of affairs" in Palestine to be prolonged because of its deliberations, and so should request Great Britain to implement all of the Mandate's provisions. Above all, the mandatory power should be asked to admit a substantial number of Holocaust survivors whose sufferings in Europe had still not been fully relieved, who longed for the haven promised them in the Mandate, and whose early admission the Anglo-American Committee of Inquiry had recommended. The mandatory's discriminatory Land Transfer Regulations of February 1940, leaving about only five percent of Palestine along the coast and in Jerusalem open to unrestricted purchase of land by Jews, should also be abolished during the interim period.

As for the UN's new Special Committee, interested parties such as the Arab States and perhaps the British government should not sit on the UNSCOP. The committee's terms of reference should include the continuing rights of the Jewish people (clearly Robinson's touch), internationally recognized under the Mandate, as well as the plight of Jewish Displaced Persons on the continent of Europe. A visit to Palestine itself for a first-hand acquaintance with the problem on the spot should take place, along with study of the Jewish problem worldwide; this was the reason for the Balfour Declaration and the Palestine Mandate, with their "clear promise" to establish in Palestine a Jewish National Home. Finally, a small committee, of about seven members, should be set up to work more effectively and reach decisions "more expeditiously" so as to complete its labors before the next regular session of the General Assembly.[20]

Four days later, Robinson focused his attention on the thorny subject of self-determination, about which the statement was often made that Zionist aspirations to Palestine were in conflict with that principle. Drawing on "positive international law and the political realities of our time," his confidential memo drew a distinction between the democratic and the ethnic principle. The democratic, first formulated in the decisions of the Yalta and Potsdam conferences, would exclude the imposition of political regimes contrary to the desire of the local population; the second would be a "powerful lever" for the creation of the so-called national states. The principle of self-determination did not appear in Article 2 of the UN charter, although references to it were made in Articles 1 and 55. The Charter did not establish self-determination of peoples in the ethnic sense as a binding principle. Neither the peace makers after the First World War nor those after the Second followed the principle of self-determination, as witness the cases of South Tyrol, Sudetenland, the prohibition of a German *Anschluss* with Austria in 1938, and Transylvania.

When the map of Europe was to be reshaped at the end of World War II, Robinson went on, one of the most frequently used methods for reaching national homogeneity was mass transfers of population (including Poles, Russians, Ukrainians, Belarusians, and Lithuanians). HMG made "ample use" of the slogan of self-determination in its latest pro-Arab statements, but it did not appear to intend to apply it to such of its possessions as the islands of Malta and Cyprus. If a free and unfettered expression of local views prevailed for Palestine, at least three points of view would surface: the Jewish community there, part of the Arab population, and great masses of Fellahin and Bedouin. In addition, the beneficiary of the Palestine Mandate was "the Jewish people as a whole," who would also have to be taken into account. In conclusion, self-determination was a "vague notion" applicable as a political criterion only for certain situations, and lacked the authority of a rule of international law.[21]

Robinson had "very grave" objections to Benjamin Akzin's idea of asking the International Court of Justice to give an advisory opinion. While the American Zionist Emergency Council's Washington representative despaired of a positive UN decision, Robinson had long been disappointed with the functioning of the League's High Court. Even if a majority could be marshaled in that Court for this end, he argued, a result which appeared improbable and would require protracted debate at a moment when no one wished to have too long a session, it would demand a tremendous concentration of all the Jewish Agency's forces when many other problems required its immediate attention. Further, UNSCOP's creation would have to be adjourned, while it was inconceivable that the International Court of Justice would be able to produce an opinion before the end of September 1947. The "whole affair" would have to be postponed until the next regular General Assembly in 1948, with no guarantees that that GA or the political climate worldwide would be more favorable than now. Moreover, full satisfaction from that Court, which had to date not tested any case and was hesitant to render judgment, was not a foregone conclusion. Even if it were to render a favorable opinion, this would not add substantially to the strength of the Agency's claim or to its legal position, and would not necessarily have a bearing on recommendations for the future. "The problem to be solved is a political problem and not a purely legal [sic]," Robinson emphasized.[22]

In another memo he spelled out the official status of the Jewish Agency. That new body had been recognized by Article 4 of the League of Nations Mandate to represent the Jewish people in relation to Palestine, with its special position stipulated in Articles 6 and 11 regarding "close settlement by Jews on the land" and developing public works, natural resources, and other services "not directly undertaken by the Administration." Summarizing the World Zionist Organization's development since its founding in 1897 under Theodor Herzl, Robinson heralded the fact that over 300,000 Jews had arrived in Palestine, the great majority assisted by the Agency. In the same short period, 200 agricultural settlements, the majority self-supporting, were established or financed, comprising a population of 50,000-60,000 people, and responsible for absorbing thousands of children from the Nazis under the Youth Aliya scheme. These varied and far-reaching activities, affecting the entire Jewish community in Palestine as well as many Jews elsewhere who desired to rebuild their lives in their own land, reflected, he asserted, both the broad, democratic basis of the Agency, its international status, and the semi-governmental character of its functions to which the British Peel Commission had drawn attention a decade earlier.[23]

As Robinson saw it, the difference between the Arab and the Jewish cases was the difference between two kinds of logic, the deductive and the inductive. Consistently, the Arabs argued that the problem was a very simple one: apply the same principle as one does to the British and the Americans—everyone is master in his own country. The Jewish attitude, inductive, charges that problems were not solved on the basis of principle but on the basis of international law realities: the facts, the existence of DPs and of a "Jewish problem," the Balfour Declaration, and other official international pronouncements. *The Jews, it had to be stressed again and again, were a nation requiring statehood.* That, he told the American Section of the Jewish Agency Executive, had to be remembered in preparing our case before the United Nations.[24]

Another issue which Robinson took on was the claim by Arab speakers that the right of Jews to immigrate into Palestine was denied by the UN Charter and the GA resolution of December 15, 1946. The latter, he observed, merely approved the constitution of a new specialized agency, the International Refugee Organization (IRO). That constitution gave "due weight" to, but did not require the previous consent of, the indigenous population to the entry of refugees or Displaced Persons to any non-self-governing country. As for the Charter, its preamble expressly enjoined the UN to respect the "obligations arising from treaties." Nothing in the Charter was of itself capable of invalidating a legal instrument like the Mandate; moreover, Article 80 clearly aimed to preserve the Mandate.

Some Arab spokesmen consciously misquoted the General Assembly's IRO December resolution ("the organization should endeavor to carry out its functions in such a way as to avoid disturbing friendly relations *between nations*"). They wished thereby to give the impression, as their resolutions read, that the UN "*disapproved* of the resettlement of displaced persons where the resettlement would be likely to disturb friendly relations with *neighboring countries*." Furthermore, the IRO Constitution was not valid for or binding on any other specialized UN agencies, not to speak of the UN as a whole or the mandatory power, while the British Government, in its struggle to stop Jewish immigration, never appealed to the Charter or the IRO Constitution for legal warrant. Finally, while the UN left the problem of resettlement to individual governments for decision, the IRO Constitution was not barred from resettling Jewish DPs in Palestine.[25]

Most significant at this stage was Robinson's very lengthy memorandum on May 14, 1947, "Fundamental Considerations in Preparing for Our Stand before the Special Committee." Required to now defend its stand before UNSCOP, as well as various world governments, and to show that its proposals were feasible, the Jewish Agency first had to prepare a paper on what the "idea of independence" would mean for the totality of Palestine's population and for the Jewish community in particular. Other Agency papers should compare the two alternatives of a Jewish and an Arab state in the whole of Palestine, as well as determine whether some form of a Mandate or trusteeship should follow, and if so, how this would operate, whether with an individual mandatory power or a collective administration. Keep in mind, Robinson cautioned, the warning of the outstanding mandate authority Professor William E. Rappard that it would be "a real international tragedy" if, in settling this "delicate" question, "the interests of the wards were to be sacrificed to the jealousies of the guardians."

Arriving at any trusteeship agreement for Palestine was fraught with difficulties, he continued. The Trusteeship Council's composition was still not complete (the Soviet Union had not yet joined); no definition of "states directly concerned" had yet been found; and the basic idea of trusteeship as "a static instrument" could be adjusted only with great difficulty to the Palestine Mandate, "a dynamic instrument." As Robinson told the American Section one day earlier, the UN Charter limited trusteeship to the benefit of a territory's current inhabitants, and he doubted that an organization like the Jewish Agency would be given sovereign status.

With the continuation of the Palestine Mandate or its conversion into a trusteeship agreement not giving the Zionist cause any satisfaction, and a *sui generis* international regime presenting obvious difficulties, Robinson raised two other possibilities. The so-called binational state, given past experience in constitutional law and government as adapted to the specific conditions of Palestine, did not justify such a solution. The clear differences between the contending Jewish and Arab communities, including the disparity in the standard of living, economic stratification, culture, and democratic institutions, would inevitability lead not to an independent system but to some supervision by an international arbitrator recalling the difficult example of the "free city" of Danzig under the League of Nations. Lastly, Robinson proposed that "most careful" consideration should be given *"to partition and various types of it."* A detailed discussion on boundaries, population, economic conditions, reciprocal protection of minorities, the fate of Jerusalem, special economic relations with neighboring countries and so on, should be prepared in time in order "not to leave the initiative to others."[26]

The major surprise of these General Assembly deliberations came that same day, when Soviet delegate Andrei Gromyko announced that while a binational state for Palestine remained the best solution, if it were not realizable because of "the deterioration of relations" between Jews and Arabs, then UNSCOP would have to consider partition of that country into "two independent autonomous states." The Agency understandably hailed this address as "an event of extraordinary importance," considering past standard Communist attacks on Zionism and the Soviet spokesman's admission now that the Jewish people's desire for a state was "natural and justified" in light of their "indescribable" and "exceptional sorrow and suffering" during the last world war.

Robinson remained skeptical, however. He cautioned colleagues that there was nothing new in Gromyko's condemnation of the Mandate as an instrument of British imperialism; that he "leaves us in the dark" concerning the rights of the Jewish people to Palestine; and he did not make clear that the Jewish DPs wished to emigrate there, nor speak of future Jewish immigration. Finally, the international law expert of the Agency's American Section pointed out, Gromyko's statement that Arabs and Jews both had "historic roots in Palestine" was certainly a long way from accepting the unique historical connection of the Jewish people with that country. Understanding, as Robinson did, that the Russian's speech left Moscow free to support either Arabs or Jews at the GA in September, Ben-Gurion informed the General Assembly that "a distinct Jewish nation" had arisen in Palestine having no conflict with the Arab people. Back home, the Agency Executive chairman told his colleagues in Jerusalem that the USSR's overarching purpose was to oust British influence from the Middle East, an assessment with which High Commissioner Alan Cunningham fully agreed.[27]

Two additional issues drew Robinson's attention at this point. First, counter to the Arab States decrying the Palestine Mandate as "illegal," "immoral," and "invalid," all of them save Lebanon stating that they never recognized the Mandate, he observed that three (Egypt, Iraq, and Lebanon) were expressly bound to it by the Law of the League of Nations. In addition, the Arab States (who failed at San Francisco to have their reservations about Palestine accepted) were fully aware of the scope and meaning of the UN Charter, wherein Article 80 safeguarded the rights of *peoples* under the mandates. Since the only people specifically cited by name in the entire mandates system was the Jewish people, their right to have its national home in Palestine constituted part of UN law.

As to the Arabs' repeated charge that the mandates had terminated with the dissolution of the League of Nations, HMG did not concur (witness its request of the GA on April 2, 1947, regarding an investigation of the Palestine Mandate). Nor did the UN Charter's Article 80; Australia's delegate at San Francisco, Minister for External Affairs and Attorney General Herbert V. Evatt, had spoken for the clear majority when stating on May 10, 1945, that "old" and "new" mandates comprised the classes of territory under discussion, and the former "obviously cannot be left to become international orphans." In addition, the Chinese resolution that the UN assume the functions of the League as to the mandates system was unanimously passed at the League's last Assembly session in April 1946. The substantive provisions of the mandates, Robinson concluded, could be terminated only through the "orderly channels" of the United Nations.[28]

The decision by Lord Mountbattten and Attlee on June 3, 1947, to partition British India spurred Robinson to warn his colleagues that nothing would be "more fateful" than drawing an analogy between the fate of that "jewel in the British crown" and Palestine. The basic idea behind the India plan was static, based on the correct fact that no substantial changes in mutual relationships between Hindu and Moslem could be accomplished, and based on respect for the wishes of the population, which required a *sui generis* plebiscite to ascertain that will in the provinces. No consideration was given to the idea of a corridor between the two parts of Pakistan, leaving it a state of two disconnected Moslem "islands" in a Hindu sea; nor to the problem of eventual transfer of minorities in order to make the populations more homogeneous; nor to the reciprocal protection of minorities.

Other issues made the scheme for India unique. The offer of Dominion status to the two warring factions; the scattered 563 Princely States (Rajistan) to decide on their allegiance; and the problem as projected against the general background of the East-West split—all further indicated that "this plan is so Indian" that to call it a plan for the partition of Palestine would ignore the dynamism of the Palestine situation, while suggesting the new idea of a state without territorial cohesion. If the India partition plan had any bearing on the Palestine question, Robinson posited, it was nothing but a confirmation of certain aspects of HMG's current Morrison plan proposing a cantonization of the Holy Land with provincial autonomy, a proposal that the Jewish Agency had fully rejected.[29]

Trusteeship under the UN Charter offered no solution, argued another Robinson memo. While Article 76 stated that the final goal was political freedom either in the form of self-government or independence, it might open the way for binational trust territories. Even if an agreement were reached, would Great Britain consider the Arab states as "states directly concerned," which would then allow them a veto on any formulation? Perhaps the "gravest" of all HMG's "aberrations" in its Palestine policy was its taking those states into account when drawing up the 1939 White Paper, then calling them in again during 1946 and

1947 to give advice on Palestine's future. In this regard, the possibility should not be excluded that one of the Arab states or the Arab League as a whole might claim to be the trustee, which in turn raised the problem of collective trusteeship, possibly the worst solution.

A collective trusteeship run by the Big Powers, Robinson observed, would invite administrative paralysis. Examples readily abounded: witness the past "endless bickerings" of the inter-allied Councils in Berlin and Vienna; the "barren negotiations" of the Council of Foreign Ministers; the "impotence" of the UN Security Council; the "present stalemate" in the GA's Atomic Energy Commission; and the "absolute deadlock" in the Security Council's Military Staff Committee. The stalemate over Trieste, in dispute between Italy and Yugoslavia over the last five months, was yet a warning of the ineffectiveness of such a trusteeship. Moreover, he added, the composition of the new Trusteeship Council consisted of government representatives—including Iraq—who decide out of political, not legal or moral, considerations. They were not prepared to offer an agreement with "dynamic provisions" for future Jewish immigration and settlement.[30]

As for an international regime for Palestine, his first tentative observations on June 25 began with the assumption that the functions should determine the regime, not the reverse. To be most fitting for the Zionists' objective, it had to secure a permanent flow of emigrants to develop the country and to carry out large settlement and development plans "until such time as a Jewish majority existed in Palestine" and the democratic processes would be able to take care of the next stage. Seeking the good of the present population and bringing about a "prospering Jewish majority as a pre-condition for a Jewish state," the solution might lie first in the strengthening of the Jewish Agency's powers and functions to be primarily responsible for "the dynamic elements" of the new regime's progress.

A second step would witness the creation of a tripartite government commission, consisting of Jews, Arabs, and a UN team, to carry out the current business of good government and to secure the uninterrupted functioning of the Jewish Resettlement and Development Authority (Jewish Agency). A "neutral" body, following the UNSCOP precedent, would be the most desirable UN team. A detachment of the UN Military Staff Committee could be stationed for security, but in the long run police and military forces should be created from local elements of the population whose loyalty to the "ultimate purpose" of the international regime was beyond the slightest doubt. Whether the Agency should initiate suggesting such details or intervene only when and if urged to do so must be reserved for further consideration.[31]

For the next few months, Robinson shifted his energies to preparing a volume on the special session of the General Assembly, held from April 28 to May 15, 1947, convened as a step towards the solution of the Palestine problem. He had first proposed this need to the Jewish Agency Executive on June 2, emphasizing that it was the first time in history that the Jewish People had been given opportunity to appear in an official capacity before the organized community of nations, and that that people spoke with one voice via the Jewish Agency. Such a study, he noted, would not only be a record of history, but also provide guidance for the next, second regular Assembly. First and foremost, the official documents of the UN and the Verbatim Records of the meetings of the General Committee, of the GA, and of the First Committee would be consulted, with a reasonable deadline for publication to be sometime in the last two weeks of August.

Given the green light, Robinson's *Palestine and the United Nations: Prelude to Solution* appeared remarkably on schedule under the imprint of the Public Affairs Press. His survey began with the San Francisco Conference and ended with the conclusion of the special session. Reviews were generally favorable, especially praising the extensive documentation and footnotes, although some found fault with his "prosecuting manner" when stating the Arab case and criticizing Ernest Bevin. Making a point of sending a copy to the UN secretariat, the chairmen of the special session committees, UNSCOP members, US Congressmen, and key UN delegations, he then returned to his legal tasks for the Agency Executive.[32]

September saw no cessation in Robinson's activity. He took part in the meetings of the American Section of the Jewish Agency Executive, and prepared an extensive review for his associates of the general debate in the GA on the Palestine question. That debate, held on September 17–22, saw the first clear expression of America's assertion of leadership in the UN with Secretary of State George C. Marshall's announcement that the United States "gives great weight" to the recommendation by the majority of UNSCOP members for the partition of Palestine. That speech shocked the Arab delegates, those of Syria and Lebanon particularly bitter against the United States' "senior representative," while the British and French held back from expressing their views. Robinson found it difficult to explain why all the other country delegates, with the exception of UNSCOP member Alberto Ulloa of Peru supporting that Special Committee's majority position, remained non-committal. For the future, he suggested that the Agency again stress the inequity being perpetuated between the two parties in the argument, the Arabs having five permanent spokesmen and the Jews none. Whether the Agency should reply to all the insinuations made until the present by the Arab states at the UN, thus "embarking upon polemics," remained up for discussion.[33]

The suggestion, put forward in a *New York Herald Tribune* article on October 7 by former US Undersecretary of State Sumner Welles, and quickly accepted by Swedish delegate Rickhard Sandler, that implementation of the GA's decision on Palestine would be carried by the Security Council particularly worried Robinson. Only a few days earlier, the Assembly's General Committee had accepted a proposal by three Arab states to consider international cooperation in preventing immigration "likely to disturb friendly relations between nations" (anti-Zionist "back door tactics," Robinson observed, that had failed the previous May regarding the IRO Constitution). Implementation of a GA decision under the UN Charter's Article 10 did not instruct the Assembly to appeal to the Council for help, he pointed out on October 13 to the Jewish Agency Executive. In addition, use of police or other armed forces was clearly implied in Article 81, which provided for the UN to be an administering authority in trust areas. Since the Trusteeship Council operated under the GA's authority (in non-strategic areas), he added, it would be for the Assembly to recruit and organize such forces.[34]

Did a recommendation of the General Assembly with regard to Palestine have legal force? In Chapter IV of the Charter, "recommendations" and "decisions" were used interchangeably. Robinson's examination of various Articles led to his conclusion on October 29 that neither the use of the word "recommendation" nor the use of recommendations in regard to various addresses was decisive for the proper legal validity of such an act. More to the point, the most recent statements of Colonial Secretary Arthur Creech Jones at the UN expressed HMG's readiness, although reserving its right to take part in implementation, to acquiesce in whatever recommendation the GA might make. Also taking into consideration that the Palestine question was within the UN's jurisdiction as affecting the future of a mandated territory, and as this was something which Great Britain admitted, Robinson concluded thus: Any GA recommendation in this matter, while technically termed a recommendation, was in essence a decision *binding* the membership of the UN and creating an obligation on all members of the UN to respect such a decision in accordance with Article 2, paragraph 2, of the Charter.[35]

Implementation of an ultimate General Assembly decision on Palestine raised a few basic issues, he hastened to note at the beginning of November. While the Guatemalan, Uruguayan, and USSR proposals envisaged a transitional period under a UN authority, the American proposal saw such an authority as but an advisory body of the UN attached to the mandatory government. Whether the British Government would cooperate in some kind of condominium with a UN committee was still uncertain. The date for termination of the mandate was also in dispute (January 1, 1948 for the Soviets, July 1, 1948 for the United States), influencing as well the evacuation of British troops in Palestine. As to what kind of UN authority should exist in Palestine in the period between the GA decision and the establishment—not necessarily simultaneously—of two states in Palestine, the GA might appoint the UN authority, to be responsible to the Security Council (the only permanent UN body). That would still leave open its composition. An international military force and deadlines, such as for the adoption of a constitution by the two states, had yet to be resolved as well.

As to a provisional government, Robinson insisted that the Jewish Agency, already in existence, nominate members; the Arab authority might well be confirmed by the UN. The mandatory power, about to leave, should not have authority (the US proposal) to prescribe the electoral provisions for a Constituent Assembly. The UN authority, as per the Soviet proposal, could approve the relevant legislation prepared by the Provisional Government. Both the American and Soviet proposals agreed, after all, that in the transition period the Provisional Government should proceed, under supervision of the UN authority, to the establishment of administrating organs of government, both central and local.[36]

While his colleagues in New York labored incessantly to corral GA delegates for a majority vote favoring Palestine's partition into a Jewish and an Arab state, Robinson raised preliminary observations regarding "a constitution for Eretz Israel." The expression "Jewish State," used throughout the UNSCOP Report, should be replaced as soon as possible by a proper name, his lengthy November 14 memorandum began. That report had recommended the adoption of a constitution as a prerequisite for the establishment of an independent state. A preliminary draft constitution should be prepared for submission to the Constituent Assembly by the spring of 1948, as the GA might meet in March and was due to conclude its work between May and July. Presenting a tentative table of contents of the constitution, together with a list of some constitutions from other countries which might be useful, Robinson noted that special consideration had to be given to the radical change in the *corps electoral* in view of the large development plans and the increase of "heterogeneous elements" through the mass immigration of Jews to the new state. The influence of the Jewish Diaspora, as well as the existence of a vast Arab minority and the surrounding Arab states, could not be overlooked either.

The committee drafting such a constitution faced many problems, he observed. Those of a general nature included, among others, the delimitation of constitutional law and ordinary legislation; whether the constitution should be made rigid or flexible, particularly in regard to amendments and revision; whether the principles of election should include literacy tests and encourage a multiplicity of political parties. Also to be examined were the question of the representative organ and the types of self-government, and whether the document should be based upon a rigid interpretation of the theory of separation of powers or whether the rule of law should be "enthroned" by way of judicial review of legislative (and/or administrative) acts.

Major specific problems could not be avoided. These included whether Eretz Israel was a national Jewish state or a "welfare state" for all its inhabitants; the relationship between the Jewish religion and the State; whether minorities should be granted autonomy in their internal affairs; the terminology of government and law in Hebrew. With common sense, knowledge of the social milieu, legal acumen, and many more qualities, primarily a spirit of cooperation, necessary to produce a constitution, the accumulated experience of other nations in this field was to be stressed in this regard. Immediate steps, Robinson concluded, should be taken to secure the help of "comparativists," and to compile a reference library on constitutions, electoral laws, parliamentary procedures, and comparative government for the benefit of the committee preparing this essential document.[37]

With obtaining the necessary two-thirds vote in the General Assembly for partition hardly a given, Robinson did what he could towards this objective. When Abe Feller, chief legal counsel under UN Secretary General Trygve Lie, advised him that the Agency might not obtain that result, he prepared a memo arguing that a two-thirds vote was not needed. Under the direction of Moshe Toff heading the Agency's Latin American department, he collaborated with famed Argentinian poet Carlos Gruenberg to achieve support in the vital bloc of Latin American and Caribbean countries. He found a sympathetic ear in the Russian delegate Semyon K. Tsarapkin, Soviet chargé d'affaires of the Russian embassy in Washington, who had spoken in the *Ad Hoc* Committee about the Nazi persecution of the Jews during World War II, and emphasized the right of the Jewish people, like the Arabs, to a state of their own in Palestine. When Syria's Faris El-Khouri and Palestine Arab Higher Committee executive Jamal Husseini made the claim that the East European Jews who wanted to go to Palestine had no connection to the Jews of biblical Israel but were descendants of the seventh century pagan Khazars of Turkish stock who had converted to Judaism, Tsarapkin proudly came to Robinson and said "Did you hear, Yaakov, I am a Khazar!" Robinson told a Yugoslav delegate who wished to vote "no" at the GA that his father, Dr. Joza Vilfan, was an old friend who had favored Jewish minority rights in Europe. The son called his father, Secretary General to Marshal Josip Broz Tito, in Belgrade. Vilfan lost no time in going to Tito. Yugoslavia would vote "abstain."[38]

On the evening of November 29, 1947, history was made in six minutes with more than the required majority vote in the Assembly to partition Palestine into two states that would become fully independent by October 1, 1948, along with Economic Union. Yet, while pandemonium swept across the Jewish world, the Arabs' launching of a civil war in Palestine and its grim consequences left Robinson and his colleagues little time to rest on their hard-earned laurels. He soon met with Constantin A. Stavropoulos, chosen by UN secretary general Trygve Lie to be in charge of all legal affairs for the secretariat advance party of the five-man Palestine Commission created to implement the GA's recommendation.

The Greek lawyer, a few years later to become undersecretary general of the UN's Legal Office, wished Robinson's assistance regarding the constitutional problems of the two states and the problems of Palestine law. Stavropoulos advised that the Jewish Agency organize immediately its own working groups to aid the Commission regarding military affairs, police, boundaries, economics, laws and constitution, and administration central and local, and to provide him with a list at the earliest possible time of civil servants in Palestine able to serve under the Commission and subsequently under the Provisional Councils of government. The secretariat's most important job, Robinson understood, was to find persons "fearless enough" to serve on the Provisional Council of the Arab state. It was characteristic that the secretariat envisaged such members being held in "protective custody," Robinson concluded his report to the Agency Executive.[39]

As 1948 dawned, Walter Eytan in Jerusalem sent Robinson his first draft of a scheme for the emerging Jewish commonwealth's foreign office. Hoping that Robinson would come to Palestine for its UN Division, the new Director of the Foreign Ministry also sought his advice as to who could issue passports and to whom they should be issued. Another important legal matter for Robinson's consideration was the issue of recognition of the new Jewish State. At what stage could such recognition be given? Did the Ministry ask for it, or did it come automatically? In any case, Eytan cabled Shertok that it was important to secure independence in the conduct of foreign relations at the earliest possible date, since this and other matters could not be conducted by the Palestine Commission.[40]

The efforts by officials in the US State and War Departments to reverse the Assembly decision, making strong use of the argument that Arab oil was vital to the nation's economic and political security, as well as to Secretary Marshall's European Recovery Plan, also sparked Robinson's concern. Writing at the end of January to Arthur Lourie, a lawyer heading the Agency's office in New York, he suggested that the time had come for the Zionists to meet increasing charges on the ground of "Un-Americanism." The connection between the pro-Arab American oil industry and these developments had to be studiously pursued, beginning with the current Congressional investigation in Washington into the exorbitant prices charged during World War II by the Arabian American Oil Company (ARAMCO) to the US Navy. A book just published by Yale University Law Professor Eugene V. Rostow, *The National Policy for the Oil Industry*, indicated that a thorough investigation of the real relationship between foreign oil, security, and domestic consumption could well establish "a tenable doctrine" for the American Zionists to justify their attitude, he urged.[41]

Faris El-Khouri's two "exceptions" to the UN Palestine Commission during a meeting of the Security Council on February 10 elicited yet another secret memorandum by Robinson to the Agency Executive. The ardent Syrian nationalist's first charge that the Commission was not elected in accordance with the Provisional Rules of Procedure, requiring secret ballot according to Rule 82 for the General Assembly, merited a few objections. The Security Council was not a body superior to the General Assembly, nor had the Council any jurisdiction at all to verify the legitimacy of subsidiary organs of the Assembly. Moreover, Robinson noted that none of the Arab delegations had raised an objection when the Commission was elected. In addition, Rule 82 in conjunction with four other Rules covered only a limited number of elections constituting something like general provisions. This interpretation was corroborated by UNSCOP, as were the UN Temporary Commission on Korea and one on Greece—all elected not by secret ballot.

As for El-Khouri's exception that the GA's November 29 recommendation had not been "adopted" by the member states, from the viewpoint of the GA, the UN, and international law in general, it was not the business of the UN to follow what measures, if any, individual states were taking in regard to resolutions passed by the Assembly. The credentials of all UN delegates empowered them to vote, "which means to commit their governments and that is all that is necessary." The "implementation" of a resolution was a legal responsibility of the UN and not of its members, Robinson emphasized; if unopposed, the resolution would be carried out by the Palestine Commission, and if opposed, it would come before the Security Council. Concluded Robinson, neither in law nor in precedent was there any support for the "exceptions" raised.[42]

The State Department rejected Robinson's legal paper about implementation and a GA recommendation regarding a territory which was an international trust. According to the view of "Foggy Bottom," he reported to the Agency Executive at the end of the month, it would be "too heavy a commitment" for the US to accept his theory that the Assembly may enforce its decision, while adopting his second approach would jeopardize the US government's hold after the war on the Pacific Islands taken from a defeated Japan. Article 43 of the Charter, Robinson noted, did provide for an explicit method to create an international force, a UN army composed of national contingents. Transitional provisions contained in Article 106 also allowed for "a joint action on behalf of the community of nations" in order to maintain international peace and security pending resolution of law and order.

In Robinson's view, US head delegate Warren Austin omitted reference to Article 106 when addressing the Security Council on February 24 because he did not wish to commit himself to this method of creating an international force, but "the doors are still open." Shertok disagreed, sensing that Austin's statement about the Council being directed to keep international peace and not to enforce a political settlement (partition) underlay the State Department's view that the Assembly's recommendations were "merely of moral weight," and not legally binding. This, he sensed, already reflected an attempt to set up the Council as an authority superceding, and possibly setting aside, that of the Assembly.[43]

Austin's announcement to the Council on March 19, 1948, declaring that, with partition no longer a viable option in view of the on-going civil war in Palestine, a temporary trusteeship for Palestine should be established, corroborated Shertok's fears, stunned the delegates, and infuriated Secretary General Lie. The American reversal, which shocked Truman, divided the Agency American Section as to future action. It agreed that the Executive in Palestine should decide whether to proclaim a Provisional Government immediately. Robinson suggested that if it so decided, no proclamation should be made of a Jewish State, since the General Assembly had done so on November 29 last, and reference to that fact should be made in the declaration of independence's preamble. In addition, the Provisional Council should declare that it would act under the UN Palestine Commission if the latter exercised its functions, and would assume full administrative responsibility with the termination of the Mandate on May 15.[44]

"Plugging away hard," in a skeptical Creech Jones's characterization, to obtain a truce and interim trusteeship, Dean Rusk, head of the UN Division of the State Department, drew up draft articles to that end on April 22 and distributed them to the Jewish and Arab representatives. The same day, Abba Hillel Silver, chair of the Agency's American section, informed the UN Political and Security Committee that the *yishuv* would establish the Jewish State officially on May 15 right after the end of the Mandate. Four days later, an official memo by Robinson and Epstein pointed to the Palestinian Jewish community's concentrating its efforts over the past five months in making the Jewish State a reality "in accordance with the Resolution of the General Assembly," while the Arab population did not set up an alternative central communal organization. The functional services created by the former, they posited, were of such a nature that they "cannot be discontinued without causing irreparable harm to the total population of the areas under Jewish control."[45]

Responding to Jamal Husseini's assertion to the GA's Committee I on April 26 that Article 28 of the Palestine Mandate offered a legal basis for an Arab-dominated state in the whole of western Palestine, yet another Robinson memo observed that that Article in no way indicated the nature of the country's future government. Palestine was not granted "provisional recognition" as an independent nation by the League of Nations Covenant or by the Mandate. Rather, Article 28's purpose was to safeguard in perpetuity the rights secured by Articles 13 and 14 concerning the Holy Places, as well as have the mandatory "fully honor the financial obligations legitimately incurred by the Administration of Palestine." That Mandate, whose primary purpose was to give effect to the Balfour Declaration, was unique in its legal nature. Upon its termination, he concluded, only such a regime could be established which would satisfy the essential purposes of the Mandate and the Balfour Declaration; the creation of the Jewish State "is the only practical device for satisfying this purpose." Shertok, countering Husseini's declaration that the country's Arabs would proclaim the whole of Palestine as an independent state on May 16 unless the GA created a temporary trusteeship that would lead to a sovereign unitary state in conformity to Arab demands, asked the UN on April 27 to prevent an invasion of Palestine by Transjordan at the Mandate's end, and rejected the American trusteeship proposal.[46]

On May 6, Shertok cabled Ben-Gurion Robinson's final opinion as to procedure when May 15 arrived. Provided that no "explicit" revocation or supersession of the partition plan would be voted by this GA special session, the Agency's Legal Counsel based his stand on the resolution adopted on April 12 by the Zionist General Council (*HaVa'ad HaPo'el HaTsiyoni*) that the "higher authority" of the Jewish State should arise with the end of the Mandate. The General Council had also approved on that date the decision of the Agency Executive and the National Council (*HaVa'ad HaLeumi*) of March 23 that a Provisional Jewish Government would operate immediately with the Mandate's end, no later than May 16, and cooperate with those UN representatives who would be present at that time in the country. A communication should state that the Provisional Government had discussed current matters, and issue a declaration regarding the protection of holy places, religious and minority rights, citizenship, international conventions, and financial obligations. Another communication would address issues of Economic Union and Transit. The term "Provisional Government," Robinson indicated, was suggested, since the new government could be established only by a Constituent Assembly. Following elections for the Assembly, his lengthy memo closed, that body could be called in after August 1, the date for the total withdrawal of all British forces from Palestine.[47]

Eight days later, Ben-Gurion declared in Dizengoff House on 16 Rothschild Boulevard in Tel-Aviv, the first Jewish city, the establishment of *Medinat Yisra'el* (the State of Israel). Two millennia had passed before this rebirth of Jewish sovereignty in the biblically covenanted Promised Land. The announcement was made at 4 p.m. that Friday so as not to violate the start of the Sabbath in Palestine two hours later. High Commissioner Cunningham left Government House in Jerusalem early that morning, his farewell radio broadcast the previous night expressing his "great sadness" that an Arab-Jewish peace had not been secured under the Mandate, alongside the constant desire that "cooperation, good-will and sanity" might be established between HMG and Palestine's inhabitants "to our mutual benefit in the future."[48]

For Robinson and his colleagues, the arc of history had at long last bent toward justice. His long-held hope that the identity of the Jewish People as a nation would receive international acknowledgment, particularly after the Holocaust, reached fulfillment on May 14, 1948. The exile of 1,800 years had come to an end, bearing the weight of revolutionary significance, and the singular role played in that drama's last act by an international lawyer of high repute had certainly proven significant in its denouement. That morning, called to the White House for the first time, Robinson had argued to its legal staff that a Jewish State would adhere to the UN Charter, and that it merited US recognition in light of the Assembly's November vote following a full debate on all aspects of the Palestine question.[49]

Using to the fullest his wide command of languages and history, Robinson would go on to serve as Counselor to Israel's Permanent Mission to the UN until his resignation in 1957. Among his outstanding attainments were the drafting of the Reparations Agreement between Israel and the Federal Republic of Germany (1952), which resulted in the payment of more than $930 million in goods and services to the State of Israel as the heir to those Holocaust victims who had no family survivors, and his legal advice to Israel as it sought to fend off diplomatic pressure while negotiating withdrawal from the Sinai after the Suez incursion (1956). He also secured the Foreign Ministry's approval after three years to sign, on Israel's behalf, the International Refugee Convention in 1954, stressing that many Jews worldwide required this protection and that the Jewish State's "moral" reputation was on the line. At the same time, from his vantage point as Israel's delegate to the UN Commission on Human Rights, he quickly became disillusioned with the world's hypocrisy when faced with the intrusion of Cold War geopolitics directly into the Middle East, mature democracies acquiescing to Egypt and other authoritarian regimes "with clear knowledge that these regimes repress human rights," and politics behind certain appointments weakening the International Court of Justice.[50]

Robinson would also serve as a pivotal special assistant to Attorney General Gideon Hausner, preparing the international law arguments used by the prosecution, at Israel's trial in 1961 of Adolf Eichmann. Sharply disagreeing with a *Washington Post* editorial (a charge repeated in other circles) that Israel had engaged in "jungle law" by abducting Eichmann from another country and that it had no jurisdiction to try the case, he posited that the concentration of Holocaust survivors, the presence of documentation, and Israel's "special Jewish character" made it "natural and proper for Israel to assume jurisdiction in a case involving the Nazi design to exterminate the Jewish people."[51] This was the first trial, he appreciated, to feature the legal theories of universal jurisdiction and genocide, and the first to rely so centrally on survivor testimony. After a four-month trial, the individual most responsible for implementing the Nazis' "Final Solution" was convicted and the conviction affirmed, and he was hanged in late May 1962, his ashes scattered at sea.

Following Robinson's retirement from the Israeli diplomatic service, he helped establish the research branch of Yad Vashem, the state's official memorial to the victims of the Holocaust. He pioneered in gathering documentation on what in Hebrew is termed the *Shoah*, edited Holocaust-related subjects for the *Encyclopedia Judaica*, and became the Legal Advisor relating to Holocaust issues for the Conference on Jewish Material Claims against Germany, the Memorial Foundation for Jewish Culture, and the YIVO Institute for Jewish Research, where he maintained an office. These activities coincided with the course Robinson gave at the Academy for International Law in The Hague (1958), his preparation of a comprehensive bibliography on international law assessing over 2,000 sources in dozens of languages (1967), and a seminal analysis about the international protection of minorities from a global viewpoint (1971). Together with his brother Nehemiah, who had assumed the IJA directorship in 1947, he also centralized the efforts of Jewish organizations around the world to coordinate Holocaust research and to support the work of prosecutors' offices investigating Nazi criminals by providing documents and locating witnesses. Typically, Robinson introduced himself as merely "research coordinator of the four Holocaust institutes." His last major bibliographic work was a comprehensive digest of the Nuremberg evidence, more than 3,000 documents submitted to the IMT, coedited with Henry Sachs (1976).[52]

At Robinson's passing on October 24, 1977, in New York City at the age of eighty-eight, Israel still lived under relentless siege and periodic war, the Arab world continuing its adamant refusal to accept Jewish legitimacy or indigenousness in Eretz Israel. Following the Popular Front for the Liberation of Palestine's two terrorist attacks in April and May 1974 inside Israel that claimed forty-five lives (including twenty-nine children), Palestine Liberation Organization leader Yasser Arafat cheered when appearing in the General Assembly that November while wearing an empty gun holster, the killing of fourteen and eighty injured in a bombing attack on Jerusalem's Zion square in July 1975, and the General Assembly Resolution 3379 of November 10, 1975, declaring that "Zionism is a form of racism and racial discrimination," Robinson had privately bemoaned the triumph of "tyranny" and the "subversion of international law." Yet the contribution of this modest and austere human being to the success of the beleaguered Jewish State's success remained strong. As Abba Eban, Israel's first Permanent Representative to the United Nations, wrote later, "Robinson did more than anyone else to educate us all in the potentialities and limitations of multilateral diplomacy." His insistence that Israel's delegations make every effort to take part in all the UN's activities and make in them "a contribution based on intrinsic quality, not on mere political power," a stance which rapidly established for Robinson a dominant position in the UN's Sixth Committee (Legal Committee), influenced future Israeli diplomats and inspired countless others.[53]

Robinson left a lasting legacy of considerable worth. His extraordinary memory, his accuracy, and his power of rational analysis—characteristics popularly associated with the intellectual leaders of Lithuanian Jewry—convinced Israeli Ambassador and Professor of International Law Shabtai Rosenne to deem Robinson "the first truly Jewish international jurist of front rank of modern times . . . placing the perceived interests of the Jewish people and its established organs first in his order of priorities." The passing of this powerful advocate for his people, a man who acted mostly behind the scenes throughout his long and productive life, evoked this judgment in a eulogy by Nahum Goldmann: Robinson was "one of the greatest figures in the [sic] Jewish history of this last half century." Given his wide-ranging achievements on behalf of world Jewry, the product of a rare scholar-activist's defining vision, many would agree.[54]

Endnotes

1. Stephen Schlesinger, "San Francisco—the Birthplace of the United Nations," *San Francisco Chronicle*, June 19, 2015; https://www.un.org/en/sections/history; "A Great Day; 1945 San Francisco Conference" (radio broadcast, 1955), soundcloud.com/united-nations-eng/1945-san-francisco-conference.
2. Monty Noam Penkower, *Palestine to Israel: Mandate to State, 1945–1948*, vol. 1, *Rebellion Launched, 1945–1946* (New York, 2019), 6–7; Robinson memo, "The Arab States and the Mandate for Palestine," May 21, 1947, CF-Robinson memos, Zionist Archives (hereafter ZA), New York City (now at the Central Zionist Archives [hereafter CZA], Jerusalem).
3. Omry Kaplan-Feuereisen, trans. Richard Mann, "At the Service of the Jewish Nation: Jacob Robinson and International Law," *Osteuropa* 58: 8/10 (2008): 157–166; Mark Lewis, *The Birth of the New International Justice, The Internationalization of Crime and Punishment, 1919–1950* (Oxford, 2014), 150–180; James Loeffler, *Rooted Cosmopolitans: Jews and Human Rights in the Twentieth Century* (New Haven, 2018), 31 and chap. 2. Improbably, the Third Reich acceded to the League's decision to honor that commitment to the Jews

of German Upper Silesia until it expired on July 15, 1937. Natan Feinberg, *HaMa'arakha HaYehudit Neged Hitler: Al Bimat Hever HaLeumim* (Jerusalem, 1957). For the Minority Treaties, see Oscar I. Janowsky, *The Jews and Minority Rights (1898–1919)* (New York, 1933); Jacob Robinson, Oscar Karbach, Max M. Laserson, Nehemiah Robinson, and Marc Vichniak, *Were the Minority Treaties a Failure?* (New York, 1943); Carole Fink, *Defending the Rights of Others: The Great Powers, The Jews, and International Minority Protection, 1878–1938* (New York, 2004).

4. Jacob Robinson, "Institute of Jewish Affairs at 25," *Scope Special*, n.d., 3–4, Series 3, Jacob Robinson MSS., US Holocaust Memorial Museum (hereafter USHMM), Washington, DC; Loeffler, *Rooted Cosmopolitans*, 125–126; Gil S. Rubin, "The Future of the Jews: Planning for the Postwar Jewish World, 1939–1946," PhD dissertation (Columbia University, 2017), chap. 1; Gil Rubin, "The End of Minority Rights: Jacob Robinson and the 'Jewish Question' in World War II," *Simon Dubnow Institute Yearbook* 11 (2012): 55–72.

5. Monty Noam Penkower, *Palestine to Israel: Mandate to State, 1945-1948*, vol. 1, *Rebellion Launched, 1945–1946* (New York, 2019), 6–7; Shabtai Rosenne, "Jacob Robinson—In Memoriam, 28 November 1889–24 October 1977," *Israel Law Review* 13:23 (July 1978): 287–289.

6. Robinson report to Office Committee, June 7, 1945, file 2A/11, World Jewish Congress Archives (hereafter WJC), New York City, now at the American Jewish Archives, Cincinnati, OH; Jacob Robinson, "From the Protection of Minorities to Protection of Human Rights," in *The Jewish Yearbook of International Law, 1948* (Jerusalem, 1949), 115–151; Lewis, *The Birth of the New International Justice*, chap. 6; Loeffler, *Rooted Cosmopolitans*, 120–124.

7. Michael R. Marrus, "A Jewish Lobby at Nuremberg: Jacob Robinson and the Institute of Jewish Affairs, 1945–1946," *Cardozo Law Review* 27:4 (February 2006): 1653–1655. Kohanski, a philosopher who taught for most of his career at the Graduate School for Jewish Social Work in New York City, also contributed to the *Universal Jewish Encyclopedia*, was managing editor of the *Jewish Social Services Quarterly*, and was active in the American Jewish Conference and the League for Labor Palestine.

8. Marrus, "A Jewish Lobby at Nuremberg," 1657–1665; idem, "The Holocaust at Nuremberg," *Yad Vashem Studies* 27 (Jerusalem, 1998): 5–41. Also see Jonathan A. Bush, "Nuremberg and Beyond: Jacob Robinson, International Lawyer," *Loyola of Los Angeles International and Comparative Law Review* 39 (2017): 259–286; Boaz Cohen, "Dr. Jacob Robinson, the Institute of Jewish Affairs, and the Elusive Voice at Nuremberg," in *Holocaust and Justice: Representation*

and Historiography of the Holocaust in Post-War Trials, ed. D. Bankier and D. Michman (Jerusalem, 2010), 81–100.

9. Jacob Robinson, "General Report," December 6,1945, https://www.trumanlibrary.gov/library/research-files/report-jacob-robinson-world-jewish-congress; Jacob Robinson, "The Nuremberg Judgment," *Congress Weekly*, October 25, 1946, 6–8; Jacob Robinson, "The International Military Tribunal and the Holocaust: Some Legal Reflections," *Israel Law Review* 7:1 (January 1972): 1–13; Jackson to Weizmann, January 7, 1946, Chaim Weizmann Archives, Rehovot, Israel. The British authorities, Robinson reminisced, probably apprehensive of the possibility that Weizmann might raise the question of the 1939 White Paper against large-scale Jewish immigration to Palestine, vetoed Jackson's suggestion (to his great embarrassment) that the aged Zionist leader testify, claiming that it would be better to have non-Jews testify in the Jewish case. Only with the Eichmann trial, Robinson ended his "legal reflections" in 1972, did the accused appear as "responsible for the Crime against the Jewish people, not only against human rights of individual Jews, but also against the collective right of a people to existence and continuity. International law doctrine accepted the new concept approvingly." Robinson, "The International Military Tribunal," 13.

10. Jackson to Institute of Jewish Affairs, September 1, 1946, Robinson MSS., Series 3, USHMM. Robison would also advise Telford Taylor, Chief of Counsel for the US Prosecution in the Flick Case of a US Military Court at Nuremberg (April–December 1947), where German industrialist Friedrich Flick was sentenced to seven years of imprisonment for his firm's use of concentration camp inmates for slave labor in its mines and factories during World War II, as well as for the seizure of plants in occupied territories, and for his membership in the Nazi party and the "Circle of Friends of Himmler." The indictment charged this use to be War Crimes and Crimes against Humanity. Another indictment, Crimes Against Humanity for the persecution of Jews and the "aryanization" of their properties, was dismissed by the court, stating that the evidence presented (which was all for cases prior to September 1, 1939) fell outside its jurisdiction as the tribunal had a mandate only for acts committed during World War II. See Lisa M. Stallbaumer, "Frederick Flick's Opportunism and Expediency," *Dimensions* 13:2 (1999): 19–23.

11. Jacob Robinson, *Human Rights and Fundamental Freedoms in the Charter of the United Nations* (New York, 1946); Loeffler, *Rooted Cosmopolitans*, 147–149; Humphrey to Robinson, Series 3, Robinson MSS., USHMM; Robinson, "General Report," December 6, 1945.

12. Robinson to Goldmann, January 18, 1946, "Summary of the Present Situation of European Jewry," World Jewish Congress Archives, London. Also see David Bankier, ed., *The Jews Are Coming Back: The Return of the Jews to Their Countries of Origin After World War II* (London, 2005).
13. *Jewish Telegraphic Agency (JTA)*, February 26, 1946.
14. Rubin, "The Future of the Jews," 76–83; Loeffler, *Rooted Cosmopolitans*, 141–142, x. Also see Nathan Kurz, 'In the Shadow of Versailles: Jewish Minority Rights at the 1946 Peace Conference," *Simon Dubnow Institute Yearbook* 15 (2016): 187–210.
15. Goldmann report, May 30, 1945; Epstein to Shareef, May 30, 1945; both in S25/5334; Goldmann report, June 25, 1945, Z6/13; Ben-Gurion to Goldmann, September 27, 1945, Z6/302; Goldmann to Shertok, June 11, 1946, Z6/18/15; all in CZA; Shertok to Myerson, April 3, 1947, 93.01/2180/1, Israel State Archives (hereafter ISA), Jerusalem; Shertok to Myerson, April 9, 1947, S25/3965, CZA.
16. Robinson interview with the author, February 13, 1975. For the 1939 White Paper, which limited Jewish immigration in the next five years to 75,000— thereafter with Arab consent—and spoke of a Palestine State within ten years (clearly with a current Arab majority), see Monty Noam Penkower, *Palestine in Turmoil: The Struggle for Sovereignty, 1933–1939*, vol. 2, *Retreat from the Mandate, 1937–1939* (New York, 2014), chap. 10. Robinson's study of the White Paper "and the subsequent measures" is in Series 3, Robinson MSS., USHMM.
17. Robinson memo, April 16, 1947; Robinson to Jewish Agency Executive (JAE) American Section, April 17, 1947; both in 93.03/2268/15; ISA; Robinson interview with the author, February 13, 1975.
18. Robinson to JAE American Section, Apr. 17, 1947, 93.03/2268/15, ISA.
19. The Palestine Arab Higher Committee executive, under the direction of former Grand Mufti of Jerusalem Haj Amin al-Husseini and his cousin Jamal Husseini, would on June 10, 1947, announce a complete boycott of UNSCOP, while the states of the Arab League, unable to do so owing to their UN membership, resolved to stand by their May 17, 1947, declaration calling for Palestine's independence, the Mandate's abolition, and the immediate stoppage of Jewish immigration.
20. Jewish Agency Executive memo, April 18, 1947, 93.03/2269/8, ISA. For the Anglo-American Committee of Inquiry, see Penkower, *Palestine to Israel*, vol. 1, chap. 3. The Balfour Declaration of November 2, 1917, pledged His Majesty's Government to facilitate "the establishment in Palestine of a national home

for the Jewish people." This was confirmed by the victorious World War I allied powers (Britain, France, Italy, and Japan) on April 25, 1920, at the San Remo Conference in a resolution on which the Palestine Mandate (the Covenant of the League of Nations' Article 22, establishing the mandates system) was based. In that document, promulgated on July 24, 1922, the League recognized the "historical connection of the Jewish people with Palestine" and the "grounds for reconstituting their national home in that country."

21. Robinson memo, "Principle of Self-Determination and Jewish Aspirations in Palestine," April 22, 1947, CF-Robinson memos, ZA.
22. Akzin to JAE American Section, April 22, 1947, 93.03/2266/13, ISA; Robinson to Akzin, April 29, 1947, Z6/93, CZA. Akzin subsequently authored a survey of the treatment of the Palestine question by the UN up to the summer of 1948. Benjamin Akzin, "The United Nations and Palestine," n.d., A401/9, CZA.
23. Robinson memo, "The Jewish Agency for Palestine," n.d., CF-Jewish Agency memos, ZA. For the Peel Commission, see Penkower, *Palestine in Turmoil: The Struggle for Sovereignty*, vol. 2, chap. 6.
24. Robinson remarks, JAE American Section, May 2, 1947, Z5/357, CZA.
25. Robinson memo, "Jewish Immigration to Palestine," May 13, 1947, S25/5365; Robinson memo, Addition I, June 2, 1947, S25/5353; both in CZA.
26. Robinson, "Fundamental Considerations," May 14, 1947, CF-Jewish Agency, Memos Robinson, ZA; Minutes of JAE American Section, May 13, 1947, ZA. As a member of the Peel Commission, Rappard had strongly advocated the partition of Palestine into a Jewish and an Arab state.
27. Monty Noam Penkower, *Palestine to Israel: Mandate to State, 1945-1945,* vol. 2, *Into the International Arena, 1947–1948* (New York, 2019), 412–415. Seven months earlier, Robinson had prepared a detailed memo for the American Zionist Emergency Council on the Soviet press's consistent anti-Zionist stand, adding that today the USSR, absent from the League of Nations, "is very much present in the United Nations and it may well be a decisive factor in some decision where a veto can frustrate everything." Robinson, "The Press of the U.S.S.R. and Zionism," October 22, 1946, Z5/1172, CZA.
28. Robinson memo, "The Arab States and the Mandate for Palestine," May 21, 1947; Robinson memo, "The Dissolution of the League of Nations and its Influence on the Validity of the Mandate for Palestine," May 21, 1947; both in CF-Robinson memos, ZA.
29. Robinson memo, "Partition of India: Implications for Palestine," n.d., file 7/1, Abba Hillel Silver MSS., The Temple, Cleveland, OH. For the Morrison-Grady plan, see Penkower, *Palestine to Israel: Mandate to State*, vol. 1, chap. 4. India's

Rabindranath Tagore, the first non-European to receive the Nobel Prize for Literature (1913), suggested the phrase "Jewel in the British Crown."

30. Robinson memo, "Trusteeship for Palestine?," June 17, 1947, CF-Jewish Agency, Robinson memos, ZA.
31. Robinson memo, "An International Regime for Palestine: First Tentative Observations," June 25, 1947, UN 1946–1948, Palestine Questions file, Hadassah Women's Organization Archives, New York City.
32. Robinson to JAE, June 2, 1947, S25/5365, CZA; Jacob Robinson, *Palestine and the United Nations: Prelude to Solution* (Washington, DC, 1947). For reviews and letters regarding this volume, see Series 3, Jacob Robinson MSS., USHMM.
33. Minutes, JAE American Section, September 17–18, 1947, Z5/59; September 27, 1947, Z5/3416; Robinson memo, "The General Debate in the Assembly of the Palestine Question," September 26, 1947, Z6/95; all in CZA; Penkower, *Palestine to Israel*, vol. 2, 478–479.
34. Robinson to JAE, October 2, 1947, S44/454; Robinson to JAE, October 13, 1947, S25/5470; both in CZA.
35. Robinson, "The Legal Force of a Recommendation of the General Assembly With Regard to Palestine," October 29, 1947, S44/564, CZA.
36. Robinson, "Basic Issues on Implementation," November 4, 1947, Z6/95, CZA.
37. Robinson, "A Constitution for Eretz Israel: Preliminary Observations," Z4/31279, CZA.
38. Robinson interview with the author, February 13, 1975; Penkower, *Palestine to Israel: Mandate to State*, vol. 2, 492–502.
39. Robinson to JAE, December 11, 1947, Permanent Files, Hadassah Archives.
40. Eytan to Shertok, 93.03/126/9, ISA. For Robinson's comments on Eytan's draft, see January 26, 1948, 93/03/128/12; both in ISA.
41. Robinson to Lourie, January 27, 1948, 93.03/129/11, ISA. ARAMCO became the chief conduit communicating Saudi Arabia's interests to its parent corporations (Standard Oil of California and the Texas Company—Texaco) and to the US government. The complex subject, particularly as regards the Palestine question at that time, still calls for full examination.
42. Robinson, "Faris El-Khouri's 'Exceptions' to the United Nations Palestine Commission," February 16, 1948, S25/5176, CZA.
43. Minutes, JAE American Section, February 25, 1948, Z5/2377, CZA; Penkower, *Palestine to Israel: Mandate to State*, vol. 2, 581–585.
44. Penkower, *Palestine to Israel: Mandate to State*, vol. 2, 619–629; JAE American Section to Ben-Gurion, March 22, 1948, S25/1703, CZA.

45. Penkower, *Palestine to Israel: Mandate to State*, vol. 2, 658–661; Robinson-Epstein memo, April 26, 1948, 93.03/95/1, ISA.
46. Robinson memo, April 28, 1948, L35/141, CZA; Penkower, *Palestine to Israel: Mandate to State*, vol. 2, 662.
47. Shertok to Ben-Gurion, May 6, 1948, S25/1559, CZA; Jacob Robinson, "The Legal Position of the Jewish State and the Jewish Government at This Moment," May 7, 1948, 41.0, 124/23, ISA. Robinson also contributed "glosses" to Hersch Lauterpacht's draft for the Israeli Declaration of Independence. Lauterpacht's draft, seeking to reconcile between cosmopolitanism and national sovereignty, was rejected by the nascent Israeli establishment. "Declaration," by H. L. (Lauterpacht) with glosses by J. R. (Robinson), n.d., file 40.1–124/21 G, ISA; Eliav Lieblich and Yoram Shachar, "Cosmopolitanism at a Crossroads: Hersch Lauterpacht and the Israeli Declaration of Independence," *British Yearbook of International Law* 84:1 (2014): 1–51.
48. Penkower, *Palestine to Israel: Mandate to State*, vol. 2, 677–678.
49. Robinson interview with the author, February 13, 1975.
50. Loeffler, *Rooted Cosmopolitans*, 180–181, 197–199.
51. Jacob Robinson, "Jungle Law," *Washington Post*, June 20, 1960.
52. Kaplan-Feuereisen, "At the Service of the Jewish Nation," 169–170; Gideon Hausner, *Justice in Jerusalem* (New York, 1966), 303; Jacob Robinson, *International Law and Organization, General Sources of Information* (Leyden, 1967): Jacob Robinson, "International Protection of Minorities: A Global View," in *The Progression of International Law*, ed. Y. Dinstein and F Domb (Leiden, 2011), 73–106; Jacob Robinson and Henry Sachs, eds., *The Holocaust: The Nuremberg Evidence* (Jerusalem, 1976). Hurt by what he considered unfair and ill-informed criticism of the Eichmann trial by Hannah Arendt and by her views on Jewish passivity and complicity during the Holocaust, Robinson published *And the Crooked Shall Be Made Straight: The Eichmann Trial, the Jewish Catastrophe, and Hannah Arendt's Narrative* (New York, 1965), which, although poorly written and organized was accurate on almost all points, made him known to a wider public. Also noteworthy is his *Guide to Jewish History under the Nazi Impact* (Jerusalem, 1960), prepared together with Philip Friedman, who is rightfully called the father of Holocaust history, and later bibliographical works that Robinson completed with other scholars under the auspices of Yad Vashem.
53. Loeffler, *Rooted Cosmopolitans*, 293; Abba Eban, *An Autobiography* (New York, 1977), 133. US Ambassador to the UN Daniel Patrick Moynihan, charging that the 1975 UN Resolution was aimed at Jews and liberal democracy

everywhere, declared before the Assembly that same day that "a great evil has been loosed upon the world." That resolution, passed by a vote of 72 to 35 with 32 abstentions (the Soviet bloc joined in favor with Arab and Muslim-majority countries and many African countries), was revoked on December 16, 1991, by Assembly Resolution 46/86, with the vote 111 to 25, and 13 abstentions.

54. Rosenne, "Jacob Robinson—In Memoriam," 292–293; Goldmann remarks, December 11, 1977, Z6/2748, CZA. Robinson was buried in the Riverside Cemetery, Saddle Brook, Bergen County, New Jersey. Curiously, a recent volume on Jewish lawyers and international law has no chapter on Robinson's major contributions to this field. J. Loeffler and M. Paz, eds., *The Law of Strangers: Jewish Lawyers and International Law in the Twentieth Century* (Cambridge, 2019). No extended study had hitherto appeared on Robinson's key role in the establishment of the State of Israel. A symposium devoted to his career, held in Kaunas (Kovno) on the occasion of the thirtieth anniversary of his death, neglects the topic as well. E. Bendkaité and D. R. Haupt, eds., *The Life, Times and Work of Jokubas Robinzonas—Jacob Robinson* (Kaunas, 2007).

3. The Crusade to Save a Jewish State

The terse telegram to the Jewish Agency for Palestine office in New York City, dispatched from Jerusalem on January 20, 1948, carried a note of urgency. Eliezer Kaplan, treasurer of the Agency since 1933, informed Henry Montor that "MYERSON PROCEEDING STATES WILLING HELP UJA NEEDS INCREASING HOPE YOUR FULL COOPERATION." Currently executive vice chairman of the United Jewish Appeal (UJA), the forty-three-year-old Montor had met Kaplan a decade earlier during his first trip to the United States. As a response to the brutal assault against German and Austrian Jewry on *Kristallnacht* (November 9–10, 1938), engineered by Hitler's government, the Agency treasurer successfully pressed at that time for a financial campaign whereby the American Jewish Joint Distribution Committee (JDC, or "Joint" for short), created in 1914 to provide substantive help to Jews in Eastern Europe and the *yishuv* (Palestinian Jewish community) in the catastrophic wake of World War I, would share the results with the Agency by a distribution of eighty to twenty percent. Two months later, the newly created UJA linked the United Palestine Appeal (UPA), the JDC, and the National Refugee Service to provide relief for European Jews trapped in the vise of war, to sustain Jews living in British-mandated Palestine, and to facilitate German Jewish immigration to safer countries. The UJA drive achieved close to $14 million that year, a remarkable record that did not, however, increase substantially to meet the pressing needs of stricken Jewry abroad during the years of World War II and immediately thereafter.[1]

Formerly the assistant editor under Meyer Weisgal of *New Palestine*, the official organ of the Zionist Organization of America, and then publicity director and executive director of the UPA, the Nova Scotia-born Montor had also established the Independent Jewish Press Service and the Palcor News Agency to bring news abroad from the *yishuv*. In early 1939, he approached Weisgal, then confidant to World Zionist Organization (WZO) president Chaim Weizmann, about Jewish participation in the New York World's Fair. The Jewish Palestine Pavilion, the first such exhibit at an international exposition in the United States, would attract record-breaking crowds, with an estimated total of more than two million visitors. Soon after V-E Day, at the request of Agency executive Moshe Shertok (later Sharett), Morgenthau committee chairman David Ben-Gurion, Montor used his UJA contacts to make possible the top Agency official's meeting with some wealthy American Jews on July 1, 1945. This, in turn, led to the clandestine Sonneborn Institute and Materials for Palestine's obtaining essential funds and particularly armaments, transferred overseas for the Hagana's future struggle against the six surrounding Arab states.[2]

Montor's well-deserved reputation as an aggressive fund raiser first achieved legendary status in 1946, when he spearheaded the UJA's breakthrough appeal. A few JDC officials had come to him the previous summer, seeking approval for an independent campaign of at least $10 million in response to the fate of European Jewry during the Holocaust. In the face of their strong skepticism, he pressed for ten times that figure. At a preliminary conference in November 1945, the brief Yiddish speech of Joseph ("Yossel") Rosensaft, who had just come out from the former Bergen-Belsen concentration camp to plead that fellow survivors get "a piece of bread," proved especially effective. Dramatically removing a shirt to show where he had been whipped by Germans, recalled Sam Rothberg, he "tore the place apart"; Rosensaft's cry "we shall not forget and will not forgive" deeply moved those present. The annual UJA meeting in Atlantic City the next month endorsed Montor's charge, with the initial major gifts contributed by the Rosenwald, Mazer, and Leavitt families. The $100 million, a staggering figure in those times, was met.[3]

One year later, Montor scored his next major coup, recruiting Henry Morgenthau, Jr. to the UJA's supreme executive rank. Secretary of the Treasury under President Franklin D. Roosevelt (FDR), the dour Morgenthau (often referred to in Washington as "Henry the Morgue"), and his staff of experts had helped steer the country through the Great Depression and ably financed the war effort. Once aware of the State

Department's consistent obstruction of succor to the endangered Jews of Nazi-occupied Europe, Morgenthau had been instrumental in Roosevelt's actually reluctant creation of the US War Refugee Board in January 1944. By then, he had fallen under Weizmann's influence as well. However, his championing a demand that postwar Germany be stripped of its industry and converted into an agricultural nation, and especially Morgenthau's wish to attend the postwar Potsdam Conference between Truman, Churchill, and Stalin and continue in the cabinet until victory against Japan were achieved, gained him no favor with Roosevelt's successor. Harry S. Truman, wishing former Congressman and poker card partner Fred M. Vinson to replace Morgenthau, orchestrated his resignation in July 1945. Just prior to that denouement, Montor and Weisgal, thanks to the latter's close connection with long-time Morgenthau secretary Henrietta Klotz, had played an important role in the Secretary's interest to secure the appointment of Earl Harrison as Truman's personal emissary to investigate the condition of Holocaust survivors in the so-called Displaced Persons (DP) camps. Montor quickly realized that the former Treasury Secretary could be a most valuable asset to the UJA. He tried, with Klotz's encouragement and support, to have her boss become General Chairman of the organization, a steady attempt that ultimately succeeded and gave Morgenthau a life filled anew with purpose.[4]

Just back from a visit to the DP camps and Poland, Montor had proposed at the UJA's meeting in Atlantic City on December 1, 1946, that the 1947 campaign be raised to $170 million. Some leading American Jews at the annual meeting strongly demanded that the UJA go back to "normal" and adopt a quota of $50 million. In what he would characterize as "the most violent and deeply-felt speech" of his career, Montor responded with extraordinary fury for over an hour that Sunday afternoon. Speaking to each leader in the room, he spoke of what they were proposing to do by abandoning European and Palestine Jewry. The meeting left him with more enemies that he had ever before accumulated, several never speaking to him again, but those in attendance ended with a quota of $125 million. Morgenthau, present as chairman of the Resolutions Committee although his father had died the same week, was touched. When the session closed, he said to Montor, "I am enlisting for the duration."[5]

His days engaged once again, Morgenthau threw himself without reservation into the UJA post, regularly arriving at New York City headquarters on 165 West Forty-Sixth St. in the morning and leaving at the day's end. He obtained a meeting of the UJA executive with Truman in February 1947 before its initial "big gifts" campaign began. Morgenthau's daily conferences with staff, telephone calls across the country, reviews of publicity, and meetings with visiting community leaders impacted powerfully on many. His keynote addresses, some drafted by Montor, yielded $650,000 in one night in Dallas, moved Edgar Stern of New Orleans to double his announced gift to $250,000, and attained in Richmond, Atlanta, and Houston twice the big gift totals of 1946 for those communities. Soon thereafter, upon visiting five cities in three days, Morgenthau achieved totals far beyond the record achievements of 1946. His innovations included the open reading of pledge cards and the public announcement of the previous year's gift. When chaplain Herbert A. Friedman's eyewitness report of the hopeless life in a DP camp galvanized a lagging campaign in mid-1947, Morgenthau charted a DC-3 for the two of them to barnstorm a few cities every day, getting his former cabinet colleague, Secretary of War Robert Patterson, to approve Friedman's staying in uniform before formal discharge from the US Army one month later. Morgenthau found a kindred spirit in Montor's relentless demands, iron will, and charisma, as well as the younger man's inability to compromise and a fierce commitment to Jewish independence in Eretz Israel. In the next three years, thanks to Morgenthau's great prestige and Montor's energetic drive, joined to American Jewry's new feeling of determined solidarity with its European roots, the UJA would raise an extraordinary figure: $465 million.[6]

At the request of Agency executive Moshe Shertok (later Sharett), Morgenthau also asked Major General John H. Hilldring, then the State Department's Assistant Secretary for Occupied Territories and a close friend of Secretary of State George C. Marshall, if it were possible for the Jewish Agency to present its case officially at the UN. The Arab nations "are in there every day crapping all over the Jews and there is nobody to answer them," he noted. State preferred, however, that both the Agency and the Palestinian Arab Higher Committee appear on an equal footing before a small committee, rather than the Agency's having a nonvoting membership in the General Assembly. Hearing this from Hilldring, Morgenthau observed that public opinion thought it not "a sporting thing" that the Arabs "have everything their way." At the same time, he thought it advisable that the Agency delegates not go "into a court where they have got to abide by its decision and the other fellow does not." In the end, the UN's First Committee resolved to grant a hearing to both and to any other organization "representative of a considerable element of the population of Palestine."[7]

As for Goldie Myerson, Montor was aware that she directed the Agency's political department once Shertok had left Palestine in early 1947 to lead the World Zionist Organization's drive at the United Nations for a Jewish state in Palestine. She had filled in for him briefly when the British imprisoned Shertok and other Agency leaders after Operation Agatha ("Black Sabbath" in the *yishuv*'s terminology) on June 29, 1946. He knew something about the Kyev-born woman, whose youth had been spent in Milwaukee before settling in 1921 with her husband in the Jezre'el Valley's Kibbutz Merhavia, later becoming an executive member of the Histadrut trade union and subsequently that of the Mapai labor party and of the Agency itself. Her evocative appeal, made as a Histadrut representative to the 1938 Evian Conference on Refugees, for Jewish sovereignty following the dismal close of that international meeting had elicited a few newspaper headlines. In March 1946, her testimony impressed the Anglo-American Committee on Palestine, with its call for Jews, as other peoples of the world, "to be masters of their own fate," to create in Palestine a free Jewish society based on mutual cooperation throughout the country and with all their neighbors. Myerson had come to America and England a few times in the nineteen thirties, speaking as secretary of the Histadrut's Women's Labor Council to its sister organization abroad, Pioneer Women. Yet in Montor's view she had been "an impecunious, unimportant representative, a '*schnorrer*' for various little funds," such as the selling of shares for a Histadrut company and building a port in Tel-Aviv. During these visits, she stayed as a guest in people's homes; hotels were too expensive. In the United States, he reasonably concluded at the time, Myerson was an unknown.[8]

On January 22, Montor cabled Myerson directly. Joining him in the reply was Isidor Coons, the main fund raiser for the JDC and a more retiring personality with whom he enjoyed an understanding relationship. Their telegram read thus:[9]

ON BEHALF ALL OFFICERS UNITED JEWISH APPEAL WE EXTEND CORDIAL INVITATION YOU VISIT UNITED STATES UNDER

EXCLUSIVE AUSPICES UJA WE URGENTLY NEED YOUR HELP IN CAMPAIGN AND STONGLY REQUEST YOUR ACCEPTANCE BY RETURN CABLE WOULD BE MOST HELPFUL TO KNOW ARRIVAL DATE AND LENGTH OF VISIT SO IMPORTANT FUNCTIONS CAN BE ARRANGED THROUGHOUT COUNTRY

Montor was unaware that Myerson herself had urged the Agency executive to have Kaplan cable him, a development that had begun in war-torn Palestine some weeks earlier. The day after the UN General Assembly voted on November 29, 1947, to recommend the partition of Palestine into a Jewish and an Arab state, the more than 1 million Arabs in the country launched a civil war. The mandatory government's casualty list for that December included the killing of 204 Jews, while the Arab world immovably rejected the *yishuv*'s appeal for compromise and its claim to sovereignty. Excoriating the mandatory authorities for not distinguishing between attackers and those attacked, Ben-Gurion declared that Palestinian Jewry would defend itself and the frontiers of the Jewish nation in this "savage war against our very existence." Yet he had to contend with an unavoidable reality: artillery, tanks, armored cars, and combat aircraft were all lacking. Ammunition for Hagana ranks was also in short supply, some fifty rounds per rifle and six to seven hundred rounds per machine gun. Huge sums of cash had to be obtained quickly if Ehud Ueberall (later Avriel), Tuvya Arazi, and others engaged in the purchase abroad of heavy weaponry were to succeed in waging the decisive battles soon to be fought for statehood. When Kaplan wired Ben-Gurion from New York on December 3 that the Keren Kayemet L'Yisrael (Jewish National Fund), exclusively focused since 1901 on the purchase of land in Palestine, should loan the Agency $3 million in this emergency, the Agency executive chairman responded angrily: He could not do this when Kaplan's office refused to do anything in the area "where the life of the *yishuv* and even our entire future lay in the balance."[10]

In mid-December, Myerson made scant headway in pressing High Commissioner Alan Cunningham to permit the Jewish Supernumerary Police to make use of armored cars on the roads against lethal Arab attack, especially on the Tel-Aviv road to besieged Jerusalem, or to discontinue police searches for Hagana arms and arrests of Hagana members on defense duty. Nor did she find an attentive ear when observing to US Consul Robert Macatee that the imposition of an arms embargo as of December 5 by the pro-Arab US State and War Departments favored the Palestinian Arabs, who were obtaining weapons from the nearby states even as 10,000 volunteer Arab guerillas poured across the borders into the country with little British intervention. The State Department's Near Eastern Division looked askance at Kaplan's request to support the Agency's approach to the Export-Import Bank seeking an initial $100 million for its four-year plan of resettlement and development, just when Ben-Gurion wired Kaplan on the 14th that the acquisition of weapons was "now matter of life and death," urging that £300,000 be sent without delay. On the 26th, an Arab ambush in Bab-el-Wad on a Jerusalem-bound convoy, whose weapons had been confiscated earlier by the British, killed seven, including Youth Aliya's acting director Hans Beyth. Myerson miraculously escaped harm on that trip. She gained no sympathy, however, in an interview three days later with the imperturbable Chief Secretary Henry Gurney. The following day, Ben-Gurion heard that Kaplan had arranged a $7.5 million bank loan at 2.5 percent, but the Agency treasurer's hope for another $5 million from private individuals, each giving $50,000, seemed uncertain.[11]

For Ben-Gurion, the next step was clear. On the last day of 1947, speaking to his executive colleagues in Tel-Aviv, he surveyed the dire situation. Another convoy in which Myerson and associates Yitshak Gruenbaum and Eliyahu Dobkin, along with Va'ad HaLe'umi president Yitshak Ben-Zvi, were traveling from Jerusalem to Tel-Aviv had been searched by British soldiers, all weapons confiscated, and later shot at by Arabs. The need for more than 30,000 draftees until the British declared exit on May 15, 1948, would cost £3 million and another £2 million for weaponry. Only in the US might these funds be attained, but a UJA drive for hopefully $200 million (£50 million) could not be available before next year. Essential weapons had to reach the *yishuv* during the next two months, paid for in hard cash to expedite matters. Under the circumstances, if no other solution could be found in Palestine, he was prepared to go to America for this purpose. The same day, Ben-Gurion released a press statement that the *yishuv* had to focus on its defense, the establishment of the Jewish state on May 15, and the boundaries—including the isolated Negev—accorded it by the General Asssembly vote of November 29. It would not recoil from any effort, suffering, and sacrifice in this war of defense until victory, which would come. He concluded: These were "the birth pangs of *Medinat Yisrael* and her redemption, and we would receive them with love, faith, and dedication."[12]

The threat to Ben-Gurion's aspirations did not abate in the next two weeks. On New Year's Day 1948 he learned that the Arab League had budgeted £6 million for the imminent war. King Abdullah of Transjordan, although promising Myerson in their secret meeting on November 17, 1947, that he would support a Jewish state if obtaining the area assigned to the Palestinian Arabs in the General Assembly recommendation, pledged that he would "lend" his British-trained and heavily armed Arab Legion to the League in the coming invasion of Palestine. Two days later, a special meeting on security accepted a recommendation by Myerson, back in Tel-Aviv after staying in Gedera to secure the release of a Hagana female warrior involved in the December 31 convoy, that the Agency office in New York give $1 million to Arazi, with Hagana finance director Levi Skolnik (later Eshkol) to prepare a list of *yishuv* institutions and individuals who would lend £2 million to its war effort. Kaplan, soon to return home, hoped that he would have $10 million from England, Canada, and the United States in a few days' time, but not all would be for armaments. The mandatory resolved to allow but two licensed guns on each Egged public bus; searches of Jewish vehicles would continue. Another setback occurred when a Hagana shipment of twenty-six cases containing an estimated 65,000 pounds of TNT, along with fifty-one cases ready for shipment on the same vessel to Jewish firms in Palestine, had been discovered accidentally by the FBI, leading to the seizure of fifty-nine tons of war surplus explosives heading for shipment from New Jersey and New York warehouses to the *yishuv*. Up to January 11, a total of 150 Jews were officially reported to have been killed in Jerusalem, and at least 350 known to have sustained injuries. All the while, reports swirled about that Whitehall and the British military chiefs, like their American counterparts, were seeking to overturn the UN's partition decision, one scheme even advocating that the Arab Legion take over all of Palestine and the *yishuv*'s cities and settlements given autonomous status.[13]

On January 12, Ben-Gurion heard from Kaplan, now back in Palestine, that $5.2 million was required immediately for arms purchases in Europe. Perhaps the *yishuv* could raise £2–3 million, but at least £7 million was needed from abroad, primarily in America. Resolving that the two of them had to travel there, an adamant Ben-Gurion decided to bring the matter to the Agency executive, sitting in Tel Aviv, on the morrow. Myerson, however, thought his offer to travel to the United States was out of the question. Ben-Gurion's presence in Palestine at this critical hour could not be denied. She offered to undertake the task, arguing that her services in Palestine could certainly be dispensed with for a few weeks. In addition, she spoke English fluently. It would also give her respite from fruitless talks with Gurney, who had the previous night again accused her and the Agency of "deception, suspicion, chauvinism," and of consorting with the dissident Irgun and Stern right-wing underground forces. Insisting on a vote of those present that evening, her arguments fell on the receptive ears of colleagues "so tired and harassed." The laconic entry in Ben-Gurion's diary entry told the result: "It was decided on Golda's trip to America."[14]

She would not depart for the United States in another nine days' time. During that interval, a Hagana force sent from Jerusalem to relieve the beleaguered kibbutz Kfar Etzion was discovered on January 16 five kilometers from its objective. After a battle that lasted seven hours against hundreds of armed Arabs who descended from the surrounding hills, the entire relief force of thirty-five under the command of Danny Mass, having run out of bullets, began throwing stones at their attackers, was massacred, their bodies brutally mutilated and stripped by the local villagers. British forces, which had made no effort to stop the fighting, later transferred the dead for a communal burial in Kfar Etzion. At the same time, London announced that His Majesty's Government would honor its treaty pledges of sending considerable armaments to Egypt, Iraq, and Jordan. On January 20, eight Jews were killed in Yehiam, and seven Jewish Supernumerary Policemen murdered who were not permitted to use armored cars out of their neighborhood near Yazur on the 22nd. Yet United Kingdom representative at the United Nations Alexander Cadogan declared to the UN Commission on Palestine that the violence in that country was due to the Jews, while mandatory Undersecretary John Fletcher-Cooke added that the Jews would have to withdraw to the coastal plain from Tel-Aviv to Haifa after the fighting subsided.[15]

With Montor's reply in hand on January 22, Myerson set off that morning for the long flight to New York City. Aware then only of his reputation, that he was "a great power and did great things," she knew not one individual either among the UJA and JDC hierarchy. More than a decade had passed since her last visit to the States. The growing despair and pessimism felt by many Palestinian Jews, especially after the slaughter of Mass's Hagana patrol, also rested on her shoulders. Yet the fifty-year-old woman, far more militant politically than the moderate Kaplan, held Ben-Gurion's trust. Myerson also possessed what she later called the *yishuv*'s secret weapon: *ein breira* ("no alternative"). One night earlier, Ben-Gurion had discussed with her what to do in America, and to instruct Arazi to purchase jeeps, bazooka-type guns, speedy motor boats, corvettes, and even an aircraft carrier, and to report by cable each week about his activities. The destiny of the 600,000 members of the *yishuv* appeared to rest on this emergency mission, perhaps a fool's errand, its end anything but certain.[16]

Myerson's overriding objective to win the hearts and pockets of American Jewry began at a moment that could hardly have been less propitious. She arrived at LaGuardia airport on January 23 in one of the worst blizzards New York City had ever known, more than a foot of snow blanketing the area. The metropolis was cut off, no trains or planes available beyond its borders. Montor was in Chicago for the sixteenth annual General Assembly of the Council of Jewish Federations and Welfare Funds. Her sister, Clara, head of the Bridgeport Jewish Federation, suggested when they met at the airport that she travel to that conclave. Yet Montor, to whom Myerson quickly conveyed the idea by telephone, was dubious. The conferees were not Zionists in the main, and the officials from Chicago themselves had objected strenuously to his UJA goals for 1946 and 1947. She stayed overnight at the Brooklyn home of her niece, the married daughter of her sister Sheyna who was still in America because of recent surgery. While Golda, Clara, and Sheyna talked through the night, Montor contacted Council executive director Harry Lurie, who turned down Myerson's desire to address the gathering as "a partisan thing." So did Sidney Hollander, past Council president. He then pressed Harry Goldenberg of Minneapolis, vice-president of the Council and chairman of the UJA national cabinet, along with a few other Zionists at the assembly, and arranged a spot for her to speak during the Sunday program. Stanley Myers of Miami, the Council president, sent off a warm invitation. A sudden break in the weather on Saturday enabled Myerson to get a plane the next day to Chicago. She walked into the Sheraton Hotel on January 25, "shaking," with "no idea of what was going to happen."[17]

Montor "took to her at once," he subsequently recalled. Myerson's features, her face, her political sincerity, her "very homeliness" made the Agency's political director, in his opinion, the ideal speaker for the "state-in-being." Her first message to the Jews of America was scheduled for delivery at the Council's business meeting after lunch. Following reports of the credentials committee, the budget and dues schedule, and the presentation of exhibit awards, Myers presented Myerson that afternoon as "our distinguished guest," an "extraordinary personality" who had played a role of "high statesmanship" in the destiny of Jewish Palestine in this "transitory period." Having "eminently carried the burdens of governmental problems in the most difficult period of the Jewish Homeland," he went on, she "epitomizes the courage and faith of the Jewish People in Palestine." Recently escaped from an Arab ambush, she appeared now with a message from "the greatest battlefront of Jewish survival today." He ended with these words: "I am happy now to introduce a splendid representative of her sex, a brilliant statesman of her people and an intrepid fighter for the freedom of Israel." Rising from their chairs, the delegates received the sudden invitee with prolonged applause.[18]

For thirty-five minutes, Myerson proceeded to speak without notes. The *yishuv*'s heroic youth, many in their teens, had no alternative but to fight against the war forced upon it by the ex-Grand Mufti of Palestine (Haj Amin al-Husseini) and his men, she began. "We can stand our ground" against them, the aid they receive from Arab states, and British policy that "for all practical purposes" helps the Arabs. The 300 people in the four settlements of the Etzion bloc northwest of Hevron had recently fought back an attack of 1,000 Arabs. Telling the fate of the thirty-five who were killed nine days earlier after more than a seven-hour battle in their attempt to come to the aid of Kfar Etzion, she declared that the Jewish community in Palestine would fight to the end. Jewry had lost 6,000,000 Jews in the Holocaust years, and it would be "audacity" on the *yishuv*'s part to worry the Jewish people worldwide because a few hundred thousand more Jews were in danger. Rather, if Palestine's Jews could remain alive, then "the Jewish people as such is alive and Jewish independence is assured." Otherwise, "we are through" for many centuries with the dream of a Jewish people and a Jewish homeland. Every Jew in Palestine believed that the *yishuv* would finally be victorious, she added, although aware that the price of life to pay would be high—over three hundred killed by now, with no doubt that "there will be more."

The valiant spirit of their youth would not falter, Myerson continued, but it could not alone face rifles and machine guns. A special campaign within the *yishuv* had raised almost $6.5 million, and soon another $2 million campaign would begin, augmenting taxes on various articles that bring in $320,000 a month. With the exception of a few babies from one settlement, not a single person left the isolated Negev settlements. Men and women have lined up for hours in order to give blood for the wounded. The time factor was most important: millions of dollars had to be obtained immediately, she emphasized, the sum of between $25 and $30 million in cash within a couple of weeks. The battle was being waged as well for those not yet in the country, including the 30,000 "illegal" immigrants detained by the British in Cyprus camps and hundreds of thousands more, and the *yishuv* had to be prepared to absorb them. While Palestine's Arabs had the nearby Arab states, the "only hinterland that we have is you." She believed that the Jews of the United States would realize the current peril, and do what they had to do. Paraphrasing Churchill's thrilling speech in June 1940 when England appeared alone to face Hitler's armed juggernaut, she asserted that the *yishuv* would fight in the Negev, in the Galilee, and on the outskirts of Jerusalem until the very end.

The *yishuv* would raise no white flag to the former Grand Mufti, she closed, but the approximately one thousand leaders present and their communities could decide whether it or Haj Amin al-Husseini would be victorious. Do not be late, Myerson begged her listeners, and "bitterly sorry" three months from now for what you failed to do today. Yet she was leaving this platform "without any doubt in my mind or my heart." The decision of American Jewry would be similar to that which had been taken by their counterpart in Eretz Israel, "so that within a few months from now we all can participate again not only in the joy of a decision being taken upon the establishment of a Jewish State," but in "the joy of the laying of the foundation, the cornerstone of the Jewish

State, knowing that every one of us, we there, and you here, have given of our best to make this dream become a reality."[19]

Spontaneously, the audience rose as one to its feet, some in the cavernous hall weeping openly. A recent biography ably captured the electric atmosphere that filled the hotel ballroom: "In her plain black dress, without a speck of makeup, her hair austerely parted in the middle and pulled tightly back, she seemed to some like a woman out of the Bible." "She had swept the whole conference," marveled Montor years later at this unique performance. The Dallas delegation, hardly a hotbed of Zionist sentiment, immediately retired to caucus, and then declared that they were going back to Texas to "get so much money that they won't know what to do with it." Loans would have to be taken in the bank, paid off later from the funds collected—so be it. Others present followed its lead, "firebrands," in Montor's phrase, who meant to light up every community they represented.[20]

The next day, Myerson returned to New York. After reporting in the morning to the American section of the Jewish Agency executive, she went to a press conference that Shertok had arranged for her at Lake Success, where UN headquarters were temporarily located in the Sperry Gyroscope plant twenty miles east of the city in northwest Long Island. Excoriating British "neutrality" for actually aiding Arab attacks, she made the *yishuv*'s stand clear: "If we are killed, at least we are killed as law-abiding citizens" who, besides defending their lives and what they had created in Palestine, had been to first implement the decision of the United Nations, which they had accepted "in good faith." The minute Arab aggression stopped, "there will be peace in Palestine." The Jewish community there would eventually be victorious, she averred, sustained by hope that "independence and a Jewish State in Palestine" will arise "before the end of a short period." The arming and recognition of a legally recognized Jewish militia was essential, together with an international force representing the entire UN to prove by its very appearance to the ex-Grand Mufti and the Arab States that the will of the vast majority of the United Nations "shall be done." The time factor was crucial, these steps ultimately to bring peace. All of Palestine's inhabitants would benefit thereby, Myerson was certain, she asserting that "masses" of Arabs would like to settle down in the Jewish State, whose new government would seek as one of its first obligations to raise their standard of life in health, housing, and education. Hearing this, Harold Beeley, the pro-Arab advisor on Palestine matters to Foreign Secretary Ernest Bevin, concluded that her appeal in effect for US military intervention in favor of the Jews and playing off America against Great Britain could only cause satisfaction to one major power: Soviet Russia.[21]

Montor had "jumped the gun" in proposing to his UJA associates that the 1948 appeal be set at $170 million, with a substantial portion of funds collected to go for Myerson's clarion call to arm the *yishuv* without delay. His focus on the centrality of the Palestine issue rather than the UJA's past emphasis on Jewish needs in Europe, a theme which Weizmann trumpeted when addressing UJA audiences at this time, won him many adversaries, such as the upright Pabst Brewery head Harris Pearlstein, chairman of its Allocations Committee. When the Administrative Committee, with Morgenthau presiding, met at Montor's request to hear Myerson present her case to them for the first time, former UJA national chairman and JDC executive William Rosenwald warned that any UJA involvement in raising money for weapons would destroy everything that it had built up through the years. "I have the greatest sympathy with Palestine and I certainly want it to be stronger," he continued. Speaking very forcefully and without stuttering in his usual manner when he had not spent a lot of time practicing a speech, Rosenwald's sincerity and effective arguments persuaded many who were sitting around the table. As he spoke, Montor saw tears rolling down Myerson's face. She knew that Rosenwald was a very powerful personality in the American Jewish community and certainly in the affairs of the United Jewish Appeal. It seemed that her mission was doomed.

At that critical moment, Morgenthau, no orator or philosopher, made what Montor later considered "the greatest statement" that he had ever heard from the usually stolid fifty-seven-year-old Jew of German ancestry. Turning directly to Rosenwald, he asserted in effect that he could not accept what "Bill" was saying. Feeling just as deeply about America as you, I tried to serve my country, he declared. But the United Jewish Appeal was here for the purpose of saving the Jewish people, and we could not save the Jewish people unless the Jews in Palestine, who were trying to defend themselves against murderers, were able to defend themselves. That is what the UJA is all about, Morgenthau concluded, and if Myerson said they have to have weapons and we are the only place where they can get the money to buy the arms, "then

3. The Crusade to Save a Jewish State

I am afraid, Bill, that you will have to accept my decision. We are going to include Myerson and her request in this year's campaign." That is how the meeting ended. Myerson was "overjoyed." There was no formal decision, but Morgenthau had his way.[22]

Nor did Myerson's plain-spoken, rousing appeal in Chicago sit well at first with JDC headquarters in New York City. Paul Baerwald, one of its founders and currently Honorary Chairman, had just submitted a memorandum to his colleagues advocating that they "husband our resources" and realize that, in light of the UN partition decision in favor of a Jewish state, the success of the 1948 campaign would be more difficult to predict. The "Joint" did not know on what basis the Jewish Agency determined the priority of the financial demands made on it for so many different purposes, nor what plans they had to meet these demands. Given that for the next few months there would be "a definite acute practical cash problem," he wondered why the Agency did not approach such organizations as the American Jewish Committee, the Zionist Organization of America (ZOA), Hadassah, and the American Jewish Congress. "We owe it to ourselves," Baerwald concluded, "to look at this question from the broadest possible viewpoint." Montor sought to have the JDC accelerate payments to the UPA out of the 1947 UJA collections, and Myerson telephoned to request an appointment with Edward Warburg, its chairman, but nothing conclusive resulted.[23]

As Myerson "did not have a dime," Montor brought her in a taxi to the office of Moe Leavitt, the JDC's executive director, on January 28. Leavitt's first reaction brought a sudden dose of reality: The UJA was a philanthropic organization which by no manner of means could become involved in a fund for obtaining weapons for the *yishuv*. In addition, he asked, if all the money collected were to go to that war effort, what would be the JDC's financial share in this emergency campaign? The "Joint," after all, was committed to helping Jews in great need throughout the world. Ultimately, after three days of intensive talks between Myerson, Montor, and the JDC Administration Committee, it was agreed to approach thirty to forty of the larger Jewish communities throughout the country with a push to convert into cash "accelerated" collections on account of 1947 UJA pledges, to advance contributions on account of the 1948 campaign, and to seek bank loans. The JDC would receive half of the monies collected, the other half going to the UPA, with the drive to cease on March 1. Since Myerson sought at least $25 million, the special UJA campaign to meet the emergency in Palestine would now be set at $50 million. JDC Board of Directors' member and investment banker Harold Linder, who immediately reached an understanding in the matter with the Chase National Bank and the Central Hanover Bank and Trust Company, would accompany Myerson to a number of key cities for this purpose. Myerson soon cabled Ben-Gurion of the JDC's "full support," noting that "without which action impossible."[24]

On February 4, after Myerson addressed the UJA executive in the presence of Morgenthau and Linder, a telegram was drafted to all members urging "as substantial a cash advance as you can make" within the next forty-eight hours towards the $10 million that had to be raised in New York within ten days. A list of the individuals in the industrial field who had already sent checks with sizeable contributions was attached, with the "dire need of cash" made clear. Two days later, a letter from Baerwald and JDC vice chairman I. Edwin Goldwasser informed leading American Jews of the emergency campaign for $50 million. Time clearly was of the essence, especially as the UN Palestine Commission's first monthly report, which had just indicted Great Britain in effect for circumventing the partition resolution, failed to make a single recommendation. The same report stated that "powerful Arab interests" were deliberately attempting to "alter by force" the General Assembly's November resolution, and urged that the Security Council provide an international armed force soon if the Commission were to be enabled to implement that resolution and maintain law and order in Palestine when the British transferred authority to it.[25]

By February 9, Leavitt could report to the JDC staff that Myerson and Linder had visited Newark and Baltimore, followed by a trip to Boston and Miami, and that the response to requests for immediate cash had been "most gratifying." In addition, Dallas had already sent in $500,000 and Milwaukee a like amount, the latter to forward an additional such amount shortly. Cincinnati and St. Louis were next on the Myerson-Linder trail. A meeting of large givers and campaign leaders would be held two days later at New York City's Biltmore Hotel to hear Myerson. Thereafter, it was planned to solicit about 1,200 of the biggest givers for advance cash contributions toward 1948 and balances on 1947 pledges. There was "a most favorable reaction to this intensified campaign," he informed the group, with everyone involved feeling that it would act as a "worthwhile stimulus" probably resulting in higher contributions for 1948 and accelerating the 1947 payments on pledges. During the first six months of 1947, total receipts of UJA on accounts of 1946 and 1947 had totaled $46 million. With the special effort now to obtain $50 million quickly in cash, and possibly another $20 million coming in from communities not included in the acceleration scheme, it was probable that $97 million would be received in the first six months of this year. Much would depend, Leavitt concluded, on the UJA "hammering away" to get as many pledges as possible.[26]

The outlines of the $50 million drive were formally announced the next day in a telephone conference with twenty-five of the largest cities, addressed by Myerson, New York State's Governor Herbert Lehman, and Morgenthau, with Council president Myers in attendance. When championing the $250 million UJA objective for 1948 at the recent conference in Atlantic City, Lehman had declared that Palestine's Jews should be "given the means to protect themselves" against overt Arab aggression intended to contravene the UN partition vote. He now "wholeheartedly" endorsed Myerson's plea, telling listeners that "we are on the threshold of a new era in Jewish life—an era that can bring the end of Jewish homelessness—an era that may mark the beginning of the end of Jewish misery and sorrow." At the close of the two-hour program at New York's WNEW Studios, Morgenthau stressed that "we dare not lose this fight," and that we, with the help of American Jewry and the Jews of Palestine "will be victorious." He immediately authorized a survey, conducted via former War Production Board planning committee chairman Robert Nathan, a committed Zionist now heading an economic consulting firm, in connection with the raising of funds in the country for Palestine's development. Not long thereafter, Morgenthau dispatched a letter to leaders in cities not covered by the WNEW broadcast, concluding thus: "Jewish lives depend on immediate action. Speed is urgent."[27]

New York City's effort on behalf of the year's national UJA campaign was launched the very next day. Some 2,500 community leaders convened at the annual Women's Division rally held at the Waldorf-Astoria Hotel. Speakers included FDR widow Eleanor Roosevelt, Lehman, liberal columnist Max Lerner, and Mrs. Jerome I. Udell, chairman of the Women's Division in the 1948 drive. Mrs. Roosevelt, a member of the US delegation to the United Nations, told the gathering that "we must ask our government to allow the importation of arms into Palestine and to raise its embargo." The Arab leaders, she added, "have done themselves a great harm in saying that they would fight a decision of the United Nations."[28]

Morgenthau's intervention proved crucial when accompanying Myerson, along with Montor, Rothberg, and Goldenberg, for a whirlwind visit in his first trip to Miami. A breakfast meeting and a luncheon went very well, and then the group flew to Miami Beach for another presentation in its biggest hotel. Although the building was owned by a Jew, fund raising was forbidden there. Coming down to the beautiful patio and seeing the guests so elegantly dressed, she froze. While drinking black coffee and smoking her cigarettes, Myerson began to cry. One thought crossed her mind: "How could I, in this beautiful atmosphere, tell what is happening at home?" I am sure, she told Montor, that when I get up to talk, they will all walk out. "I understand perfectly how you feel," Morgenthau interrupted. "I will get up, never mind what the manager of the hotel said about not having any fund raising here, and say 'Friends, you're here on a vacation which you deserve. Nobody has the right to trouble you, and since I don't want to keep you here under a false pretense, I have to tell you that we intend to do business tonight. Anybody that wants to walk out, we'll do nothing against them; you can just get up and walk out.'" He proceeded to speak. No one left the room. That evening, about $1.5 million in cash was raised, to be the highlight of her many trips across the country. "I think we ended that day in Miami with about four or five million dollars," the *yishuv* visitor subsequently recalled.[29]

That same month, Montor arranged for a TWA plane, with the UJA "Star of Hope" emblazoned on it, to pick up thirty-five major Jewish leaders in various cities. The group then went on a tour of European and Palestinian communities. The trip spread over a four week period and garnered much publicity. At a meeting in the Vatican, Pope Pius XII gave his blessing to their $250 million "Destiny Drive." When the group returned home, they participated in "The Flying Caravans" at functions across the United States. In their new capacity as organizers and speakers, they proved to be highly effective solicitors. This select group thereby became "one more link in the American Jewish communal chain," which, thanks to Montor's unique gifts of ingenuity and temerity, brought the UJA to record achievements.[30]

On February 24, a two-day national conference in Washington, DC set in motion the $250 million UJA national campaign for overseas relief and Palestine needs. Aiming for $50 million in cash within the next ten days for the *yishuv* emergency, keynote speaker Morgenthau dubbed this the "Ten Days of Decision." Neither a Jewish state in Palestine nor peace would be possible if the UN failed, he averred, and he hoped that American Jewry would have the "backbone and the stamina" to help realize the Jewish dream of centuries. Saying that President Truman regarded the UJA campaign as "one of the most important undertakings that any group ever embarked upon," Attorney General Tom Clark compared Palestine's Jewish settlers with the early American pioneers, and expressed the view that "the troubles that now best this new Jewish state set up through the UN will soon be overcome." A Jewish commonwealth would not only help reduce "the problem of the homeless and displaced Jews in Europe," Warburg declared, but also benefit millions of others by expanding industry, agriculture, and opportunity in the Middle East. UPA national chairman Israel Goldstein went further, charging that much larger resources in the form of government grants would be needed for "the settlement of a million Jews in Palestine," but it was important that the Jews themselves should be the first to respond.[31]

Was $50 million in such a short time remotely realistic? Gottlieb Hammer, who was then acting as comptroller of the Jewish Agency's New York City headquarters with full power of attorney on Kaplan's behalf, cabled Kaplan on February 14 that "prospects indicate" the UPA would receive $15 million, possibly $20 million. Years later, the *yishuv*'s emissary to the United States in those critical weeks confided the JDC officials' belief that the agreed upon amount "was 'nuts' anyhow," that they would not even get $25 million. Myerson felt at the time, however, that it made no difference: "we might as well ask" for double that figure. Montor, she added, thought that perhaps $10 to $12 million would be collected. Yet he worked very hard, preparing before each community visit a list with the Council of Jewish Federations of how much they could ask for. Stalwarts from the JDC and UJA executive ranks besides Montor who often joined these trips included Warburg, Rosenwald, and Rothberg. While she crisscrossed the United States, from coast to coast, with every day in a different city, they could not keep up with that demanding schedule. Her companions changed off, but the pace never slackened. Myerson was a woman possessed.[32]

Already by February 10, Gideon Ruffer (later Rafael), a member of the Agency delegation to the UN, could report to a colleague in Tel-Aviv that Myerson was going "from strength to strength and from million to million." Given this mission, which had "no equal in importance," he and associates were delighted in her success at winning the hearts and opening the pockets "to a degree hitherto indescribable." The same day, just when Ben-Gurion informed his security committee that the *yishuv* "might be able to stand up to the Arab armies" if it could hold on for two to three months until essential weapons arrived, Myerson wired him that $15 million had been obtained, with at least $20 million likely to be guaranteed by the month's end. The situation in Palestine had greatly worsened, he immediately replied, the armies of the Arab states far better equipped and financed at present than the *yishuv*. Palestine's Jewish community would be under siege very soon, with some "islands" of settlement, particularly the Negev, as well as the Upper Galilee and Jerusalem, cut off. Other than the detailed list of armaments and other pressing needs which were attached to the letter, he asked that $1.5 million be immediately sent for the purchase of a boat to rush a delivery of the weapons so desperately sought.[33]

The increasingly grave situation prompted Ben-Gurion to cable Shertok on February 12 that "serious attacks" were likely from the well-trained and equipped Arab bands invading across Palestine's northern and eastern frontiers, assisted by mainly German technicians. The next six weeks were "extremely critical if not fateful," as "goods" from Ueberall and Arazi could only be expected at best after six to eight weeks. He urged the immediate arrival of an international force or at least the dispatch of military equipment by the UN or the United States, a demand which Agency representative in Washington Eliyahu Epstein (later Elath) lost no time in sending to Marshall, the UN Palestine Commission, and the members of the Security Council. The Secretary of State, however, gave no encouragement to Eleanor Roosevelt's personal letter seeking that the arms embargo be lifted, with the Jews and any UN police force to be equipped with modern armaments as "the only thing which will hold the Arabs in check." Both Jews and Arabs were committing acts of terror, Marshall replied. Moreover, her suggestions would lead to further bloodshed, and the problem should be approached through the UN rather than unilaterally. When soon asked at a press conference on February 19 if the United States would continue to support partition, Marshall replied thus: "The whole Palestine matter "is under consideration."[34]

The descent into further killing and chaos in the biblically covenanted Promised Land did not allow, however, for tempered deliberation. While Goldenberg could inform the Council of Jewish Federations executive committee that $17 million in cash had already been sent in by February 23, with over $40 million pledged, an attack one day earlier aided by some British deserters and orchestrated by local Palestinian commander Abd al-Qadir al-Husseini in Jerusalem's densely populated Ben Yehuda Street had killed fifty-eight people, almost all civilians, and seriously wounded thirty-two more. The same day, His Majesty's Government announced that it would block Palestine's sterling balances of about £100 million, thus curtailing Jewish imports from sterling area countries, as well as causing avoidable credit stringency and thus a probable rise in the domestic cost of living. The *yishuv* would emerge victorious against the Arab forces provided that weapons arrived before May 15, Ben-Gurion wired Shertok on February 27, but that remained unsure, even as Hagana intelligence possessed proof that the British in Palestine were recruiting for the Arab Legion. The next day, after a British constable and three Arabs in uniform entered the Hagana position at the HaYotzek factory opposite Holon and confiscated all weapons, Arabs who had gathered outside immediately opened fire: eight Hagana men were killed and "subsequently butchered."[35]

Nor did this deadly pace slacken in the first two weeks of March. Entering Palestine on the 6th with a large, well-armed contingent, former military leader in the Arab Revolt (1936–1939) and pro-Nazi collaborator Fawzi al-Kaukji announced that the Arab Liberation Army was fighting for "the annihilation of the Zionists," a phrase Haj Amin repeated in declaring that the Arabs would continue fighting "until the Zionists were annihilated and the whole of Palestine became a purely Arab state." At a meeting the following day of the UJA Administration Committee, at which Morgenthau announced that cash contributions to meet the emergency developments in Palestine would reach the $50 million mark by the early part of the next week, Myerson warned that the Jews in Palestine "are fighting a war of survival… which they must fight to a victorious end to save their a lives and homes as well as to safeguard the rights of the homeless Jews of Europe find a home in the Jewish state in the Palestine future." On February 11, an Arab explosion partially wrecked the Jewish Agency headquarters in Jerusalem, killed ten people and wounded ninety others.[36]

The same morning, Myerson departed LaGuardia airport for Tel-Aviv. Ending her five-week American tour the previous day at a dinner meeting with a group of outstanding Washington newsmen and radio correspondents, she declared that attempted conciliation with the Arabs at this time would result only in strengthening their resistance to the UN decision on partition, since they regarded the lack of firm action by the UN as encouragement to proceed with violence. If Haj Amin were removed from the scene, she went on, influential Arabs now terrorized by his Arab Higher Committee would come forward for negotiation; non-aggression pacts had been concluded even now between Jewish and Arab villages in Palestine. The British, she charged, far from practicing the impartiality which they continuously professed regarding the implementation of partition, had helped to arm Arab guards, let the Arab Legion remain in Palestine, and replenish the Arab war budget by a long-deferred payment of $1.2 million to the Moslem Supreme Council run in fact by the former Grand Mufti. The decisive factor remained the spirit of the Palestinian Jewish community and particularly of its young people, determined to fight and needing weapons. Only a token UN international force was desired, she declared, since the *yishuv* wished no one else to do their fighting for them. The distinction between maintenance of peace in that war-torn country and enforcement of partition, raised by the United States at the Security Council, Myerson termed "a legal quibble." She would now fly home.[37]

Myerson's mission had achieved a resounding success, indeed nothing short of incredible. On March 29, two days after forty-six members of the Hagana were killed in a convoy to kibbutz Yehiam, and ten days after US delegate Warren Austin shocked the Security Council when announcing that a temporary trusteeship should be established for Palestine, Montor could report to the JDC staff in New York that $43 million had arrived in cash, with outstanding pledges of about $7.5 million—the $50 million goal actually to be oversubscribed. The availability of these dollars was "providential" for the *yishuv*'s situation, he and Coons told the UJA executive committee, the American Jewish community's "genuine spirit of consecration" evident in its response to this "unique and historical call for statesmanlike action to meet a crucial situation." With funds shifted by Hammer via a credit account with Manufacturers Trust Bank to the Anglo-Palestine Bank in Jerusalem (later Bank Leumi) and to Geneva, where the Jewish Agency's Chaim Posner (later Pazner) transferred them at higher black market rates to Ueberall in Prague, vital Czechoslovak armaments reached the beleaguered Hagana just in time to launch its first battle offensive on April 1. Safer convoys from Tel-Aviv to Jerusalem, as well as the capture of Tiberias and Haifa, sparking the flight of thousands of Arabs in those areas, soon followed. Fierce assaults against kibbutzim Mishmar HaEmek and Ramat Yohanan failed, the surrounding Arab villages razed. A general collapse of Arab morale in Palestine, especially after the death of Abd al-Qadir al-Husseini at the key al-Qastal village dominating the western entrance to Jerusalem and the Irgun's killing of close to 110 Deir Yassin villagers, ensued.[38]

Ben-Gurion, having secured a 6 to 4 vote on May 12 of the *Minhelet HaAm* (People's Administrative Council) to reject an American truce proposal and Marshall's admonition to Shertok not to declare statehood at this time, moved ahead with a proclamation of independence. Two days earlier, Myerson had sharply rejected Abdullah's appeal during their second secret meeting that the Jews delay for one year announcing sovereignty, after which the country would be united with Jordan in a "Judeo-Arab" kingdom where Jewish membership in the Parliament and Cabinet could reach fifty percent. On May 14, 1948, upon declaring in Tel-Aviv's Museum of Art on 16 Rothschild Boulevard that *Medinat Yisrael* would stand for "the principles of liberty, justice and peace as conceived by the Prophets of Israel," be open to "the ingathering of exiles," give full citizenship to the Arab people of Israel, and extend the hand of peace to all the neighboring states, Ben-Gurion, the fifty-two year old resolute leader, became the first to sign a typed document marking the end of 1,888 years of exile from Jewry's birthplace. Of the thirty-six who followed in Hebrew alphabetical order, two were women: WIZO pioneer Rachel (Kagan) Cohen, head of the Va'ad HaLeumi's Social Welfare Department, and the individual whom Ben-Gurion had persuaded his Mapai colleagues to include in the Provisional Government "as an historic act," "G. Myerson." Sitting in her best black dress, with Shertok holding the document, she could not stop crying when thinking of all those who should have been present but were not. News had also just been received that the Etzion bloc had fallen with heavy losses. A few minutes after midnight, Myerson was filled with "joy and relief" upon hearing that Truman had quickly recognized the State of Israel, she thinking it "like a miracle coming at the time of our greatest vulnerability, on the eve of the Arab invasion.[39]

Morgenthau acknowledged this revolutionary moment in Jewish history after Warburg had objected to a press release by issuing a statement to American Jews as UJA General Chairman that appealed for their financial support, hailing this "source of great spiritual excitement," knowing that "a new chapter in world Jewish history has been opened," and "convinced that this new state will add stature to Jews everywhere." Earlier that spring, he had played a decisive role as well in the Jewish Agency's obtaining a special loan of $10 million from Manufacturers Trust. With Montor in tow, he had accompanied Hammer to see the chairman of the board, Harvey Gibson, at the bank's headquarters in New York City. Although Gibson did not have cordial relations with Morgenthau during World War II when serving as president of the American Red Cross, the former US Secretary of the Treasury bluntly took over the meeting, candidly declaring that the funds might well be used for military purposes and pressing for the loan. His forthright manner overcame Gibson's initial insistence that the bank did not finance wars, and the board chairman's coolness gave way to declaring that an exception would be made in this instance. In subsequent years, Hammer reminisced, the Agency's relationship with Manufacturers Hanover, the bank's successor, proved to be "smooth and fully responsive to our requests." For his "outstanding leadership' in the UJA program, Morgenthau now received the 1948 award for "distinguished service to Jewry" from the National Federation of Jewish Men's Clubs.[40]

Two days after the historic proclamation in Tel-Aviv, Montor cabled Myerson urging that she return quickly to the United States even for a short tour, convinced that her presence might well sway American Jewry to give another $50 million to the new State of Israel. After consulting with Ben-Gurion, who insisted that she, like other State officials, Hebraize her name, Golda Meir took the next plane available for LaGuardia Field. In city after city, at UJA lunches, dinners and teas, and at parlor meetings, she repeated one theme: "We cannot go on without your help." Meir's audiences, she reminisced, answered with "unprecedented generosity and speed." Most commitments were made by private figures, but Jack Benny (born Benjamin Kubelsky) sent a check to fellow radio star Eddie Cantor (Edward Israel Itzkowitz), then hosting Meir's appearance at his home, with the note "Eddie, fill in this check for whatever you need." Cantor filled in the check for $25,000, which he knew was the minimum that Benny, whose popular program made stinginess the most famous part of his persona, would have given.[41]

The fifty percent gained now for Israel in the UJA drive for 1948 (the other fifty percent going to the JDC) enabled the well-armed Israeli Defense Forces (*Tzahal*) to eventually turn the tide against the five invading Arab armies. Upon hearing in January about her "fairly grim picture of immediate needs," Jewish Agency executive secretary in New York Arthur Lourie had written an associate in Jerusalem that "it is too early to say whether her mission here will be successful, but she has determination and courage and if anyone can do the job I think it will be she." Meir's initial triumph, augmented by the second trip to the States, gave Ben-Gurion good reason to tell this to the *yishuv*'s emissary upon her return: "Someday when history will be written, it will be said that there was a Jewish woman who got the money which made the state possible."[42]

On July 1, upon receiving an urgent request from the Provisional Government of Israel to reach Truman, Morgenthau wrote to the President asking that he take every available step to rush relief supplies to Jerusalem, the embattled city cut off from normal communications. At least a hundred tons of milk power and fifty tons of eggs were needed within a week's time, children particularly suffering because of the blockade. Israel was prepared to pay for these essential supplies with its own funds for goods available from the US government stocks in Europe. While receiving no reply, he wrote one week later to Kaplan and Ben-Gurion advising that a US committee be formed without delay to coordinate all funds raised for Israel. To be known as the American Friends of the State of Israel, it would have a quasi-official recognition from the Israeli authorities as the "sole clearing house" for all collections of funds in America, the monies transmitted to the treasury of the new government. During the balance of 1948, he continued, the UJA should be authorized to deposit funds that normally would go to the UPA to the new state's fiscal agent directly. He was transmitting this confidential suggestion through the good offices of Montor, the message ended, who would bring the plan to them and explain it in greater detail.[43]

Morgenthau strongly endorsed Montor's charge that the current American Zionist leadership sought to use funds raised in the United States as a lever with which to change or dominate Israel's social structure, which led Montor to resign that September as UPA executive vice-president after many years of service and sparked his effort to create a new organization to raise funds for direct transmission to the Jewish state. With UPA chairman Abba Hillel Silver pressuring the Jewish Agency executive in Jerusalem by control of the flow of these funds, Hammer sought to eliminate the role of the UPA as the organization that transmitted funds from the UJA to the Jewish Agency, and found an ally in Rose Halprin of the Hadassah Women's Zionist Organization presidium. Quietly, she conferred with Morgenthau, then attending a UJA conference in New Orleans. He and Montor, resenting Silver's "overbearing manner" and his determination to "to control every situation," agreed with legal counsel Maurice Boukstein's idea to incorporate the Agency's New York office as an entirely new organization, to be called The Jewish Agency, Inc. Montor prevailed upon his volunteer leadership to recognize this entity as the recipient of funds intended to be used in Israel. Silver resigned and the crisis came to a swift close. The UPA, soon to be renamed the United Israel Appeal and drawing more easily through the local welfare funds, shifted the burden of fund raising to the non-Zionist communal leaders and thereby reduced the ZOA's conservative influence, this to the understandable satisfaction of Ben-Gurion and others of the Labor Party which led the Israeli government.[44]

Taking his first trip to Israel that October, focusing on how UJA funds could aid in meeting the state's future needs, Morgenthau pressed this cause with Ben-Gurion and Kaplan. Upon landing, he declared that "Israel's struggle for independence has greatly increased the dignity and stature of Jew everywhere," and that Israel's struggle concerned "all freedom-loving peoples" and was "a test of the United Nations." He hoped that the US government would play the fullest role in the prompt establishment of peace in Israel on the basis of justice, and asserted that American Jews were determined to give every support for the Jews now in Israel and also for the hundreds of thousands in Europe whose future depended on the new commonwealth. He happily introduced as his traveling companion young Curtis Roosevelt Boettiger, the late President's grandson, who had come as the special representative of Mrs. Eleanor

Roosevelt, "who is keenly interested in the successful establishment of the Jewish state as a stronghold of democracy in the Middle East."[45]

The ten-day visit, including a brief tour of the battlefront lines, deeply impressed Morgenthau. He marveled at how the "Burma Road" was carved out of the rock of the Judean hills: "It could not have been made possible if the young men and women who built it were not motivated by an unquenchable search for freedom and peace." He noted the care that Israeli soldiers took protecting Arab mosques and shrines in Ramleh. "The state of Israel without Jerusalem would be like the Jewish people without its history," he asserted after a surprise visit to that city. On the first celebration in the new state of Simchat Torah, Morgenthau joined Ben-Gurion in dancing with a Torah scroll to the cheers of spectators. Distanced from religious practice since youth, he then wiped tears from his eyes. Just before Morgenthau's departure, the new government expressed its gratitude to the UJA General Chairman by conferring its highest honor—naming the former Palestinian Arab village Khirbat Bayt between Gedera and Latrun, a *moshav* populated by Jewish immigrants from Greece, Poland, and Turkey, Tal Shachar ("Morning Dew," taken from the German word Morgenthau). Calling this occasion "one of the greatest moments of my life," he told the crowd that by showing the Israeli Jew to be "a fighting man," "you have raised the standard of the Jew in the Christian world." "You will have to depend on your own strong right arm," he cautioned, because the young republic had "very few friends in the outside world." This was the kind of "exultant militancy," future UJA board chairman Herbert Friedman remembered, which inspired both the American and the Israeli Jewish communities.[46]

From then onward, Morgenthau became an unabashed champion of the State of Israel. Immediately upon returning home, he proclaimed that the US government "should have a policy of its own towards Israel and not follow the British Foreign Office." "The State of Israel is stronger than ever. They are going to win," he confidently added when disclosing that the Israeli Navy had intercepted one vessel carrying a great shipment of weapons to Syria. One month later, he appealed to British Prime Minister Clement Attlee and predecessor Winston Churchill to press for the release of 11,000 Jews interned by British authorities on the island of Cyprus. Declaring that "their only crime is that they are Jews who escaped death at the hands of Hitler and sought to find life among their own people in Israel," Morgenthau charged that "these men, women and some 600 babies have been subjected to the most inhuman forms of degradation." He added that "if the British people could see the intolerable conditions under which the Cyprus refugees live, they would demand that the refugees be freed to leave for Israel at once." The people and government of Israel were eager and anxious to receive the Cyprus "prisoners," and give them an opportunity to build new lives. Of the 11,000 Jews held in prison camps on Cyprus, at least fifty percent have been there for two years, another twenty-five percent for more than eighteen months and the remainder for at least six months, he stated.[47]

Morgenthau played a decisive role as well in preserving the UJA's income tax exemption status when the anti-Zionist American Council for Judaism filed an affidavit and brought a suit declaring that the UJA was in effect an agent of a foreign government. Characteristically, Morgenthau took charge, and called in Randolph E. Paul, a former member of his staff who became a part-time Special Assistant to Truman for tax policy and later the President's envoy to the negotiations between Switzerland and the Allied Powers on Nazi assets in that country. Hammer and Agency legal counsel Boukstein, as well as Morgenthau and Montor, worked over the next few months with Paul in meeting the charges. These were successfully refuted to the satisfaction of the Internal Revenue Service (IRS) with one provision: the Jewish Agency must indicate that any funds transmitted and received in Israel from the UJA would not be sent directly and be used solely for humanitarian (not military) purposes. Ben-Gurion then signed a resolution adopted by the Agency executive that it would never violate IRS regulations. Few ever knew of Morgenthau's intervention.[48]

The UJA leadership's involvement in Truman's upset victory over New York State's Governor Thomas E. Dewey in the 1948 presidential election also remained a secret for many years. Determined to overcome a deficit in the polls, the American Chief Executive traveled more than 30,000 miles by rail to bring his message to the people in large cities and eke out a victory. During this "whistle-stop tour," begun in September aboard a seventeen-car train called "The Magellan," Truman spoke at 352 places aided by talking points that seven young men, one of whom having escaped Nazi Germany just in time, sent him by air courier to a runner from the train. This localized, popular approach had to be paid for. Abraham (Abe) Feinberg, former president of Americans for

Hagana, resolved to raise the necessary funds in gratitude for Truman's support for Israel and the President's promise on May 27 to Weizmann, then accompanied to the White House by Feinberg, of a large loan to the new state. Montor asked Friedman to work towns along the train route, raise cash, and bring it to the train each day. A carefully selected list of people connected to the UJA campaign was drawn up for each location on the schedule, and the money collected once Friedman made his appeal placed in a brown paper bag. With this as the only serious fund raising taking place on his behalf, Truman was not embarrassed to tell Friedman how much he appreciate the effort. "The Magellan" thus kept to schedule, returning to Washington just before election day.[49]

Montor was also instrumental in the creation of a new financial instrument to aid Israel in the spring of 1950. A major problem had arisen from the confluence of several events: the massive immigration of almost 1,000 Jewish refugees which reached the state's shores each day, doubling the pre-war population to 1.2 million; a precipitous drop in UJA funding owing to American Jewry's apparent inability to grasp that the Israeli government would continue its mission of *kibbutz galuyot* ("the ingathering of exiles"); and a shortage of food that led to rationing. Ben-Gurion and Kaplan convened a Jerusalem conference that September to determine a strategy for meeting this crisis at which Sharett, Meir, and Jewish Agency chairman Berl Locker sat down with the American delegation: Montor, Rothberg, Myers, Halprin, Nathan, Friedman, Feinberg, US businessman Joseph Meyerhoff, and WZO president Nahum Goldmann. "Fiercely intense and persistent," Montor opened by declaring that the UJA was doomed, and he proposed in its stead that the State of Israel issue bonds to finance its operations. Usually "ice-cold and tightly reined in," Montor railed at those who feared a bond drive, who he claimed were hiding their fear behind a pious concern for the health of the UJA. The more moderate Friedman advocated trying both the bond approach and strengthening the UJA under the new chairmanship of Joseph J. Schwartz, former JDC director in wartime Europe, in order to reach a goal of $1.5 billion for the next three years. The conference adopted this position, assigning $1 billion to come from the United States.[50]

Montor left the UJA to organize the new campaign for the American Financial and Development Corporation for Israel, soon to be called Israel Bonds, Ben-Gurion tapping Meir to present this to a national conference in Washington, DC that October. She offered skeptical listeners the "gilt-edged security" of the people of Israel and their children, who were growing up "proud, safe, self-respecting Jews," the debt to be paid back with interest. The ZOA pledged on that occasion to purchase $100 million of the bonds. When Morgenthau received Truman's blessing for the new venture, the President understanding the need for long-term financing for economic growth, the assembly voted to proceed. The chances of success improved greatly when Morgenthau agreed to leave the UJA and serve as chairman of the Board of Governors. In May 1951 Ben-Gurion kicked off the first campaign in Chicago, with a rally of 100,000 at Soldier's Field and a ticker-tape parade down State Street. The first year brought in $52.5 million. When launching the drive in January 1953, Ehud Avriel, now Director General of Israel's finance ministry, declared that the proceeds of the Israel Bond issue had made it possible for the State of Israel to embark on "many vital projects linked to its primary objective of achieving economic independence within the shortest possible time." The next month, the Soviet government newspaper *Izvestiia* charged that Morgenthau, along with fellow Jews US Congressmen from New York Emanuel Celler and Jacob Javits, had worked out plans to make Israel the major anti-Communist stronghold of the United States in the Middle East. He stayed on as board chairman until the end of that year, deciding to bow out because he objected to Israel's financial policies. Morgenthau chose to do so gracefully, as he jotted down the very last entry in his Presidential Diaries, "and not look for anything or expect anything further from the Government of Israel."[51]

The man whom Meir later considered "far more influential than Ben-Gurion, Kaplan, Montor and myself put together" in championing Israel Bonds after leading the UJA's postwar success, who never received any compensation "whatsoever" from either organization, now faded from the spotlight. A brief feature story carried by the Jewish Telegraphic Agency in early 1958 quoted Morgenthau's statement that Israel's victories by "a handful of soldiers" in the 1948 war, followed by its lightening success in the Sinai Campaign at the end of October 1956, enhanced the prestige of the Jewish commonwealth and of Jews throughout the world. He refused to comment when asked whether he thought the United States would come to Israel's aid if that state were attacked, but asserted that he had no fears for Israel's future.

He expected to visit Israel the following March, a plan that would not came to fruition.⁵²

On the night of February 7, 1967, after suffering a heart condition and a long illness, the seventy-five-year-old Henry Morgenthau, Jr. died at the Vassar Brothers Hospital overlooking the Hudson River in Poughkeepsie, New York. Funeral services were held two days later at Reform flagship congregation Temple Emanu-El on Sixty-Fifth St. and Fifth Ave. in New York City, the survivors his widow, the former Marcelle Puthon Hirsch, and three children from a first marriage to Elinor née Fatman, a close friend to Eleanor Roosevelt. Only three hundred people came that morning to pay their last respects. The eulogies by Senior Rabbi Julius Mark and John M. Blum, the Yale University historian and a fellow Jew who had edited Morgenthau's diaries, did not say a word about his activities on behalf of Jews or of Israel, although he had openly asserted two months after the state's establishment that "the most important Jewish issue before the Jews of America is the success of the State of Israel," and that "any element which would retard or defeat that success must have our unyielding opposition." Montor, seated next to Klotz, served as an honorary pallbearer, as did Rosenwald, Sonneborn, Friedman, and Schwartz. That evening, writing as Morgenthau's "right hand" during their joint efforts at the UJA and Israel Bonds, Montor noted to US District Attorney Robert Morgenthau what his late father's dedication and enormous prestige had done in creating "unity and harmony" in American Jewry, as well as in helping to establish the atmosphere within which huge sums were raised on behalf of the Palestinian Jewish community and then the State of Israel. He "encouraged the timid, converted the indifferent, and gave new vigor to the old stalwarts," Montor concluded, "a great American but also a great Jew. Few have equaled his commitment to both causes."⁵³

Montor paid additional tributes to "the old man" in public and in private. In the Israeli daily *Ma'ariv*, "Henry on Henry" thought it conceivable that Morgenthau's German-Jewish origin explained why something in his personality did not generate friendship. Yet beneath the cold exterior, there was a feeling of warmth, and without him it was doubtful that Israel would have been able to raise such large sums of money for the state's urgent needs. A few months later, writing to his UJA assistant, Montor described "a naïve, uninformed man" but one "dedicated to the tasks at hand." These included "frenetic efforts" to save Jews during the Holocaust, and having "an uncanny skill" when Secretary of the Treasury in surrounding himself with superb civil servants who were "able and incorruptible." In a more candid, long missive three weeks later, Montor recalled Morgenthau's attractive smile, the curious maneuvering with his hands, his quick rise to anger, and his equal return to serenity. He had an intuition and a sensibility that were "truly remarkable." Like political Zionism's founder Theodor Herzl, Morgenthau came of a totally un-Jewish background but was "moved by particular events to become a Jew." When he did, Montor added, "he was neurotic, indefatigable, unashamed in trying to save Jews." Under the pressure, encouragement, and emotion of Klotz, who goes completely unmentioned in Blum's three volumes of the Morgenthau diaries, he went "racing after any hope" that could be found to save those who were "suffering solely because they were Jews." Montor did not add Morgenthau's deep suspicion, confided to a few, that Truman had rejected his presence at the Potsdam Conference because he was a Jew and could succeed to the presidency, although there is no indication of this in anything Truman said or wrote.[54]

Montor's passion and fierce will strongly influenced many, notably Rothberg, who became chief officer of Israel Bonds, but his dictatorial style and "self-confidence to a fault" increasingly created friction with UJA even after he retired as chief executive officer of Israel Bonds in May 1955. Reports of frequent conflicts with local Jewish community leaders and particularly UJA chairman Schwartz, the two men quarreling over the timing of the two campaigns and competing for volunteer manpower, reached Levi Eshkol. Israel's third Prime Minister unsuccessfully sought to resolve the situation by calling a meeting in Jerusalem. Frustrated at the dashing of his hope that he had settled the problem, he cabled Montor, then in Rome on his way back to the States, to return for further discussions. When Montor refused, a sign of what Friedman subsequently dubbed his "mercurial volatility," Eshkol fired him without further ado.[55]

From then on, Montor took up residence in Rome and Jerusalem. In the Eternal City, so called because ancient Romans believed that no matter what happened to the world or how many empires came and collapsed, Rome would go on forever, he established a consumer finance company. His Finanza Popolare also developed branches in Milan and Turin. Contacts with the Zionist establishment dwindled, although Weizmann had cabled him immediately upon Montor's break with the UPA in October 1948 with this message: "Regret hearing your resignation. Feel confident Israel will continue to have benefit of your loyal, devoted, brilliant service. Warm regards." Looking back at those years, Meir judged Montor's share to be "critical" in the UJA's achievements, his ability to work "limitless," and his knowledge of what every Jew had, what his problems were, and how much he should give nothing short of "incredible." And in 1960, on the occasion of the tenth anniversary celebration of Israel Bonds, Ben-Gurion, the man who willed a state, declared that Henry Montor's name was high among "a list of ten individuals most responsible for the creation of the State of Israel."[56]

Montor died of leukemia on April 16, 1982, in Jerusalem's Hadassah hospital, a son and a daughter his immediate survivors. The "dynamic and sometimes controversial figure on the American Jewish scene," read the obituary notice by the Jewish Telegraphic Agency, "was widely respected for his vision and innovative methods." He was "at times considered a thorn in the side of the Jewish establishment because of the zeal with which he sought increased funds for Israel. His effectiveness as an advocate of the primacy of Israel as a new home for the survivors of the Holocaust often placed him in the role of a leading spokesman for Israel as it stood on the threshold of independence." Thanks in great measure to his aggressive and novel, creative style, the UJA and Israel Bonds had raised more than $14 billion for Israel's social, welfare and economic development programs. Now, without fanfare, burial took place on the Mount of Olives just east of Jerusalem.[57]

To American Jews, Myerson/Meir embodied the collective will of the embattled *yishuv*, prepared to defend its home to the very end against an Arab world committed to its destruction. Morgenthau, breaking with his staunchly anti-Zionist father's final piece of advice that he not have anything to do with Jews, brought his great prestige and sincerity to win over various influential circles, his personality giving "substance and power" to the campaigns. He surely merited the B'nai Brith gold medallion, which read "Lover of Israel," for his outstanding contributions to the World War II effort and refugee relief.[58] Montor provided important contacts, publicity skills, and zealous drive, his unrelenting pursuit of the revival of Holocaust survivors and of Israel's rebirth vital to eventual triumph. Meir would go on to become the first ambassador of the State of Israel to the Soviet Union, Knesset member, Minister of Foreign Affairs, Mapai secretary general, and Prime Minister before her death on December 8, 1978. Most fittingly, her final resting place would be on Jerusalem's Mt. Herzl alongside other leaders of *Medinat Yisra'el*. Morgenthau's contribution would be acknowledged in Tal Shahar and on a street sign in Jerusalem. Montor's gravestone, simply giving in Hebrew his places and dates of birth and death, is his only memorial in Israel. The Mt. of Olives registry lists that one plot as *muznah* (neglected).

Meir's legacy is deservedly enshrined in Israel's memory, while that of Morgenthau is dimly remembered and that of Montor forgotten. In their crusade to save a Jewish state during the short interval as the clock inexorably neared May 14, 1948, the three had confronted considerable odds to success. Yet, working assiduously in concert and with some dedicated JDC-UJA executives, they touched the hearts of American Jews who "gave as Jews," such as the thousands at a rally in New York City's garment district who heard her offer them a choice between meeting in Madison Square Garden to rejoice in the establishment of a Jewish state or to meet there at another memorial meeting for the Jews in Palestine "who are gone."[59] The Jews of America were eager to take part in the tectonic shift which ultimately brought their people back onto the world's center stage with sovereignty in Israel after two millennia. During the Montor/Morgenthau era, the center of philanthropy moved from Europe to Israel, bringing non-Zionists as well to assume the significant role of active partners in the drama.

Nothing was certain at that point in time. Many years later, Gideon Rafael recalled that when he, Sharett, and a secretary, then comprising Israel's entire foreign office, tried at 2 a.m. on May 15, 1948, to send out telegrams announcing the creation of the new state, only after the approval of the expense by the man appointed by the British to handle the transition was Israel's independence pronounced to the world.[60] A new journey in the odyssey of Jewish history had begun.

Endnotes

1. Kaplan to Jewish Agency New York for Montor, January 20, 1948, S25/1701, Central Zionist Archives (hereafter CZA), Jerusalem; Henry Montor, "Hashpa'ato Al Yahadut America," in *Eliezer Kaplan, Chazon U'Ma'as*, ed. Y. Shapira (Tel-Aviv, 1973), 137–141. *Kristallnacht*, the "Night of Broken Glass," an unprecedented orgy of destruction and terror, methodically

targeted Jewish shops, synagogues, orphanages, and dwellings; led to the death of almost 100 Jews and hundreds wounded; the deportation of more than 30,000 Jews to concentration camps (where several hundred would die in the following weeks); and soon a Central Office for Jewish Emigration headed by SS *Obersturmbannführer* Adolf Eichmann for all Jews to fall under the Third Reich's control. See Monty Noam Penkower, *The Swastika's Darkening Shadow: Voices before the Holocaust* (New York, 2013), 83–85, 213–220.

2. Henry Montor interview with the author, June 8, 1977; Barbara Kirshenblatt-Gimblett, "Performing the State: The Jewish Palestine Pavilion at the New York World's Fair, 1939/40," in *The Art of Being Jewish in Modern Times*, ed. B. Kirshenblatt-Gimblett and J. Karp (Philadelphia, 2008), 98–115. The Hagana, first formed in 1920 against Palestinian Arab attacks, served under the aegis of the Jewish Agency as the paramilitary defense arm of the *yishuv*.

3. Montor interview, May 5, 1977; Sam Rothberg interview, May 4, 1976; both in UJA Archives, New York City; Gottlieb Hammer, *Good Faith and Credit* (New York, 1985), 213–214.

4. Monty Noam Penkower, *The Jews Were Expendable: Free World Diplomacy and the Holocaust* (Urbana, 1984), chap. 5; idem, "The Earl Harrison Report: Its Genesis and Its Significance," *American Jewish Archives* 68:1 (2016): 1–75; Montor interview with the author, June 15, 1977.

5. Montor to Meltzer, February 15, 1967, A371/34; Montor to Kaplan, December 5, 1946, S63/333; both in CZA.

6. Montor interview with the author, June 8, 1977; Marc Lee Raphael, *A History of the United Jewish Appeal* (Brown University, 1982), 30; Herbert A. Friedman, *Roots of the Future* (Jerusalem, 1999), 226, 337, and chap. 16; *Jewish Telegraphic Agency* (hereafter *JTA*), February 8, 1967.

7. April 30, 1947, and May 1, 1947, vol. 8, Presidential Diaries, Henry Morgenthau, Jr. MSS., Franklin D. Roosevelt Library, Hyde Park, New York; Monty Noam Penkower, *Palestine to Israel: Mandate to State, 1945–1948*, vol. 2, *Into the International Arena, 1947–1948* (New York, 2019), 405–409. One month later, he telephoned Truman asking that the Chief Executive intercede against the British cabinet's decision to send the 4,554 Holocaust survivors aboard the *Exodus 1947,* who had sought entry into Palestine in the face of restrictive British immigration law, back to their original exit port from France. Morgenthau's private intervention raised the President's ire; the State Department soon declared that it could not intervene because His Majesty's Government carried "full responsibility" for maintaining peace and order in Palestine. Ibid., 446–447.

8. Montor interview with the author, June 8, 1977; *JTA*, March 26, 1946; Montor interview, May 5, 1977, UJA Archives.
9. Coons-Montor to Myerson, January 22, 1948, S25/1558, CZA.
10. Penkower, *Palestine to Israel*, vol. 2, 546, 552; Kaplan to Ben-Gurion, December 5, 1947; Ben-Gurion to Kaplan, December 8, 1947; both in S25/1700, CZA.
11. Myerson-Cunningham interview, December 17, 1947, S25/22; Myerson to Shertok, December 16, 1947, S25/1700; both in CZA; *Foreign Relations of the United States, 1947*, vol. 5 (Washington, DC, 1971), 1090–1096; Ben-Gurion to Kaplan, December 14, 1947, S25/1700; Myerson-Gurney interview, December 29, 1947, S25/7725; both in CZA; David Ben-Gurion, *Yoman Milchama, Milchemet Ha'Atsmaut, 1948–1949*, vol. 1, ed. G. Rivlin and E. Oren (Tel-Aviv, 1984), 88. For the US arms embargo, see Amitsur Ilan, *The Origin of the Arab-Israeli Arms Race* (London, 1996).
12. Ben-Gurion, *Yoman Milchama*, 92–96.
13. Ibid., 100, 107–108, 121, 122; Penkower, *Palestine to Israel*, vol. 2, 547, 551 554.
14. Ben-Gurion, *Yoman Milchama*, 135–143; Myerson to Shertok, January 13, 1948, S25/1701, CZA; Golda Meir, *My Life* (New York, 1975), 211–212.
15. Penkower, *Palestine to Israel*, vol. 2, 555–556, 565. In August 1949, kibbutz Netiv HaLamed Heh (Path of the Thirty-Five) was founded by former *Palmach* members of the Hagana at a key point along the route which the convoy had traversed that fateful night. A few months later, the decomposed bodies, twelve identified by Rav Aryeh Levin by means of a rarely performed biblical lottery attributed to the Vilna Gaon, were brought in November to the Mt. Herzl cemetery in Jerusalem and buried in a separate section.
16. Meir interview, June 8, 1975, with Hodes, Nardi, and Kaufman, in *Living UJA History: Irving Bernstein, An Oral History Anthology* (Jerusalem, 1995); Meir-Bethell interview, May 24, 1977, P-1784, Israel State Archives, Jerusalem; Ben-Gurion, *Yoman Milchama*, 168.
17. *Living Jewish History*, 6–7, Montor-Kaufman interview, April 15, 1976, UJA Archives. In a field staff memorandum more than a year earlier, Lurie had stressed that the Council's "greatest strength" was its "non-political and non-partisan" character, that it expressed "no preference on controversial and ideological issues." Memo, November 7, 1946, Council of Jewish Federations and Welfare Funds Archives, New York City.
18. Montor to Steinglas, March 12, 1969, A371/549, CZA; Memorandum, January 24–26, 1948, Council of Jewish Federations and Welfare Funds Archives, New York City.

19. Myerson address, January 25, 1948, MRD-1, 37/2, UJA Archives. A briefer version was published twenty-five years later in Marie Syrkin, ed., *A Land of Our Own: An Oral Autobiography by Golda Meir* (New York, 1973), 73–79.
20. Francine Klagsburn, *Lioness: Golda Meir and the Nation of Israel* (New York, 2017), 305; Montor-Kaufman interview, April 15, 1976, UJA Archives.
21. Minutes, January 26, 1948, Z6/50; Myerson statement, January 26, 1948, Z5/411; both in CZA; Beeley note, January 27, 1948, Foreign Office records 371/68533, Public Record Office, Kew, England.
22. Montor interview, May 5, 1977, UJA Archives; Montor to Meltzer, March 12, 1969, A371/34, CZA.
23. Baerwald memo, January 21, 1948, Paul Baerwald MSS., Herbert Lehman MSS., Columbia University, New York City; Leavitt report, Administration Committee, January 27, 1948, JDC Archives, New York City.
24. Montor interview with the author, June 8, 1977; Montor to Steinglas, March 12, 1969, A371/549, CZA; Leavitt to Montor, February 2, 1948; JDC Staff Meeting, February 2, 1948; both in JDC Archives; Myerson to Ben-Gurion, February 2, 1948, S25/1702, CZA.
25. Executive meeting, February 4, 1948, MRD-1, 33/1, UJA Archives; Baerwald-Goldwasser letter, February 6, 1948, Lehman MSS.; Penkower, *Palestine to Israel*, vol. 2, 566–567. Montor had secured from the JDC the joint goal for the 1948 UJA drive of $250 million (of which less than $150 million would be raised), with the UPA getting forty-five percent of the first $50 million, fifty-five percent of the next $75 million, and at least seventy-five percent of the remainder. Raphael, *A History of the United Jewish Appeal*, 33.
26. JDC Staff Meeting New York, February 9, 1948, JDC Archives.
27. Lehman to Stern, January 21, 1948, Herbert Lehman MSS., Columbia University, New York City; UJA executive, January 4, 1948, MRD-1, 33/1, UJA Archives; February 11, 1948, vol. 8, Presidential Diaries, Morgenthau MSS.; Morgenthau letter, February 18, 1948, MRD-1, 34/1, UJA Archives.
28. *JTA*, January 19, 1948.
29. Meir interview, June 1975, UJA Archives.
30. Raphael, *A History of the United Jewish Appeal*, 34–35; *JTA*, February 10, 1948.
31. *JTA*, February 24, 1948.
32. Hammer to Kaplan, February 14, 1948, S25/1558, CZA; Meir-Hodess interview, June 1975, UJA Archives.
33. Ruffer to Sharef, February 10, 1948, 93.03/64/18, Israel State Archives; Security Committee, February 10, 1948, S25/9346; Myerson to Ben-Gurion,

February 10, 1948, S25/1702; both in CZA; Ben-Gurion to Myerson, February 10, 1948, *Yoman Milchama*, 232n.

34. Penkower, *Palestine to Israel*, vol. 2, 576–578.
35. Executive meeting, February 23, 1948, Council archives; Penkower, *Palestine to Israel*, vol. 2, 582–585, 591.
36. Ibid., 601; *JTA*, March 7, 1948.
37. *JTA*, March 11, 1948.
38. Staff meeting, March 29, 1948, JDC Archives; Montor-Coons report, March 26, 1948, Council archives; Gottlieb Hammer interview with the author, December 6, 1977; Chaim Pazner interview with the author, June 20, 1979; Penkower, *Palestine to Israel*, vol. 2, 617, 644–646, 649. Hammer would continue to send Posner requested funds until the State of Israel's independence. See Z5/3491, CZA.
39. Penkower, *Palestine to Israel*, vol. 2, 670–672, 678; Ben-Gurion, *Yoman Milchama*, 281–282; Meir, *My Life*, 216–230. Myerson had already, after returning from the United States, urged her Mapai colleagues on March 20 to declare statehood, even if a provisional government. *Akhshav O Le'Olam Lo*, ed. M. Avizohar and A. Bareli (Beit Berl, 1989), 357–358.
40. Montor to Steinglas, September 2, 1967, A371/547; UJA Bulletin, May 16, 1948, A371/356; both in CZA; Hammer, *Good Faith and Credit*, 89–90; *JTA*, May 30, 1948.
41. Meir, *My Life*, 214, 223–225; Lawrence J. Epstein, *The Haunted Smile: The Story of Jewish Comedians in America* (New York, 2001), 63–64.
42. Lourie to Kohn, January 27, 1948, S4/565, CZA; Meir, *My Life*, 214. For the totals raised by the *yishuv* towards its War of Independence, of which Meir's UJA campaign, bringing in $129 million—with a little over $40 million spent for defense or fifty-five percent of the financing of foreign purchases, see Yitzhak Greenberg, "Financing the War of Independence," *Studies in Zionism* 9:1 (1988): 63–80; Haim Barkai, "*HaAlut* HaReialit Shel Milchemet *HaAtsma'ut* 1948–1949," in *Milchemet Ha'Atsmaut, Diyun M'Hudash*, ed. A. Kadish (Tel Aviv, 2004), vol. 2, 759–791; Moshe Naor, "From Voluntary Funds to National Loans, The Financing of Israel's 1948 War Effort," *Israel Studies* 11 (2006): 62–82. Also see Doron Almog, *HaRekhesh B'Artsot HaBrit 1945–1949* (Tel Aviv, 1987); Doron Rozen, *B'Ikhvot HaOtsar HaAmerika'i: Pe'ilut HaHaganah B'Artsot HaBrit 1945–1949* (Tel Aviv, 2008).
43. Morgenthau to Truman, July 1, 1948; Morgenthau to Kaplan and to Ben-Gurion, July 8, 1948; both in Presidential Diaries, Morgenthau MSS.

44. *JTA*, October 15, 1948; Hammer, *Good Faith and Credit*, 130–132; Urofsky, *We Are One!, American Jewry and Israel* (New York, 1978), 279–286.
45. *JTA*, October 21, 22, 25, and 26, 1948; November 3 and 11, 1948; Ben-Gurion, *Yoman Milchama*, 757, 769, 771–772, 780.
46. *JTA*, October 25 and 26, 1948; Friedman, *Roots of the Future*, 338. The "Burma Road" was a makeshift bypass road between Kibbutz Hulda and Jerusalem to counter the Arab attacks on the Tel-Aviv road to Jerusalem, built under the supervision of visiting US General "Mickey" Marcus during the 1948 Arab siege of Jerusalem.
47. *JTA*, November 2, 1948; December 21, 1948.
48. Montor to Kaplan, May 6, 1948, Z5/3115, CZA; Montor interview, May 5, 1977, UJA Archives; Hammer, *Good Faith and Credit*, 95–96.
49. Philip White, *Whistle Stop: How 31,000 Miles of Train Travel, 352 Speeches, and a Little Midwest Gumption Saved the Presidency of Harry Truman* (New York, 2014); Friedman, *Roots for the Future*, 145–146; I. L. Kenen, "Abraham Feinberg," February 16, 1973, courtesy of I. L. Kenen (in the author's possession).
50. Friedman, *Roots of the Future*, chap. 20.
51. Meir, *My Life*, 269–270; Melvin I. Urofsky, *We Are One!*, 201–203; Friedman, *Roots of the Future*, 170; *JTA*, January 19 and 30, 1953; *JTA*, February 25, 1953; Decrmber 9, 1953, vol. 8, Presidential Diaries, Morgenthau MSS. While the Israel Bonds Organization sold a total of $19 billion by 1998, the UJA, contrary to Montor's attack as to its uselessness, raised about $700 million in its annual campaign that same year.
52. Meir, *My Life*, 270; Montor to Steinglas, January 14, 1969, A371/548, CZA; *JTA*, January 16, 1958.
53. *JTA*, February 8, 1967; Morgenthau statement, July 4, 1948, MRD-1, 4/3, UJA Archives; Montor to Steinglas, February 11, 1967; Montor to R. Morgenthau, February 9, 1967; both in A371/547, CZA. A plain memorial stone in Mount Pleasant Cemetery, Hawthorne, Westchester County, marking the graves and Morgenthau and his first wife, just gives the respective years of birth and death.
54. *Ma'ariv*, February 24, 1967; Montor to Steinglas, December 25, 1967, A371/547; Montor to Steinglas, January 13, 1968, A371/548; both in CZA; Penkower, "The Earl Harrison Report," 62. At the time, without Truman having named a Vice-President, and before a constitutional amendment altering the order of succession, the Secretary of the Treasury would succeed if Truman and Secretary of State James Byrnes, both of whom were traveling

to Potsdam, had died. For Klotz's decisive influence: Klotz interview with the author, March 4, 1977; and Henry Morgenthau III, *Mostly Morgenthaus, A Family History* (New York, 1991).

55. Friedman, *Roots of the Future*, 226; Hammer, *Good Faith and Credit*, 231-232. Rothberg was especially influenced by his trip to the DP camps in early 1947. Sam Rothberg report, February 1947, UJA Archives.

56. *JTA*, April 16, 1982; *JTA*, November 3, 1948; Meir interview, in *Living UJA History*, 13; *New York Times*, April 16, 1982.

57. *JTA*, April 16, 1982; *New York Times*, April 16, 1982. Montor gave his own assessment in a private letter some years later: "I know that I rendered a great service to the State of Israel, but I am not such a fool as to think that I deserve enshrinement because of it. It was something I was able to do, and it was something I urgently wanted to do. The reward that I got in terms of self-satisfaction, in terms of transformation of hopes into reality, was very substantial and it nurtures me even today." Montor to Meltzer, March 3, 1967, A371/34, CZA.

58. Morgenthau, *Mostly Morgenthaus*, 411; Montor to Steinglas, February 15, 1967, A371/34, CZA; *New York Times*, November 8, 1945.

59. Meir interview, in *Living UJA History*, 12.

60. *New York Times*, February 12, 1999.

4. Clark M. Eichelberger, Champion of the UN and of Israel's Rebirth

On March 19, 1948, less than four months after the General Assembly of the United Nations with a vote by more than two-thirds of its members had recommended the partition of Palestine into a Jewish and an Arab state, the head of the American delegation to the UN announced that the Security Council was not prepared to go ahead with efforts to implement this plan. The Jews and Arabs of Palestine and the British mandatory power could not agree to carry out that proposal "through peaceful means," Warren Austin observed, and the loss of life in the Holy Land "must be brought to an immediate end." With "the maintenance of international peace" at stake, the Security Council had an inescapable responsibility and full authority to take all necessary steps to bring about a cease-fire in Palestine and a halt to the armed incursions being made into that embattled country. The United States Government proposed, in addition, that a temporary trusteeship for Palestine be established under the UN Trusteeship Council to maintain the peace, and to afford the contending communities there, "who must live together," further opportunity to reach an agreement regarding the future government of that country. Such a trusteeship would be "without prejudice" to the character of the eventual political settlement, which Washington hoped could be achieved "without long delay." An immediate special session of the General Assembly should be convened to consider this end, with the UN Palestine Commission to suspend its efforts to implement the proposed partition plan.[1]

The Jewish Agency for Palestine delegation sat dazed, Security Council secretary general Trygve Lie considered resignation, and even the non-Zionist *New York Times* sharply criticized the "inept" shift which caused American prestige to suffer a "severe blow" with the government's reversal of policy. Jewish War Veterans' commander Brig. General Julius Klein, noting the support of the American Legion as well for partition, publicly warned that this example of the United States' "broken faith" and "ignoble surrender" played into the hands of Soviet Russia, reenacted the appeasement by the British and French governments of Hitler at Munich in 1938 with the grant of the Sudeten German territory of Czechoslovakia, and rewarded the former Palestine Grand Mufti Haj Amin al-Husseini, the oil interests, and power politics. The Big Four powers in the Council had no right to modify the Assembly's partition recommendation, which should be fulfilled, stated USSR representative Andrei Gromyko.[2]

US President Harry S. Truman, shocked, as he jotted in a diary, that the "striped pants conspirators" in the State Department had "pulled the rug from under me today," had just the previous day told World Zionist Organization avatar Chaim Weizmann during an off-the-record meeting in the Oval Office that he would work for the establishment of a Jewish State including the Negev. Truman had actually approved a draft of Austin's statement on March 8 without fully realizing its full significance, and, as emerged from a meeting which he convened with close advisors on March 20, had assumed that Austin would announce the alternative plan after a Council vote had demonstrated the "impossibility" of putting over partition. While sending advisor Samuel Rosenman to quickly tell Weizmann that there would not be "any change in the long policy" they had just talked about, Truman issued a statement five days later that trusteeship was not proposed as a substitute for partition, but as an effort to fill the vacuum soon to be created by the Palestine mandate's termination on May 15. An immediate truce had to be reached between the country's warring peoples, he added, "if we are to avert tragedy," and the United States was prepared to take its share of responsibility if the UN agreed to its proposal.[3]

David Ben-Gurion minced no words in reacting to Austin's political bombshell. "It is we who will decide the fate of Palestine," asserted the feisty chairman of the Jewish Agency executive after an emergency meeting at his home in Tel Aviv: "We cannot agree to any sort of trusteeship, permanent or temporary—the Jewish state exists because we defend it." The creation of the Jewish commonwealth was actually not dependent on the General Assembly's partition vote of November 29, 1947, he averred, although that decision "had great political and moral value." The *yishuv* (Palestinian Jewish community) would refuse to surrender to "the terrorism of Arab gangs, armed by the British Foreign Office and brought to Palestine by its sufferance." He warned that Jewish action against Great Britain would result if the mandatory administration showed signs of failing to withdraw from Palestine according to plan. "Only by our strength, if we are ready and have enough time to use it in full," Ben-Gurion emphasized, "will the Jewish state be established."[4]

The Arab leadership welcomed Austin's statement, Emil Ghoury of the Palestine Arab Higher Committee executive wishing that the UN would be able to find a Palestine solution "acceptable to all." Yet it remained adamant against any consideration of a Jewish state. Syrian President Shukri al-Quwatli was hopeful for a new basis of Arab-American cooperation, George Wadsworth, the former US Minister to Syria and Lebanon and now a member of the US delegation to the UN, informed Secretary of State George C. Marshall—for partition could never be accepted by the Arabs. Lebanon delegate Camille Bey Chamoun said the same to the Council after Austin's speech, declaring that the Arabs would insist on "total independence for Palestine undivided and democratic." Abdul Raham Azzam Pasha, secretary general of the Arab League, announced that the Arabs wanted peace but would fight if the Jews did. The Arabs would accept a brief UN trusteeship, but would never agree to shelving independence for Palestine indefinitely. They would accept a compromise, he informed the British ministry in Beirut, "when and if [the] Zionist spirit had been well and thoroughly broken." British Foreign Secretary Ernest Bevin received from Haj Amin "an Arab Charter for Palestine," which declared that the country's Arabs were determined to see that the Jewish "hordes" from foreign lands over the past twenty-five years, "instigated and directed by the international Zionist cabal," would never succeed in establishing their sovereignty "on one inch of Palestine soil."[5]

Few were as scathing in their attacks on the American government's reversal over Palestine as Clark M. Eichelberger. Director of the American Association for the United Nations (AAUN), officially launched in February 1945, he deemed it "a shocking and tragic betrayal of the United Nations and the good faith of the United States." The most tragic result of Washington's conduct over the last few weeks, his public release read two days later, had been the "sabotage" of that world organization by a narrow interpretation of the UN Charter. The Charter gave ample authority to the Assembly and the Council to assume responsibility for the maintenance of peace and security and the development of the general welfare. Yet the American government appeared unwilling to bear the burden necessary to enable full support of the UN. The government's statement that the UN "does not automatically fall heir to the responsibilities either of the League of Nations or the mandatory power in respect to the Palestine mandate" represented a denial of the "moral concept" of trusteeship and the responsibility of the Assembly and the Council for the maintenance of law and order.

While in the case of Trieste, Greece, or Korea, and probably soon in the case of Czechoslovakia, Washington had and would insist on the spirit as well as the letter of the Charter, Eichelberger's lengthy statement continued, it had "so whittled down" the moral and legal responsibilities of the UN as regards Palestine's fate that this would rise to "plague this country" in the future when it would wish the UN to assume "bold and courageous responsibility." It was all too evident that the Charter was a document to be interpreted liberally when it suited Washington's convenience and interpreted narrowly when it did not, and that the UN was not "the foundation of American foreign policy," but an instrument to be used "to the full, in a restricted sense, or not at all at our convenience" in its containment strategy against the Soviet Union. Not one word had been issued by the US government sharply condemning the threats of aggression by the Arab states against Palestine's Jews; rather, it had "meekly bowed" to those threats. Furthermore, "despite the fact that six million Jews lost their lives in gas chambers and in concentration camps," "not one kind or sympathetic word" was raised by the American government in support of "the moral and spiritual right of the few remaining Jews to have their homeland with a voice in the United Nations."

The AAUN was aware of the "overhanging tension and danger" to which President Truman had referred in his message on March 17, delivered before both Houses of Congress, when speaking of the threat to the freedom of Eastern and Central Europe by the "ruthless" aggression of the Soviet Union, such as its recent seizure of Czechoslovakia, and its "constant abuse" of the veto at the UN. However, if our government was to be strong and take a lead in preserving the peace of the world, what Truman had on that occasion called "the establishment of the rule of law in international affairs" as expressed in the UN Charter, it must meet each issue courageously and keep each promise as the occasion arose. "Above all it must support a strong United Nations," Eichelberger emphasized. If the US government were to throw away collective security for whatever it hoped may be strategic or economic advantage in the Arab countries, it will have made "a most tragic exchange to the detriment of American security." Truman's message to Congress had declared that the United States supported the UN and that we must work to strengthen it. "Our retreat in the Palestine issue," Eichelberger closed, "would seem to be a retreat from his words."[6]

Born on July 29, 1896, in Freeport, Illinois, to parents who descended from pre-American Revolutionary Swiss and English settlers, Eichelberger interrupted his political science studies at Northwestern University to serve in France during World War I. While spending most of his military service as a corporal loading boxcars in central France and witness to much of the war devastation there, he had developed an enthusiasm for the League of Nations, which was reinforced by a winter visit to the fledgling world organization in 1923. Impelled consequently to take the job of a lecturer on national and international affairs for the Radcliffe Chautauqua System, the talented orator spoke on the League in every state. Five years later, he became director of the Midwest office of what would be called in 1929 the League of Nations Association, and then that organization's national director in 1934. The highly regarded editor of the *League of Nations Chronicle*, also a consultant in 1936 to the League of Nations secretariat, the indefatigable Eichelberger transformed the Association as its "sparkplug" into the country's most dynamic internationalist group and assumed the leadership of the non-pacifist wing of the peace movement. While domestic and international circumstances, as well as its own internal weaknesses, limited the effectiveness of the Association, the group under Columbia University professor James T. Shotwell, its president, did keep the internationalist option before the public and provided valuable assistance to the State Department and White House in conflicts with isolationists in the US Congress.

Disturbed by the League of Nations' collapse and by the challenge from Germany, Italy, and Japan to democracy and world order, Eichelberger strove in the fall and winter of 1937–1938 to construct an internationalist coalition advocating collective security and revitalized peace machinery. Following President Franklin D. Roosevelt's speech in Chicago of October 5, 1937, calling for an international "quarantine" against the "epidemic of world lawlessness" abroad (which Eichelberger may have inspired in a conversation with Roosevelt in July), he formed the Committee for Concerted Peace Efforts to publicize that address. In early 1938 he was instrumental in alerting the Roosevelt administration to the perils of the Ludlow amendment, which sought a national referendum on any Congressional declaration of war—except in cases when the United States had been attacked, and he successfully marshaled opposition to its passage by Congress. In March 1939 he oversaw the reorganization of the Committee as the American Union for Concerted Peace Efforts, which under his direction spearheaded an abortive attempt to revise the US Neutrality Act of 1937 in the direction of collective security.

With the outbreak of World War II in September 1939, the League of Nations Association, under the auspices of the newly created Commission to Study the Organization of Peace as its research affiliate, brought together a group of authorities on international affairs for an intensive examination of the fundamentals of a reformed society of nations to be established at the end of the global conflict. Since he thought that the US had to do everything possible to defeat Nazi Germany, Eichelberger soon called for assistance to Germany's enemies, played a pivotal role in 1940 in the formation of the influential Committee to Defend America by Aiding the Allies (becoming its director and chairman), and, after the Japanese attack on Pearl Harbor on December 7, 1941, called for a "great crusade" to build a new international order. Eichelberger collaborated in the preparation of reports and statements by the Commission to Study the Organization of Peace, and participated in 1942 and 1943 as a member of the State Department's Advisory Committee on Post-War Foreign Policy, chaired by Undersecretary of State Sumner Welles, in the drafting of a constitution for a world organization.

Probably no private citizen did more in the period which climaxed in the ratification of the United Nations Charter by the Senate on July 28, 1945, asserts historian Robert D. Accinelli, to mobilize public opinion, gain congressional support, and direct a series of national coalitions to secure this objective. Two years earlier, Eichelberger's United Nations Association had organized congressional speaking tours championing a future world organization, a step endorsed on November 1, 1943, by the United States, Great Britain, the USSR, and China in the Moscow Declaration and passed by a Senate resolution five days later, with the 1944 Dumbarton Oaks conference outlining the framework of the international body. A widely circulated pamphlet by Eichelberger immediately pointed out what subjects were postponed at that conference for later decision. He was among the leaders of a group of non-governmental organizations which acted as semi-official consultants to the US delegation at the San Francisco United Nations Conference on International Organization, and who were responsible for the inclusion of several important provisions in the United Nations Charter focusing on human rights and trusteeship. In that capacity, he was a member of the five-man committee that prepared the first US working draft for that historic document.[7]

In February 1945, the name of the League of Nations Association was changed to the American Association of the United Nations, which Eichelberger would continue to serve as executive director until 1964. A prolific writer, he consistently advocated for the United Nations as a means of achieving world peace. Already in 1939 he wrote that the road to world peace was to be found in "a highly developed society of nations," and that some future generation may live in a world in which national sovereignty "counts for much less than it does today" and in it there will be "new forms of group loyalty and patriotism." Reviewing books by James Shotwell, Sumner Welles, and Walter Lippmann about a future world order, he asserted in 1944 that in today's world of shrunken distance, "there is not room for several sets of moralities and rules of international conduct." In the tradition of League of Nations' champion President Woodrow Wilson, he added this: "Above and beyond any natural groupings must be universal law, and a common morality, and a universal organization."[8]

His career turned into a personal credo supporting the aims of the League of Nations, Eichelberger regularly took note of his belief that in the future "all the men, in all the lands, may live out their lives in freedom and want." In this statement, he observed to friends, "there is only one word with more than one syllable." He and associates perceived a world of interlocking interests and relationships in which the peace and prosperity of any one nation were dependent on the well-being of all. The walls of his East Side apartment in New York City were hidden behind more than 3,000 books on foreign policy and on railroading, a subject for which he maintained a lifelong enthusiasm. Beginning in the 1940's, he also was a radio broadcaster, his program called "The U.N. is My Beat," for WMCA and subsequently WNBC. He became a familiar and respected figure at UN headquarters in New York and among advocates of the UN in his own country and abroad. He was active as well in the World Federation of the United Nations Association. Eichelberger's lodestar remained crystal clear after the San Francisco Conference: a faith in the UN and in the capacity of the United States for global leadership. Although fully cognizant of the UN's deficiencies and that it was sometimes "neglected, bypassed, or defied," he believed that it made the difference between an uneasy pace and a third world war.[9]

Since the Cold War between East and West colored practically every dispute before the UN after 1945, Eichelberger stressed the importance of reducing tension and differences between Moscow and Washington. Having consistently emphasized the essential need for negotiation and compromise between the two superpowers within the mediating form of the UN, it is not surprising that Eichelberger and the AAUN strongly endorsed the General Assembly partition vote on Palestine as a UN triumph, which found hostile rivals United States and the USSR bloc joining in the majority for the first time. The civil war launched against the *yishuv* by Haj Amin's Arab Higher Committee and infiltrating Arab guerilla bands the day after that vote led the AAUN board of directors, in turn, to call upon the Security Council on January 28, 1948, to immediately create under Articles 39, 41, and 42 of the UN Charter an International Police Force for Palestine composed of national contingents, and the US government to lift its arms embargo on the Middle East "in favor of those parties in Palestine who are willing to abide by the General Assembly resolution." This would greatly assist the Palestine Commission, appointed by the Assembly, in carrying out the partition resolution, which "has been hailed as the best possible solution that could be made under the circumstances." That proposal, the AAUN statement went on, was "an indication of the courage and determination of the United Nations to meet a most difficult problem," and an "encouraging" sign of Soviet-American accord. The decision gave hope "that a very tragic problem would be met most decisively," and that these hopes "must not be shattered by inaction or timidity at the present time."[10]

To John Foster Dulles, a member of the US Mission to the UN, Eichelberger observed that the Assembly decision for Palestine's partition, discussed over the years and arrived at after "deliberate and thorough" Assembly procedure, "was not a quick improvised arrangement." Increasing disorders in Palestine presented the Security Council with the need of fulfilling its responsibilities for the maintenance of international peace and security. Neither the UN nor its individual members could permit the Arab states to feel that "constant threat, intimidation, violence and invasion" could "scare them" from going through with the plan which they had supported. The courage with which the Council faced this problem, he went on, would be determined by the "decisiveness and leadership" of the United States, yet many observers felt that there had been an "anomalous silence" in Washington since the Assembly vote was taken. Would Dulles sign the AAUN statement with approximately ten other influential citizens? Eichelberger asked. It would be used in the press and in whatever appropriate ways to bring it to the attention of the greatest number of people. As the decision could no longer be delayed, the AAUN felt it imperative that action be taken as quickly as possible.[11]

Dulles did not sign, but Eichelberger was gratified a week later to be able to inform Lionel Gelber of the Jewish Agency's UN team that Eleanor Roosevelt, Welles, and former New York Governor Herbert H. Lehman would do so. Gelber, an authority on international and British Commonwealth affairs and formerly on the faculty of the University of Toronto, had, as Political Advisor to the Agency, addressed the AAUN earlier that month at a large all-day conference. The AAUN statement, he was now told, was to be circulated to 100,000 leading American citizens in the shape of a letter. Eichelberger attached great importance to the views of Major George Fielding Eliot, whose recent pro-Zionist articles were noteworthy. Reporting to Moshe Shertok (later Sharett), who was then heading the Jewish Agency's case at the UN, and colleague Nahum Goldmann, Gelber called Eichelberger "an old friend" who was not seeking official contacts. Most of the AAUN national director's sphere of interest was international rather than national in character. When and if concrete measures of cooperation were required, he would suggest to Eichelberger the "appropriate quarters" where this might be obtained.[12]

On February 10, 1948, Senators Robert F. Wagner (D, NY) and Elbert D. Thomas (D, Utah) joined Roosevelt, Welles, and Lehman in signing Eichelberger's revised AAUN statement. Sharper in criticizing the "intransigence" of the Arab leaders against the General Assembly partition vote, it wondered what confidence could be placed in the UN's ability to meet and master future crises if these weak states in the Middle East successfully challenged the world organization's authority. Calling for a UN International Police Force or Constabulary and noting that the Security Council had the power, in accordance with Article 39 of the Charter to determine "a threat to the peace, breach of peace or act of aggression," to immediately do so, it also called for lifting the US arms embargo in favor of those parties in Palestine (the *yishuv*) willing to abide by the Assembly resolution. The police force, composed of national contingents for service in Palestine, should be ready to move in when British troops leave or earlier, if requested, and remain "until peace and security are assured."[13]

The very next day, an Eichelberger memorandum to AAUN chapters and cooperating groups charged that the UN was facing "the most serious crisis of its existence," as there was "grave danger" that the Assembly's resolution might be thwarted, with a "very major blame" then placed on the US government. Many deaths had resulted from the Arab states making it clear that they intended by force to prevent the carrying out of that resolution, and 15,000 soldiers from neighboring Arab countries were supposed to have infiltrated the Arab part of Palestine. The United States was in danger of indicating that the UN was a venue to be resorted to when convenient. Particularly in this case, where Washington had urged "so strongly" the passage of the partition plan in November, what nation was left in which the world might have faith if this country should refuse to carry out its obligations under the Charter? The argument made in Washington that carrying out the partition plan might antagonize the Arab States and imperil our oil supply was "far outweighed" by "the value of a strong UN supporting collective security." For the United States to destroy that possibility would imperil its own security "much more so than would making the Arabs angry." The time had come "for a great wave of moral indignation," a time when "the highest statesmanship must be based on moral considerations." Eichelberger's memorandum closed thus: We had to indicate as a people and insist that Washington demonstrate by performance that the UN "is the foundation of our foreign policy and that we intend to carry out our obligations."[14]

A letter on February 10 to Secretary Marshall from thirty members of the House of Representatives, initiated by Jacob K. Javits of New York City's Twenty-First District, echoed the AAUN's appeal for discontinuing State's arms embargo at a time when extensive sales of weapons by Great Britain to the neighboring Arab nations was reported. The group believed that grave danger would ensue if the UN Palestine decision might be jeopardized and the UN itself made "ineffective," and wondered if the Arab nations' activities, in their "announced violent resistance" to the UN partition decision, endangered the maintenance of international peace and security in the terms of the UN Charter. What was the US government prepared to do to help in implementing the Assembly's vote on Palestine?—the Congressmen queried. Marshall replied two days later, declaring that Washington had no information indicating that to date the continuance of British treaty shipments had interfered with the carrying out of the partition recommendation. Nor had the Council determined that there been thus far any "overt acts" to endanger international peace and security. Meanwhile, the mandatory power was responsible for preserving peace and security in Palestine. The US Government could not determine what steps to possibly take in that regard until the Palestine Commission reported, but it was working with other Council members in preparing a draft statute for the trusteeship of Jerusalem. As President Truman and I have made clear on several occasions, Marshall concluded, we regard the solution of "this immensely difficult problem" as a UN solution, "and our contribution to that end will be as a member and steadfast supporter of the United Nations."[15]

Morris S. Lazaron, Reform rabbi of the Baltimore Hebrew Congregation and a long-time AAUN member, strongly disagreed with Eichelberger. A major voice and founding member of the anti-Zionist American Council for Judaism (ACJ), an organization created in June 1942 to support the "rehabilitation" of Palestine but to oppose political Zionism in favor of a universalist interpretation of Jewish destiny as "a religious community wherever we may dwell." Its solution to the so-called "Jewish problem" rested on equal rights for Jews worldwide and a democratic, autonomous Jewish-Arab state in Palestine, much like the binational commonwealth advocated by Hebrew University president Judah Magnes. Reacting to the partition vote, Lazaron publicly warned that the American Jewish community was being drawn into "hazardous political activities whose end in Palestine cannot be foreseen and, in America, constitutes a thrust against our democracy." Wondering why the opinion of (anti-Zionist) specialists in the State Department was overridden on November 29, 1947, he cautioned against "a civil war to conquer a land against the will of the majority of its inhabitants."

The train of events thus set in motion in Palestine, Lazaron wrote on January 31, 1948, to the Baltimore Jewish Council's executive director, might "imperil the peace of the world." It was a "salutary thing" that Gentile and Christian fellow-Americans knew that there were Jews determined to have no part in "the hazardous Zionist adventure." The Zionists had "disturbed the peace of American Israel and endangered the peace of the world." Lazaron intended to speak the truth as he saw it, decrying the Zionists for having destroyed "that wholesome atmosphere which is the only basis for stable and peaceful living for Jews and everyone else in Palestine and everywhere."[16]

AAUN member Virginia C. Gildersleeve, the Dean of New York City's Barnard College from 1911 until her retirement in 1947 and co-founder of the International Federation of University Women (1919), concurred. The sole female US delegate to the San Francisco Conference, she claimed in her letter on February 10 to the *New York Times* that the General Assembly had the power only to recommend, the International Court of Justice at The Hague seeming to be "the suitable tribunal" for a Council request of an advisory opinion on the Palestine conundrum. The Council now had to consider, given that the Arabs would not cooperate in setting up a state in partitioned Palestine, "some revision" of the Assembly partition plan. Having long been associated with the missionaries and teachers of American educational institutions in the Near East working for peace and friendly cooperation between peoples, she considered it their duty to share personal knowledge of that region with our fellow citizens here, and avail ourselves of every "legitimate device" for a peaceful settlement before sending in armed forces which would provoke in the Near East "intense and prolonged war, bringing misery alike to Jew, Moslem and Christian." "I believe," she wrote separately to Eichelberger, that the AAUN's stand was wrong, and "I prophesy that you will soon realize this."[17]

The same day, Gildersleeve added her name to a memorandum entitled "The Palestine Problem for Americans," calling for the immediate suspension of all efforts to implement the existing partition plan by military force. The signees made up an impressive list: Henry Sloane Coffin, president emeritus of the Union Theological Seminary; Harold L. Hoskins, director of the School of Advanced Studies and of the Middle East Institute (both in Washington, DC); Kermit Roosevelt, Jr., a grandson of President Theodore Roosevelt and O.S.S. intelligence officer during and after World War II; author Harold Lamb; John A. Wilson, director of the University of Chicago's Oriental Institute; and Walter L. Wright, currently professor in Princeton University's Department of Oriental Languages and Literatures. Foreseeing "a confused and bloody war," which would more likely end "sooner or later with the annihilation of the Jews than of the Arabs," as well as with the loss of American educational and commercial interests (particularly oil concessions) in the region to the benefit of "its Communist competitor," the group called for the possible ordering of a cease-fire and the Security Council to request the International Court of Justice to seek a settlement of the long-standing legal dispute. Finally, the Council was advised to persuade the Arab and Jewish communities to "take the next logical step" and form a comprehensive federation, a system of checks and balances conserving the essential interests of each and yet securing the "necessary and inevitable unity of this small country."[18]

Kermit ("Kim") Roosevelt, Jr. fully agreed. Having the previous month criticized in the *Middle East Journal* the Zionist lobbying tactics to secure the Assembly's partition vote, he observed in a radio broadcast on February 10 over the Mutual Broadcasting System's American Forum of the Air that the minority votes represented 500 million people, far more than those of the majority, and people more directly concerned with Palestine. Some Soviet agents among Jewish refugees from Eastern Europe would likely enter Palestine; Syrian fighter Fawzi Kaukji, active in the 1936–1939 Arab Revolt, the 1941 Iraqi revolt against British rule, and now leader of the Arab Liberation Army infiltrators, together with Palestinian Arabs trying to defend their country "against imperialist domination," could not be "blamed too much for concentration on their own interests first." Partition, he concluded, was "unworkable" and "unjust." If we try to enforce it, the Arabs will retaliate against us and the UN, and the United States would lose its oil concessions, vital to our security and the success of our European Recovery Program against the spread of Communism. "Unworkable" because the proposed division was economically and politically "hopeless" and could only be imposed by large-scale military power; "unjust" because it would force on Palestine territorial "mutilation" against the will of a majority of its inhabitants. Furthermore, it would project the Jews into a war which can only be disastrous to them, and it would encourage Jewish "displaced persons" to look for refuge in the one place where they "certainly cannot find the peace and security they deserve."[19]

On that same broadcast, Walter L. Wright, past president of Robert College in Istanbul and former O.S.S. Director for the Near East, assented to Roosevelt's stance that partition was "morally indefensible" for it contradicted the principles of self-determination and self-government of peoples. To place nearly half a million Arabs as a minority under the rule of the proposed Jewish state would create more problems that it would settle. The world's greatest reservoir of oil, in Arab lands, had to remain "on this side of the Iron Curtain." Compromise between Jews and Arabs was the only possible solution; they alone could settle this problem. The General Assembly had "merely recommended" partition to the Security Council, the sole authority which could really reach a decision on this point. The cause of freedom, peace, and justice in the world could not be served by using armed force to establish Zionist rule over half of Palestine and half a million of the world's forty million Arabs.[20]

Senator Owen Brewster (R, Maine) and Emanuel Neumann, president of the Zionist Organization of America, countered during the broadcast that appeal from the partition vote on the basis of Arab armed resistance was "utterly incompatible" with the entire conception of an international body that should peacefully resolve problems within the scope of its constituted authority. The Security Council should immediately, in accordance with the recommendation of the Palestine Commission, respond to its call for adequate force to carry out and implement the Assembly's decision to partition Palestine. The Assembly had not merely recommended, but appointed a Palestine Commission and directed the Trusteeship Council to work out a statute for Jerusalem. The partition vote notwithstanding, Saudi Arabia king Ibn Saud did not cancel oil concessions to American companies. The 600,000 Palestinian Jews have been joined by more than 700,000 Arabs as the result of the Jewish cultivation that had taken place since Jewish settlement there over the past six decades. The bogey of Communist agents entering Palestine was contradicted by Zionism's persecution under Soviet rule for twenty-five or fifty years, and none have been found among the many Jews imprisoned in Cyprus camps by the British for their "illegal" attempt to reach Palestine's shores. The US arms embargo should be lifted, permitting the 30,000 Palestinian Jews who served in the British Army during World War II to have the weapons with which they could now defend their country while the British supply the Arab countries with arms. Finally, the UN was bound, in the interest of its own authority and prestige, as well as the cause of world stability and peace, to "apply its full weight" behind the Assembly decision.[21]

Eichelberger found a welcome champion in Sumner Welles, who took a forthright stand on February 17 with a column in the *New York Herald Tribune* entitled" "U.S. Stand in Palestine Viewed as Starting U.N. on League's Path." Attacking what he termed "counselors of caution" acting much like the appeasers of dictators in the previous decade, the former US Undersecretary lashed out against the US government's renouncing "every semblance of leadership" by not insisting that the UN must be enabled to enforce the Assembly's partition decision. This refusal, he insisted, would pave the way for what Army and Navy officials, supported by some in the State Department, feared most—the extension of Soviet control with its military forces over the Middle East. The arguments on oil were just as unrealistic: oil resources would not be available to Western Europe or the United States in case of war, while the Arab governments would hardly oppose their exploitation by American companies in time of peace. Far more fundamentally, in this rare instance of US-Soviet concurrence on the Palestine partition vote, the Palestine question "is a test case": Was the UN "the foundation of American policy" to halt aggression in the world, a test at which the League of Nations had failed? Should the United States persist in its "blind inaction," Welles warned, it would be preparing the way for the failure of the new international organization, and the one hope that humanity possessed today for the rule of law, for the freedom and progress of mankind, and for the establishment of a peaceful world order "will vanish with it."[22]

"Profoundly discouraged" over hearing in Washington that considerable discussion of a retreat from the Assembly resolution seemed calculated to pave the way for that about-face, on February 19 Eichelberger pressed Dean Rusk, State's Director of the Office of Special Political Affairs, to have the US government take whatever steps were necessary to carry through the partition resolution. He had already warned Rusk that if the Arabs and the British flouted the partition plan, "this may be the Ethiopia of the United Nations, and we shall not have Italy to blame." The Security Council was charged with the duty of maintaining peace and security, he pointed out now, and it would be a narrow interpretation of Articles 10, 11, and 14 in the UN Charter and Chapter VII not to set up an international police force in Palestine to do so. The US government had no hesitancy in branding Albania, Yugoslavia, and Bulgaria as threats to the peace of the world even though they were never charged with formally invading Greece, yet had raised no protest against the invasion of Palestine by Arabs from neighboring countries.

This "actual breach" of international peace and security could not be overlooked, Eichelberger declared, particularly as Washington and Moscow had agreed on partition. "Military strategy is on pretty dangerous ground when divorced from moral considerations," with the destruction of collective security under the UN striking a greater blow to American security than by temporarily offending the Arab states. This is "the most critical moment" in the UN's history, Eichelberger averred, British conduct reflecting a desire to sabotage the Assembly's decision and the United States mandated to stand up against Arab "bluffing and intimidation" and have law and order prevail.[23]

With no reply received from Rusk, serving as State's point man to the US delegation at the UN, Eichelberger cabled Marshall three days later, on the eve of determining American policy for the Council's meeting to deal with Palestine. The AAUN urged the Secretary to give "unqualified support" to the Assembly's resolution, which was passed under American leadership, and support its implementation by an international police force and by whatever other steps were necessary. "American leadership is required," and it would be "an incredible situation" if the UN should be blocked and the will of this country thwarted by Arab threats. The argument of those US military authorities opposed to partition was "very shortsighted," the possible following of a policy that would wreck collective security a much greater blow to American security than antagonizing Arab states. The AAUN urged Marshall to "brush aside" all counsels of "delay, timidity, and legal hair splitting," and give vigorous leadership to the UN Security Council in this crisis.[24]

To Lazaron, Eichelberger expressed his great sorrow that he disagreed with the rabbi on the Palestine issue, particularly since the two men had been in agreement on almost every other subject. He remained convinced, having followed the Palestine debates closely and read the documents, that the partition settlement was "the only feasible one," and one which should be carried out with an international army and whatever force was necessary. The Arabs had been "bluffing to a considerable extent," and had our government shown firmness and determination from the moment of the Assembly resolution's passage, only a small armed militia would have been necessary to carry out that decision. Scrapping this resolution now would be a blow to the UN "too serious to be described," and it still could be carried out. Closing, Eichelberger hoped that they would have a chance for a long visit soon.[25]

Eichelberger found the remarks of Warren Austin, speaking for the US delegation at the Council on February 24, extremely weak and unconvincing. The argument of the former Senator from Vermont, the AAUN national director's notes read, was "altogether too legalistic," and "overstressed" the fact that the Council had authority to maintain peace and security but not to enforce an Assembly decision. It did not recognize that since the British had asked the Assembly to take action on Palestine, that body had a greater authority in this instance than if it were making a recommendation regarding a sovereign territory, nor did it acknowledge that the Arab invading bands were in "actual violation" of peace and security. Austin did not criticize the British refusal to permit the Palestine Commission to open a port for Jewish immigrants on February 1, or to permit that advance group to arrive before May 1, as provided for in the partition resolution.

Nothing was said in Austin's remarks about lifting the arms embargo in favor of the *yishuv* for its carrying out the resolution. The "moral indignation and fervor" prevalent in the American delegate's remarks in the Ad Hoc Committee on Palestine and in the Assembly were missing, too. Austin called for a committee of the five great powers to be set up for new consultations with the mandatory power and the two Palestinian communities, but the British had clearly stated that His Majesty's Government "would not budge" and the Arabs had never attended any consultations. Making this now a "big power affair," Eichelberger observed, would have the procedure end up "a Russian-American job," rather than an international militia created on the broadest possible basis, to a very great extent from the smaller states.[26]

Unaware that State's Policy Planning Staff under George Kennan had just advised Marshall and Undersecretary of State Robert Lovett to approve "a fairly radical reversal" of US policy regarding partition, Eichelberger organized a massive Emergency Conference two days later at New York City's Waldorf Astoria Hotel to endorse the AAUN's stand. Sixty-two national organizations, including the American Federation of Labor and the Congress of Industrial Organizations, unanimously pledged their support for implementing the Assembly's Resolution 181 (II) on partition as "the best workable solution of a most difficult problem." That resolution, now "openly challenged by force and violence" by members of the UN and by "turbulent elements" within Palestine, required the Council to take "affirmative action" against this blow "to the integrity and very existence of the United Nations itself."

Immediate steps had to be taken to counter "a threat to the peace of the world." These steps, which must be taken, included an international police force and—a new idea—recognizing the Provisional Government of the Jewish Section of partitioned Palestine, to be effective as of April 1 in accordance with the Assembly's resolution. Finally, the Jewish Agency should be permitted to immediately purchase military equipment and the shipping of this equipment carried out in the custody of UN representatives to Palestine, there to be held by a Jewish militia in implementation of the UN decision as determined by the Security Council or by the Palestine Commission. Eichelberger quickly sent the resolutions to Rusk, asking that he show these and the list of organizations to Austin as well.[27]

Austin's speech of February 24 and subsequent resolution hinted at State's move towards a retreat from partition, reflecting "double talk" in *Nation* publisher Freda Kirchwey's view. "Outrageously hypocritical," declared Brooklyn Congressman Emanuel Celler, while American Jewish Committee president Joseph Proskauer deemed it "inexplicable wobbling"; Robert Goldman, president of the Union of Hebrew Congregations, agreed with Proskauer that the "very life" of the UN and the "good faith" of the United States were involved. Secretary General Lie publicly warned that failure to carry out partition would injure UN prestige and lead to a general loss of confidence in its ability to solve world problems. Yet Marshall declared off-the-record at a press conference on February 26 that there would be "no bending" by his department when guiding its UN delegation; it would leave matters entirely to Austin so that there would be "no confusion so long as I am Secretary of State." Confidentially, Lovett told Near Eastern desk chief Loy Henderson the next day that if the Security Council could do nothing "constructive" about the Palestine problem, a special Assembly session might make a new recommendation along the lines of a possible trusteeship. The US military and the new Central Intelligence Agency (CIA) concluded, as had the British Chiefs of Staff Committee, that partition could not be implemented, and that any solution would have to be acceptable to the Arabs.[28]

Sears, Roebuck and Company head Lessing Rosenwald, president of the American Council for Judaism, made his organization's continued opposition to partition clear to Marshall. Recent "troublesome" developments, he wrote to the Secretary of State, indicated that earlier assumptions underlying the Assembly decision were incorrect or inadequate: Arab resistance on the part of a majority of Palestine's inhabitants had been underrated. Forthright steps had to be taken so that the "legitimate, full, equal, and exclusive participation" in the newly created Jewish and Arab states by their own citizens "and by no others" would not be negated. The UN trusteeship for Jerusalem should be extended to the entirety of Palestine, and continue until all "the elements" in that territory agreed upon its replacement by a form of independence satisfactory to them. This trusteeship could be validated on the grounds that Palestine was unique, a Holy Land to hundreds of millions of people throughout the world, while the bloodshed in Palestine offered "clear demonstrations" of their leaders' "unfitness," at this time, for complete independence. Such trusteeship should allow for the maximum development of home rule.

Finally, the ACJ repudiated the slander around the claim of a so-called "Jewish vote" regarding the Palestine issue. Americans of the Jewish faith cast their ballots, as did all other devoted Americans, in accordance with their broad, not sectarian, political interests. Hopefully, Rosenwald declared, a bipartisan American foreign policy would be arrived at, along with the admission of a fair share of the displaced persons of all faiths into the United States. The ACJ was certain that such policy would win the overwhelming support of the American people.[29]

Virginia Gildersleeve and Kermit Roosevelt were not idle either, pressing forward with *Christian Century* associate editor Garland Evans Hopkins to create a new organization advocating a reconsideration of the Assembly's partition decision. On February 22, they invited Lazaron to join others in forming a committee of 100 prominent Americans seeking a "just and durable" settlement in Palestine. Desiring the "best interests" of Jews and Arabs, the committee's purpose was to uphold international law and democratic principles as the "only defensible basis" for solving the Palestine problem, and to emphasize that decisions reached "under compulsion" and contrary to these principles endangered the peace of the world and could be enforced only to the detriment of the United Nations. Conciliation over Palestine and US cooperation in the displaced persons problem were their objectives.

Lazaron was happy to join but unable to attend the meeting on March 2 in Washington, DC's Foundry United Methodist Church because of speaking engagements in the West and Middle West. He suggested to Roosevelt dropping the words "under compulsion" as possibly irritating the State Department, and adding some phrase indicating the organization's belief that Palestine's Jewish population would be protected. In addition, he thought that an emphasis on democratic compromise, the Zionists to be satisfied with cultural autonomy on the Swiss model and the Arab fears of domination to be allayed by speaking of "a reasonable, economically absorbable" Jewish immigration, would have many rally behind such a program.[30]

Eichelberger did not let up, writing privately to Austin on March 3 that if law and order were maintained, the Palestine Commission could carry out the mandate of the General Assembly. If the Assembly could not decide what shall be done with a territory which is really "a ward of the community of nations," Palestine would be a land without legal status, in a condition of anarchy and lawlessness. Austin's Chicago address on January 16, 1947, had asserted that the UN Charter "has a capacity for development, an unfolding quality, that we have not yet begun to explore," which the United States demonstrated by interpreting the Charter in a most liberal way regarding the Assembly's recommendation on the election in South Korea but interpreted narrowly regarding that body's authority vis-à-vis Palestine. In addition, the US government had not criticized either the Arabs' open intention to prevent carrying out the partition decision, or the British doing everything possible to hinder the Palestine Commission from carrying out the schedule provided for it. "Sabotage" on the part of the British and "timidity" on the part of our government after November 29, he closed, had encouraged Arab violence and "dangerously weakened" the authority of the UN.[31]

"Nothing could be more painful to me," Eichelberger wrote the next day to Gildersleeve, than to be on the other side of the fence from you on the Palestine issue. The statement just issued by her new Committee for Justice and Peace in the Holy Land was discussed that afternoon by a group of organizations, which paid tribute to her support of human rights at the San Francisco Conference and her contribution to the UN Charter. Yet, as he had written several times in the press, Eichelberger felt that partition was "the judgment of the world" after careful investigation and debate, and was the only workable solution for Palestine's future. Arab aggression was threatening world peace and security. The Assembly was clearly within its rights in making the recommendation and, since a mandate area was involved, had the right to assume "an executive function" and require that the Security Council maintain peace and security and help carry out the decision. Moreover, Eichelberger felt "deeply" the right of the Jewish people to an independent homeland. With "six million of that tragic people" destroyed in gas chambers and concentration camps, "is it too much atonement for the world to give this small territory and the right to be represented in the councils of the nations?" No solution of the displaced persons, seventy-five percent of whom were non-Jews, would meet this need, he declared.[32]

The argument to Gildersleeve did not meet a receptive ear, her new committee colleagues intending to lobby against Palestine's partition in the belief that it went against America's national interests and common justice, and to advocate the resettlement of Holocaust survivors in the United States and elsewhere. In a letter to the *New York Herald Tribune* on March 5, she charged that the UN Charter's Article 14 gave the General Assembly in such matters only the power to make recommendations, not a final decision. The Security Council's duty now was to consider and pass judgment on the wisdom and practicality of the partition recommendation as a way towards peace and security, and to study its possible implementation in the light of recent developments. It would not ruin the UN's prestige if the Council changed the recommendation, any more than it ruined the prestige of the US government if the Senate did not approve a bill passed by the House of Representatives. At this "very difficult and perplexing moment," it was "urgently desirable" to find a solution of the Palestine problem which would bring peace and well-being to the Holy Land. Yet it was even more important, she declared, that we should set up and understand the proper constitutional procedure for dealing with such problems under the Charter.[33]

Proskauer did not relent either, writing at length to Lovett with arguments that echoed those of Eichelberger. The UN, successor to the League of Nations and having received the Palestine mandate from the British, had the power and the duty to prescribe for the government of this captured Turkish province in World War I. A UN force could surely stop the Arabs from using violence that threatened world peace; partition would then implement itself. Washington was aiding Greece and other countries by military assistance—why not Palestine to maintain consistency in our position and save the UN from "destruction"? As the American Jewish Committee president had suggested heretofore, an affirmative policy by Washington might also involve recognizing the Jewish state as of April 1 and lifting the arms embargo. The AAUN Emergency Conference's resolutions of February 26 gave these ideas "explicit expression"; he had personally excised from them "bitter criticism of our Government." As a loyal American and a loyal UN supporter, Proskauer was confident that the "headache will be infinitely worse" if such affirmative action were not taken. The only way to get rid of that kind of headache, he urged, was "to face up to the situation and act boldly."[34]

Appreciating these "thoughtful comments" on the legal effect of the Assembly's partition resolution, Lovett replied that he was sending a copy to Austin, who might have occasion "in due course" to address the Council on some of the subjects covered by Proskauer. As for the use of force with regard to the Palestine question, he hoped Proskauer would agree that Austin's February 24 statement and the subsequent US resolution made it clear that the Council was obligated to take all measures necessary "to prevent breaches of the peace, threats to the peace, and acts of aggression." Not persuaded, Proskauer urged Austin on March 15 to make it "unmistakably clear" to the public about the Council's obligations, leaving then no factual doubt that there were breaches of and threats to the peace, and acts of aggression in Palestine. I have never been "a fanatical Zionist," he noted, my object rather always to get immigration into Palestine, "but America decided this question and led the vote in the Assembly." He had spent an hour with Marshall before the Assembly partition vote in November, at the conclusion of which the Secretary had asked him to talk to US delegation member General John H. Hildring about a way that a force might be organized to implement partition. Believing that "consistency is a virtue of great minds," Proskauer hoped that Austin would stand firm for some such program as envisaged in the full-page advertisement of Clark Eichelberger's organization in the newspapers of that morning.[35]

Lovett's concluding paragraph in his letter to Proskauer, greatly appreciating that he and other "good citizens" were behind the State Department in its effort to "do what is right" under the UN Charter, prompted Proskauer to call his attention, as against the department's possible future conduct with respect to Palestine, to certain "fundamentals." As Proskauer had declared in his annual address on January 18 last to the American Jewish Committee, its political fealty was only to "our own America," and nothing should be done regarding Palestine which in any degree constituted a violation of the laws of the United States of America. While obligated to conform to the US government and the UN organization authorities, he enjoined the Committee in that address to have "the heart, the wisdom and the courage to give all that is in us to aid in reaching a right solution as God gives us to see the right." He wished to maintain the kind of relationship which had existed to date between Lovett's Department and the Committee, in part to the end that in working out Palestine's future, we may both have the benefit of such a relationship. Envisaging the possibility, and he hoped it only a possibility, of some "fundamental shifts," the Committee desired to be helpful. His private communication ended thus: "I hope they won't come."[36]

The AAUN's position received a substantial boost with two articles by Benjamin V. Cohen, former Counselor to the State Department, in the *New York* Herald *Tribune* on March 16–17, which posited in legal terms that the Security Council had the authority to carry out the Assembly's recommendation. Attending the 1919 Paris Peace Conference on behalf of the American Zionist movement, Cohen had helped to negotiate the League mandate for Palestine; worked in tandem with Thomas Corcoran in drafting key legislation for the Roosevelt Administration's domestic New Deal; assisted in the drafting of the 1944 Dumbarton Oaks agreements leading to the UN's establishment; and served as the

US chief draftsman at the Potsdam Conference. The implications of the American stand regarding Palestine, he averred now, would "impair" the UN's Charter. Dissenting from Austin's February 24 address before the Council, Cohen observed that its implications would make the Charter "impotent" and relieve the UN's members of any real responsibility thereunder. Articles 24, 37, 39, and 40 of that document called upon the Council to intervene for the sake of world peace, and "if the Charter is to live, we must not exalt the letter which killeth and destroy the spirit which giveth life."

The Assembly recommendation, Cohen observed, was not only supported by more than two-thirds of the members but accepted by the mandatory power, its resolution not essentially different legally from the creative plan for the Free Territory of Trieste. (That territory, recognized by a peace treaty in February 1947, had been set up by the Council in order to resolve territorial claims between Italy and Yugoslavia, as well as to accommodate a mixed population there.) If the partition resolution were not recognized, a legal vacuum would exist, and anarchy and terror would prevail, a condition which the principles of the Charter could not and did not tolerate. The Jewish Agency's Hagana defense force, committed to support partition, should, with proper equipment and direction, be able to protect the Palestine Commission and, on its behalf, maintain order in Palestine. The Council's first step was to encourage the Commission to organize a well-equipped Palestine militia. To achieve this result and to preserve the UN's authority, Cohen concluded, the US government could do much if those in our government charged with the responsibility "have the will and resourcefulness to do so."[37]

Eichelberger had the AAUN reprint Cohen's two articles for wide circulation, a gesture hardly meeting with Gildersleeve's approval. "I am trying to help secure what Dr. Magnes seeks," she wrote the national director on March 17, "but must the AAUN take sides so violently and officially?" With deep regret, she tendered her resignation from the organization's membership that same day, giving four reasons for doing so. First, it was "improper" for an organization of this type to take sides officially, and to carry on "vehement propaganda" on such "a very controversial question" as the partition of Palestine. Second, her own opinion and public position were opposite to those adopted by the Association. Third, some of the statements issued by the AAUN seemed to her "seriously to misinterpret" the Charter. Lastly, in a sentence which Gildersleeve underlined, the Association was "endangering the prestige of the United Nations by proclaiming that the United Nations cannot survive unless it carries out a recommendation of the General Assembly which now, it seems fairly obvious, cannot possibly be carried out." Whatever mistakes we make, her letter to AAUN president William Emerson closed, she hoped that the UN would go on "to strength and success."[38]

One day after Austin declared in the Council that his government now proposed a trusteeship for Palestine, Emerson accepted Gildersleeve's resignation "with great reluctance," and would so advise the board of directors at its next meeting on April 2. The executive committee had just reaffirmed the position taken by the Association, his letter began. It did not consider the Palestine issue as controversial: the Assembly vote reflected months of investigation and general debate, and he was shocked that some American citizens defended the Arab States' threat of war and use of force in "flagrant violation" of the UN Charter. The AAUN had said that if the UN could not carry through on the partition recommendation, it would be "weakened" and the American leadership "compromised." We believe, continued the first dean of the Massachusetts Institute of Technology's Architecture School, that "partition is a fact and will be carried out," the firmness of the UN and the good faith of the Arab countries determining whether there would be "bitter and bloody controversy" over the boundaries. The AAUN rested on the legal opinion presented in the *New York Herald Tribune* by board member Benjamin V. Cohen. It "deeply regretted" their divergence of viewpoints with Gildersleeve's interpretation of the Charter, and hoped with her that the UN would go on to strength and success.[39]

The reversal of US policy found a few adherents. The ACJ kept in touch with Loy Henderson, who urged its leaders to send a strong letter of support to Marshall. Rosenwald wrote in praise to Austin; Lazaron spoke on radio across the country favoring Washington's retreat from partition, and shared his views with the receptive Samuel McCrea Cavert, general secretary of the Federal Council of the Churches of Christ in America. Gildersleeve explained the stand of the Committee for Justice and Peace in the Holy Land to Senator R Taft (R, Ohio) and others. Judah Magnes wrote to the anti-Zionist historian of nationalism Hans Kohn that the United States was finally "on the right track," and his colleague Ernst Simon pressed for their Ihud Association's binationalist program. Hearing of Henderson's private explanation for the endorsement of a trusteeship, British Ambassador Lord Inverchapel conveyed to Bevin his view that Truman and Marshall had felt constrained to give "greater weight" to the views of Secretary of Defense James Forrestal and the Joint Chiefs of Staff in light of a rapidly deteriorating international situation, as well as their realization that voters would overwhelmingly object to any shedding of American blood in a Jewish cause and Truman's possible loss of patience with all domestic pressures which had militated against an assessment of the Palestine problem "on its own merits."[40]

Eleanor Roosevelt reacted far differently, writing on the March 22 to Marshall with an offer to resign her post on the UN Human Rights Commission because she felt compelled to air her thoughts in public. Aside from the United States' "moral obligation" to the Jews under the 1917 Balfour Declaration, in which Britain pledged her support to facilitate the establishment of "a Jewish national home in Palestine," to which the United States and other victorious allies had assented in the San Remo Declaration (1920) and the Palestine mandate (1922), her greatest concern was the damage done to the UN itself, which at the present time the United States had "more or less buried." She sent Truman a copy of the letter the same day, decrying as well the American readiness to prepare for "an ultimate war" against the Russians, with whom she thought some arrangements could be made by using US economic power to obstruct their political advance. Realizing that her resignation would be a calamity for the embattled White House in a presidential election year, Truman implored her not to take this step, arguing that the UN was humanity's best and perhaps only hope for peace; it and the United States needed her. His heartfelt letter moved Roosevelt deeply, and she resolved to remain at her post, although criticizing trusteeship in her *My Day* column shortly thereafter.[41]

Professor Quincy Wright of the University of Chicago's Committee on International Relations, author of the magisterial *A Study of War*, preparer of several reports of the Commission to Study the Organization of Peace, and an advisor on international law to the US member of the Nuremberg War Crimes tribunal, was disturbed by the AAUN's stand. This board member had suggested during the Assembly deliberations that its executive committee take no position on the Palestine matter, and always thought that the partition recommendation was "unjust" to the Arabs and "unworkable." Nevertheless, Wright wrote to "Kim" Roosevelt's mother, Belle, he hoped that she and perhaps Gildersleeve would reconsider their resignations and that the AAUN board would take "a reasonable position" at its April 2 meeting, getting "on the right track" before anything was done which might weaken its general purposes.[42]

Receiving a copy from Wright, Eichelberger quickly reminded him that the AAUN's stand was based on the board's January resolution and subsequent meetings of the executive committee, and that the recommendations to which Gildersleeve objected were formulated at its Emergency Conference of February 26 and approved by the executive committee that afternoon. The board had stated clearly that the UN would not survive if it could not make decisions and carry them out. He failed to see Wright's point that the partition resolution might have violated the domestic jurisdiction clauses of the Charter, for Palestine was not a sovereign state, but a mandate about to be surrendered by the British, who had asked the General Assembly to determine that country's future government. Consequently, Eichelberger thought that the Assembly had the right to make any disposition of the area it wished, and that partition was the only arrangement which more than a majority of its members felt was "workable." He imagined, the letter ended, that "we shall have a very thorough discussion of the whole question" at the board meeting next week.[43]

Emerson's letter to Gildersleeve drew strong encouragement from two formidable sources. James P. Pope, former Democratic Senator from Idaho whose 1935 resolution that the United States join the League, a position Eichelberger's organization supported, had lost to isolationist sentiment in Congress, as did his call to join the World Court, now served as a director of the Tennessee Valley Authority. He was in "hearty agreement" with that letter, thinking Austin's February 24 statement "timid, legalistic, and defeatist in character," and he thoroughly agreed with Benjamin Cohen's recent public analysis. The US representative's subsequent statement that the US would not favor the use of force in any way to implement partition Pope considered even more distressing, for without the UN's ability to use armed forces against violence, there could be no more hope of permanent order and peace in the world. Sumner Welles wrote in similar vein to Emerson, considering

Gildersleeve's public position to have "helped gravely to confuse public opinion" as to the true issues in the Palestine question, the clear-cut provisions of the Charter, and the scope of the authority of the UN. Your letter, he added with "very warm congratulations," made wholly plain what the objectives and policy of the Association should be. Were the AAUN ever to become "merely a supine agency" of the US Government, it would prove to be "wholly useless as an instrument for good both in this country and in the world at large."[44]

Feeling that a crisis had developed in the relationship of the United States to the UN, Emerson and Eichelberger sent a long "personal and confidential" letter on March 26 to the board of directors' membership a few days before their critical meeting. Ample evidence demonstrated, they began, that this government was using the UN as an instrument of power politics. Truman's request from Congress of an American loan to Greece and Turkey (the Truman Doctrine) and the Marshall Plan to arrest the spread of Communism in Europe were both put into action while ignoring the UN, but the government's "vacillation and retreat" over partition brought our country's prestige to "a new low" in that international forum, our high position of leadership among the nations now "destroyed." The narrow interpretation of the Charter regarding the Council's authority vis-a-vis Palestine, repeated in Washington's refusal to return Yugoslav gold by resort to the UN Economic and Social Council, was "dangerous" for American security. The United States properly insisted on the Security Council's right to discuss the Soviet coup in Czechoslovakia through a liberal interpretation of the Charter, and it should continue to assure the success of the UN and American security in the Palestine question by reaffirming the Assembly's vote for partition. On May 16, 1948, the provisional government of the Jewish State will be proclaimed; the United States should recognize this government. Partition, having been once promised in November and with the Jewish Agency "so far along" in the establishment of a provision government, partition could not now be withheld: "Indeed, partition is a fact."

"The way is dark," the pair acknowledged. The lines between the Soviet Union and the western world had become more sharply drawn. Millions of people were disheartened because the UN had not taken certain decisions in the field of political security and carried them out. Yet the "poignant desire" shared by millions of people that the UN succeed was still present. We believe, concluded Emerson and Eichelberger, that the AAUN's mission was now "to lead a crusade for the establishment of the United Nations as the foundation of American foreign policy."[45]

A few board members persisted in strongly opposing the AAUN's stand on Palestine. Its policy permitting the organization "to engage in propaganda," Belle Roosevelt wrote Emerson, would defeat the high purpose of the organization and in a sense be a "betrayal" of the people who had worked with and for the AAUN. The Association must continue to interpret the UN Charter to the public, providing full and unbiased information on all problems which come before the UN, but not bring pressure for or against specific action. The UN should have the greatest freedom of action with its Charter, and be prepared for admitting an error and undertaking to correct it, allowing the "potentiality for just and corrective action." She sent this letter to fellow board members. Dana Backus did the same with a memorandum objecting to the AAUN's taking "an intransigent position" on Palestine, and wishing the Association to urge that Washington give "a forthright and specific description" of what "appropriate means" it would be prepared to use in cooperation with other nations to keep the peace in Palestine.

Helen Davis, writing to Emerson, asserted that the AAUN should not be participating in "agitation for the immediate use of force" and "arousing emotions at any time as to a political situation." Harsh criticism of our government, she observed, lent strength to its enemies within and without "and may be most unwise." An opponent of the partition resolution, Davis (like Quincy Wright) thought that the Association should be "a purveyor of facts" and take no position for or against that Assembly decision. All three women would attend the AAUN board meeting of April 2. So would Lazaron, who, while not wishing to resign, thought the AAUN's "staking" its "entire future" on the Palestine matter "a grave error."[46]

In response to Lazaron, Eichelberger informed him that Gildersleeve was the only board member who had resigned to date, and one who had been a member for a few months but never attended a meeting. Only in the case of Palestine, the AAUN national director charged, had our government made "a most cowardly retreat" in the face of evident threats by the Arab states. The previous day, forty-six Hagana men in a convoy on the road from Nahariya to Kibbutz Yehiam and another fifteen near Neveh Daniel were killed, individuals "who only wished to have a small piece of the Middle East as their homeland." The reason I came to believe in a Jewish State entitled to membership in the UN, Eichelberger revealed in his letter of March 29, was that "no effective voice in opposition to the persecution of Jews throughout the world will ever be raised by any other country, but when such a voice can be raised in the UN, the situation will be quite different." Bayard Dodge's recent claim in the *Reader's Digest* that Palestine might not accommodate more than a million more immigrants and there would be nine million left "is about as subtle an appeal to antisemitism as I have ever heard." Palestine was the only plan that the Assembly concluded seemed workable. One could not say that partition failed, Eichelberger closed: "It has not been applied" because the British set out to sabotage it and the American Government, in the face of Arab threats, "has been as ignominious in retreat as in any similar action in our history."[47]

Conveying his further thoughts in another letter to Eichelberger, Wright continued to believe that, the partition resolution a mistake, "it is better to rectify it than to cling blindly to it." Restoring law and order through a trusteeship agreement, leaving the future in "considerable measure" open, should be emphasized now; for the moment neither the Jews nor the Arabs were ready to give up the "irreconcilable positions" which they have taken. The legal arguments over Articles 2, 52, and 80 in the UN Charter were certainly "sufficiently cogent" to allow the Arabs' request for an advisory opinion from the International World Court (as Gildersleeve thought); the ten abstentions on the partition vote were notable. "Caution and moderation" were expedient; the United States certainly will not "play into the hands of the Soviet Union," and without US support partition was not going to be effected. The AAUN should not "make itself a martyr to consistency, especially when conditions have changed. In a follow-up communication, Wright made some suggestions as to a final board statement favoring an impartial trusteeship to restore peace in Palestine. In his view, these pointed the direction in which peace might be restored, British cooperation reestablished, and the way opened for ultimate solution by agreement.[48]

With twenty-three board members in attendance on the afternoon of April 2 at the AAUN headquarters, an elegant six-story townhouse on 45 East Sixty-Fifth St. in Manhattan's Lenox Hill neighborhood right near Central Park, Welles began the proceedings by asserting that the Association had come to "a determining point" in its history. The US reversal of its previous policy on Palestine, he declared, "will render the

Security Council impotent and prevent the United Nations from achieving the high objectives for which it was created," and the board had to speak out on this and other such basic issues. A draft resolution having the AAUN speak, as "the conscience of the American people" toward the UN, on behalf of "a stronger UN to enhance world security," any minority opinion on major issues to be publicized as well, was then adopted without opposition. Another stating that the UN should be "re-established as the cornerstone of American foreign policy in place of the present policy of regarding the United Nations as an instrument to be used or ignored as expediency may dictate" was also passed with no opposition.

The discussion on Palestine then commenced with Emerson reading letters from Eleanor Roosevelt, who had recently joined the board, James Pope, and Herbert Lehman, all expressing their approval of the Association's stand on the contentious issue. Speaking on behalf of the AAUN's draft resolution on Palestine, Emerson reiterated that the US reversal had an "overshadowing" effect, not only giving the impression that Washington was attempting to restrict the powers and authority of the international organization, but had discouraged all the people in the democracies as to the efficacy and future potentiality of the UN as an agency for peace. Benjamin Cohen then noted that what almost amounted to "unilateral action" by our government in asking for a special session, without disclosing how a trusteeship could overcome the same difficulties currently faced under the partition settlement, left one seriously in doubt whether an arrangement could be reached on any other subject. Welles took issue with the suggestion from Wright (who was not present) for a joint Anglo-American trusteeship as most dangerous: if the United States sent soldiers and the British troops remained, the pressure of the Soviet Union upon Iran, Turkey, and other countries would be "overwhelming."

The dissenters then took the floor. While regretting the "vacillation" of the United States, Helen Davis believed that every effort should be made to do nothing which would hinder the possibility of a cessation of hostilities in Palestine. In her view, it would be a mistake to issue a resolution calling for volunteers and lifting of the US arms embargo. The AAUN or individuals of the Association should do everything possible to see that the United States and other countries admit their fair share of displaced persons. Lazaron doubted that partition would solve the problem of the Jews or displaced persons. Carrying out the partition plan against the will of the majority of Palestine's inhabitants would "destroy everything" that had been built in Palestine. The draft resolution, he thought would hinder, not help, a solution.

Eichelberger next spoke of the "open and flagrant" statements on the part of Arab leaders and the uncooperativeness of the British. The Jewish Agency, he said, was the only body that was, "step by step," carrying out the General Assembly resolution. If a trusteeship should be voted, he thought that the Palestine Commission would be the logical authority to administer it. He favored economic union and political independence, as advocated in the partition recommendation, as the end solution for Palestine. Victor Elting wondered if it would not be better to wait until after the special session before coming out with any recommendations, but Alger Hiss, currently president of the Carnegie Endowment for Peace, declared that the draft resolution offered a "constructive approach" to our government and to the UN. It did not attempt to prophecy what the UN would do; rather, it indicated a course of action that would be consistent and within the authority of the UN. Dana Backus questioned pointing "too much scorn" in the first point of the resolution, and hoped that in redrafting the ultimate resolution the idea of a non-Palestinian force would be brought in. Malcolm W. Davis, long associated with the Carnegie Endowment for International Peace, also hoped that the idea of an international force would be added to the resolution. Worried that a minority report would weaken the Association, Oscar A. de Lima and Hugh Moore hoped that an effort would be made in the final resolution to bring the board into harmony.[49]

At the end of three and a half hours, an "overwhelming" majority of those present at the well-attended meeting approved the draft resolution, with Eichelberger announcing that he would see to it that the committee appointed to revise the resolution in the light of the discussion met quickly. Operating on the mandate that no publicity be given until this had been completed and the board members heard from, a group consisting of Cohen, Hiss, de Lima, and John I. Knudson convened the next afternoon. Also taking into account Wright's suggestions, the new resolution appealed for all parties in Palestine to respect the truce in spirit and in fact, urged that the trusteeship be effectuated through the UN Palestine Commission, and called for lifting the arms embargo under the UN's authority and for volunteer troop enlistments from abroad. Partition was endorsed, but those who were in disagreement, Eichelberger wrote to Wright, were "protected" by the phrase that "a substantial majority" favored this solution. Belle Roosevelt and Lazaron, the latter making at the board meeting "as pro-Arab a speech as though he was a member of the Arab Higher Committee," would probably not like the end result, he added, but both were too friendly to the AAUN and to many of us personally to resign. Emerson lost no time in informing the board on April 4 of the redrafted resolution, confident that it expressed the wish of the "overwhelming majority" of its members, and hoping that they would signal whether or not it met with their approval so that the AAUN could make suggestions to the American government before the Assembly's special session began on April 16.[50]

Wright did not approve, noting to Eichelberger that with the Security Council "eminently wise" in calling on April 1 for a truce and a special session to consider further the question of Palestine's future government, the present resolution "sounds like supporting a lost cause." Moreover, he thought that, if given publicity, the AAUN's declaration might injure the prestige of the UN and lesson the influence of the US and of the Association itself. If the AAUN got in "violent public controversy" with Gildersleeve's new committee, which included a number of persons who had in the past been active with the Association and whose support the AAUN certainly ought to have, it would be "unfortunate." Still voting "no," Helen Davis went much further, calling the Balfour Declaration "unwise"; Jewish "foreigners" to a large extent in Palestine by "illegal entry"—the Arab forces' invasion to be deplored, yet the former "invasion in a different form"; the Christian nations "remiss in their duty to the Jews," but that offered no reason for "insisting that the Arabs fulfill that duty"; and the Americans advised not to urge the arming of a group "who used terrorist methods before any Arab invasion took place." She would like to see the Association dedicated to have the UN work out a plan which could be accepted by both the Zionists and the Arabs. If that were achieved, "we could set up a milestone in world history."[51]

Lazaron took the lead for the opposition, appreciating the "fine" attitude of Eichelberger and Emerson to his wish for preparing a minority statement that would be sent to the board and given simultaneous publicity with the ultimate resolution of the majority. While also deploring the "hesitation and vacillation" in US foreign policy with regard to Palestine which had "created confusion" and weakened the UN's authority, his own contribution on April 7 began, the current draft did not take account of the Security Council's stand of six days earlier, and it called for recognizing "a non-existent Zionist state" even while the final disposition of the problem was pending in the UN. In his view, such recognition would "unquestionably stiffen Arab opposition, permit bloodshed and civil war, foment instability and unrest throughout the Middle East, endanger our national security, and threaten the peace of the world."

The US government, Lazaron's statement proposed, should guarantee the Arabs "against Zionist domination," allowing for Zionist immigration of 75,000 at once and an agreed upon immigration in successive years, while telling the Zionists that the Balfour Declaration had not specified a state. Moderates on both sides should be encouraged, with a UN trusteeship giving equal rights for all and cultural autonomy for a democratic Palestine commonwealth erected by the labor of Arab, Zionist, and Gentile, the US government urged to implement this position through the UN. Finally, Washington should reaffirm its support of a measure to permit displaced persons' immigration into the United States and to take the lead in the UN in providing for the settlement of displaced persons of all groups.[52]

On April 10, the AAUN board, "by a substantial majority," adopted its recommendations calling for support of the Assembly partition resolution, the authority of the Palestine Commission, and assistance from the UN to provide that body with "whatever forces it may deem requisite." That included the recruitment of "the necessary forces to maintain law and order," with no sacrifice of citizenship for enlistees. It asked that the US government assume this time "its appropriate share of the responsibility" for the carrying out of any decisions of the forthcoming Assembly, and that, pending action by the special session, this country recognize the provisional governments of the Jewish and Arab states as soon as each was set up and that the US embargo on the shipment of arms to the Near East be lifted. All parties involved should respect the Council's call for a truce. While expressing "grave doubts" that the temporary truce proposed by the United States would be carried out more successfully than partition with economic union, the AAUN urged that any trust agreement be effectuated through the UN Palestine Commission. The Assembly's November 29 resolution for a trusteeship over the city of Jerusalem should remain unchanged, thereby preserving the peace and security of the Holy Places there. A minority of the board, the statement concluded, objected to the reaffirmation of the wisdom of partition, and a minority statement was drafted by Rabbi Morris Lazaron of Baltimore, a board member.[53]

Amazed that only the majority statement appeared in the *New York Times* account, Lazaron asked Eichelberger why the minority one was not sent to the board members, approximately half of whom were not present at the April 2 meeting and all of whom had received a copy of the majority resolution. He "profoundly" believed that the Association had made "a grave error' in staking its prestige of this Palestine issue, the more so since it permitted other opportunities, "when it might have spoken prophetically," to go by without a word. "Morris" wished "Clark" to have this immediate word of his "grievous disappointment at the entire procedure." In a separate letter, he, joined by Belle Roosevelt and Helen Davis, asked all the members to sign their dissenting statement and return it to him at once if they agreed.[54]

Emerson countered three days later with a letter to the board members, noting that Lazaron had drafted his own statement in the office on April 6, which, in accordance with their understanding, was sent to members who had voted against the majority statement, five in all. So far, only one of these recipients had notified Emerson and Eichelberger of his acceptance of it. Another resolution adopted at the April 2 meeting had stated that the minority statement would be circulated among the members, sent to the chapters, and released to the press in case of a "close division" on a matter of major importance. Five persons voting against a resolution out of a board of forty-five hardly seemed to be a "close division." However, Emerson noted, Lazaron's statement was indeed sent to the chapters, to the board members, and was available to the press.[55]

The minority statement elicited but a few positive responses. Convinced that the Assembly's partition resolution was the "best solution" of the "very difficult" Palestine problem that could be arrived at and "a source of much gratification" and "tremendous relief" everywhere in view of US-Soviet support finally on one important matter, Pope added that the Arabs had deliberately defied the UN, and the US change of policy dealt a "terrible blow" to the prestige and power of the international organization. Even Dana Backus noted to Lazaron that the dissenting statement did not acknowledge the final resolution's acceptance of the truce proposal and that it called on the United States to assume its share of responsibility "for the carrying out of any decisions of the forthcoming assembly." While she tended toward partition with economic union simply because that solution had "come up on top" most often as a result of various investigations over a period of years, Backus felt that the AAUN should not pass formal resolutions on questions that were under discussion in the UN, which it had now done in this one instance with detailed recommendations on the Palestine question. Come April 21, only James Shotwell and Monroe E. Deutsch, Provost of the University of California, had joined the dissenters.[56]

Eichelberger brought the controversy to an end with a letter to Lazaron on April 28, pointing out the rabbi's misstatements of fact. The committee appointed to prepare a revised resolution had done so, and its draft had been sent to all members of the board on April 4 for vote by mail. Lazaron certainly must have received Emerson's letter of that date before arriving in the office two days later to draft his minority statement. It was therefore "absolutely unfair" for Lazaron to say that it was regrettable that he was not informed of the procedure. In addition, Lazaron, Roosevelt, and Davis had left the meeting of April 2 immediately after his speech, which was, of course, "regrettable."[57]

One week later, Eichelberger received a request from *Nation* editor Kirchwey to join an eminent group of Americans in signing an advertisement that would occupy a full page in the *Washington Post*. (His friend had already cabled Truman on April 14 that the US truce proposal "dishonored" his pledged word that the administration was still committed to partition, the same day that Herblock's scathing cartoon in that newspaper showed an American spokesman at the UN standing on his head while explaining US policy on Palestine, bewildered delegates looking on.) The text, drawn largely from the Nation Associates' memorandum to the UN entitled *The British Record on Partition* about the mandatory's sabotage of the Assembly decision, would take the form of an open letter to the President "in view of our privileged knowledge that a very strong effort is being made to secure a return to partition." Truman, according to their information, had come to realize belatedly that "he has been double-crossed," and the appointment of General John H. Hilldring to join the US delegation to the UN was "an earnest [sign] of that understanding." Yet events were moving so rapidly in the UN and a victory for the British was entirely possible, Kirchwey cautioned, if a presidential directive did not override the State Department, "which is playing ball with the British." The signees hoped that this advertisement might be helpful in giving impetus to Truman and his advisers. Eichelberger readily agreed to join.[58]

Lazaron made one last public effort as the date of the Palestine mandate's termination drew nigh. Speaking at length at a rally sponsored by the American Council for Judaism in Washington's Hotel Shoreham on May 6, he warned that current Zionist agitation would destroy what had been built in Palestine; would make extended Jewish immigration into Palestine impossible; place the 800,000 Jews living in other Arab or Muslim lands in jeopardy; prejudice the position of American Jews; and threaten the security of the United States and endanger the peace of the world. A cultural Zionist, he decried "the dangerous currents of a chauvinist nationalism, foreign to the spirit of the faith of my fathers," which would "vitiate the sympathy for Jews these heart-breaking years have evoked for them throughout the Christian world." The unilateral declaration of the Jewish Agency, apparently dominated at present by Zionist extremists, to establish a state on May 15 was "a challenge to warfare." He, as did Dr. Judah Magnes, supported the US truce proposal, which would stop the bloodletting and safeguard the vital, continued flow of oil from the Arabian peninsula to the West; imposing partition against the will of the majority of Palestine's inhabitants "will destroy the United Nations." The Zionist state, facing the "implacable enmity" of the Arab world, could never stand on its own feet, and would "badger" by future pressures every Jewish community in the world.

A Jewish homeland could be secured if the Zionists would drop the state issue, Lazaron proposed, while Jew and Gentile could unite on a platform to empty the displaced persons camps this year by settlement in Palestine, the United States, and other lands. The only hope of preserving what had been built in Palestine and of extending it rested on cooperation with the Arab majority there. He appealed to the Arabs and the Zionists to lay down their arms. The Arabs faced no danger of Zionist domination: they outnumbered the Zionists two to one; the Arab birthrate was much higher than theirs; the Arabs had gained by Zionist efforts and would stand to benefit by further Zionist immigration into and development of Palestine. The Jews had not been promised a state in the Balfour Declaration. There should be "measureable and continued" Jewish immigration and the right of land purchase. Each community autonomous in the culture area, and working on great economic projects and cooperating in self-government, could, in the end, erect together the "democratic commonwealth" of Palestine, a "bastion of freedom" in the Middle East. If extremists on both sides persisted in fighting, the United States should recognize the claims of neither, and an arms embargo put on the entire area and its ports blocked. The moderates strengthened thereby, it would not be long before the extremists would "lose stomach for the fight and the conditions for equitable solution would be present."

Above all, Lazaron concluded, the Jewish and Christian tradition gives our life dignity, nobility. Judaism, one of the great cultural and spiritual insights of the world, spoke an eternal language appealing to mind and heart. It pointed to love and purpose in the universe, and proclaimed the glory of the free spirit as an instrument of God's revelation. Crying out against injustice and hate, it maintained the soul of the Jew with "majestic hopes of glorious human destiny not only for Israel, but for all mankind." "Out of our loins have come other dreamers, and our sons and daughters of Christendom and Islam have helped to spread the deathless truth. God is one and all men are brothers." "This is the banner I would lift for Christians and Jews," his emotional peroration ended, "in our day of doubt and strife."[59]

Boston Herald editor Frank W. Buxton, Pulitzer-prize winner and a member of the Anglo-American Committee of Inquiry on Palestine, sharply disagreed. Writing to ACJ president Rosenwald two day later, he did not regard partition, a fait accompli "for good or ill," as a sort of "capricious act" which could be lightly dismissed on the "dubious theory" that the Assembly had erred. Numerous prominent individuals agreed with him that any other solution had been "made impossible by the train of events," and certainly "an overwhelming preponderance of opinion" favored partition "as the only course now." He had read "shocking" remarks by Rabbi Lazaron, which "might better have come from a close friend of the Grand Mufti or from such figures as G. L. K. Smith and the persons who used to circulate the *Protocol* [sic] *of the Elders of Zion*." He did not include Dr. Magnes in this assemblage, strongly opposed though the Hebrew University president was to partition. The fact that most of my Jewish friends in Boston, Buxton noted, men and women who had been ardently anti-Zionist in the past, acquiesce in partition and resent the implications of various arguments set forth by the extreme champions of non-partition "has impressed me deeply."[60]

Kirchwey's "privileged knowledge," as she put it to Eichelberger, that a very strong effort was being made to secure partition, with Truman "belatedly" realizing that he had been "double-crossed," accurately reflected the latest developments at 1600 Pennsylvania Ave. Partition advocate Bartley Crum, a member of the Anglo-American Committee of Inquiry whom she had also asked to endorse the advertisement in the *Washington Post*, reported to the Jewish Agency that his private talk with Truman on May 10 had been promising. Clark Clifford, Truman's Special Counsel who had filed a copy of Cohen's articles of March 16–17 favoring partition on legal grounds, advised the Agency to "go firmly forward" with its declaration of independence. Clifford had the "definite impression," Shertok was informed on May 11, that the President was considering recognition of the new state.[61]

Indeed, after a stormy meeting in the Oval Office the next afternoon, during which Marshall announced that if Truman accepted Clifford's advice, he would vote against the President if he cast a vote in the coming November elections, Clifford successfully pressed Lovett to have State approve *de facto* recognition by the White House. A humanitarian concern for the Holocaust survivors' wishes; the Jewish domestic vote and widespread public support for sovereignty; promises to former business partner and long-time friend Eddie Jacobson and to Weizmann; a desire to strengthen the fledgling UN and to forestall the Soviets in recognizing a new state that had already proven itself on the battlefield; resentment against what he called the State Department's "striped-pants boys"; and the devout Baptist's strong belief in the biblical sources about the Divine giving the Land of Canaan to Abraham and his descendants—all melded into Truman's own decision to recognize the State of Israel only eleven minutes after Ben-Gurion's announcement of a free *Medinat Yisra'el* on May 14, 1948.[62]

The American delegation then engaged in General Assembly deliberations on Palestine was caught unawares by the sudden denouement, and Marshall, who ordered Rusk to fly to New York and prevent the delegation "from resigning *en masse*," later told Truman that his department felt the United States "had hit its all-time low before the UN." Arab delegates spoke harshly at the UN against Truman's action, while Eleanor

Roosevelt would write to Marshall that the President's speedy action had created "complete consternation" in the Assembly hall. Calling on the American Council for Judaism to follow Magnes's example in seeking peace between Jews and Arabs on binationalist lines and criticizing the new Jewish commonwealth "severely" once the Israeli state was established, Lazaron acknowledged the ACJ's failures to convince the majority of American Jews that to follow Zionism would "isolate us from our fellow citizens" and to "stave [off] the national influences which have slowly disintegrated Judaism and transform all of its branches into a national religion for Jews only."[63]

Gildersleeve would repeatedly testify before Congress and urge Truman to deny American support to Israel, and described herself as "struggling ardently against" the creation and later the continued existence of the Jewish State. Her Committee for Justice and Peace in the Holy Land would merge in 1951, under Kermit Roosevelt's leadership, into the pro-Arabist American Friends of the Middle East, which one historian asserts was financed by the Central Intelligence Agency and ARAMCO. "Kim" Roosevelt would play a key role in the CIA's successful effort in August 1953 to overthrow Mohammad Mosaddegh, the democratically elected prime minister of Iran, in favor of strengthening the monarchical rule of the Shah, Mohammad Reza Pahlavi, as an imagined counter to Communism in the Cold War.[64]

As for the AAUN, its pro-partition stance vindicated with Truman's recognition of the State of Israel, Eichelberger would go on to appear before Congress and to author books on the UN's ten, fifteen, and twenty years. His memoir appeared in 1977, *Organizing for Peace*, a personal history of the founding of the United Nations. The Assembly's adoption in December 1948 of the Universal Declaration of Human rights contained many of the same provisions proposed by the AAUN's Commission to Study the Organization of Peace nearly two years earlier. The Association received an unexpected windfall when Eleanor Roosevelt, who had just resigned from the UN Human Rights Commission, walked into Eichelberger's office shortly before Dwight D. Eisenhower's inauguration and, in a modest tone, offered her services as an "educational volunteer." Barnstorming the country on its behalf, and expressing herself forcefully on the broad issues that came up at AAUN staff and board meetings, she focused on creating new chapters and the raising of the budget. She would also be a valuable ally in Israel's first diplomatic battles, objecting to UN Mediator Folke Bernadotte's plan to transfer the Negev to Transjordan in exchange for the Jewish state's getting unfertile lands in northern Galilee, championing Youth Aliya's effort there for the education and social integration of many displaced, homeless Jewish children, and getting the sultan of Morocco in 1956 to allow the Jews of Casablanca to go to Israel. The woman whom Truman called "the first lady of the world" would willingly pursue efforts on behalf of the AAUN until her death in November 1962.[65]

Eichelberger continued to insist that the untapped potential of the UN, whatever that world body's imperfections, could be used to transform it into a universal society under law. The UN had to adjust to changing circumstances and new problems, he believed, leading to an extension of its authority to the seabed, outer space, and Antarctica. When the AAUN merged with the United States Committee for the United Nations to form a new organization called the United Nations Association of the USA, he served as its president from 1964 to 1968. During the same years, the individual whom former Undersecretary of State George W. Ball called "the Dean of the corps" of those few Americans "who have tried untiringly to spread the word that our nation dare not refuse an active involvement in world affairs" became chairman of the Commission to Study the Organization of Peace and then its executive director until 1974, when he retired. To his last years, this prolific writer, expert publicist, and superb organizer saw the UN as an evolving international society, a "unifying moral force" in which the American people and their government played a very important part towards the maintenance of peace. Believing that, in the long run, the UN's success was dependent upon the force of public opinion, he never tired in advocating that all nations must make the UN the foundation of their foreign policies.[66]

One year before his death on January 26, 1980, Eichelberger deposited his papers with the New York Public Library's Manuscripts and Archives Division. A statement issued by the library declared that his contributions "spanned a crucial period in American history from 1920 to 1977," and that "his relentless crusade for universal, rather than regional, peacemaking methods had been rewarded with the establishment of the United Nations following World War II." Eichelberger's energetic championing Israel's rebirth as well by honoring the General Assembly's partition resolution was in keeping with his staunch credo.

Although rarely accorded mention hitherto in studies on the creation of the Jewish state, his and the AAUN's persistent activity on its behalf also deserves acknowledgment. The AAUN should be remembered as the United States' most dynamic internationalist group and only American interest group devoted exclusively to supporting the United Nations. Eichelberger's conviction, pointedly put to Morris Lazaron in March 1948, was unequivocal: "No effective voice in opposition to the persecution of Jews throughout the world will ever be raised by any other country, but when such a voice can be raised in the UN, the situation will be quite different." More than seven decades later, Eichelberger's help in granting the Jewish people, after suffering over millennia, a sovereign seat at the diplomatic table of the family of nations, something he deemed "a moral and spiritual right," remains another commendable legacy, indeed.[67]

Endnotes

1. *UN Doc. S/P.*, vol. 271, March 19, 1948.
2. Monty Noam Penkower, *Palestine to Israel: Mandate to State, 1945–1948*, vol. 2, *Into the International Arena, 1947–1948* (New York, 2019), 619–620. *New York Times* publisher Arthur Hays Sulzberger, long opposed to a Jewish state and insecure over his Jewish identity, endorsed the General Assembly's partition recommendation in order to strengthen the hand of the United Nations. See Monty Noam Penkower, *Twentieth-Century Jews: Forging Identity in the Land of Promise and in the Promised Land* (Boston, 2010), chap. 5.
3. Penkower, *Palestine to Israel*, 608–609, 621–622, 628–629, 633.
4. *New York Herald Tribune*, March 21, 1948.
5. Ibid.; Penkower, *Palestine to Israel*, 630–631.
6. Eichelberger press release, March 21, 1948, box 66, Carl M. Eichelberger MSS., Manuscripts and Archives Division, New York Public Library (hereafter NYPL), New York City. Also see Robert D. Accinelli, "Pro-U.N. Internationalists and the Early Cold War: the American Association for the United Nations and U.S. Foreign Policy, 1947–52," *Diplomatic History* 9:4 (Fall 1985): 347–362. For Truman's address to the joint session of Congress, calling for speedy action on the European Recovery Program (the Marshall Plan), restoration of the draft, and enactment of universal training legislation to maintain US armed forces at their authorized strength, see "Special Message," March 17, 1948, Harry S. Truman Library (HSTL), Independence, MO.

7. Robert D. Accinelli, "Militant Internationalists: The League of Nations Association, The Peace Movement and U.S. Foreign Policy, 1934–38," *Diplomatic History* 4:1 (Winter 1980): 19–38; Smith Simpson, "The Commission to Study the Organization of Peace," *American Political Science Review* 35:2 (April 1941): 317–324; Robert A. Divine, *Second Chance: The Triumph of Internationalism in America During World War II* (New York, 1967); Andrew Johnstone, *Dilemmas of Internationalism: The American Association for the United Nations and US Policy, 1941–1948* (Burlington, 2009); Clark M. Eichelberger, with William T. Stone, *Peaceful Change: The Alternative to War* (New York, 1937); Clark M. Eichelberger, "Next Steps in the Organization of the United Nations," *Annals* 228:1 (July 1, 1943): 34–39; idem, *The Time Has Come for Action* (New York, 1944); idem, *The United Nations Charter: What Was Done at San Francisco* (New York, 1945).
8. "Model UN and UNA-USA," Selous Foundation for Public Policy Research, 2018; Clark M. Eichelberger, "Plans for World Security," *Virginia Quarterly Review* 20:4 (Autumn 1944).
9. Alfred E. Clark, "Clark M. Eichelberger Dies at 83: Led American U.N. Association," *New York Times*, January 27, 1980, 20; Robert D. Accinelli, "Clark Mell Eichelberger," in *Biographical Dictionary of Internationalists*, ed. Warren F. Kuehl (Westport, 1983), 235–239; Clark M. Eichelberger, *Proposals for the United Nations Charter—What Was done at Dumbarton Oaks* (New York, 1944).
10. AAUN statement, January 29, 1948, Z5/409/1, Central Zionist Archives (hereafter CZA), Jerusalem; Clark M. Eichelberger, "Editorial," *Changing World* 19 (December 1947): 2.
11. Eichelberger to Dulles, January 28, 1948, box 66, Eichelberger MSS.
12. Gelber to Shertok-Goldmann, February 3, 1948, Z6/4/5, CZA. Other than Gelber's contributions to leading newspapers, this forty-year-old former Rhodes scholar at Balliol College, Oxford, had authored *The Rise of Anglo-American Friendship* (1938) and *Peace by Power* (1942), both published by Oxford University Press.
13. AAUN statement, February 10, 1948, box 66, Eichelberger MSS.
14. Eichelberger memo, February 11, 1948, box 66, Eichelberger MSS.
15. Congressmen to Marshall, February 10, 1948; Marshall to Javits, February 12, 1948; both in box 2, Hyman A. Schulson MSS., Manuscripts and Archives Division, NYPL.
16. Monty Noam Penkower, "The Genesis of the American Council for Judaism," *American Jewish History* 86 (June 1998): 167–194, reprinted in idem, *Twentieth-Century Jews,* chap. 4; Thomas A. Kolsky, *Jews Against Zionism*

(Philadelphia, 1990); Lazaron to Sachs, January 31, 1948, file 28/14, Henry Hurwitz MSS., American Jewish Archives, Cincinnati, Ohio.
17. Gildersleeve letter, February 10, 1948; Gildersleeve to Eichelberger, February 10, 1948; both in box 66, Eichelberger MSS.
18. Bridgeman to Gildersleeve, with memo attached, February 10, 1948, Virginia Gildersleeve MSS., Rare Book and Manuscript Library, Butler Library, Columbia University, New York City.
19. Kermit Roosevelt, "The Partition of Palestine: A Lesson in Pressure Politics," *Middle East Journal* 2:1 (January 1948), 1–16; Roosevelt remarks, The American Forum of the Air, February 10, 1948, Zionist Archives, New York (now at the Central Zionist Archives, Jerusalem). For Kaukji's activities, see Laila Parsons, *The Commander: Fawzi Al-Qawuqji and the Fight for Arab Independence 1914–1948* (New York, 2016).
20. Wright remarks, The American Forum of the Air, February 10, 1948.
21. Brewster and Neumann remarks, ibid.
22. Sumner Welles, "U.S. Stand on Palestine Viewed as Starting U.N. on League's Path," *New York Herald Tribune*, February 17, 1948.
23. Eichelberger to Rusk, February 19, 1948, box 67; Eichelberger to Rusk, February 1, 1948, box 20; both in Eichelberger MSS. A border incident between Ethiopia and Italian Somaliland gave Fascist dictator Benito Mussolini an excuse to intervene and invade Ethiopia on October 3, 1935. Hundreds of thousands of Ethiopian civilians died as a result of the Italian invasion, which included the use of mustard gas against civilians by the Italian army. The country was formally occupied on May 9, 1936; Emperor Haile Selassie went into exile. On June 7, 1936, he addressed the fifty-two nations of the League, charging that "international morality" and collective security were at stake. The League's ineffectiveness was apparent. Its members condemned that act and voted to impose economic sanctions on the aggressor. Yet the British and French governments, more concerned about the growing power of the Third Reich, viewed Italy as necessary to restrain German power. President Franklin D. Roosevelt, whose country was not a League member, declared that the United States was neutral, and he invoked the Neutrality Act to place a blanket ban on all weapon shipments to Italy.
24. Eichelberger to Marshall, February 22, 1948, box 67, Eichelberger MSS.
25. Eichelberger to Lazaron, February 24, 1948, ibid.
26. Eichelberger notes, February 24, 1948, ibid.; Penkower, *Palestine to Israel*, 585.
27. Penkower, *Palestine to Israel*, 585; AAUN press release, February 26, 1948; Eichelberger to Rusk, February 27, 1948; both in box 67, Eichelberger MSS.

28. Penkower, *Palestine to Israel*, 587–588, 593–594, 596.
29. Rosenwald to Marshall, February 21, 1948, file 107, American Council for Judaism Archives, University of Wisconsin Library, MD.
30. Cable to Lazaron, February 22, 1948; Lazaron to Roosevelt, February 25, 1948; both in box 3044, Lazaron MSS.
31. Eichelberger to Austin, March 3, 1948, box 120, Eichelberger MSS.
32. Eichelberger to Gildersleeve, March 4, 1948, ibid.
33. Gildersleeve to the Editor of the *Herald Tribune*, March 5, 1948, ibid.
34. Proskauer to Lovett, March 1, 1948, box 8, Joseph M. Proskauer MSS., American Jewish Committee Archives, New York City.
35. Lovett to Proskauer, March 10, 1948; Proskauer to Austin, March 15, 1948, both in box 8, Proskauer MSS.
36. Proskauer to Lovett, March 18, 1948, ibid.
37. Benjamin V. Cohen, "The United Nations and Palestine," *New York Herald Tribune*, March 16–17, 1948; William Lasser, *Benjamin V. Cohen: Architect of the New Deal* (New Haven, 2002); Cohen interview with the author, July 22, 1973.
38. Gildersleeve to Eichelberger, March 17, 1948; Gildersleeve to Emerson, March 17, 1948; both in box 120, Eichelberger MSS.
39. Emerson to Gildersleeve, March 20, 1948, ibid.
40. Penkower, *Palestine to Israel*, 626–627.
41. Ibid., 627–628.
42. Wright to Belle Roosevelt, March 23, 1948, box 120, Eichelberger MSS.
43. Eichelberger to Wright, March 25, 1948, ibid.
44. Pope to Emerson, March 24, 1948; Welles to Emerson, March 24, 1948; both in box 120, Eichelberger MSS. Also see David L. Porter, "James Pinckney Pope, in W. Kuehl, *Biographical Dictionary of Internationalists*, 584–586.
45. Emerson-Eichelberger to members of the board of directors, March 26, 1948, box 120, Eichelberger MSS.
46. Roosevelt to Emerson, March 27, 1948; Backus memo, March 30, 1948; Davis to Emerson, March 31, 1948; all ibid.; Lazaron to Eichelberger, March 26, 1940, box 3046, Lazaron MSS.
47. Eichelberger to Lazaron, March 29, 1948, box 120, Eichelberger MSS.; Penkower, *Palestine to Israel*, 634; Bayard Dodge, "Must There Be War in the Middle East," *Reader's Digest*, April 1948, 34–45. Dodge was then president of the American University of Beirut and a supporter of Judah Magnes's binationalist views on Palestine.
48. Wright to Eichelberger, March 30, 1948, and April 1, 1948; both in box 120, Eichelberger MSS.

49. Meeting of the board of directors, April 2, 1948, box 49, CRIA papers, Carnegie Council on Ethics and International Affairs MSS., Rare Book and Manuscript Library, Butler Library, Columbia University, New York City. Lehman, whose letter of endorsement for the AAUN's favoring the Assembly partition resolution concluded with the hope that the Association would "distinguish between a change in time schedule and the fundamentals of the settlement," had days earlier, as honorary vice-president of the American Jewish Committee, joined Proskauer and Executive Committee Chairman Jacob Blaustein in a public statement favoring the "still-binding" partition resolution of the Assembly on November 29, 1947. They also expressed the Committee's "keen regret" at the US government's "modification" of its earlier positive position on that date. In their view, the government's reversal had resulted in "a loss of international prestige by the United States and has been a blow to the United Nations." Statement, March 28, 1948, MRD-1, 20/2, United Jewish Appeal Archives, New York City.
50. Eichelberger to Wright, April 5, 1948, Emerson to board members, April 4, 1948, both in box 120, Eichelberger MSS.
51. Wright to Eichelberger, April 6, 1948; Davis to Eichelberger and notes, April 6, 1948; both ibid.
52. Lazaron statement, April 7, 1948, ibid.
53. AAUN press release, April 10, 1948, ibid.
54. Lazaron to Eichelberger, April 12, 1948, box 3046, Lazaron MSS.; Lazaron, Roosevelt, and Davis dissenting statement, April 12, 1948, box 120, Eichelberger MSS.
55. Emerson to board members, April 15, 1948, box 66, Eichelberger MSS.
56. Pope to Lazaron, April 15, 1948; Backus to Lazaron, April 15, 1948; Davis to Emerson, April 20, 1948; Lazaron to board members, April 21, 1948; all in box 120, Eichelberger MSS. Also see Harold Josephson, "James Thomson Shotwell," in Kuehl, *Biographical Dictionary of Internationalists*, 673–676.
57. Eichelberger to Lazaron, April 18, 1948, box 120, Eichelberger MSS.
58. Kirchwey to Eichelberger, May 5, 1948, file MC280/237, Freda Kirchwey MSS., Schlesinger Library, Radcliffe College, Boston; Kirchwey to Truman, April 14, 1948, file 129/1093, Israel State Archives, Jerusalem; Herblock, "We Want to Make Our Position Perfectly Clear," *Washington Post*, April 14, 1948. The candidacy of Hilldring, who had advocated partition in November 1947 as a member of the US delegation to the UN and was in regular touch with Jewish Agency's Eliyahu Epstein (later Elath), was supported by close advisors to Truman Clark Clifford and David Niles. He agreed to serve after numerous

telephone calls from Weizmann, one from Eleanor Roosevelt, and a cable from Henry Morgenthau, Jr. Penkower, *Palestine to Israel*, 643.
59. Lazaron address, "The United States, Palestine, and American Jewry," ACJ 1948 files, Zionist Archives (now at the CZA).
60. Buxton to Rosenwald, May 8, 1948, A300/16, CZA. Gerald L. K. Smith, founder of the Christian Nationalist Crusade, heralded white supremacy and antisemitism, denied that six million Jews had been murdered in the Holocaust, and would lobby for decades for the release of all Nazi war criminals convicted in the Nuremberg Trials. *The Protocols of the Elders of Zion*, an antisemitic forgery purporting to describe a Jewish plan for global domination, was first published in Russia in 1903, translated into multiple languages, and disseminated internationally in the early part of the twentieth century and beyond.
61. Lourie to Shertok, May 11, 1948, S25/1553, CZA; Cohen articles, March 16–17, box 14, Clark Clifford MSS., HSTL.
62. Penkower, *Palestine to Israel*, 673–680.
63. Ibid., 680–681; *National Jewish Post and Opinion*, May 16, 1948. Lazaron's continued stand after Israel's creation eventually led to his severed relationship with, and resignation from, the Baltimore Hebrew Congregation as rabbi emeritus. The American Council for Judaism rapidly declined in political activity and influence following Israel's resounding victory in the Six-Day War of June 1967, the *New York Times* declaring that the organization was effectively "consigned to irrelevancy." Samuel G. Freeman, "American Jews Who Reject Zionism Say Events Aid Cause," *New York Times*, June 25, 2010. For Magnes's final efforts, see chap. 6.
64. Virginia Gildersleeve, *Many a Good Crusade: Memoirs of Virginia Gildersleeve* (New York, 1980), 187, 289, 412; Robert Moats Miller, *Harry Emerson Fosdick, Preacher, Pastor, Prophet* (Oxford, 1985), 192; Kermit Roosevelt, *Countercoup: The Struggle for the Control of Iran* (New York, 1979); Hugh Wilford, *America's Great Game: the CIA's Secret Arabists and the Making of the Modern Middle East* (New York, 2013). ARAMCO became the chief conduit communicating Saudi Arabia's interests to its parent corporations (Standard Oil of California and the Texas Company, Texaco) and to the US government. The Shah would rule for the next twenty-six years until he was overthrown in the Iranian Revolution.
65. Clark M. Eichelberger, *UN: The First Ten Years* (New York, 1955); idem, *UN: The First Fifteen Years* (New York, 1960); idem, *UN: The First Twenty Years* (New York, 1970); idem, *Organizing for Peace, A Personal History of the Founding of the United Nations* (New York, 1977); Harold Josephson, *James T. Shotwell and the Rise of Internationalism in America* (Cranbury, 1975), 286–287;

Joseph P. Lash, *Eleanor: The Years Alone* (New York, 1972), 220–221, 338–339; Monty Noam Penkower, *The Holocaust and Israel Reborn: From Catastrophe to Sovereignty* (Urbana, 1994), chap. 11; Raffaella Baritono, "Eleanor Roosevelt and the United Nations: 'Diplomacy from Below' and the Search for a New Transatlantic Dialogue," *European Journal of American* Studies, 12:1 (Spring 2017); Lester B. Orfield, "UN: The First Ten Years," *Indiana Law Journal* 31:3 (1956), 433–436.

66. George Ball, "Foreword," in Eichelberger, *Organizing For Peace*, x; Clark M Eichelberger, "World Government via the United Nations," *Annals* 264:1 (July 1, 1949): 20–25; Clark M. Eichelberger, "The United Nations and the Bed of the Sea," *San Diego Law Review* 6:3 (July 1, 1969): 339–353; *United Nations Association of the United States of America, Chapter Handbook* (2019); James Wurst, *The UN Association-USA: A Little Known History of Advocacy and Action* (Boulder, 2016).

67. Alfred E. Clark, "Clark M. Eichelberger Dies at 83," *New York Times*, January 27, 1980.

5. A Truce and Trusteeship for Palestine

On April 1, 1948, the United Nations Security Council, by a unanimous vote at its 277th meeting and "in the exercise of its primary responsibility for the maintenance of international peace and security," adopted Resolution 43 calling upon the Arab and Jewish armed groups in Palestine to cease acts of violence immediately. Requesting that the Arab Higher Committee and the Jewish Agency for Palestine make representatives available to the Security Council (SC) for the purpose of arranging a truce, it emphasized "the heavy responsibility" which would fall upon any party failing to observe such a truce. The Council also adopted by nine affirmative votes and two abstentions (the Soviet Union and Ukraine) resolution number forty-four requesting Secretary General Trygve Lie, in accordance with Article 20 of the UN Charter, to convoke a General Assembly (GA) special session starting April 16 to consider further the question of Palestine's future government.[1]

The two resolutions, proposed the previous day by American head delegate Warren Austin, had their genesis in the retreat of the US State and War Departments from the GA majority vote on November 29, 1947 (Resolution 181-II) to partition Palestine into a Jewish and an Arab state at the end of the British mandate. Fearing the danger of Communist infiltration into the Near East and jeopardizing US oil needs by alienating the six governments comprising the Arab League, G-2 Army Intelligence, the Central Intelligence Agency, and State's Near Eastern and African Affairs division and Policy Planning Staff had all concluded (as had their counterparts in London) that partition could not be implemented. In their judgment, an alternative solution had to be found. Secretary of State George C. Marshall received from President

Harry S. Truman on March 8, the same day that Truman announced his decision to run for the presidency in November, approval "for use and if necessary" of State's draft for a projected Austin speech calling for a Palestine trusteeship if a GA special session found conciliation unsuccessful. Austin exploded the political bombshell when addressing the Council on March 19. A shocked Truman, having given World Zionist Organization (WZO) president Dr. Chaim Weizmann in their secret meeting on the 18th in the White House an understanding that he would work for the establishment of a Jewish State, confined his deepest feelings to a diary entry: "I am now in the position of a liar and a double-crosser. I've never felt so in my life."

While sending adviser Samuel Rosenman to tell Weizmann that "there was not and would not be any change in the long policy he and I had talked about." Truman issued a public statement on March 25 explaining his stand. Repeating Austin's point that trusteeship had been put forward because partition could not be carried out by peaceful means at the present time, he emphasized that trusteeship was not proposed as a substitute for partition, but as an effort to fill the vacuum soon to be created by the mandate's termination on May 15. An immediate truce had to be reached between the two contesting communities in Palestine "if we are to avert tragedy," and the United States was prepared to take its share of responsibility if the UN agreed to its proposal. Open warfare was "just over the horizon" otherwise, his declaration ended, and the country's regard for the UN, for the peace of the world, "and for our own self-interest" did "not permit us to do less."

At a press conference the same day, Truman remarked that his past position favoring large-scale Jewish immigration into Palestine had not changed, but he believed that the first thing to do was to restore peace in the country and arrange a settlement that would halt the bloodshed. He also hoped that trusteeship would produce the kind of peaceful settlement that would result in there not being any need for the proclamation of "the Jewish Government." The US policy, the president concluded, was to back up a UN trusteeship by all possible means, but that did not necessarily mean sending American troops to Palestine.[2]

One hour later, Marshall publicly reiterated State's search for peace in Palestine through a trusteeship, but avoided discussion on the military force needed for its implementation. He tried to persuade Jewish Agency representatives Moshe Shertok (later Sharett) and Eliyahu

5. A Truce and Trusteeship for Palestine

Epstein (later Elath) of State's sincere designs, but they thought the truce would not solve "anything basic," and displayed considerable doubt that the trusteeship would help the situation. Responding to what he considered Russian delegate Andrei Gromyko's "irresponsible" charge at the Council on March 30 that Austin's statements were preparing the ground to "bury" the partition plan which the USSR continued to support, Undersecretary of State Robert A. Lovett felt it "most desirable" to get the maximum number of Council votes possible and obtain the United Kingdom's support for the US proposal calling for a special GA session.

Shertok's impassioned plea to the Council on the afternoon of April 1 that it was not yet too late to implement the GA's partition recommendation, and that the US truce proposal gave the false impression that both sides were at fault while 7,500 armed Arabs had invaded Palestine and Arab states were voting appropriations to supply arms and men for the Palestine conflict, fell on deaf ears. In reply, Egypt's Mahmoud Bey Fawzi emphatically denied participation of the Arab states in the Palestine struggle, and declared that the Arabs would oppose any truce meant to keep the peace by armed force during the partition of the country.[3]

Pablo de Azcárate y Flores thought the American stance totally removed from the Palestine reality. Leading a six-man advance team of the UN Palestine Commission that had been created at the time of the November 1947 partition vote to transfer the present British administration to the new regimes at the end of the mandate, he quickly concluded that partition appeared "the most reasonable formula." The former Spanish Republic Ambassador to the Court of St. James and a longtime senior member of the League of Nations secretariat, this experienced diplomat had already written in mid-March to Ralph Bunche, primary advisor to the 1947 UN Special Committee to Palestine (UNSCOP) and now principal secretary to the Commission, that the Arabs could not "destroy or get rid" of the present Jewish population of 600,000; an Arab state containing the *yishuv* (Palestinian Jewish community) as a "minority" was "simply unworkable." Indeed, the boundaries between the "real war zones" of the two warring native peoples showed that partition was being carried out in fact and "making progress every day." The Jews, in particular, Azcárate added, were prepared to take over a great number of public services without any difficulty whatsoever. The

Commission's military expert on the advance team, Colonial Roscher Lund of Norway, concurred, even advising that Shertok suggest to the Security Council that the Scandinavian force of 10,000 men at present in Germany under British command should be utilized for the task of policing Jerusalem.[4]

Talk of trusteeship, Azcárate informed the Commission and Bunche that month, just when the two contenders in Palestine were already fighting and ready to engage in open war as soon as the mandate ended, sounded "at least unreal." Partition was an on-going fact, the Arabs and the Jews controlling their own respective zones while "killing and destroying each other." The only practical possibility of avoiding this war, in his opinion, would be for Washington and London to pressure the Arab states to accept partition and halt arms deliveries to their kin in Palestine, and to prevent all possible acts of aggression or provocation of the Jewish armed forces against the Arabs. Personal experiences in the Spanish Civil War dominating his whole thinking, Azcárate told Jewish Agency liaison Walter Eytan, he was "desperately eager" to save Palestine from the suffering which Spain had undergone a decade earlier. An international administrative nucleus in Jerusalem, he thought, could be "a sort of common platform" for eventually covering parts, or even all, of the country.[5]

This turn of events drove Lie into a sense of hopelessness. He had already told Austin that the American delegation's insistence that partition had to be implemented by peaceful means was impossible, and if it were not enforced, "the UN would go downhill rapidly to nothing." Stunned at the US reversal with Austin's speech of March 19, he had reminded the Council at the time that UNSCOP had discussed the question of trusteeship for Palestine and dropped the idea once concluding that both Arabs and Jews would oppose it, thus requiring larger UN forces to enforce a settlement. Skeptical at Austin's assurance, in response to his question that day, that the Americans were "of course" ready to back up any UN decision, and now witness to scheduling a GA special session (thus suspending the Palestine Commission's efforts to implement partition), he sought—unsuccessfully—to persuade Austin that they both should resign in protest; Gromyko expressed to Lie his hope and that of his government that the dramatic step would not be taken. Like Azcárate and Lund, Lie personally believed that no truce would be achieved in Palestine, but that increased fighting would again erupt there.

The secretary general's pessimism was conveyed by Byron Price, his administrative assistant, to Marshall on April 3. Both Security Council officials felt strongly that Washington's activities concerning the Palestine question were "seriously threatening" the life of the United Nations. Three days later, Shertok cabled Agency Executive colleague Goldie Myerson (later Golda Meir) in Jerusalem about Lie's impressions of the situation within the meetings of the Nine-Power Council: "confusion, absence of leadership."[6]

Shertok, leading the Jewish Agency's case at the United Nations, could not evade great pressure at this point. As a first response on April 1, he took a seat at the Council gathering to declare that, counter to its resolution to have all political and military activities suspended during the truce by both parties to the dispute and to set up a trusteeship, the Jews of Palestine would not relinquish creating a state: "We have passed, in fact, the threshold of statehood. We refuse to be thrown back." Nor would they halt obtaining necessary weapons for their defense against open Arab aggression, he averred. Yet the same day, he received a letter from Alfonso López, the current Council president, who cited resolution 43 requesting that Shertok make representatives available to the Council as soon as possible towards arranging a truce in Palestine. Five months earlier, López, Colombia's former delegate for the GA vote on partition, had pressed Bogotá for a "no" and received permission to "abstain." Contacted on November 28, 1947, by the British and some Arab leaders, he had proposed postponing a final decision for a couple of months; US head delegate Herschel V. Johnson had to nudge Austin to vote "no" to this sudden move. On the decisive morning of November 29, López had tried again to advance the Arab agenda with the support of the Chilean delegate, but the latter changed his mind and refrained from doing so.

More recently, on February 24, 1948, López had offered a resolution to the Council for appointing a committee of its members to see if an agreement between the Jewish Agency and the Arab Higher Committee (AHC) could be reached, as well as to consider a GA special session for the purpose of "reconsidering" the Assembly's partition resolution "as a whole or in part." He also recommended that the United Kingdom postpone its termination of the mandate to July 15, 1948, and, accordingly, its arrangements for the evacuation of its troops from Palestine. This had forced Austin that same day to introduce an initial US draft resolution at the earliest moment which hinted at the American delegation's imminent reversal, reaffirming as it did support for Resolution 181 (II), but also asking the Council's five permanent members to look "at once" into the question of possible threats to peace arising out of the Palestine question, and to call on all governments to take all possible action to prevent or reduce "the disorders" now occurring there. López's consistent bias did not augur well for his impartial chairing of the Council's new talks on a truce for Palestine.[7]

The UN Palestine Commission resolved to continue its work, including the selection of Provisional Councils of Government. For Panama member Eduardo Morgan, no difficulty existed regarding the creation of such a council in the Jewish state, and he thought that the Security Council should take action against "the aggressor" Arab groups resorting to force against the UN resolution. Azcárate recommended to Bunche on April 1 that a truce, beginning with Jerusalem, be sought between the Jewish Agency and the Arab League, not the AHC; that the present administrative structure of Palestine in which *de facto* partition had been to a considerable extent carried out be respected and maintained; and that Jewish immigration be limited during the truce negotiations to the Jews interned by His Majesty's Government (HMG) in Cyprus. The Commission's legal expert on the advance team, Constantin A. Stavropoulos, thought that trusteeship was an "entirely unreal solution," telling Eytan that it was being put forward simply to gain time, because America "had got itself so tied up in knots" on the Palestine question and simply did not know what to do next. He regarded partition and the "virtual independence" of the Jews in Palestine as "unalterable facts," and thought that the *yishuv* would be well advised to increase its manpower and economic strength within the framework of trusteeship as long as it lasts, "as in the end the issue was sure to be settled by fighting." Palestine is in a "state of chaos," the Commission announced, with only a two weeks' wheat supply on hand on May 15.[8]

Responding to Shertok's request for an official reply to López's letter of April 1 about representation on the truce talks, three days later the Jewish Agency executive in Jerusalem welcomed the Council's efforts to produce a cessation of hostilities in Palestine and to prevent a continuation of bloodshed in the future. Noting that the *yishuv* had to defend itself against the Arabs' launching a series of attacks ever since the GA partition vote, it charged the mandatory for having failed to preserve law and order. HMG had not stemmed the invasion of Palestine by organized guerilla bands from neighboring Arab countries, had continued providing weapons to the Arab states, and had "suffered these foreign invaders" to establish themselves in military camps in Palestine, from where they disrupted communications in various parts of the country and besieged the Old City of Jerusalem.

The Agency, this April 4 document went on, would gladly agree to a military truce which would put an end to all acts of violence, and restore unhindered movement on all roads and highways, as well as free access to the Holy Places. All foreign troops and guerillas would have to be withdrawn, and all units of the British-trained Arab Legion of Transjordan removed from Palestine, preventing as well such incursions in the future. An international commission must supervise execution of the truce, the Agency not able to rely upon the British authorities in this respect. Finally, a military truce could not impede Jewish immigration, or affect preparations now in progress to assure essential public services and for "the establishment of an autonomous government in the area of the Jewish State immediately after the termination of the Mandate on May 15."[9]

The same day, even as 50,000 US veterans of all faiths swung down New York City's Fifth Ave. to the cheers of some 250,000 spectators in protest against the US reversal of policy on Palestine, Shertok wired Myerson and David Ben-Gurion, chairman of the Jewish Agency executive, that the meeting on April 6 of the Actions Committee (HaVa'ad HaPo'el HaTsiyoni) should stick to the joint declaration against trusteeship and do the utmost to defeat it at the special session, even if the chances would be "extremely uncertain." To some young members of the Agency's political department who sharply criticized the *yishuv* leadership's military response, particularly in view of Jerusalem's dire position "verging on catastrophic," and called for pulling out of some isolated Jewish settlements slated to be in the Arab state, Shertok replied that the *yishuv* had a "deep-rooted aversion" to abandoning any position "to very last." As regards a truce for Jerusalem and having women and children leave the Old City, the US line merging Jerusalem with the "general problem" delayed possible action. He was "fully alive" to the necessity for a respite, but that depended also on the "other party." He doubted the Arabs' readiness to compromise after political advantage would be gained. It was very important, Shertok advised Eytan on

April 5, that the Palestine Commission immediately issue a report summarizing Azcárate's experience. This should emphasize that partition "in fact exists"; that it could have been implemented in accordance with Resolution 181 (II) had the British remained "genuinely neutral and not in fact obstructing"; and that the *yishuv* was ripe for independence and determined to establish the Jewish State.[10]

The British persisted in their official stand that HMG would continue to adhere to its neutral attitude, much to the disappointment of Marshall and his department. Harold Beeley, main advisor on Palestine to Foreign Secretary Ernest Bevin, had advised Colonial Secretary Arthur Creech Jones at the end of March that little if any hope existed as to a temporary trusteeship, although a truce and suspending the Palestine Commission's work were steps in the right direction, leading to a GA special session. Bevin and his colleagues, reported the High Commissioner for Canada to his superior, were "really obsessed" with the special tasks and responsibilities that concurrence in any new compromise might thrust upon them beyond May 15. "HMG's policy is now simply to get out of Palestine as quickly as possible without regard to the consequences," Alan Cunningham, the country's last High Commissioner, wrote despairingly to Creech Jones on March 25. Ben-Gurion told Cunningham of his eagerness "to have an agreement that everybody in Jerusalem should go freely about their business," but the AHC's Hussein Khalidi stated emphatically that the Arabs would gain nothing from a truce. "The Jews are the only ones to welcome it," emphatically stated this highest ranking AHC executive member in Jerusalem, because they would like to see [the] 100,000 Jews in the Sacred City in perfect security so that the Hagana gangs would not have to worry about them."[11]

Hoping to obtain a cease-fire considering that "many innocent lives have been lost and much that has been achieved in the progress of many years has been destroyed," Cunningham appealed in a radio broadcast on the evening of April 3 to the two "contending parties" to arrive at some arrangement to bring a halt to bloodshed. Pointing out that the British were due to remain in the country only "for a short time longer," he offered his services to the leaders of both sides to negotiate an armistice. Unable to leave Jerusalem for the Agency executive's meeting in Tel-Aviv, Yitshak Ben-Zvi, head of the *Va'ad HaLeumi* (National Council), urged the executive to accept the High Commissioner's plea in order to save Jerusalem, "without doubt our weak point." The city had been cut off from supplies for ten days, his fearful, somber letter noted, with the Jewish Quarter in the Old City under siege for the past four months and the southern and northern outskirts holding out with difficulty. Demoralization was spreading among considerable sections of the Jewish population. The Arabs did not want a cease-fire, Ben-Zvi conceded, but the British, for humanitarian, political, and prestige reasons, were in favor. While adhering to the executive's formal reply of April 4 to López's request, he closed, a cease-fire was essential to save the Jews of Jerusalem from "annihilation and destruction" pending the UN's political decision.[12]

The Agency should devote all its energies to securing a trusteeship that would be "as compatible as possible" with the ultimate creation of a Jewish State, Azcárate advised Eytan on April 5. Speaking as a friend, he warned that, as the situation in 1936 Spain had shown, "non-intervention" would occur if the Jews resisted trusteeship, and they could not afford to fight both the Arabs and contend with non-intervention by the Western Powers. In the course of the imminent GA special session debate, the Zionists' putting forward helpful proposals for Palestine's future would gain the sympathy and support of most of the delegations. Rather than continuing to harp on their past grievances and indulging in recriminations against the British—although "fully understandable"—which would do no good in the Assembly or anywhere else, they should engage in constructive political work at the UN headquarters in Lake Success. Later on, within the framework of that trusteeship, they should use every opportunity to build up their strength, the more effectively done the sooner they would obtain a Jewish State. Azcárate assured Eytan that he would be proud to play some part in the future administration of affairs in Palestine.[13]

A few hours later, the US delegation submitted its fifteen-point formulation of General Principles regarding a temporary trusteeship for Palestine. Austin invited the Council members (excepting the USSR and Ukraine) to his office, where he presented the plan while announcing that it did not commit the United States at this stage. Perhaps most contentious were the points that the agreement would be of "indefinite" duration subject to "prompt termination" whenever the Arab and Jewish communities agreed upon the country's future government, and that a Governor-General would be given the authority to call upon other governments when necessary towards the maintenance of security in Palestine. Most of the Council members present initially criticized the plan's vagueness, France's Alexandre Parodi especially critical that all questions of substance, such as immigration, were evaded, and that the crucial question of enforcement had been shirked. While HMG's V. G. Lawford remained non-committal, Columbia's Gonzales Fernandez stressed the shortness of time, and urged a truce and prolongation of the mandate. Syria's Faris El-Khouri, declaring that the Arab States were "parties directly concerned," assumed that the Arabs and Jews would fight it out, in due course "get tired," and compromise. China's Tingfu Tsiang argued that unilateral termination of the Mandate was unlawful. Canada's permanent delegate, A. G. L. McNaughton, wrote to Secretary of State for External Affairs Lester B. Pearson (who agreed) that a trusteeship agreement could not even be concluded without United Kingdom's concurrence.[14]

A worried Lawford, pressed at the April 5 meeting to take a stand on the trusteeship proposal, given Article 79 of the UN Charter requiring the mandatory's consent if the GA approved that measure, asked the Foreign Office for clarification. Even his friend Parodi had told him privately after the meeting that he had with difficulty restrained himself from pointing out that Lawford's attitude really rendered the whole discussion "futile." Bevin replied two days later, ordering Cadogan first to repeat his earlier statement to the Security Council that HMG would relinquish all rights as mandatory on May 15. He should then say that if the GA approved a trusteeship before that date, the British would *not* make use of the "veto" which their position as mandatory power might be held to confer on them. Cadogan, at the same time, had to make it absolutely clear to the Council that this statement did not commit London in any way to take part in the administration or enforcement of a trusteeship or of any other settlement.[15]

The US delegation sought a truce, declared Dean Rusk to the UN Division of Public Liaison on April 5, because the Arabs were better armed, and the Jews would "undoubtedly be slaughtered" in the event of large-scale fighting. In the forefront of the American delegation's effort and aided by his deputy, Robert McClintock, Rusk, State's director of the Office of United Nations Affairs, had already recommended in a "top secret" memorandum to State on February 3 that the United States should support any measures "falling short of the use of armed force" by the Security Council to restrain external aggression against Palestine from the contiguous Arab states. Yet, he continued at the time, if partition could not be implemented without force, the US should then support calling a GA special session to reconsider the entire problem, with the probable outcome that a UN trusteeship would be proposed and "terminable" when the Jewish and Arab communities in Palestine could agree on a *modus vivendi* for a unitary federal state or for partition. Immediately following Austin's speech of March 19, Rusk had made a strong appeal to Britain's UN adviser, Gladwyn Jebb, for HMG's support, noting that it would at least keep the Russians out of Palestine except to the extent that the USSR would participate in the Palestine trust if they chose to join the Trusteeship Council. He hoped that if London did back the American scheme, the British might reconsider their proposed dates for evacuation.[16]

Few Security Council delegates were more censorious of the US plan than Parodi. France's first ambassador to the United Nations openly expressed to the Agency's Aubrey (later Abba) Eban his government's resentment at being called to follow the Americans "blindly into a cul-de-sac." Having voted for partition the past November on the false assumption that American support would be steadfast, France could not again commit her vote to the United States if there were no certainty of "an equitable and stable settlement." Given the lack, among other matters, in the General Principles of clear enforcement, which had "wrecked" the partition solution, he could not envisage his superiors in Paris voting for the proposal in its present form. Perhaps the Americans would in three months "traverse the whole journey" which HMG had accomplished in the period culminating in the 1939 White Paper, in which case they would then commit themselves to a "frankly" pro-Arab resolution; France would then "disengage herself," not prepared to be a party to the "violent suppression" of Jewish rights which the GA had so recently approved.

While relaxing nothing of its "vigilant preparation," Parodi advised Eban that the Jewish Agency should seek to work for improved provisions in the trusteeship agreement. A two-thirds Assembly vote might ensue if there were no other plan available for adoption. He indicated a readiness to work for an agreement on immigration, within the terms of the trusteeship proposal, based on the entry of 200,000 Jews in three years. He agreed with the Agency's point that the constitutional provisions of the American plan, going against everything that experience and judgment had proved, were based on the unitary majority proposal (favoring the current Arab population). If Jewish immigration were to be absorbed, he agreed with Shertok's exposition of the Agency's need to control economic policy. In Eban's view, Parodi favored a trusteeship superimposed upon a territorial partition within which Jews and Arabs exercised fairly complete autonomy, this territorial delimitation following the lines of the Assembly's November plan. The Frenchman's strong reservations about the present proposal, Eban advised his colleagues, coupled with Soviet opposition and British detachment, would seriously undermine the "great-power basis" of US policy. Furthermore, the task of enforcement would imply a unilateral responsibility, which might not be "palatable" to American public opinion.[17]

Loy Henderson, chief of State's Near Eastern division, did not sit idly by awaiting the Council members' official response to the American truce/trusteeship proposals. He suggested to Lovett that "moderates and temperate" individuals like Judah Magnes, Hebrew University president and binationalist advocate, and Arab League secretary general Azzam Pasha be invited to the United States as soon as possible to possibly break "the present log jam" in the UN. The "extreme public positions" taken by the Jewish Agency and the Arab Higher Committee regarding sovereignty, Henderson argued, made it increasingly difficult for them to modify their positions sufficiently for arranging a UN truce and interim governmental machinery after May 15. (At the same moment, the Agency's Vivian [Chaim] Herzog heard from military correspondent George Fielding Eliot that Marshall was loathe to regard the American Zionist leaders as representatives of the *yishuv*, while Senator Arthur Vandenberg [R, Michigan] told *Detroit Jewish News* publisher Philip Slomovitz in deepest confidence that the Secretary of State was prepared to resign because of their pressure unless Truman yielded to him.) Lovett, having requested Bevin and French Foreign Secretary Georges Bidault on April 9 to join in sponsoring the American proposal, approved Henderson's suggestion the next day, and telegrams to that effect were dispatched to Jerusalem and Cairo.[18]

While Azcárate thought Ben-Gurion's March 21 public assertion against a trusteeship of any duration a "most unwise and imprudent statement," the Arab attitude towards trusteeship did not offer much solace either. In a talk with Azcárate, the Egyptian Consul favored a maximum period of two or three years, but with the 30,000 imprisoned Jewish "illegal" immigrants in Cyprus, transported there by the British Navy's halting their overcrowded vessels which sought to reach Palestine's shores, to be absorbed within the Arab states. Husseini notified the Security Council on the 9th that the Arabs would not negotiate any truce with the Jewish Agency because the AHC did not consider the Agency as representing Palestine's Jews. AHC chairman Haj Amin, the former Grand Mufti of Palestine who had spearheaded the Arab assaults against the *yishuv* since April 1920, violently rejected any truce outright. The struggle in Palestine would continue until the Arabs realized their national objective, he told a Cairo newspaper, a point he repeated at the Arab League meeting of April 10. Writing to the three foreign consuls in Jerusalem, Haj Amin added that all of Palestine was a holy place to the Arabs, not just Jerusalem alone, to be protected against the intruder. Prime Minister Mahmoud El Nokrashy Pasha advised US Ambassador Pinkney Tuck in Cairo that the definite duration of the trusteeship had to be stipulated together with guarantees against an increase in Jewish armaments, numbers, and land purchases in Palestine, accompanied by an assurance that trusteeship would not jeopardize Arab "national aspirations" towards final, complete independence as a "united Arab nation."

The Arab League, Azzam Pasha would soon declare to Tuck, did not support the American plan of temporary trusteeship, which it considered would serve only "to create a new regime and bring about another phase of trouble between Arabs and Jews." The League favored, as a practical matter, a continuance of the British Mandate, since HMG military forces aided by the UN's "moral and material backing" could lead to the final disarmament and creation of "a new Palestine state." Azzam added to British Ambassador Ronald Campbell that Jewish immigration had to cease in the meantime, and if civil war broke out in Palestine the Arabs were confident of success, although it might take years, owing to their "inexhaustible" manpower reserves.[19]

Shertok, quickly pointing out to the Canadian delegation and others that the temporary trusteeship plan would "perpetuate outside rule," was encouraged by the "glaringly negative character" of the American scheme. In his opinion, it facilitated mobilizing opposition and the United States' own possible retreat in the event of failure. Gromyko informed Shertok that his group would vote against trusteeship, and the Agency delegation hoped that several Latin American representatives would do likewise. While informing Palestine Commission chairman Karel Lisicky of Czechoslovakia about the grave food situation in Jerusalem, given the mandatory government's utter failure to maintain law and order on the highways, Shertok took comfort from a growing conviction in UN circles that the American trusteeship proposals would not win the necessary two-thirds majority. Still, as reported to him by Agency political secretary Leo Kohn on April 7, all efforts at a truce in Jerusalem had failed so far owing to the "adamant attitude" of Haj Amin, who opposed any Jewish state in Palestine.[20]

Azcárate's reservations about the fifteen points' General Principles, which he transmitted to Bunche that day, began with its call for a cabinet and a democratically elected legislature, which he considered unreal, given the "very wrong and dangerous" impression that elections could be held at once. In addition, "locally recruited police and volunteer forces" would be insufficient from the first moment of the truce; an international police force of volunteers was "indispensable" at the very start. Immigration and land purchases should not be negotiated in consultation with the two warring communities, but left in the Governor-General's hands. Arrangements to provide the trusteeship with a solid and stable financial basis had to be made at once. The trusteeship's "indefinite duration," a formula difficult to be accepted by either side, should be changed to one year. The Jews might conclude that all possible partition was eliminated by the plan, Shertok observed, while that suggestion contradicted point one's assertion that a temporary trusteeship would not prejudice the "rights, claims, or position of the parties concerned" or the character of the eventual political settlement.[21]

Privately, while convinced, as he had written to Bunche on more than one occasion, that the fact of partition was becoming "plainer every day," Azcárate sadly told Eytan that he saw no hope nor even advisability of resisting the new US proposals; if these were American policy, they could not be resisted. Almost with tears in his eyes, he made a very moving plea to urge the Zionist leaders to face this issue squarely. Their policy of uncompromisingly opposing any trusteeship, whether temporary or permanent, would lead them "straight to disaster." Their "purely destructive criticism," even if every word were true, would avail them "nothing." He advised Eytan to press his superiors to accept a limited trusteeship, no more than for one or two years, and during that time gather all their strength in order to be ready for "the final struggle"—political or military—when it came. Trusteeship would allow them "to fight another day." He and Lund, whom Eytan described as "behaving like real bricks," shared these views.[22]

AHC executive member Jamal Husseini, refusing on the afternoon of April 7 to sit down at the same table with Shertok when López convened the first meeting to discuss a truce, took an unequivocal stand. The UN Charter required the application of "strictly democratic principles" in Palestine, and *all* illegal Jewish immigrants (those who entered without the permission of the existing authority) and those militant, right-wing "elements" in Palestine which the Jewish Agency admitted were beyond its control should be expelled from the country. If these immigrants were to leave, then the Arabs could "insure" that the non-Palestinian Arabs who entered Palestine "illicitly" would also leave. Otherwise, Husseini emphasized, not as a threat but "merely a fact," the outside Arab incursions would continue. Article 22 of the Covenant of the League of Nations required the mandatory to establish as quickly as possible a local government to represent the people and to hand over power to this government, as HMG had done in the case of Transjordan. The British had no right to leave a vacuum on their departure, and the Arabs would not ask them to stay one day later than May 16. They would "defend their country with their blood," but a definite solution must be found. "The Arabs would cooperate," Husseini closed, "but only on a lasting basis."[23]

Called in an hour later, Shertok noted to López that he had already indicated to the Security Council and to Lie the Jewish Agency's attitude regarding the truce proposals. The *yishuv* leadership was prepared for an unconditional truce immediately provided that the current 7,500 foreign Arab troops and the 3,000 men of the Arab Legion leave Palestine forthwith, with all such future incursions to cease under the supervision of an international body. Palestine's Jews were forced to defend themselves; there was "a false equality" by putting on an equal footing armed Arab incursion with so-called illegal Jewish immigration. Indeed, the term "illegal immigration" with regard to the Arabs' opposition was irrelevant because the Arabs "do not recognize the right of the Jews to any form of immigration." Three things had to be borne in mind, Shertok emphasized: the international guaranteed right of the Jews to immigration into Palestine; over the past sixty years they had come to live there; and they continue to come unarmed. "We will not accept of our free will any imposed settlement," he wished to make it clear, and "we stand on the compromise settlement of November 29." To López's comment that the Jews should enter into these negotiations with an "open mind," Shertok responded that they could not accept a truce which would serve as "a preparatory stage" for further Arab aggression, and it should not be assumed that peace in Palestine would be achieved by a "considerable reduction" of Jewish rights and interests.[24]

With Husseini's objection to Jewish sovereignty and Shertok's insistence that the GA resolution of November 29 was (as he summarized the meeting to Ben-Gurion and Myerson) "our irreducible minimum," the first meetings had ended inconclusively—as would the second. Husseini asserted to López the next afternoon that the Arabs wanted a declaration that the Palestine problem would be solved according to the strict principles of democracy and self-determination in accordance with the UN Charter. Jewish immigration, a breach of faith by the British and counter to the 1939 White Paper, had been forced upon the Arabs, and if it continued after May 15 "it would be impossible to restrain" the Arab people from counteraction without the use of armed force. Jewish immigration from Cyprus and the countries of Eastern Europe after the mandate ended would alone contribute largely to the renewal of fighting. Nor was López's suggestion for limiting Jewish immigration during the truce reasonable: all immigration should cease. There was a "most acute" housing and food shortage in Palestine, which had two hundred inhabitants to the square mile and half of this area could not be cultivated, while there was a very great increase of population. As their conversation drew to a close after two hours, López expressed his regret that there had not been as much progress as he had expected. To reporters Husseini declared that he had refused to consult with any Jewish Agency representative as the AHC had never recognized the Agency "and never will."[25]

That evening, Shertok remarked to López that the longer a truce lasted the better, but it was not for the Agency to express any wish as to the best approach since the Jews had not started the fighting. Arab bands had to be removed and incursions had to stop. As for the cessation of "political activity" mentioned in the Council's first resolution of April 1, which López took to mean keeping "in abeyance" preparations to implement the partition plan pending a GA decision, Shertok quickly noted that "the Agency was already the government," and it would be "insane" not to continue making preparations for carrying out Resolution 181 (II), which entailed the setting up of an authority. These developments showed "the natural logic" of the partition plan. Both Lie and Azcárate had declared that partition already existed.

A truce for Jerusalem might be possible, Shertok went on, including safety of food and water: a large Iraqi military unit was camped on that city's water supply and the mandatory had not intervened. The Jews would be ready for cooperation with the Arabs after May 15 as regards food supply and other common services, such as post and railway, for the whole of Palestine. In the absence of a mandatory government or any alternative, it was "a matter of self-preservation" for the Jews to control the area in which they were vitally interested. On November 29, 1947, the General Assembly had conferred certain rights on the Jews, "and they refused to renounce these rights or to see them impaired." Immigration was "the crux of the matter," Shertok noted, and there was no possibility of linking it to the truce: the Jews would not yield under threat of violence. They had refused to halt it during the Arab Revolt of 1936–1939, and they would refuse now.[26]

A second private meeting in Austin's office, held that same day again in the absence of Gromyko, yielded little consensus. No one had done "any work" on a possible trusteeship. Cadogan conveyed the Foreign Office's cable of that date regarding a "veto" if a GA trusteeship were approved before May 15, and his colleague Trafford Smith indicated that the local Palestine police forces could not maintain law and order in mixed Arab-Jewish areas. El-Khouri declared that the Arabs would honor a truce so long as "activities for partition are not continued." Austin opined that a unanimous Council resolution endorsing the General Principles before May 15 would be "a great uplift to the world," but Parodi again noted the vagueness regarding implementation and immigration. Only El-Khouri made specific comments on all of the fifteen points, which he said should have been put forward the previous November, and again emphasized that "all States directly concerned" had to agree to the terms of the Trusteeship Agreement. After the meeting, Smith told Canada's Michael Ignatieff that he agreed with Parodi's criticisms: progress would likely not be made unless the United States made a more definite commitment as to outside forces, immigration, and guarantees for minorities. The Americans, this Colonial Office's representative thought, were trying to leave the United Kingdom with the major commitment for Palestine, and avoid as far as possible "assuming any commitment itself except in the most generalized form."[27]

Shertok's meeting with Lovett and Rusk on April 9 and another with Rusk the same day did not shake his resolve. He emphasized the Agency's uncompromising opposition to trusteeship, and that any truce should focus on military, not political, matters. The Agency might make a declaration not to bring in armed male immigrants, but would continue with setting up a central administration to function as of May 16 in the entire area assigned the Jewish State by the GA's November 1947 resolution. It would oppose an indefinite trusteeship; a truce for a fixed period would be easier, but not to prejudice Jewish rights. As to Lovett's wish to "avoid anarchy" on May 15 and have "a breathing spell," Shertok asserted that State exaggerated Arab strength, and if the United States "took care" of Jerusalem "we would hold our own," particularly if the Hagana was helped with weapons. Obtaining a two-thirds vote for trusteeship was "doubtful," Shertok declared, and "improbable" if the US delegation did not exert itself to achieve that end. An international police force for Jerusalem on behalf of "the world and civilization" did not involve difficulties that could arise for policing the entire country. Finally, the Agency's ability to control Jewish underground dissidents and enforce truce discipline depended on the conviction that a truce did not affect Jewish statehood. "Conversations inconclusive," he wired Ben-Gurion.[28]

Rusk's stand during his second talk with Shertok carried ominous overtones. The United States was a civilized government and would have to take action, he declared. Wanting to halt the probability of intensified bloodshed in Palestine, the State Department had decided that "they must tide the situation over in some way, come what may." It stood by the public statements of Truman and Marshall on March 25, wishing above all to prevent "a major conflagration." The Jews might be able to hold out in the beginning, but "in the long run" would be "overpowered." All rights would be preserved under a trusteeship, but he finally admitted that State wanted the truce to go on during the trusteeship, "so that in the nature of things it amounted to the same." Rusk still believed that the Arabs might accept a continuance of immigration. As for Jerusalem, he warned that the Arabs would fight if the

Jews did something for that city which was strictly in accordance with the GA's November recommendation. State would therefore have to produce a different solution, which might include, for example, access to a port, possibly Haifa. Shertok's understanding of this comment was confined to his summary of their meeting: "Such a provision would cut the Jewish State in two."[29]

Charles Fahy, State's former Legal Counselor and now on retainer for the Jewish Agency executive's American Section, found Rusk staunchly holding to his views. According to his report to section chairman Abba Hillel Silver of his meeting with Rusk the same day, Fahy heard the department's director of UN Affairs say directly that a truce in fighting was impossible without a suspension "for the time being" of the creation of the Jewish State. Accompanying a truce might be joint Jewish and Arab commissions or boards of some sort, but failure to arrange a truce "gravely endangers" the Jewish population of Palestine. Moreover, the resulting bloodshed would set in motion "a chain of events," the end of which could not be foreseen in terms of world peace. This would create "a grave domestic and international problem" for the United States.

The Zionists, Rusk charged, were not in a position to argue (as Fahy did then) that the United States should not exert pressure to push through its present proposals, given the "influence exerted" by the Jewish Agency for the GA resolution of the previous November. The Assembly had approved the resolution, which was subsequently not given a chance to work, Fahy retorted. The current General Principles "certainly could not be said to be workable," he asserted, and the United States' position would be doubly weakened if after abandoning the November resolution it pressed through another which would be found to be unworkable. At this point, Rusk responded that he would like to review the situation, and emphasize the truce as the matter which must be pressed, not the proposals of trusteeship.[30]

On April 10, the Palestine Commission reported to the GA that it could not fulfill its assignment because of the "armed hostility of both Palestinian and non-Palestinian Arab elements, the lack of cooperation from the mandatory power, the disintegrating security situation in Palestine," and the Security Council's not furnishing it the necessary armed assistance. The previous day, Cadogan told Austin that HMG doubted whether there was any prospect of agreement based on the US trusteeship proposals, and he cited his superiors' estimate that five divisions together with several aircraft squadrons and a fairly large naval force would be needed to impose a trusteeship regime.

At the same time, López had informed the members convening again in Austin's office that his two meetings with Husseini and Shertok had produced no common ground, "illegal" Jewish immigration the heart of the problem. He suggested that, under these circumstances, the Security Council should appeal for a truce and ask the United Kingdom to keep the mandate for some time longer. Both sides, López thought, were "too worked up emotionally" to listen to reason, and he doubted that an Arab-Jewish agreement would be reached at the present time. The only specific suggestion made at the meeting was Austin's stressing that the truce should be on "a stand-still basis," including immigration, and that it should not be employed to impose any political statement, but only to institute peace and order, and to establish a temporary government in Palestine to take over from the mandatory.[31]

Gromyko, absent at the first two informal meetings in Austin's office, had received instructions on April 9 from Soviet Foreign Minister Vyacheslav Molotov to defend the partition resolution. He was to point out that the Security Council had not exhausted all the resources at its disposal to put this into practice, and to charge HMG with hampering the Commission's work in Palestine. As for the US trusteeship proposal, by repealing the November majority decision it would aggravate the Jewish-Arab struggle in Palestine and "intensify unrest" in the region, compromise the GA's position, and leave the country in a "semi-colonial position." Finally, trusteeship contradicted the principle of autonomy, and was marked by distrust of the local population to organize Palestine's administration independently on a democratic basis.

When Gromyko did attend the third private meeting at the US delegation's headquarters on April 12, at which the Palestine Commission's role was debated, he protested the discussion of a truce at such a venue, and wondered if this was done to have some delegations avoid embarrassment. López countered that he was fully within his rights to take advice from the other Council members in this manner. The same day, Australia's Herbert V. Evatt informed Austin of his country's continued support for partition, that recommendation's lack of success due less to fighting in Palestine and more to the "vacillation" that had taken place in the attitude of some of the powers most concerned and to the absence of "positive restraints" on the Arabs, which all UN members had the duty to exercise in carrying out the GA November resolution. New Zealand's Prime Minister, Peter Fraser, sent similar instructions to his minister in Washington and to the country's UN Department, hoping as well that the "great powers" would give partition their support.[32]

The mandatory administration, Cadogan admitted at López's next meeting on April 13 (to which Gromyko was not invited), had "disintegrated" to the point where it was not possible for the British further to delay their departure. Yet the Security Council, a frustrated Bunche informed Azcárate, had given the Palestine Commission no instructions or guidance to date, while the United States' fifteen-point plan was "general and often vague." Pressing for a truce and an international trusteeship, Azcárate continued to favor partition as the formula which "reduces to a minimum" the friction between Arabs and Jews. His cable along these lines to Lie and Bunche the next day ended thus: "Consider most unfair for Jews continue encouraging establishment state without providing appropriate international military assistance to defend it against Arab attack." Not surprisingly, the Commission's unanimous report to the GA, published on April 14, charged the mandatory with rejecting "any progressive transfer of authority," including refusing to let it arrive in Palestine earlier than May 1 and to organize Jewish and Arab militias in advance, as well as taking measures such as blocking Palestine sterling balances (thus limiting what Bunche considered the flow of essential imports to Palestine) without consulting the Commission.[33]

The Arabs had started attacking the Jews, the Jewish Agency executive stressed in replying to Cunningham's personal appeal for a cease-fire, and if they halted this the Agency would as well. It is understood, Kohn communicated to the High Commissioner, that a cease-fire implied freedom of movement on all roads in town and in country. Reiterating the Agency's demand to the mandatory government, he posited that as long as the British authorities were in the country, their duty was to prevent the incursion of armed bands from across the frontiers and to expel those which had entered. The very fact of the invasion of military personnel and of guerilla bands, as well as the import of arms and ammunition from across the frontiers was, in the *yishuv*'s view, an act of aggression and a danger to its security. If in the Security Council's current deliberations this expulsion and future prevention of incursion were not assured, the *yishuv* would reserve for itself "freedom of action to insure its security."[34]

Given the mounting violence in Palestine, a troubled Shertok began to search for some possible concessions on the Jewish Agency's part. If the executive in Jerusalem considered it advisable, he had wired Ben-Gurion on April 9, perhaps Shertok might "informally and without prejudice" probe the possibility of dropping the condition on the removal of existing outside Arab bands, and insist only on the prevention of future incursions. While maintaining so far both conditions "as absolute," he saw great advantage in securing a truce by this concession should it prove possible. Two days later, having received no response, he sent a second telegram to Ben-Gurion, expressing his view that truce negotiations should not be broken off. He strongly urged the executive to refrain from "demonstrative acts proclamations" pending May 15. All resolutions should be kept regarding the Agency's preparation in taking over internal matters, except for measures rendered imperative by the necessity to maintain essential services in the interim. He awaited an immediate reply.[35]

Weizmann resolved at this point to write to Truman in the hope of inducing the President to recognize the Jewish State, whose establishment the US Government was at that moment trying to prevent in the UN. He was fully aware that the Jewish Agency and the American Zionist Emergency Council under Silver's chairmanship were mounting an offensive against the trusteeship proposal, fully agreeing with the private warning of Uruguay's UN permanent representative, Enrique R. Fabregat, fervent partition champion at the UNSCOP deliberations and the Assembly vote, that any new victorious plan would ultimately mean that the *yishuv* would be "completely liquidated," and the Jews should therefore not yield "one inch" on partition's "irrevocability." Yet the seventy-four-year-old, ailing Zionist chief, having received Truman's earlier pledge in their March 18 meeting, wished to make his own appeal with a letter on April 9. The logic of partition, the private communication began, compelled him to go on record against the idea of trusteeship, "a leap into the unknown." Asking the British to carry on, as the State Department was rumored to be considering, he thought would be "the worst possibility of all."

Deciding to add a paragraph to Eban's first draft, Weizmann went on to confide his trembling to think of "the wave of violence and repression which would sweep Palestine" if rule continued under the British or indeed any foreign reign. Certain that Truman would not be a part to the "further disappointment of pathetic hopes" shared by the 100,000 Holocaust survivors still present in the Displaced Persons camps in Europe, he declared that the choice for the Jewish people was "between statehood and extermination." "History and providence have placed this issue in your hands," Weizmann concluded, "and I am confident that you will yet decide it in the spirit of the moral law." He sent a copy to Marshall, expressing regret that the two could not meet, as Weizmann had wished to give him information that would have "been of use and prevented difficulties."[36]

Truman chose not to answer the letter. (Lovett, sent a copy by Weizmann, would acknowledge it after two weeks with the expressed hope that the UN's action would lead to the "restoration and peaceful conditions" in Palestine and to agreement between Arabs and Jews resident there "on their future government.") The President and Marshall had recently received from James V. Forrestal, the country's first Secretary of Defense as of September 1947, the estimate of the Joint Chiefs of Staff, who thought that a complete effective truce was impossible because of the "extremists" on both sides; that 100,000 troops, aside from destroyers and considerable air support, would be needed to impose and supervise trusteeship; and that even if the US provided 46,800 of these soldiers, it would necessitate at least partial mobilization, over-extend the army, require a supplementary budget, and could not be fully deployed prior to May 15. In addition, the Standard Oil Company of New Jersey's board directors had just released a public statement (which Rusk deputy McClintock placed in State's "Palestine File") about the vital necessity of Middle Eastern oil for Western Hemisphere oil supplies and the European Recovery Program. The latter, more popularly known as the Marshall Plan, had just begun with the intention to improve prosperity on the Continent and prevent the spread of Communism on that soil.[37]

On the other hand, sharp rising domestic criticism was heard from such as the independently minded Senator Wayne Morse (R, Oregon), who warned that reversals by the United States and others would prevent the UN from surviving as an instrumentality for maintaining peace, a charge echoed in young Boston Congressman John F. Kennedy's public castigation of the trusteeship plan as "one of the most unfortunate reversals in American policy" and in his demand to lift the US arms embargo against shipments to the Middle East, instituted on

November 14 last, so that the Jewish people in Palestine could "defend themselves and carve out their partition." Truman also had to contend with a movement within the Democratic Party to champion Dwight D. Eisenhower's candidacy for the presidential election come November. On April 9, he declared at his weekly press conference that he had no comment to make about Palestine other than that it was pending before the UN, or whether the Administration was considering any modification of the arms embargo. McClintock, hearing that the lack of detail in State's General Principles "considerably disturbed" informed Austin that Lovett had personally signed off on the truce proposal, and that it had been cleared by the White House. At the same time, Truman quietly gave permission to Eddie Jacobson, his former haberdashery store partner, to tell Weizmann that the President stood by his earlier promises to the Zionist leader.[38]

When Austin, joined by American UN delegation colleagues John C. Ross and Philip Jessup, visited Weizmann's sick-bed at New York City's Waldorf Astoria Hotel to say how dangerous it would be for peace if the Jews of Palestine proclaimed a state on May 15, they received a sharp rejoinder. Palestinian Jewry "would be off its head if it postponed statehood for anything as foolish as the American trusteeship proposal," Weizmann shot back. Further, he considered the *yishuv*'s intention to proclaim statehood as soon as the Mandate ended "thoroughly justified and eminently realistic," a conviction which he repeated when Parodi conveyed to him the "veiled threat" that the United States would send cruisers to the Mediterranean in order to enforce the arms blockade. Quoting a remark of Baron Edouard de Rothschild, he told Trafford Smith that "*Les Americains sont les gens qui vous lâchent*," and expressed amazement that they had not produced a single great man since President Woodrow Wilson. When Truman adviser Rosenman, also a member of the small committee planning the President's re-election campaign, approached him with an offer to help on condition of strict secrecy, Weizmann readily agreed. Various short memoranda were given him to brief this "newcomer" for action at the appropriate moment.[39]

While what Azcárate had characterized to Bunche as the "minor war" between Arab and Jew in Palestine rapidly escalated, particularly with the Hagana's radical turn to offensive operations as of April 1 aided by a first secret delivery of Czech weapons, Eban delivered to Ross on April 12, as well as to Lie and Azcárate, the Jewish Agency's observations (actually his authorship) on the General Principles. First, the Agency found it necessary to discuss the general applicability of trusteeship to Palestine. As to the former, the US proposal prejudiced Jewish rights, while any plan would not meet with the Arabs' acceptance "until they are confronted with the Jews as a permanent and equal factor with which they have to come to terms. The Jews will accept no position of subjection to the Arabs and will continually press on towards independence."

Eban then turned to criticize the specific American proposal. The unique Statute of Jerusalem was not bound in any way by the trusteeship provisions of the UN Charter, and so provided no precedent or justification for establishing permanent foreign rule over the country as a whole. The provision for a "democratically elected legislature," the gravest feature of the entire proposal, ignored "the dual character" of Palestine's national composition, two separate nations which "do not hold the ends of life in common or agree on the central purposes of the state." There was no end in sight of trusteeship's enforcement, while the provisions envisaged for immigration and land purchase were not specified, thus ignoring the "inseparable connection" between the concepts of Jewish statehood and Jewish immigration.

As to the applicability of trusteeship to Palestine, Eban's lengthy memo observed, both peoples had "an urgent desire for national freedom," a fact acknowledged by the 1937 Peel Commission, UNSCOP, and throughout the General Assembly's second regular session. The movement to set aside Resolution 181 (II) had already weakened the GA's moral authority, and revealed the Security Council as a body unable either to secure UN Charter observance or to resist aggression. The Palestine Mandate, *sui generis*, recognized world Jewry's rights in that country, rights derived from the Mandate, preserved under Article 80 of the Charter, and confirmed by the GA partition vote, which were to be continued in force until such time as that Mandate was replaced by a new agreement. British policy in the Near East, firmly wedded to the alliance with the Arab League, had been "sharply directed" against those fundamental Jewish interests which the Assembly had recently approved and recognized Palestinian Jewry "as a nation fit for imminent independence."

Henceforth, the memo continued, the "violent reversal" of the historic vote on November 29, 1947, would have the Jews think of no other "political idiom but that of national sovereignty." In the *yishuv*'s politics, economy, defense, and other major spheres in the daily routine of life, "an existing tendency of Jewish autonomy" existed and would continue to flourish. (Its Provisional Government would be established on April 13.) While Palestine was moving forward "inexorably" towards partition in a pattern of growing decentralization across the country, the US proposal "comes on the scene in an attempt to galvanize a dying mandate into life or to build a new trusteeship on the wreckage of the old." Because the very concept of trusteeship is "so flagrantly out of accord with the general principles and current realities of the Palestine situation," the Agency's "observations" declared, no improvement in these proposals could make them a useful starting-point in the quest for a political settlement.[40]

López, never to be deterred in his course, brought a proposal on April 15 as Colombia's delegate to the Security Council for a truce regarding all military and political activity in Palestine, HMG to use "its best efforts" for as long as it remained the Mandatory Power had been aggravated to effectuate this desired end. While America and Canada expressed their acceptance, both Shertok and Husseini strongly objected. Gromyko charged that the proposal ignored the Jews' right to immigration and that Arab irregulars had to leave the country. With a few corrections, the truce proposal was adopted one day after the special session began, the mandatory named to supervise the truce. The USSR and Ukraine abstained.[41]

A secret State Department cable to the Foreign Office actually accused the British government of "an abdication of its responsibilities" rather than cooperation with its strongest ally. Reading this, British Ambassador in Washington Lord Inverchapel wrote to Bevin that he had naturally been "at pains to remind State Department officials of the strength and unity of public feeling in Britain on this issue as a result of our heavy casualties and sacrifices, and to recall how much Britain's difficulties as the Mandatory Power have been aggravated by the irresponsible back-seat driving of the US Administration, Congress and public opinion." To the sympathetic American Ambassador to the Court of St. James, Lewis W. Douglas, Bevin responded that British public opinion would not support any longer keeping troops in Palestine, nor was he sure that troops would be necessary at all if a firm decision were reached for the creation of a unitary Palestinian State. Could the US Government not really send in their troops? he asked. The Jews, the Foreign Secretary thought, would be much more reluctant to fight against American troops than against those of other countries.⁴²

On April 16, Cadogan pledged to the Security Council that the Arab Legion would be withdrawn from Palestine before May 15, drawing the Agency's reaction that the British were handing over to the Legion vast quantities of military stores, ammunition, and equipment. While rejecting a plea to immediately recognize the Hagana, form a Jewish militia in Palestine under UN authority and allow it to acquire weapons, British Prime Minister Clement Attlee stated that he doubted HMG's small and infrequent supply of arms to the regular Arab forces by treaty were or would likely "be put to an improper use in Palestine." HMG would not recognize the Jewish Agency after May 15, announced Bevin in the House of Commons. The true explanation of UK policy, Beeley confided to the Canadian delegation, was his government's wish that the Middle East remain outside the Soviet sphere of influence. Dropping the Palestine Mandate, "a festering sore" which if allowed to continue might have forced the Arab world into the Soviet camp, would "consolidate" the UK's position in that region. A policy of non-intervention would most likely lead to heavy bloodshed in Palestine, with the Jews, in Beeley's opinion, left in complete control of the Tel Aviv-Haifa seaboard area. Jerusalem and outlying Jewish communities he judged to be "indefensible."⁴³

Not able to "simply stand aloof" when confronted by the dire prospect of a deteriorating situation in Palestine, especially when the Mandatory Power proved unwilling "to assume helpful responsibilities," Lovett explained in considerable detail to Fahy on April 16 why the United States came to propose a truce and a trusteeship. These seemed "the best possible" proposals to avoid the likelihood of increasing violence and chaos in the weeks preceding May 15, without the United States abandoning the GA November resolution "as the ultimate solution it desired." The delegation would exhibit no "unusual exertion" for approval of the trusteeship proposal; the matter was up to the Assembly. If that proposal did not receive acceptance, he seemed to feel that one for Jerusalem to protect the Holy Places should be urged, and indicated that the United States might move in that direction "at the appropriate time." The activities of some Jewish organizations in the United States and their pressure tactics were "harmful," he opined. Behind Lovett's real concern in this regard, Fahy concluded, was the feeling that the US government was doing all that it could under the circumstances, and that more confidence by the "Jewish elements" in the country "is desirable."[44]

For Palestine's imperturbable Chief Secretary Henry Gurney, never one to let the country's descent into chaos prevent his golf game, the Zionists did not "care two-pence" for the United Nations while Husseini even refused to sit in the same room with Shertok. The mandatory officers had "given all they've had," but now the British were "merely fed up" with Palestine. (Perhaps not surprisingly, Gurney refused to ask London to free funds for the import of necessary fuel and fuel products after the shutdown of the Haifa oil refineries.) Everyone knew that the UN was not in a position to take action, Truman's recent announcement motivated not by the interests of peace but focused on the US election year, and the Palestine Commission at Lake Success "a really surprisingly incompetent body." If the Security Council were put on the Greek stage, Gurney imagined, it would have Austin suggesting "something that commits nobody to anything at all," Truman repeat "I am still backing partition," the British delegation chorus declare HMG was leaving "this thoroughly wicked child" on May 15th, Shertok and Husseini adhering to their uncompromising lines, and the play ending with loud catcalls from the chorus of Guatemalans and Uruguayans, thunder and lightning, and the arrival of a herald bearing the agenda for the next meeting of the General Assembly on disputed Kashmir. The UN discussions, Gurney concluded, "seem to be more and more futile and unreal."[45]

Although hearing from Ben-Gurion on April 16 that the *yishuv*'s grim fortunes had dramatically shifted to victories, especially regarding control of Jerusalem's hills and the greatly outnumbered Hagana's rout of Fawzi al-Kaukji's Arab Liberation Army at kibbutz Mishmar HaEmek, the Agency executive chairman certain that the fate of Palestine's Jews depended on the arrival of military equipment rather than on developments at Lake Success, Shertok persisted in the truce negotiations. These had been conducted, he cabled Ben-Gurion three days later, not in order to provide ourselves "with alibi for non-compliance," but in an earnest effort to achieve a truce, "which we need badly." The Agency had to avoid the impression that it was deliberately flouting the truce, and observing the truce did not involve evacuation of the Arab positions now occupied by the Hagana. No conditions were set in that respect, after all, while the Agency's condition regarding the evacuation of outside Arab forces had not been accepted.

Ben-Gurion agreed with Shertok that the "most dangerous" aspect of the truce proposals was the mandatory's supervision of its terms. He replied on April 19, one day after he was appointed head of the People's Administration and also head of the *yishuv*'s security matters, that while the Agency executive informed Cunningham that if the Arabs agreed to a cease-fire they would act likewise, the High Commissioner had not received any intimation of agreement from the other side. In fact, the Arab attacks continued without respite, particularly in Jerusalem. Finally, "this does not mean acceptance truce conditions." Shertok sent Ben-Gurion's cable to López without its final sentence.[46]

The same day, the Palestine Commission decided to suspend its efforts to set up a provisional council of government for the proposed Jewish State, while also learning that its efforts to create a volunteer police force consisting of Britons for Jerusalem's security had failed. Without an adequate international police force to implement partition, a despairing Azácarte cabled Lie and Bunche, he considered the advance group's presence in Jerusalem "unnecessary and undesirable." He remained convinced, as he told Cunningham, that partition was "the formula" that reduced to a minimum the friction between Arabs and Jews. That would make easier their collaboration, in his opinion, and the only possible way for the Arabs to achieve "their very legitimate claim" to national independence and sovereignty.[47]

On April 20, Austin presented the GA Political and Security Committee "tentative suggestions" for a temporary trusteeship in Palestine, administered by a Governor-General to continue for three years or until such time as the Jews and Arabs agreed on the future government of Palestine. At the same time, he stated that the United States was prepared to discharge its share of responsibility in providing troops to carry out trusteeship, provided that other countries took part and a truce prevailed. Carl Berendsen (New Zealand), Gunner Hagglof (Sweden), John Hood (Australia), and Gromyko proposed a reversion to partition, Berendsen particularly eloquent in calling for the UN to follow the course set on November 29, 1947, or the alternative "is inevitable confusion and dismay." A British spokesman reiterated that HMG would end the mandate on May 15, that there would be no British troops left in Palestine after August 1, and that between those dates there would be no enforcement by British forces not having the consent of both communities.[48]

The Jewish Agency again requested, in a letter to López, the immediate withdrawal of the Arab Legion, whose units had actively participated recently in an attack on the Jewish settlement of Neveh Ya'akov. Jessup's attempt on the 21st to railroad through the US trusteeship plan by its referral to the Trusteeship Committee failed, six delegations arguing that it represented an attempt to achieve implicit approval of the American proposal. The same day, Austin requested the Security Council to take up again the question of implementing the truce resolution of April 17, and a meeting of the Council was set for six days later.[49]

Truman continued to feel very strongly that he would "try to do something" about Palestine before the GA special session ended. While prepared to appoint his own representative to the UN delegation (a step pressed for by the Zionists) as a counter to some pro-Arab advisers there, he told two top leaders of the Democratic Party that carrying out the partition resolution would not garner sufficient votes in the Security Council. Rosenman's transmission of memoranda favoring a truce for Jerusalem as an aid to the Jewish State's success and warning the Arab states not to commit aggression, documents supplied by Weizmann's associates, made their mark; he reported to Weizmann soon thereafter that Truman would intervene regarding Jerusalem. The President, "horrified" at the Arab massacre of seventy-eight Jews in a Hadassah Hospital convoy on April 13, with no intervention from a mandatory garrison two hundred yards away, was also perplexed by Zionist "inflexibility" regarding the truce negotiations. He soon defended Austin's announcement about supplying US troops for a Palestine police force in his role as America's Commander-in-Chief, the same day that Austin, responding to a petition from about 5,000 members of the bar protesting the US reversal of support for partition, replied that "all of us should get together to patch up" the Palestine government "and administer it until some arrangement can be made."[50]

The pertinent UN bodies pressed forward during April 21–22 on a truce and a trusteeship, with little success. The Trusteeship Council, with the Americans' Francis B. Sayre taking the lead against the opposition of the delegates from New Zealand and Australia, declared that it would take no action for UN rule over Jerusalem — as stipulated in Resolution 181 (II) — until the GA had reached a conclusion. Parodi asked the Political and Security Committee to appoint a governor to recruit a special police force to protect the Holy City of Jerusalem; Hood introduced a resolution directing the Palestine Commission to create one or both provisional councils of government, the Arab League states to prohibit their nationals from activities designed to obstruct the November 29 resolution. Silver, who already on April 1 had declared the US truce proposals "wholly unsatisfactory and futile," informed the Security Council that the Jews would establish their state officially on May 16.

Austin revealed that the United States had not been able to get any country to agree to send troops to Palestine if no truce was agreed upon. El-Khouri charged the Jews with terrorism in Haifa, sparking Guatemala's Jorge Garcia-Granados, avid Zionist ever since his UNSCOP participation, to ask the Syrian delegate whether the Arabs in Palestine were throwing flowers at the Jews. "The only morally sound position for the secretariat now to take was to support partition," Bunche told his colleagues on April 22, "since the partition process had already gone very far." At the moment, Lie concluded this meeting in his office, it looked as though the Jews and Arabs would be left to fight it out, which he considered "a terrible prospect."[51]

Assuming that the Security Council's proposal for a truce would succeed, the interim period of trusteeship therefore not requiring a great amount of force to support it, on April 22 Bevin's staff prepared the outline of a revised plan for an interim government to continue for at least one year. A Council of Ministers, composed of an equal number of Jews and Arabs under a non-Palestinian Governor appointed by the UN and with a non-Palestinian volunteer police force, would work towards a final settlement. The existing Land Transfers Regulations of 1940 under the White Paper should be maintained, and Jewish immigration fixed at a rate of 4,000 per month for two years or for the duration of the interim government, whichever was the shorter period. Cantonal frontiers, drawn in such a way as to make possible an exchange of rural populations, should prevail, the cantons having the right of secession five years after the independent state was established. However, Lord Listowel, deputizing for Creech Jones (then at the UN), pointed out the unreality of the scheme, "not the least chance" that the representative Arab and Jewish leaders would agree to sit together in such a Council at the present time or accept this plan. Pressed by Ambassador Douglas to "fill the breach in Palestine until a UN solution had been found," Bevin would go no further than say that HMG would give "immediate consideration" to an agreement if one were reached between Jews and Arabs.[52]

April 23, 1948, marked significant shifts in this drama. The Security Council passed a US resolution (which Truman had approved earlier that day) that the consuls in Jerusalem of France, Belgium, and the United States join as a Truce Commission to supervise compliance with the Council's truce call of the 17th and report to López within four days. (Russia, Ukraine, and Colombia abstained in the vote.) Even as the Hagana set up its rule over Haifa, Cadogan told the Council that the Arabs had brought on that decisive defeat because large numbers of them had filtered into the city. King Abdullah of Transjordan urged all Arab nations "to join my army in a movement to Palestine to retain the Arab character of that country," while Lebanese UN delegate Charles Malik declared that the Arabs would oppose anything except a unitary state. Creech Jones, addressing the Political and Security Committee, declared that there could be no settlement in Palestine at present unless it were backed up with a "very substantial" means of enforcement; the Colonial Secretary did not indicate the British attitude toward the American proposal.[53]

Late that same afternoon, Weizmann received electrifying news from Rosenman. Truman had just told this well-placed adviser "I have Dr. Weizmann on my conscience." The President went on to aver that he had not realized on March 18 when speaking to the Zionist leader that the State Department had gone so far in abandoning the partition plan. He wished to "find his way back" to the GA resolution of November 29, and if the special session could be "surmounted" without reversing partition, and if a Jewish state were declared, he would recognize it immediately. Truman stipulated one absolute condition: he would deal only with Weizmann. For that reason, Weizmann had to postpone his departure for about three to four weeks so that Truman could receive him as soon as he was ready for an official announcement. Weizmann shared this report "in absolute secrecy" with closest associates upon returning to his hotel suite that evening. He soon sent Rosenman a confidential memo for Truman's attention asserting that the President's intentions might be thwarted by the "rapid developments" of events transpiring in Lake Success towards a UN trusteeship, and that he should intercede with London regarding the Arab Legion and Abdullah's threat of invasion.[54]

The Hagana's conquest of Tiberias and of Haifa, sparking a large exodus of Arabs from the two cities, raised yet another clash at the UN between the Arab and Jewish representatives. El-Khouri charged on April 23 that this mass flight reflected the Jewish policy to "destroy" the Arab population within the area accorded the Jews in the GA partition resolution. With information from Eliyahu Sasson, the top Arab specialist in the Agency's political department, Shertok countered that this phenomenon was apparently not the consequence of "only fear and weakness." Rather, it was being organized by followers of the AHC's Husseini leadership and carried out with the cooperation of invading Arab forces in order to vilify the Jews, and create in the Arab world and world opinion the impression that such invasion was not in defiance of the UN November 1947 decision but to rescue persecuted Arabs in Palestine. The foreign Arab commanders' actual disappearance in the initial stage of every serious battle, under the pretext that they were going to bring reinforcements, left the native inhabitants to their fate, spreading chaos and panic—and flight.

Addressing both the Security Council and the GA Political and Security Committee on this issue, Shertok stressed that the Jews did not wish to chase the Arabs from the homes, but desired that the Arabs live in "full security" in the Jewish State. Brigadier I. N. Clayton, adviser on Arab affairs at the British Embassy in Cairo, thought *au contraire*, telling the US Embassy's First Secretary that the Arab Legion's march into Palestine after the British evacuation offered the best guarantee for security, with the amalgamation of Transjordan and Palestine an "excellent" solution to the Palestine problem.[55]

Rusk did not give up hope, sending from April 22 through the next two weeks a total of five drafts of a US truce and trusteeship proposal to the representatives of the Jewish Agency and of the member states of the Arab League. (McClintock had drafted a first draft as early as April 11.) To Judge Joseph M. Proskauer, president of the non-Zionist American Jewish Committee who, keenly interested in a cease-fire for Jerusalem, encouraged this objective with Lovett and Rusk, State's Office of UN Affairs director had stressed on the 19th that it was essential to have a truce—"if only [the] Jewish Agency wouldn't insist on declaring *State* on May 15." Proskauer replied that he was "sick and tired of hearing you ask [the] Jewish Agency to give up without indicating what [the] Arabs are to give. Jamal refused to sit down at [the] same table with Shertok." Towards the end of that meeting, Rusk suggested two "reasonable" people with whom the Agency might sit down: the

Turkish representative and Fawzi of Egypt. The latter choice appeared qustionable, given that the delegate from Cairo had told the Near East Division's Samuel Kopper on April 6 that the Arab States were willing to go along on truce arrangements provided that these did not allow for an independent Jewish State and that that illegal Jewish immigration ceased "forthwith."[56]

A joint memo by Jacob Robinson, the Agency's Legal Counsel, and Epstein pointed out serious flaws in Rusk's first draft, yet Proskauer thought otherwise. He was persuaded by an initial "provisional draft" on April 27 (to which he contributed), and urged Shertok that day to accept a truce limited in duration. It would stop bloodshed; allow "cooling time" for working out some modification of the partition plan; strengthen the *yishuv* (its political factions not an "undivided house") militarily; and gain goodwill with the US government and the UN. "The Jewish Agency cannot fight the world," Proskauer cautioned, "and brave words may result only in the death of brave men."[57]

The American pressure did not let up. Rusk had Douglas again emphasize to Bevin that if the situation developed whereby the Soviets could use Palestine as a point of entry into the Middle East, American public opinion would "compel" Washington to "reconsider" the value of their commitments in Greece, Turkey, and Iran against Soviet influence. Rusk had to admit on April 26 to organizations accredited to the UN that the US had found no "takers" to cooperate in the sending of troops, and Husseini insisted at the Council on the "wicked" Mandate being replaced by "the whole of Palestine as one unit." Yet Lovett, worried that the Palestine situation might easily lead to a "general conflagration" with terrible repercussions on the world scene, made a thinly veiled threat to the Agency executive's Nahum Goldmann two days later.

In an off-the-record meeting with Goldmann on April 28, Lovett warned that if the Zionists prevented a truce in Palestine, the United States would block any military and financial help being given to the *yishuv*, and publish a White Paper incriminating them (along with the British and the Arabs), which would do "great harm" to America's Jews and increase antisemitism in the country. Shertok immediately cabled Ben-Gurion this disturbing news. (One week later, two State Department officials quietly drafted a resolution for the Security Council to impose economic and other sanctions against any Palestine organization or government failing to comply with the truce.) The same day, Cadogan sent

Palestine Commission chairman Lisicky a letter marked "secret" insisting that British assets in oil supplies, commercial interests, foodstuffs, and military stores be safeguarded and guaranteed after the mandate ended. To make sure that they would have enough to cover an anticipated deficit of almost £9 million, the British impounded the funds of the Palestine Currency Board, totaling almost £50 million.[58]

Douglas's appeal, following the request from Rusk, that HMG shift from her present attitude to cooperate with the US truce/trusteeship proposal received a frigid reception. Was Abdullah to stand "idly by," Attlee and Bevin insisted to him on the 28th, when the Jews "were allowed to be aggressors on his co-religionists and fellow-Arabs in the State of Palestine?" The number of Arabs who are infiltrated into Palestine was not large, and any acts they had committed "had been exaggerated. After all, Palestine was an Arab country." "Was it aggression for Arabs to come into Palestine from their own countries," they queried, "and non-aggression for Jews to come in by sea to the tens of thousands?" The Jews entered as unarmed immigrants, Douglas responded, leading Attlee to immediately remark: "That was just Hitler's method"; they were soon armed once they got in. When the Ambassador finally asked if HMG would be willing to "play a part" after May 15, they answered that London would give no undertaking before knowing whether the truce terms had been accepted by both sides. "We feared that we would be left to carry the whole weight again," the pair concluded, "and this we would not and could not undertake to do." London had requested the Arab governments not to invade Palestine providing the Jews ceased their attacks, and they thought that Washington should take the same action with the Jews. "After all," Bevin told Douglas the next day, "the present Jewish action was the direct outcome" of US policy, and therefore HMG felt that the Americans, and they alone, "could really remedy the situation."[59]

While the Agency and the AHC contemplated a Trusteeship Council formulation by the Belgian delegation to obtain a cease-fire for Jerusalem's Old City, Parodi proposed a special police form of 1,000 volunteers for Jerusalem. On April 28, the chairman of the Truce Commission warned Abdullah that any warlike decision or action by his forces to march shortly across the Palestine frontiers would be the cause of "the gravest censure" by the Security Council and the entire UN as a possible threat to peace. Shertok, however, had to hasten writing a letter to Marshall in order to clear up a "serious misunderstanding." The previous day, the Secretary of State had declared at an off-the-record press conference, drawing upon a McClintock memo which Lovett had requested, that an agreement for truce had virtually been reached between the Agency and the Arab League on thirteen of Rusk's fourteen points—immigration the exceptional issue. This statement disturbed Shertok greatly.

Shertok had already indicated leading the Jewish Agency's cause at the UN, had already indicated a number of difficulties and objections to the truce draft when shown it on the previous evening. He had repeated these to the Security Council on April 27, primarily the truce's deferment of statehood and rendering its attainment in the future "most uncertain." In addition, the Agency could never accept British supervision of a truce or the "gross inequality" of a US arms embargo, which left the Jews at a decided disadvantage compared with the Arab states. Shertok quickly pointed this out to Proskauer as well, in reply to the judge's urgent letter of the previous day. Concurrently, a telegram from the Truce Commission described the rapid deterioration of the general situation in Palestine, noting to the Council that the "intensity of fighting is increasing steadily."[60]

As April drew to a close, Arthur Lourie, directing the Agency's office in New York, concluded to Eytan that the GA Political Committee's discussions "are almost incredible in their apparent futility," wrangling for days over questions of procedure and "an atmosphere of cynicism and gloom" hanging over the whole meetings. Hosting a private meeting of the representatives of the Western Hemisphere, Austin forcefully stressed that the United States was deliberately seeking collaboration from other UN members, not under any circumstances aiming to "throw their weight about" and impose a solution. Upon his return to New York for consultations, Azcárate had announced that partition was a fact, and the only question was how long it would be before the fact is recognized. Reporting home, Cunningham declared that the Arabs in Jerusalem were either under no control or acting under the orders of a number of Iraqi and Syrian military leaders without coordination, looting common and the AHC "virtually not functioning." Greatly disappointed as the local British administration disintegrated and worried for the safety of his people, the High Commissioner even suggested to Creech Jones an earlier termination of the mandate, only to be told that this would bring "general dismay, a very serious loss of reputation here with intensification of malicious criticism," and "possibly bring to naught" the efforts of those laboring to bring "some alleviation to the current situation and future prospects there."[61]

Proskauer, finding support from Goldmann—which a satisfied Rusk conveyed to Lovett—persisted, pressing Ben-Gurion to accept the truce. Yet at that same moment, Abdullah publicly advised the Jewish bodies in Palestine to halt their aggression, and accept citizenship in a Palestine State under his rule. For its part, the British UN delegation informed its Agency counterpart that all pressure from the State Department to persuade HMG to prolong its tenure had failed. It seemed absurd, Eban wrote to a colleague in Paris, for Parodi to hail a US scheme which its original sponsors did not seem to regard very highly themselves.[62]

Indeed, on April 30 the US delegation modified its plans for Palestine, and proposed to the Trusteeship Council a "simple and temporary" trusteeship for Jerusalem. (That did not prevent State mandarins, responding to Jessup's request, from preparing two possible alternative plans for UN action establishing a provisional government for all of Palestine.) In disagreement, Britain's UN Counselor John Fletcher-Cooke suggested instead that the present government of Jerusalem, headed by District Commissioner R. M. Graves, should be replaced by a neutral chairman appointed by Cunningham. Australia's delegate, dissenting, called all such plans illegal, and suggested a return to the Security Council's draft statute for Jerusalem. Husseini agreed with the Britisher's proposal, but Shertok did not, saying that the Jews could not undertake a formal cease-fire there unless the Arab siege was lifted. Separately, he suggested to Ben-Gurion to publish a "modest communiqué," indicating that the *yishuv*'s government actually existed, so that if by accepting truce terms the Agency would be precluded from proclaiming sovereignty on May 16 its position was not prejudiced, and it could argue that the government was already in "full working order" when the truce agreement was concluded.[63]

The Arabs stood firm. The AHC had still not responded to Cunningham's appeal for a cease-fire, Khalidi having left early that month for Damascus and not returned to Jerusalem. On April 26 Husseini declared to the Political Committee that the country's Arabs would proclaim the whole of Palestine an independent state on May 16 unless in the meantime the GA created a temporary trusteeship that would lead to a sovereign unitary state. On April 28, Saudi Arabia's Prince Feisal spoke on behalf of all the Arab delegates meeting in his apartment when telling Rusk and Jessup that Jewish immigration could at most continue at the British legal quota of 1,500 per month, but it had to "cease altogether" after the truce. (One week earlier, Feisal had told Jessup and Kopper that Palestine had already received its "fair share" of Jewish immigrants, and that those coming for some time from Eastern Europe "had been of a communist nature.")

Azzam Pasha said the same thing to the British in Cairo as had Feisal about Jewish immigration. This was the same Arab leader who had frankly told Eban and the Agency's David Horowitz in September 1947 that the Arab peoples viewed Palestine's Jews as "an alien organism," which the Arabs would eventually eject in the same manner as they had the European Crusaders after two hundred years of living uninvited in their midst. Arab Legion units, at the same time, fired on Jerusalem's Talpiyot and Mekor Hayim neighborhoods, and exchanged artillery shelling for three days against the Hagana's taking control of the Gesher police station in the Beit Sh'an Valley until ordered to return to their barracks.[64]

Truman, as he told Rusk on April 30, wished to get the Palestine matter "settled" rather than approach it from the point of view of personal political considerations. He agreed with State that an immediate truce there seemed to be the government's basic objective. In addition, it was "fundamental" that the truce should not be used as "a cloak" for a change in the military position of either warring side. After Rusk pointed to "extremists" like Silver, who, unlike Goldmann, Shertok, and some Jewish leaders in Palestine, made "a formidable war party" which "complicated" the department's task considerably, the President remarked that he wished Marshall to know that he was ready to take whatever steps the Secretary thought would hasten the completion of a truce, prepared to "go the limit" in helping the UN bring this about. "If the Jews refuse to accept a truce on reasonable grounds they need not expect anything from us" he replied to Rusk's statement that the Arabs might accept the truce and the Jews would not, which might then create "difficult problems" for him. The Arabs should be told that our policy was firm, Truman concluded, and be reminded that "we have a difficult political problem within this country." Expressly stating his concern over the Russian aspect of the situation, he ended by saying to Rusk "go and get a truce"—there was no other answer to this situation.[65]

The same day, Bevin informed Creech Jones that, from the point of view of HMG's relations with the Americans, he would be "glad" to see the increasingly "unreal" US trusteeship plan "die of its own accord rather than for us to intervene to finish it off." He preferred that the British concentrate for the time being on the positive work of furthering the local truce for Jerusalem, thinking that as May 15 approached, "eleventh hour considerations" might make the two parties "rather amenable to reason," and that the truce offered the best way out. If the Colonial Secretary were to mention in the Security Council "limiting the struggle," Bevin thought it better for him not to specifically refer to arms embargoes: Britain's position as regards the supply of weapons to the Arab States was in American eyes "particularly vulnerable."[66]

On May 1, while the Hagana took almost full control of Jerusalem's strategic Katamon neighborhood and Syrian army troops attacked the Dan, Dafna, Kfar Szold, and Lehavot HaBashan settlements in the Upper Galilee, the thirty-three-year-old Eban explained directly to the GA's Political Committee why the defeat of the US trusteeship plan was important and urgent, asserting that Jewish sovereignty was already a reality in everything but name. The world Zionist movement, having created solid, coherent institutions in Palestine over the years, was now poised on the threshold of sovereignty, and it also possessed a certificate of national legitimacy from the UN. Further, the Americans' "violent reversal" of policy ran counter to mankind's conscience haunted by the spectacle of Jewish survivors still languishing behind barbed wire in Europe, whose capabilities and ideals "will be fully at home" in the Jewish state, and above all reflected a blatant acceptance of illicit force as the arbiter of international policy, thereby covering the UN in "universal derision." The time had come, his address ended, for the emancipation of "two historic peoples from a long period of tutelage" and allowing for a vision of mutual cooperation. "Congratulations," Gromyko soon told Eban in his booming bass voice during a luncheon at Lie's Forest Hills home, "you have killed American trusteeship."[67]

At this point, while Shertok declared to the Trusteeship Council that the Agency was "utterly opposed" to the American plan for the duration of any time period, trusteeship had no takers either in the Arab camp. Husseini and Iraq delegate Awni al-Khalidi saw it as an attempt to impose partition indirectly. The Arab states might have to enter Palestine to establish "law and order" after May 15, Fawzi told Rusk, while Feisal added in another interview that they "could not ever" accept a Jewish state, which would be "an abscess to the political body of the Arabs." A scheme to have Jerusalem placed under the International Red Cross flag and a truce for the entire country drew Husseini's quick response: "No Partition!" Conceding the absence of governments' willingness to supply forces to implement a trusteeship, the American plan (so Creech Jones wrote to Bevin) was "now dying a natural death," The Colonial Secretary gave Rusk on May 2 his opinion that the Jews would agree to sovereignty in a coastal state running from Tel Aviv to Haifa, with Abdullah's forces partitioning the country along a line across to and including Jaffa, Aqaba going to Saudi Arabia monarch Abdul Aziz Ibn Saud, Syria getting the northeastern corner of Palestine, and "liquidating" Haj Amin. Cuban delegate Guillermo Belt, who had cast "no" at the November 29, 1947 vote, proposed that a subcommittee create a provisional UN regime after May 15, pressing for an agreement based upon "a free and independent state in Palestine."[68]

On May 6, a GA vote of 35 to 0 (with 17 abstentions) approved the Trusteeship Council resolution to have the mandatory appoint a neutral Special Municipal Commissioner to take over the entire Jerusalem administration ten days hence. Berendsen saw no point in this "man of straw," while Julius Katz-Suchy, Poland's delegate and a Jew, continued to back partition and questioned the legality of this appointment. Parodi, the new Security Council president, proposed that a provisional government last only a few months; Tsiang deemed trusteeship "reactionary" and in general unpopular; Russia's Semyon Tsarapkin thought that even bare consideration of the French proposal in effect ignored the November 29 resolution. The same day, the US delegation's Ross relayed to State that after a meeting with Parodi and Creech Jones, "a basis for agreement on truce terms has not been found." Hearing the Colonial Secretary declare that recent military successes had made the Jews determined "not to budge" from statehood and unlimited immigration, while "inflamed Arab opinion" would sweep any Arab government in compliance with UN decrees, Parodi confided to Austin that his government would never permit French boats to do what the British Royal Navy had "done to the Jews" seeking entry into Palestine. Creech Jones offered nothing further to a closed meeting of the subcommittee the next day than saying that "at this late hour, what is not possible by consent is not possible at all."[69]

Rusk had tried another tack. On the morning of May 3, he proposed to Lovett that an immediate cease-fire begin in Palestine two days hence, with the Mandate extended for ten days, and an airplane furnished by Truman fly to the Middle East with representatives of the AHC, the Arab States, and the Jewish Agency joining members of the Truce Commission to conclude a truce during that time. The President agreed to make his plane "Sacred Cow" available, a receptive Shertok was informed, and US Consul Thomas Wasson in Jerusalem transmitted the message to the Jewish Agency. Upon consulting his colleagues in Jerusalem, Shertok wrote to Rusk the next day that they did not consider warranted the "somewhat spectacular proceeding now suggested." This persuaded Rusk to inform Lovett that the Agency, in light of the Jews' present military superiority in Palestine, would prefer to "round out" its commonwealth after May 15, thereby becoming the "actual aggressors" against Palestine's Arabs. He thought Creech Jones's May 2 partition solution "the wisest course of action." The United States was doing "everything it can," Truman told the press on May 6, to get the Palestine problem settled peacefully. Bevin turned down flat Rusk's idea, however, declaring in Commons that HMG would not depart from its position to retain the Mandate until May 15, despite Marshall's expression to Inverchapel of "very strong hope" that London would agree to an extension "in the great interests of peace."[70]

The State Department found encouragement in Marshall's private talk with Magnes and Rusk's with Goldmann, who separately had each urged the United States to press for a truce and a trusteeship. The Secretary set up an off-the-record meeting for Magnes with Truman on May 5, during which the President praised the Anglo-American Committee of Inquiry's report for a binationalist state and wide Jewish immigration as the best solution; expressed bitterness that the Jewish and Arab leaders had rejected his "Sacred Cow" offer; and pledged that it was "our duty" to "find a way" of solving the Palestine quagmire. The next day, Truman approved State's draft of proposed articles for a three-month cease-fire under the Truce Commission's authority, during which neither side could take steps to proclaim statehood or to seek international recognition to that end. He remained bitter, and so told *New York Times* publisher Arthur Hays Sulzberger, about the British and "New York Jews" (which he conflated with "New York Zionists," to Sulzberger's discomfort), also deeply concerned, as was Lovett, about the development of antisemitism in the United States as a result of Zionist activism.[71]

Yet reports still circulated in the State Department and the White House to the effect that Shertok had agreed to conditions for a military truce and "political standstill" in Palestine, forcing him to write to Marshall on the 7th at Epstein's suggestion that his letter of April 29 had made clear the Agency's objections to the proposed US truce. Private individuals (a hint to Proskauer, Magnes, and Goldmann) who took an opposing line, he pointed out, did not represent Palestinian Jewry, bore no constitutional responsibility for its future, and were not in a position to give effect to what they advocated. He was about to fly home for consultation with the Agency executive, which alone would have to decide on its immediate course of action. Epstein handed over a copy of this letter to "Dave" (David Niles), an Administrative Assistant in the White House, to give "his Chief" (Truman).

The next day, accompanied by Epstein, Shertok made his final case to Marshall. Realizing that the Agency was prepared to gamble on a "now or never" basis to declare a Jewish commonwealth on May 15 and on the possibility of an arrangement for partitioning Palestine with Abdullah, the Secretary warned, as a military man, that it was very dangerous to base long-range policy on temporary successes in the field of battle. Should the tide turn against the Jews in the long run, he said bluntly, they had no warrant to expect help from the United States. Thanking Marshall for "his sincerity and wisdom," Shertok promised to convey this admonition to his associates in Jerusalem.[72]

Clark Clifford, Truman's forty-one-year-old Naval Aide and trusted adviser, had by then prepared some penciled notes about the question of American recognition of the anticipated Jewish state. With suggestions from Niles and Max Lowenthal, who had been legal counsel for Senator Truman during the Senate Special Committee to Investigate the National Defense Program in World War II, he had on March 8 drafted a lengthy memo to Truman advising that, uninfluenced by election considerations, endorsing the GA partition recommendation was "in complete conformity with the settled policy" of the United States and "best for America." Implementing partition, he had stressed then, was crucial to the UN's future and to the country's cementing alliances with South

5. A Truce and Trusteeship for Palestine

America and Western Europe, a position also taken by the American Association for the United Nations. Now, receiving Clifford's notes that the Jewish state, to be set up shortly, was "inevitable" ("We must recognize inevitably. Why not now?"), Truman telephoned Marshall for his views. Hearing the Secretary's strong objections, Truman said that he wished to have a meeting the next week on the subject. Telling Clifford that Marshall would likely take a very strong position at the meeting, he wished the young Missourian to make the case for recognition. "You know how I feel," the President added: "I want you to be as persuasive as you can possibly be."[73]

The showdown at the Oval Office on the afternoon of May 12, the same day that both Jewish and Arab UN representatives rejected the plan for establishing a UN Central Commission for Palestine as a temporary interim regime, appeared to end in Marshall's favor. While Clifford supporters Niles and Truman secretary Mathew J. Connelly sat by quietly, as did McClintock and Fraser Wilkins of State's Near East division (the latter two replacing Rusk and Henderson because Lovett thought their presence in the same room as Clifford would be "too inflammatory"), Lovett and especially Marshall criticized the Jewish Agency's hardening attitude, and argued that the United States should continue supporting the UN trusteeship resolutions and defer any decision on recognition. When Clifford responded that partition had taken place, Lovett immediately countered that the Security Council was still discussing a truce, and that premature recognition of a state whose nature would be unknown ("buying a pig in a poke") would be "highly injurious" to the UN and, as a "very transparent" attempt to win the Jewish vote in the November election, also to the President. Reiterating some of these points, Marshall, his face "reddening with suppressed anger," interjected that Clifford's counsel was based on domestic political considerations, while the Palestine problem was international. Should the President follow Clifford's advice, he would vote against Truman if he cast a vote in the coming elections this November.

Knowing that he had to stop the meeting, the Secretary's last statement coming very close to an explicit threat to resign, Truman declared that he would deal with both sides of the problem himself. To a very agitated Marshall, he said that he was "inclined to side with you in this matter." He then initialed the State Department's resolution, mainly drafted by Rusk and Jessup, for a truce and a UN Commissioner for

—211—

Palestine. Ninety minutes had passed. When Marshall left the room, Truman suggested that Clifford "let the dust settle a little—then you can get it again and see if we can get this thing turned around. I still want to do it. But be careful. I can't afford to lose George Marshall."[74]

To Clifford's surprise, Lovett called him shortly after the tense conference had ended, and asked that they meet for drinks that evening to see if a solution could be found to avoid a Truman-Marshall "break over this issue" just in these most difficult months of the Cold War. When Clifford insisted that the President, whose views he had accurately presented, was not going "to give an inch," Lovett responded, "let's see what can be done at State." A pleased Truman advised Clifford the next morning that he keep encouraging Lovett "to work on the General," while telling Niles "I was sorry to have to decide against you fellows yesterday." He agreed with Niles that the "western" (US) recognition should precede the Soviet bloc's recognition, so as to give it "the right slant from the beginning." That afternoon, Lovett suggested a new approach: recognize the state but delay announcing or implementing it for an unspecific period. Without even consulting Truman, Clifford shot back that the President was "rock solid" in his basic view. Lovett then suggested *de facto*, rather than full *de jure*, recognition. Again without consulting Truman, Clifford said that this was an issue on which he felt his group could yield to State.[75]

The next day, Jessup's proposal for a UN Mediator was forwarded to the Political Committee for voting on May 14. The proposal had first been approved with the British and Canadian delegations after the United States dropped its trusteeship proposal, Bevin approving the selection of Sweden's Count Folke Bernadotte. This reduced role from the earlier US resolution for a UN Commissioner authorized the Mediator to promote a "peaceful adjustment of the situation." Just then news arrived of the biggest massacre of Jews in the Palestine armed conflict, two Arab Legion companies—still under the orders of the General Officer Commanding British troops in Palestine, Gordon MacMillan—joining hundreds of Arabs from nearby villages in the assault against Kfar Etzion. Jessup's step did not stop Niles, Jacobson, former New York Governor Herbert Lehman, influential politicians Jacob Arvey (Chicago) and Edward J. Flynn (New York), and Bartley Crum of the 1946 Anglo-American Commission of Inquiry on Palestine from pressing Truman to recognize the emerging Jewish state. The Jewish War

Veterans of America, under the command of Major-General Julius Klein, kept up its public pressure campaign. Weizmann's letter to Truman on the 13th, which reached him through Niles, made a personal plea, expressing his thought that the world would regard Truman's action "as especially appropriate that the greatest living democracy should be the first to welcome the newest into the family of nations."[76]

While Ben-Gurion was making preparations to declare the new Jewish commonwealth in Tel Aviv's Museum of Art on May 14 at 4 p.m. as its Prime Minister and Defense Minister, the Minhelet HaAm (People's Administrative Council) having decided two days earlier by a close vote of 6 to 4 to reject the US trusteeship proposal, implying a proclamation of sovereignty for the newly named "Israel," Clifford told Lovett that Truman would be satisfied if Marshall agreed not to oppose the President's recognition. On his own, he also asked Epstein that afternoon to prepare an official letter to Truman, with a copy to Marshall, requesting that the United States recognize the new state but claiming nothing beyond the borders outlined in the November 29 resolution.

With no time to consult Jerusalem other than cabling Shertok that State insisted upon this "procedural point," although no evidence was yet available that the request would be "complied with" if submitted, Epstein turned to lawyer David C. Ginsburg for help in drafting the letter for US recognition. Receiving this request with the new name "State of Israel" penciled in by Epstein at the last minute, Clifford, with Niles's help, replied to Epstein's letter and prepared a statement for Truman's use. During lunch he turned down Lovett's proposed statement that Truman was considering the subject of recognition, and said that speed was essential to preempt the Russians' likely move to do so. Lovett still sought delay of a day or two, but Clifford said that Truman was under "unbearable pressure" to recognize the Jewish state promptly.[77]

Lovett, to whom Marshall had deputed the entire Palestine dilemma, and his colleagues at State arrived at the language of a White House release one-half hour before the Mandate would come to an end that Friday. (Cunningham had left Government House in Jerusalem that morning for departure at midnight from Haifa aboard the cruiser HMS *Euryalus*.) Lovett asked that the announcement be delayed until Austin got advance word of it and the GA session would end about 10 p.m., but Clifford, who was with Truman at the time, relayed that the President had decided to issue the statement shortly after 6 p.m. A stunned Rusk pointed out that this would "cut right across a standstill," for which the US delegation had been working for weeks at the UN, and for which State already had forty votes. Nevertheless, Clifford replied, these were Truman's instructions. Rusk called Austin, who, disgustedly, slammed down the telephone, and simply left for home without telling his associates.

At 6 p.m. Marshall, who also had been kept in the dark as to the secret Clifford-Lovett talks, informed Bevin and representatives of other capitals of the impending move. The British Foreign Secretary remained certain that a loose central authority such as the one proposed in the Morrison-Grady plan of provisional autonomy would eventually bring all "into a harmonious whole." Truman's *de facto* recognition, penned by Clifford and White House secretary Charles Ross even before Epstein's letter arrived, came at 6:11 p.m.—only eleven minutes after Ben-Gurion had declared Israel's independence. (Little notice was paid when Granados then went to the GA podium to announce Guatemala's *de jure* recognition of the new Jewish state.) Epstein raised the Israeli flag for the first time on US soil outside the Jewish Agency's Washington office at 2210 Massachusetts Ave., Mrs. Woodrow Wilson also present "to see the fulfillment of the idea [the Balfour Declaration] supported by her husband in 1917." A formal acknowledgment from Marshall to the earlier Epstein letter that afternoon, quoting Truman's statement of recognition, evoked the Jewish Agency representative's feelings at that time: "Hope had justified itself, had finally vanquished all the doubts and fears that had been assailing me."[78]

Truman, thinking of his April pledge to Weizmann, said to an aide: "The old Doctor will believe me now," convinced, as Truman said years later, that he had done "what I thought was right." At that same moment, "pandemonium" (Rusk's description) struck the GA hall. Silver had silenced his audience briefly when announcing the creation of the Jewish State, yet debate had been continuing on the resolution posed by Jessup for the appointment of a UN Mediator. A US delegate had to literally sit on Belt's lap to keep him from going to the podium to withdraw Cuba from the UN. Four minutes later, Marshall ordered Rusk to fly to New York and "prevent the US delegation from resigning *en masse*." Some of the Secretary's friends advised him to step down from his office, but Marshall replied that "you do not accept a post of this sort and then resign when the man who has the Constitutional authority to make a decision makes one. You may resign at any time for any other reason but not that one." Fawzi, el-Khouri, and Malik spoke harshly against Truman's action, while the delegates of Canada, China, and a number of Latin American states felt that they had been "double-crossed." Eleanor Roosevelt of the US delegation would write to Marshall that Truman's speedy recognition had created "complete consternation" in the UN, and her associates would have wanted prior knowledge and "a very clear understanding beforehand with such nations as we expected would follow our lead."[79]

The US resolution for a UN Mediator was adopted at 8:30 that evening by a vote of 31 votes to 7 (the Arab and Muslim nations) with 16 abstentions (the Soviet bloc), but the proposal for a temporary trusteeship over Jerusalem was defeated by 20 affirmative and 15 negative votes with 19 abstentions (including the British delegation). Jessup hurried back to Manhattan in his car, feeling that "the record of the United States was sullied." In the Foreign Office's view, so Beeley reported to Austin, it was "not correct to consider" that the November 29 GA resolution established a legal basis for the creation of a Jewish commonwealth. Marshall later told Truman that State felt the United States "had hit its all-time low before the UN," while Roosevelt wrote him that seldom had she seen "a more bitter, puzzled, discouraged group of people" than the American delegation, "just non-plussed by the way in which we do things." "There was not much else to be done," the President replied to her, given "the vacuum in Palestine" and the Russians "anxious to be the first to do the recognizing." In his memoirs, Truman added that some of the State Department's career men should not have been surprised at his decision if they had "faithfully supported my policy." "They almost put it over on you," Lovett said to him after Truman's announcement on recognition.[80]

At 5:00 the next morning, having been awakened a few hours earlier to hear of Truman's recognition, Ben-Gurion woke again to broadcast from a Hagana transmitter while the bombing by Egyptian spitfires over Tel Aviv, killing one and injuring five, echoed into his microphone. He fully appreciated that, in the words of Eban's later reminiscence, the US President's step came to the embattled Jews of Palestine "as an unexpected act of grace": "They were no longer forsaken and alone." Ben-Gurion sent a telegram, joined by Myerson, Agency treasurer Eliezer Kaplan, and Va'ad HaLe'umi executive member David Remez, to Weizmann's hotel suite. Acknowledging that he had "done more than any other living man" towards the creation of the State of Israel, they looked forward to his becoming its first President.[81]

The Jews could harbor no illusions about their adversaries' true, venomous intent. Abdullah's Order of the Day had informed his troops on May 4 that they would shortly have to join the "holy war" (*jihad*) to save Palestine, and on this war "depends the honour and the glory of the Arab States." Haj Amin's spokesman, Ahmed Shukairy, just announced the Arabs' goal as "the elimination of the Jewish State." "This will be a war of extermination and momentous massacre which will be spoken of like the Mongolian massacre and the Crusades," predicted Azzam at a Cairo press conference. As to the attacking armies, "generally reliable" French intelligence in Beirut informed the Agency that five Arab states would invade simultaneously on May 15 with some 30,000 forces, including 5,000 of the heavily armed Arab Legion. Lie, who like many had foreseen the chaos that now came to fruition, described the outcome as a "fiasco." The inevitable, first Arab-Jewish War had begun.[82]

Endnotes

1. "Resolutions adopted by the Security Council in 1948," United Nations Security Council, https://www.un.org/securitycouncil/content/resolutions-adopted-security-council-1948.
2. Monty Noam Penkower, *Palestine to Israel: Mandate to State, 1945–1948*, vol. 2, *Into the International Arena, 1947–1948* (New York, 2019), 550, 557–563, 568–570, 577–578, 585–589, 593–594, 602–609, 619–624, 628–629. It is possible that Truman, contending at the same time with the Soviet *coup d'état* in Czechoslovakia, Moscow's aggressive designs in Germany and elsewhere, and his call to Congress for a US selective service recruitment law, did not realize the full significance of the draft of Austin's statement when he had approved it on March 8. In addition, as emerged from a meeting which Truman convened the next day, he had assumed that Austin would announce the alternative plan *after* a Council vote had demonstrated the impossibility of putting over the partition plan.
3. Ibid., 633, 635–636. For Shertok's April 1 address, see Moshe Sharett, *B'Sha'ar HaUmot* (Tel Aviv, 1964), 173–191.

4. Penkower, *Palestine to Israel: Mandate to State*, vol. 2, 597–598.
5. Ibid., 632.
6. Ibid., 602, 619–620; James Barros, *Trygve Lie and the Cold War: The UN Secretary-General Pursues Peace, 1946–1953* (DeKalb, 1989), 189–190; Shertok to Myerson, April 6, 1948, S25/1558, Central Zionist Archives (hereafter CZA), Jerusalem, Israel.
7. Shertok remarks, April 1, 1948, UN Trusteeship Council, S/PV.277; Shertok to Ben-Gurion, April 2, 1948, S25/1704, CZA; Penkower, *Palestine to Israel, Mandate to State*, vol. 2, 513, 515, 518, 585–586.
8. Ibid., 638; *Jewish Telegraphic Agency* (hereafter *JTA*), April 1 and 4, 1948; Eytan report, April 2, 1948, 93.03/125/16, Israel State Archives (hereafter ISA), Jerusalem.
9. Executive to Shertok, April 4, 1948, S25/1704, CZA.
10. *JTA*, April 5, 1948; Shertok to Ben-Gurion and Myeerson, April 4, 1948, S25/1704; Berman, Eytan, Kohn, and Herzog to Shertok, March 28, 1948, S25/1558; Shertok to Sasson, April 4, 1948; Shertok to Eytan, April 5, 1948; both in S25/1551; all in CZA. That same moment, a lengthy Hagana intelligence report detailed the mandatory government's obstructive steps against implementing the GA partition decision. "Sekirat Teneh," April 6, 1948, S25/9671, CZA.
11. Penkower, *Palestine to Israel: Mandate to State*, vol. 2, 632–633; Efraim Karsh, *Palestine Betrayed* (New Haven, 2010), 169. Beeley had admitted on April 1 to a US Embassy official in London that he could not suggest a better plan than that of the United States, the alternative apparently to let the Jews and Arabs "fight it out" until some kind of an arrangement was reached. Jones to Rusk et al., April 1, 1948, File 1, Robert McClintock MSS., State Department records, National Archives (hereafter NA), Suitland, MD. The Hagana, created in 1920 as a response to Arab attacks in Jerusalem and elsewhere, served as the Agency's defense force.
12. *Palestine Post*, April 4, 1948; Ben-Zvi to Jewish Agency Executive, April 5, 1948, S40/8/1, CZA.
13. Eytan-Azcárate meeting, April 5, 1948, S25/5634, CZA.
14. General Principles, April 5, 1948, 93.03/95/14, ISA; Shertok to Myerson, April 6, 1948, S25/1704, CZA; Eban to Fischer, April 7, 1948, 93.03/126/6, ISA; Kopper to Marshall, April 5, 1948, File 1, Dean Rusk MSS., State Department records, NA; Penkower, *Palestine to Israel: Mandate to State*, vol. 2, 636–637; Pearson to Wrong, April 6, 1948, RG 25, series A-12, vol. 2093, part 5, Public Archives of Canada (hereafter PAC), Ottawa, Canada.

15. Lawford to Foreign Office, April 5, 1946; Foreign Office to New York, April 7, 1948; both in Foreign Office records (hereafter FO), 371/68541, Public Record Office (hereafter PRO), Kew, England.
16. Penkower, *Palestine to Israel: Mandate to State*, vol. 2, 637, 567, 625. For McClintock's overall views on the Palestine conundrum and its impact on US oil needs, with large-scale fighting between Jews and Arabs "inevitably" to open the way for Soviet penetration of Palestine, see Memo, April 7, 1948, File 1, McClintock MSS.
17. Eban to Fischer, April 7, 1948, 93.03/126/6, ISA.
18. Penkower, *Palestine to Israel: Mandate to State*, vol. 2, 637. From April onwards, Magnes had shared his support of a truce and trusteeship with Austin, American Consul in Jerusalem Thomas Wasson, Azcárate, and supporters in the United States, particularly the American Jewish Committee, Judge Jerome Frank, and former Barnard College dean Virginia Gildersleeve, a founder of the anti-partition Committee for Justice and Peace in the Holy Land, who told *New York Times* publisher Arthur Hays Sulzberger that he had impressed her "profoundly." Magnes to Austin, April 4, 1948, file 4-1751, Ernst Simon MSS.; Magnes to Wasson, Ms.Var. 350/7, Martin Buber MSS.; both Jewish National Library, Jerusalem; Azcárate to Bunche, April 20, 1948, DAG-3/3.1.1., box 1, UN Archives, New York City; April 12, 1948 draft, box 73, Jerome Frank MSS., Sterling Library, Yale University, New Haven, CT; Gildersleeve to Sulzberger, May 3, 1948, Palestine and Zionism-2, Arthur Hays Sulzberger MSS., *New York Times* Archives (now at the New York Public Library). For Magnes's binationalist views for Palestine, see chap. 6.
19. Penkower, *Palestine to Israel: Mandate to State*, vol. 2, 638; Sasson to Shertok, April 8, 1948, S25/5634; Report of Arab League meeting, April 11, 1948, A116/87I; both in CZA.
20. McNaughton to Pearson, April 7, 1948, MG 26, J1, vol. 440, PAC; Shertok to Ben-Gurion, April 6, 1948, S25/1704, CZA; Shertok to Lisicky, April 6, 1948, DAG-13/3.1.0:4, UN Archives; Gass to Epstein, April 7, 1948, 93.01/2180/14; Kohn-Cunningham meeting, April 7, 1948, P563/1; both in ISA; Kohn to Shertok, April 7, 1948, S25/1704, CZA.
21. Penkower, *Palestine to Israel: Mandate to State*, vol. 2, 639.
22. Eytan to Shertok, April 8, 1948, P573/1, ISA.
23. López-Husseini meeting, April 7, 1948, 93.03/94/8, ISA. For the refutation by the Agency's legal advisor of Husseini's claim regarding the League of Nations Covenant, noting that Palestine was not granted "provisional recognition" as an independent nation by the Covenant or by the Mandate (which gave the

Jewish Agency special status to speak for world Jewry in creating a Jewish National Home in Palestine), see Jacob Robinson memo, April 28, 1948, L35/141, CZA.
24. López-Shertok meeting, April 7, 1948, 93.03/95/1, ISA.
25. López-Husseini meeting, April 8, 1948, 95/1—Chet-Tzadi 93, ISA; Husseini statement, April 8, 1948, L35/65, CZA. For the restrictive 1939 White Paper, which limited Jewish immigration during the next five years to 75,000—thereafter with Arab consent—and foresaw a Palestine state within a decade (thus an Arab majority), see Monty Noam Penkower, *Palestine in Turmoil: The Struggle for Sovereignty, 1933–1939*, vol. 2, *Retreat from the Mandate, 1937–1939* (New York, 2014), chap. 10.
26. López-Shertok meeting (two reports), April 8, 1948, 95/1—Chet-Tzadi 93, ISA; Shertok to Ben-Gurion and Myerson, April 8, 1948, S25/1704, CZA.
27. McNaughton to Pearson, April 7, 1948, MG 26, J1, vol. 440, PAC; New York to Marshall, April 7, 1948, File 2, Rusk MSS.
28. Shertok-Lovett-Rusk meeting, April 9, 1948, 130.2414/22; Shertok to Ben-Gurion, April 11, 1948, 93.2180/14; both in ISA.
29. Shertok-Rusk meetings, April 9, 1948, 93.03/129/6; Shertok to Ben-Gurion, April 11, 1948, 130.9, 2337/4; all in ISA.
30. Fahy to Silver, April 10, 1948, 93.03/126/10, ISA.
31. Penkower, *Palestine to Israel: Mandate to State*, vol. 2, 640; Austin to Marshall, April 12, 1948, File 2, Rusk MSS. Two days later, the British informed Bunche that "there was no question" of the proposed military force coming "into being" before May 15. Fletcher-Cooke to Bunche, April 12, 1948, RG 25, vol. 84–85/19, PAC.
32. Penkower, *Palestine to Israel: Mandate to State*, vol. 2, 640–641. Gromyko's presence elicited the same day a worried memo from the director of the State Department's Office of European Affairs about the danger of a Soviet contingent in a UN security force for Palestine. Hickerson to Lovett, April 12, 1948, File 1, McClintock MSS.
33. Penkower, *Palestine to Israel: Mandate to State*, vol. 2, 641; Bunche to Azcárate, April 13, 1948, DAG-3/3.1.1., File 1, UN Archives; *Palestine Post*, April, 14, 1948; Bunche to Fletcher-Cooke, May 6, 1948, DAG-13/3.1.0.1, box 2, UN Archives.
34. Kohn to Fox-Strangeways, April 9, 1948, P673/1, ISA.
35. Shertok to Ben-Gurion, April 9, 1948; Shertok to Ben-Gurion, April 11, 1948; both in S25/1704, CZA.
36. Penkower, *Palestine to Israel: Mandate to State*, vol. 2, 641–642; Weizmann to Marshall, 93.03/67/6, ISA.

37. Penkower, *Palestine to Israel: Mandate to State*, vol. 2, 642.
38. Ibid., 642–643. For the official US arms embargo, which discriminated against the Jews, see Amitsur Ilan, *The Origin of the Arab-Israeli Arms Race* (London, 1996).
39. Penkower, *Palestine to Israel: Mandate to State*, vol. 2, 644.
40. Azcárate to Bunche, April 1, 1948, DAG-13.3.1.0.1, File1, UN Archives; Eban to Ross, April 12, 1948, 93.03/95/14; Shertok to Ben-Gurion, April 12, 1948, 130.9, 2337/4; both in ISA; *HaAretz*, April 13, 1948. Under Article 80, a provision of international law, Jewish rights to Palestine and the Land of Israel were not to be altered in any way unless there had been an intervening trusteeship agreement between the states or parties concerned converting the mandate into a trusteeship or trust territory. Among the most important of these Jewish rights were those contained in Article 6 of the Mandate, which recognized the right of Jews to immigrate freely to the Land of Israel and to establish settlements thereon.
41. Schedule, MC280/238, Freda Kirchwey MSS., Radcliffe College, Cambridge, MA; *Yearbook of the United Nations (1947–48)*, 414–415.
42. Rusk to Lovett, April 16, 1948, file 2, Rusk MSS.; Inverchapel to Foreign Office, April 17, 1948, MG 26, J4, vol. 310, PAC.; Bevin to Inverchapel, April 19, 1948, FO800/487, PRO.
43. Schedule, MC280/238, Freda Kirchwey MSS.; New York to Pearson, April 19, 1948, MG 26, N1, vol. 64, PAC. A week later, Beeley thought that the Jews could consolidate a state of restricted size running from Tel Aviv to Haifa "and going inland fifteen or more miles." Austin to State, April 27, 1948, file 2, McClintock MSS. For the Agency's modification of the truce draft, see Shertok to López, April 16, 1948, 93.03/94/5, ISA.
44. Fahy-Lovett meeting, April 16, 1948, 93.03/126/10, ISA.
45. Gurney diary, April 6–23, 1948, St. Anthony College, Oxford University, Oxford, England; Condensed survey, February–May 15, 1948, A289/125, CZA. In the introduction to a private "Postscript" in the diary, Gurney would claim that "no evidence existed" to substantiate the statement that 6,000,000 Jews had been killed in Europe, and "whether or not this is true, it was open to Jews there to resume life in their own countries."
46. Ben-Gurion to Shertok, April 16, 1948, 93.03/117/20; Shertok to Ben-Gurion, April 19, 1948, 93.01/2180/14; both in ISA; Shertok to Ben-Gurion, April 19, 1948, S25/1551, CZA.
47. Azcárate to Lie and Bunche, April 19, 1948, DAG 13/3.1.0/box 5-B; Azcárate to Cunningham, DAG 13/3.1.0/box 5-A; both in UN Archives. At this point,

Bevin advised the Colonial Secretary to perhaps suggest to Austin that any Palestine settlement should include the responsibility of UN members to accept refugee Jews throughout Europe, and that the best contribution any outside state could make if fighting ensued in Palestine would be to prevent the entry of additional arms or reinforcement for either side—ideally involving "sealing the land and sea frontiers of Palestine." Bevin to Creech Jones, April 19, 1948, FO371/68543, PRO.
48. Schedule, MC 280/238, Kirchwey MSS.
49. Reports, April 20–21, 1948, Anne Robison MSS., New Jersey (courtesy of Anne Robison); McClintock to Lovett, April 20, 1948, file 1, Rusk MSS.; *JTA*, April 21–22, 1948, Schultz diary, April 22, 1948, MC280/238, Kirchwey MSS.
50. Penkower, *Palestine to Israel: Mandate to State*, vol. 2, 649–651.
51. Schedule, MC 280/238, Kirchwey MSS.; *New York Times*, April 21, 1948; Secretariat meeting, April 22, 1948, DAG 1/1.1.3, box 1, UN Archives.
52. Interim Government plan, April 22, 1948; Listowel to Bevin, April 23, 1948; both in FO371/68548, PRO; Douglas to Marshall, April 22, 1948, 501.BB/Palestine/4-1548, State Department records, NA.
53. Truce Commission resolution, April 23, 1948, M. Medzini, *Israel's Foreign Relations, Selected Documents, 1947–1974* (Jerusalem, 1976), 134–135; Schedule, MC 280/238, Kirchwey MSS.; Report, April 23, 1948, Robison MSS.
54. Penkower, *Palestine to Israel: Mandate to State*, vol. 2, 652–653.
55. Shertok to Zaslani, April 22, 1948, 130.09/2337/4, ISA; Sasson to Shertok, April 23, 1948, S25/8182, CZA; Sharett, *B'Sha'ar HaUmot*, 202–208; Tuck to Marshall, April 25, 1948, file 3, Rusk MSS.
56. McClintock draft, April 11, 1948, File 3, Rusk MSS.; Proskauer letter to the *New York Times*, April 12, 1948; Rusk draft, April 22, 1948; Proskauer-Lovett-Rusk negotiations, April 19, 1948; both in 93.03/85/16; all in ISA; Austin to Marshall, April 24, 1948, file 3, Rusk MSS.; Kopper memo, April 6, 1948, File 1, McClintock MSS. Privately, Rusk told Beeley that in pressing the Security Council to follow up its previous resolution in favor of a truce, the US delegation hoped to make it quite clear" to public opinion that it was "impossible" to stop the conflict in Palestine. Beeley to Burrows, April 24, 1948, FO371/68546, PRO.
57. Robinson-Epstein memo, April 26, 1948, 93.03/95/1, ISA; Jewish Agency Executive, American Section, April 1948 minutes, Z5/2387, CZA; McClintok to Lovett, April 26, 1948, file 3, Rusk MSS.; Proskauer to Shertok, April 27, 1948, box 8, Joseph M. Proskauer MSS., American Jewish Committee archives, New York City. Earlier that month, Proskauer had pressed the pro-Zionist James

G. McDonald, one of the US members of the Anglo-American Committee of Inquiry on Palestine, to intercede with the Pope for the internationalization of Jerusalem. Proskauer to McDonald, April 1, 1948, box 8, Proskauer MSS. For Robinson's vital contribution to the Agency ever since the British turned to the UN in April 1947 for recommendations regarding Palestine's future, see chap. 2.

58. New York to Foreign Office, April 27, 1948, FO371/68649, PRO; Penkower, *Palestine to Israel: Mandate* to State, vol. 2, 658–659; Report, April 26, 1948, Robison MSS.; *JTA*, April 27, 1948; Shertok to Ben-Gurion, April 28, 1948, S25/1558, CZA; Bancroft to Rusk, May 5, 1948, file 3, Rusk MSS.; Lillie Shultz, "Britain's Stake in an Arab Victory," *The Nation*, May 29, 1948, 595–598. Years later, Rusk denied that any such threat had been made, declaring that "if there's one thing that an Assistant Secretary of State cannot do it's to affect a transfer of funds for philanthropic purposes anywhere." Yigal Lossin, *Pillar of Fire: The Rebirth of Israel – A Visual History*, trans. Z. Ofer (Jerusalem, 1983), 537.

59. Record of Conversation, April 28, 1948, FO800/487; Bevin-Douglas talk, April 29, 1948, FO371/68546; both in PRO.

60. French resolution, April 26, 1948, file 3, Rusk MSS.; *JTA*, April 29, 1948; Nieuwenhuys to Abdullah, April 28, 1948, 93/125/15, ISA; Shertok to Ben-Gurion, April 28, 1948, 93.03/95/1, ISA; Shertok to Marshall, April 29, 1948, File 13, Clark Clifford MSS., Harry S. Truman Presidential Library, Independence, MO; McClintock to Rusk, April 28, 1948, file 3, Rusk MSS; Sharett, *B'Sha'ar HaUmot*, 208–223; Shertok to Proskauer, April 29, 1948, box 8, Proskauer MSS. For Abdullah's reply to the Truce Commission's warning, Kirkbride to Foreign Office, April 30, 1948, FO371/68646, PRO. At this point, Weizmann's views were "closely in accord" with those expressed by the Jewish Agency. New York to Pearson, April 27, 1948, MG 26, J1, vol. 440, PAC; Report, April 28, 1948, Robison MSS.

61. Shertok to Ben-Gurion, April 27 and 28, 1948; both in S25/5176, CZA; Lourie to Eytan, April 30, 1948, 93.03/126/9, ISA; New York to Pearson, April 28, 1948, MG 26, J 1, vol. 440, PAC; Memo, April 27, 1948, box 20, Frank Corrigan MSS., Franklin D. Roosevelt Presidential Library, Hyde Park, New York; Penkower, *Palestine to Israel: Mandate to State*, vol. 2, 659; Cunningham report, April 25, 1948, FO37168545, PRO; Austin to State, April 29, 1948, file 3, Rusk MSS.; Creech Jones to Cunningham, April 29, 1947, FO371/68546, PRO.

62. Proskauer to Ben-Gurion, April 30, 1948, S25/1558, CZA; *Palestine Post*, April 26, 1948; Eban to Fischer, April 29, 1948, 93.03/126/6, ISA. For Goldmann's views immediately after the Security Council had adopted the US proposal for

a truce and trusteeship in Palestine, see Lichtheim to Agronsky, April 1, 1948, A209/29, CZA. Goldmann's views remained unchanged when addressing the US Jewish organization's Political Advisory Committee one month later. Meetings, May 3–4, 1948, file 32, Religious Zionist Archives, Mosad HaRav Kook, Jerusalem.

63. Schedule, MC 280/238, Kirchwey MSS.; Memo, April 29, 1948, file 3, Rusk MSS.; Shertok to Ben-Gurion, April 29 and 30, 1948; both in S25/1588; Shertok to Ben-Gurion, April 30, 1948, S25/5176; all in CZA. As early as April 9, Azcárate had advised that if no agreement had been reached by April 25 about the whole of Palestine, "all efforts must be concentrated on Jerusalem." Azcárate memo, April 9, 1948, DAG-13/3.1.0.5, UN Archives. Also see R.M. Graves, *Experiment in Anarchy* (London, 1949).

64. Chronological Account, April 25, 1948, 93-125/15, ISA; Penkower, *Palestine to Israel: Mandate to State*, vol. 2, 660–662; Memo, April 21, 1948, file 2, Rusk MSS.; David Horowiz, *State in the Making* (New York, 1953), 234–235. In reply to Feisal's expressed concerns, Rusk suggested to the Saudi prince that the Truce Commission deal with such questions as immigration and repatriation during the period of the truce itself, permitting on "compassionate grounds" up to 4,000 Jewish displaced persons per month, immigration not to be used to alter the military position of either community in Palestine. Rusk to Feisal, April 29, 1948, file 3, Rusk MSS.

65. UK Delegation UN to Foreign Office, May 1, 1948, FO371/68546, PRO; Meeting, May 2, 1948, file 32, Religious Zionist Archives; Penkower, *Palestine to Israel: Mandate to State*, vol. 2, 662. Truman also appointed John Hilldring, without consulting State, as his special representative to the US delegation at the UN. This delighted the Zionists, who knew of his key support for Holocaust survivors and then for partition as part of the US delegation last autumn at the GA. Forrestal threatened to resign in protest, but Marshall assured him that the appointment was not going to "neutralize" Loy Henderson, whom Forrestal greatly liked and respected. Hadow to Mason, May 2, 1948, FO371/64849, PRO. For Hilldring's earlier hand in keeping Europe's borders open to the survivors seeking entry to American DP camps, see Monty Noam Penkower, *After the Holocaust* (forthcoming, Boston, 2021), chap. 3.

66. Bevin to Creech Jones, April 30, 1948, FO371/68546, PRO.

67. Shertok to Parodi, May 5, 1948, 93.03/94/5, ISA; Eban address, May 1, 1948, Jewish Agency files, ZA; Abba Eban, *Personal Witness: Israel Through My Eyes* (New York 1992), 142–143; Linton to Brodetsky, May 2, 1948, Z4/20029B, CZA.

68. Penkower, *Palestine to Israel: Mandate to State*, vol. 2, 664–665; Creech Jones to Bevin, May 2, 1948, FO371/68648; Creech Jones to Bevin, May 8, 1948, FO371/68650; both in PRO. Henderson confided to Beeley that he thought the trusteeship plan was "probably dead," but at least it had served the purpose for "enabling them to avoid attempting to implement partition." Beeley to Burrows, May 3, 1948, FO371/68565, PRO.
69. Penkower, *Palestine to Israel: Mandate to State*, vol. 2, 665. At this point, the Agency's American Section split in favor of considering a deferment of sovereignty in favor of a truce on certain conditions, the vote 9 to 7. Jewish Agency NY to Jewish Agency Jerusalem, May 7, 1948, 93.01/2180/15, ISA. Discussion on May 11 in the GA Political Committee for a new subcommittee to recommend measures for the protection of Jerusalem, the United States' Francis Sayre again championing the American trusteeship plan of April 16, was inconclusive. UK to Foreign Office, May 11, 1948, FO371/68551; Report, May 11, 1948, Robison MSS.
70. Penkower, *Palestine to Israel: Mandate to State*, vol. 2, 666; Rusk proposal, May 4, 1948, S25/5176, CZA. It had always been HMG's hope, Bevin told the US Ambassador, that the Jews would "act sensibly" and keep within their own zones, that Jerusalem would be put under a truce, and that Abdullah "might use his forces temporarily to maintain order in the Arab areas," this allowing time for discussion and possibly for a settlement to be found. Bevin-Douglas talk, May 10, 1948, FO800/487, PRO. Ben-Gurion objected to any prolongation "even for ten days" of the mandatory regime, which "is responsible for bloodshed in Palestine, armed invasion of country and wrecking U.N. decisions." Ben-Gurion to Shertok, May 4, 1948, S25/1553, CZA. Ben-Gurion made the same point at the first meeting of the Provisional National Administration. *Palcor*, May 5, 1948. Privately, Bevin urged the Arab states to accept the truce, as, militarily, economically and politically they were "in no position" to take their "intransigent line." Foreign Office to Arab capitals and Jerusalem, May 6, 1948, FO371/68548, PRO.
71. Penkower, *Palestine to Israel: Mandate to State*, vol. 2, 667, 703; Magnes memo, May 2, 1948, file P3/162, Central Archives for the History of the Jewish People, Jerusalem; Truman-Sulzberger interview, May 8, 1948, box 58, Arthur Krock MSS., Department of Rare Books and Special Collections, Princeton University Library, Princeton, New Jersey. For the publisher's insecurities as a Jew and its impact on his newspaper's reporting of the Holocaust and of Zionism, see Monty Noam Penkower, *Twentieth-Century Jews: Forging Identity in the Land of Promise and in the Promised Land* (Brighton, 2010), chap. 5.

72. Penkower, *Palestine to Israel: Mandate to State*, vol. 2, 668–670; Epstein to Jewish Agency NY, May 7, 1948, 93.03/126/7, ISA. Worried that the establishment of a Jewish state would give the Arabs no "way out" but to attack, Azcárate advised the Agency's Vivian (Chaim) Herzog to "lessen the tempo and give the Arabs a chance to recover some form of prestige," go ahead to create the state *de facto* with a view to having it recognized after some six to eight months. Herzog meetings, May 11, 1948; Eytan meetings, May 12, 1948; both in S25/5634, CZA.
73. Penkower, *Palestine to Israel: Mandate to State,* vol. 2, 603, 669; Lowenthal Diary, May 5-15, 1948, 1885/4-P, ISA; Lowenthal to Clifford, n.d., box 13, Clifford MSS.; Lourie to Shertok, May 11, 1948, S25/1553, CZA. Fahy reported that Rusk told him the US delegation would not press further the truce or other proposals, reconciled as they were to an "inevitable" Jewish statehood proclamation. Rusk added a warning to Fahy that if the Arab Legion attacked the new Jewish state, it would be difficult for the United States to intervene on behalf of the embattled Jews. Lourie to Shertok, May 11, 1948, 93.03/2180/15, ISA.
74. *JTA*, May 13, 1948; Clark Clifford with Richard Holbrook, *Counsel to the President, A Memoir* (New York, 1991), 9–14; Penkower, *Palestine to Israel: Mandate to State*, vol. 2, 673–674. At this point, former Undersecretary of State Sumner Welles warned the Jewish Agency not to postpone the mandate's termination date and to establish a provisional government regime. He had reliable information that postponement was intended for the establishment of an Anglo-American condominium along the lines of the Anglo-American Morrison-Grady plan, which in July 1946 had proposed a division of Palestine into four zones under British administration, with autonomy accorded to the Jewish and Arab areas. Both the Jews and the Arabs opposed that plan, and Truman's lack of support ended its chances for adoption. Monty Noam Penkower, *Palestine to Israel: Mandate to State, 1945–1948, vol. 1, Rebellion Launched, 1945–1946* (New York, 2019), chap. 4.
75. Penkower, *Palestine to Israel: Mandate to State*, vol. 2, 674–675; Lowenthal diary, May 13, 1948.
76. Penkower, *Palestine to Israel: Mandate to State,* vol. 2, 675–676; UK NY to Foreign Office, May 13, 1948, FO 371/68552; Bevin to UK Delegation, May 12, 1948, FO371/68551; both in PRO; Ginsburg to Silver, May 11, 1948, 93.03/69/5, ISA; *JTA*, May 14, 1948; Report, May 14, 1948, Palestine 1948 file, Jewish War Veterans Archives, Washington, DC. The Arabs killed 24 badly outgunned Kfar Etzion defenders on April 12, murdering the next day 106 men and 27 women, including some after they had surrendered. Only

four survived the attack. For the Anglo-American Commission of Inquiry on Palestine, see Penkower, *Palestine to Israel: Mandate to State*, vol. 1, Chap. 3.

77. Penkower, *Palestine to Israel: Mandate to State*, vol. 2, 677–679; English translation of the Israeli Declaration of Independence, released at 4 p.m. Palestine time, S44/567; Epstein to Shertok, May 14, 1948, L35/120; both in CZA; Diary, May 12–14, 1948, Eben A. Ayers MSS., Harry S. Truman Presidential Library. Epstein turned to Ginsburg a day or two earlier to prepare a memo on the international law of recognizing states, and the Washington, DC lawyer came up with the fact that the United States had recognized Panama before it was created out of Colombia in the days of President Theodore Roosevelt.

78. Penkower, *Palestine to Israel: Mandate to State*, vol. 2, 679–680, 701; Wilkins interview with Jessup, July 21, 1988, Library of Congress, Washington, DC; Eliyahu Elath, "That Year in Jerusalem," *New York Times*, May 4, 1973.

79. Truman speech, December 3, 1961, file SC-12465, American Jewish Archives, Cincinnati, OH; Penkower, *Palestine to Israel: Mandate to State*, vol. 2, 680–681.

80. Ibid, 681; UK NY to Foreign Office, May 14, 1948, FO371/68552, PRO; McNaughton to Pearson, May 15, 1948, MG26, J4, vol. 397, PAC; George M. Elsey, at the time an assistant to Clifford and later Administrative Assistant to Truman, later claimed that Truman's recognition of Israel's sovereignty was, like his instruction to Secretary of Defense Forrestal on February 2, 1948, to desegregate the US armed forces "as rapidly as possible," taken from his personal belief that this was "the right thing for the nation, for the American people." Elsey interview with Michael T. Benson, December 4, 1997, in "Harry S. Truman and the Recognition of Israel," Harry S. Truman Library Institute for National and International Affairs (1998).

81. Abba Eban, "Tragedy and Triumph," in Chaim Weizmann, *A Biography by Several Hands*, ed. M. W. Weisgal and J. Carmichael (London, 1962), 312.

82. *Palestine Post*, May 5, 1948; Penkower, *Palestine to Israel: Mandate to State*, vol. 2, 682; Barros, *Trygve Lie*, 191. Three days later, the UN Palestine Commission, after holding seventy-six meetings, adjourned *sine die*.

6. Judah Leib Magnes: The Last Year

On October 28, 1948, one day after the passing of Judah Leib Magnes, a long obituary in the *New York Times* took note that he was one of the modern builders of the liberal tradition in America and for forty years "an outstanding cultural leader in American and world Jewry." The obituary went on to mention services as the spiritual leader of Temple Emanu-El (Reform) and Congregation B'nai Jeshurun (Conservative)—both of which he left because he preferred a more Orthodox Judaism; his chairing of the New York City Kehilla organization and its Board of Jewish Education; his association with American labor causes; and his vocal pacifism during World War I. In 1922 Magnes immigrated to Palestine, where he became chancellor of the Hebrew University three years later. The obituary noted that his hope was for the first Jewish university to serve as a permanent home for the tradition of science, learning and ethical dedication among the Jews, "not to achieve nationalistic aims but to enable Judaism to carry on its historical role as an interpreter and mediator among nations." This meshed with his calling for cooperation with the Arab population toward a binationalist Palestine state, which would take its place within an Arab federation in the Middle East.[1]

Magnes's proposal for Palestine was one of many competing positions during that time. In fact, Magnes had chosen not to join forces with the like-minded Brit Shalom (1925–1933), a small group founded by philosophers Samuel Hugo Bergman and Martin Buber, historian Hans Kohn, Kabbalah scholar Gershom Scholem, and Palestine Land Development Company head Arthur Ruppin. The group advocated one state based on parity between the contending Arab and Jewish populations. Magnes favored the British mandatory's proposed scheme in

1936 for a legislative council, which Jewish Agency for Palestine political director Moshe Shertok (later Sharett) feared would give the *yishuv* (Palestinian Jewish community) permanent minority status. In June of that year, together with a few prominent individuals, Magnes drew up a Jewish-Arab agreement. This agreement included Arab nationalist Musa al-Alami's proposal that the Jews reach forty percent of the total population after ten years. Subsequently, the British Peel Commission came forward with a plan to partition Palestine into an Arab and a Jewish state. Arthur Hays Sulzberger, publisher of the *New York Times*, objected to this, instead championing Magnes's plan when objecting to the British Peel Commission's subsequent offer of partitioning Palestine into an Arab and a Jewish state. First Palestine High Commissioner Herbert Samuel, former Palestine Attorney General Norman Bentwich, Kedma Mizraha founder Chaim Kalvariski-Margalioth, American philanthropist Felix Warburg, and a few other eminent figures also endorsed Magnes's position, as did the British Colonial and Foreign Offices. Yet the sustained Arab Revolt in Palestine (1936–1939), accompanied by slight prospects for true reconciliation from Grand Mufti Haj Amin al-Husseini and other leaders on the Arab side, soon put paid to any such hopes.[2]

"I am personally ready to yield Jewish political sovereignty in Palestine," Magnes wrote in October 1937 to Rev. John Holmes in New York City, "if through that I can secure—over a long period of years and over large stretches of the Arab world—the settlement of large numbers of Jews and their peaceful living and working together with the Arabs." He joined with leaders of some *yishuv* parties, former Brit Shalom and Kedma Mizraha members, and others to establish the League for Jewish-Arab Rapprochement and Cooperation, whose March 1939 pamphlet, *Al Parashat Darkeinu* (At Our Crossroads), embraced the binationalist banner. Five months later, Magnes expressed his doubts to Edward Norman, an American Jewish philanthropist. Norman had proposed a plan to transfer a large number of Palestine Arabs to Iraq's unsettled, fertile valley between the Tigris and Euphrates rivers, thus facilitating considerable Jewish entry into the biblical Promised Land. That way, Magnes objected, "many more" Jews could be settled in Palestine "if we insist upon a Jewish state or a Jewish majority in Palestine," but certainly not in Arab lands. The German *Wehrmacht*'s swift invasion of Poland, unleashing World War II, would not alter his overall perspective.[3]

Magnes's strictures aligned with those of Morris Lazaron, rabbi of Baltimore Hebrew Congregation. Their opposition to militant Zionist nationalism—especially in light of the 1941 pro-Nazi revolt in Iraq and German General Edwin Rommel's grave threat vis-à-vis the Suez Canal—suited the anti-Zionist mandarins in the US State Department's Near Eastern Division and its head, Wallace Murray. At the end of July, Sulzberger enthusiastically publicized Magnes's credo for a binationalist Palestine within an Arab federation. This, in turn, evoked American Zionist elder and American Jewish Congress president Stephen Wise's lament that "we have a man of [Magnes's] influence and power more concerned with messianic union with the Arabs than insuring the little for which we ask and to which we are more than entitled."[4]

Magnes signed the majority, binationalist conclusions of the Jewish Agency's Committee on the Arab Question, remarking that "if there is no other way then the whole thing is not worthwhile," In August 1942 he led the way to the formation of the Ichud (Union) party, which continued his earlier efforts to create a religious society that would be politically engaged, focusing on shared moral sensibilities that could result in reconciliation between communities in conflict. At the Ichud's first meeting, Magnes condemned the Jewish Agency's embrace of the Biltmore Program, whose recent call for a Jewish state in Western Palestine would lead to a war that might destroy the *yishuv* or create "a pagan state like all the nations." Joining Magnes's condemnation were many of his fellow League activists: Buber; Kalvariski; Farmer's Federation head Moshe Smilansky; educator Ernst Simon; Rabbi Binyamin (Yehoshua Radler-Feldman); the journalist Gavriel Stern; and Hadassah founder Henrietta Szold, Justice A. Valero, and leaders of the left-wing Hashomer HaTsa'ir party. Lazaron, active just then in the incipient formation of the anti-Zionist American Council for Judaism (ACJ), publicized—without authorization—Magnes's private letter to him critiquing current Jewish nationalism as "unhappily chauvinistic and narrow and terroristic in the best style of East European nations." Magnes's article a few months later in the prestigious journal *Foreign Affairs*, calling for an imposed Anglo-American binational solution, delighted the State Department's secret postwar planning staff, which worried over Arab unrest and was skeptical of Palestine's capacity for additional immigration.[5]

At the end of World War II in Europe, however, no responsible Palestinian Arab leader had ever endorsed a binationalist state. Already in the 1930s, Palestinians al-Husseini, al-Alami, and Auni Bey 'Abd al-Hadi, together with Saudi Arabia's King Abdul Aziz Ibn Saud and other Muslim rulers, had voiced strident opposition to Zionism. In a letter to Magnes one week after the Japanese surprise attack on Pearl Harbor, Rashid al-Haj Ibrahim, former leader of the Istiqlal Party (the first native Palestinian group to urge collaboration with Italy and Germany in the 1930s), dismissed even Magnes's solution by publicly listing his people's demands: "Non-recognition and cancellation of the Balfour Declaration, total opposition to Jewish immigration, non-recognition of any Jewish rights whatsoever, and further promotion of Arab aims at this time and at all times to come until our freedom and independence are fully restored." Haj Amin's alignment with Hitler during the war notwithstanding, an Arab League had been created with British encouragement, and five Arab independent nations could bring great weight to bear on Palestine's future. Seen in this context, Ichud's dream of peaceful coexistence in one small country increasingly appeared a chimera.[6]

The pressing plight of Holocaust survivors had a strong impact on Magnes, who in October 1945 flatly told US Consul-General Lowell Pinkerton in Jerusalem that, counter to the stringent British quotas of the May 1939 White Paper, he would help "with all the means at his disposal" any Jewish refugees who arrived. Yet that same month, the Royal Institute of International Affairs's Chatham House—former home to Harold Beeley, Foreign Minister Ernest Bevin's chief advisor on Palestine—began preparing a paper for the Anglo-American Committee of Inquiry on Palestine that started with Magnes's binationalist views coupled with an extension and adaption of the Ottoman millet system, which gave Arab and Jew a measure of autonomy. On the other hand, it was precisely the need to transfer Europe's Jewish masses as soon as possible to Palestine and achieve a Jewish majority that led Eliyahu Epstein (later Elath), the Agency's Washington representative, to urge Shertok in January 1946 to press for partition. Epstein argued that partition was the only realistic alternative to the binationalism that Magnes and HaShomer HaTsa'ir advocated, which would require a permanent international trusteeship or soon develop into an Arab state.[7]

Magnes appeared before the Anglo-American Committee of Inquiry on Palestine in Jerusalem's YMCA building on the afternoon of March 14, 1946. His delivery, preceded by Buber's presentation of their Ichud Party's platform, appealed to most of the committee. His approach when calling for a binational state with Jewish and Arab parity held his audience "almost breathless"—US member James G. McDonald's phrase—for more than two hours. All found his statement eloquent at times, deeply moving, and showing a moral courage that, according to a *Palestine Post* editorial, would not find its Arab counterpart. Many listeners had tears in their eyes, and US Chair Joseph C. Hutcheson went up to congratulate him, quoting from *John* 1:46 "here truly is an Israelite in whom there is no guile." However, some, including McDonald, thought Magnes's advocacy not at all practical—a "utopia," in British member Richard Crossman's judgment, unless all the Jews were as patient and rational as Magnes, the Arabs uncertain that the British were on their side, and all of His Majesty's Government's key Middle Eastern officials replaced by men who believed in the Jewish National Home promised in the Balfour Declaration and in helping Arabs and Jews to work together. In fact, Magnes himself, in reply to British member Wilfrid Crick, objected to altering his institution's name to "the University of Palestine," and advocated continued Jewish immigration (much as Mordekhai Ben-Tov of HaShomer HaTsa'ir joined it to binationalism in a private talk with the sympathetic Hutcheson). For Crossman, the difference between moderates, such as Magnes and World Zionist Organization president Chaim Weizmann, and militants, such as Jewish Agency Executive chair David Ben-Gurion, was one of principle. (Arab spokesmen thought Magnes more dangerous than Ben-Gurion.) It was all, he concluded, a question of tactics.[8]

Magnes welcomed the Anglo-American Committee's recommendation of a binational state and the immediate admission of 100,000 Holocaust survivors to Palestine. At the same time, he cautioned Palestine's sympathetic High Commissioner, Alan Cunningham, that the *yishuv* could not be asked to renounce its right to self-defense—the proviso announced by Prime Minister Clement Attlee—if the report were to be accepted, given its "unhappy bitter experiences" of Arab attacks. Yet the public tide in America, as in Palestine, was steadily running against the moderation called for by Magnes and Weizmann; for example, Magnes was unable to persuade Eleanor Roosevelt to drop her sponsorship of Ben Hecht's pageant-drama *A Flag is Born*, a defiant call for Jewish statehood that was sponsored by the right-wing Irgun Tsva'i Le'umi-allied American League for a Free Palestine. Further, Magnes's testimony on July 15, 1947, before the UN Special Committee on Palestine (UNSCOP) made less of an impression than that of the Jewish Agency's Shertok, who noted that the two fundamental events in modern Jewish history—the destruction of European Jewry and the *yishuv*'s renaissance in Palestine—were "two poles which, between them, galvanized the Jewish national will into action." Permanent stability in Palestine could only come, Shertok emphasized, by "satisfying the craving of the Jewish people" for sovereignty in their historic homeland. UNSCOP's majority partition report on September 1, welcomed even by the dissenting HaShomer HaTsa'ir, Achdut Ha'Avoda, and Revisionist Zionist parties as forming a basis for negotiation, brought Magnes to tears. It would mean war, he told a close friend, and the end of everything for which he and his followers stood against; the result would be a "dismembering" of the country.[9]

Seeking to secure Ichud's political objectives, Magnes backed, with some revisions—as he explained to colleague Ernst Simon—the UNSCOP minority report of a unitary, confederated state with two autonomous areas as the basis of discussion. He listed these alterations in a letter to the *New York Times* at the end of September: The boundaries should constitute a form of partition, divided into counties for purposes of local administration. The two peoples should have political parity, and the Federal Court of Appeals on constitutional matters should be composed of an equal number of Jews and Arabs. Jewish immigration should be permitted in all parts of Palestine up to parity with the Arabs. His original draft added that Sami Taha and Fawzi Darwish al-Husseini had called for binationalism before their assassination at Arab hands, reflecting "the true vision of the Holy Land to guide the United Nations, not the despair of the defeatists and chauvinists." "Give these two peoples the chance they never had of self-government *together*," he asserted, "and through systematic work day by day, year by year, their response will be increasingly joyous and constructive."[10]

In a letter to Cunningham, he posited that Britain had a moral obligation not to leave with "nothing to replace her." Together with Buber and Smilansky, he cabled General Assembly president Herbert Evatt of Australia to encourage work towards Ichud's program for a binational Palestine in a league of Middle East states, which would be represented at the UN by an equal number of Jews and Arabs. That single, independent entity would offer complete political equality between Jew and Arab; Jewish immigration and continued settlement would be according to the country's economic capacity determined by a board of three Jews, three Arabs, and three UN-appointed delegates; and it would allow for the fullest national cultural autonomy of both peoples. This would be preceded, the trio added, by "generous immediate immigration [of] Jewish displaced persons."[11]

Magnes was convinced that attacks on British troops and Arab citizens by the dissident Irgun and Stern group forces were, as he put it to Simon, the "decisive factor" leading to the partition recommendation. He condemned these assaults that the extremists defended as an effective method of reestablishing a Jewish commonwealth. On October 29, at the opening of the twenty-third year of the Hebrew University, Magnes condemned Zionist "totalitarianism," which he said was trying to bring the entire Jewish people under its influence "by force and violence." Those who did not speak out against the "foul deeds" of "this new pagan leadership" were also to be held responsible. He called for voices to raise the alarm, not because of anxiety for "the national discipline" but of anxiety concerning discipline to "the spirit of Israel and the timeless values of Israel's tradition." The *New York Times*, which had also declared that all Jews in the United States must share in this guilt, featured his condemnation.[12]

Simon, then on leave to teach at the Jewish Theological Seminary in New York City, questioned the propriety of the dissenter continuing individually to attack the recommendation of the majority, even though it was "for the sake of Zion." Such behavior, he wrote to Ichud member and veteran agricultural pioneer-pacifist Natan Hofshi (formerly Frankel) of Nahalal, carried the quality of the "lyrical," not reaching the realm of actuality. We have failed, he concluded, in that Ichud's ideas were appropriated by the anti-Zionists; "we were wrong in depending upon them." Magnes disagreed, asserting that as long as partition remained an uncertainty, his tactics were to oppose it—at the opportune moment publicly, and when times were not propitious, then privately.[13]

Accounts that the special session of the General Assembly might save his beloved Jerusalem from partition gave Magnes some hope in the third week of November. The city's "unifying influence" might in time heal the "surgical operation" on the rest of the country, he thought. "It has been a fearful experience for me all these weeks and days" that the "sacred land" was being bargained over and being cut up "like a piece of beef," Magnes wrote to Maurice Hexter, Federation of Jewish

Philanthropies executive in New York. It was not just a wound in his own heart, Magnes was certain, but in that of Jewish history. "Time will tell," he concluded wistfully.[14]

On November 27, Magnes cabled Sulzberger requesting that he distribute to the General Assembly delegates—without necessarily identifying himself with its message—a telegram in case deadlock over Palestine ensued, but not to publish the document without further approval. It read:

> Listened attentively Palestine debate astonished contention that Arabs Jews cannot live together and that partition or Arab dominated state or chaos only alternatives. Jews and Arabs do live and work together today and despite all contrary statements don't desire separation but union. Real alternative bi-national united Palestine based upon equal political rights and national autonomy both peoples and Jewish immigration and settlement according economic capacity as determined and developed for entire population by economic board consisting three Jews three Arabs three United Nations appointees. If special U.S. status practicable for Holy City of Jerusalem with 200,000 Jews Arabs and others why not for whole undivided Holy Land? Meanwhile pending definitive arrangements homeless Jews yearning for Zion should be admitted without further delay. Such bi-national compromise would guarantee vital interests both peoples and would be accepted by them without bloodshed and welcomed by men of goodwill everywhere. Please cable.

Sulzberger chose not to fulfill the request.[15]

The next morning, Pakistan delegate Zafrullah Khan proposed a unitary federal state with cantons, and praised Magnes's "noble and wise" steps in this respect. Former UNSCOP member Jorge García Granados of Guatemala rebutted immediately with an attack on the British mandatory's failures; charged that the Arab Higher Committee under Haj Amin would never agree to concessions; declared that the world had an obligation after the Holocaust to the Jewish people; and lauded the Zionist enterprise for already having laid the foundations for the spiritual, social, and political independence of a Jewish commonwealth in Eretz Israel. The die was cast the following day; the vote was thirty-three to thirteen in favor of partitioning Palestine into two independent states, with ten abstentions and one absent. "Any line of partition drawn in Palestine will be a line of fire and blood," shouted Arab League secretary Azzam Pasha as the furious Arab delegations left the hall.[16]

"We have failed 'for all eternity,'" Judah L. Magnes wrote to his Ichud colleagues on November 30, 1947. That sense of defeat, he explained, rested not only in the General Assembly's vote one day earlier to partition Palestine into two separate Jewish and Arab states. The committee's plan of championing Arab-Jewish reconciliation by means of a binationalist Palestine had not even achieved the appointment of a special United Nations subcommittee to study this scheme and its implementation. In light of Ichud's failure to achieve its primary political objective, the committee now had to consider if it yet had special tasks, such as continued engagement in moral and educational efforts, to justify its existence. Magnes, who had led the organization's creation five years earlier and served as its chair, considered himself responsible for its failure. Although he would be happy to work with such "dedicated, enlightened" friends should the organization continue, he no longer felt qualified to serve as its leader. He hoped that they would understand the validity of taking the present step: resignation.[17]

That same day, Palestine's Arabs launched a civil war. Unlike Magnes, who stood ready to resign over the defeat of all for which he stood, Ben-Gurion issued a statement declaring that the General Assembly's vote to give his people a sovereign commonwealth in part of its ancient homeland was "an act of historic justice, compensating at least partly for the unparalleled wrong to which the Jewish people were subjected for 1,800 years." It represented a "great moral victory" for the very conception of the UN, he thought, the international body standing for cooperation in the cause of peace, justice, and equality all over the world.[18]

In the aftermath of the General Assembly vote for two states in Palestine, Magnes wrote to Hexter shortly thereafter that the "political impotence" exhibited by Ichud, Hashomer HaTsa'ir, and particularly himself led to their suffering a defeat "for which we are hardly to be forgiven." The United States "pinch[ed] the arm" of enough dependent countries to have partition go through, and many delegates erred in averring that there were no alternatives to partition or chaos; the minority report and binationalism did offer other options, he thought. The British mistakenly pointed to the Arab Higher Committee as the authoritative representative of the Palestine Arabs; Cunningham threatened chaos; and London officials did not try to have the problem settled through the Trusteeship Council, as provided for in the UN Charter. The Arabs' own "intransigence as usual" attitude—that Palestine must be an Arab state or nothing—contributed to the unfortunate result, while the Jewish Agency, which had placed "all its cards" on partition, was only too eager to have the delegates believe that chaos was the sole alternative to partition.[19]

Magnes, meanwhile, focused on another reason to blame himself for the failure of binationalism. The previous February, the seventy-year-old, who had been diagnosed with a heart condition, heeded doctors' orders not to travel. Therefore, he did not go to London, where he might have changed the British attitude in favor of Ichud's binationalist proposals. Nor was he given the green light to travel to the United States in November to participate in the General Assembly discussions, where binationalism was omitted from the order of business, and country after country stated that there was no alternative to partition. To Magnes, a man trying to achieve political results "must kick the doctors into the pit and go," and not having done so, he believed, constituted a failure on his part.

Despair seized the worried man. At present, the "same business" had begun all over again in Palestine, Magnes wrote to Hexter. Convoys continued to guard for potash lorries, stonings of the University-Hadassah Hospital bus to Har HaTsofim (Mount Scopus) went on, convoys were needed for funerals of those killed by Arab gunfire. Road blocks, children lifting closed fists, strikes—it all reflected "the same harbingers of a spring-time of blood." As for Ichud's future, Magnes acknowledged to Simon that it lacked administrative strength. Perhaps, he suggested, its ranks should now disband and seek other organizational venues.[20]

On January 29, 1948, he, Buber, and David W. Senator, a former member of the Jewish Agency Executive who had resigned years earlier to protest the increasing activist militancy of his colleagues, issued a ringing declaration of moral protest and an appeal to "the people of Jerusalem" and, "more particularly to our Jewish brethren" to desist from mob violence and reprisals. The *Palestine Post* considered their public *cri de coeur* "a Quislingism and a stab in the back of the Jewish cause," and refused to publish the following:[21]

> Acts of barbarism have been multiplying with startling rapidity throughout the country. The aged, women, children have not been spared. Happily there are instances where Arabs have risked their lives to save Jews, and Jews to save Arabs. But men, women and children, innocent of all crime, are being murdered in increasing numbers before the very eyes of passers-bye [sic]; and even in the presence of the security forces themselves.
>
> We appeal, more particularly, to our Jewish brethren: do not desecrate our name and honor! If we also follow the rabble and the incited mob, not only shall we achieve nothing positive, but we shall only be contributing to the worsening of the situation, to an increase of hatred, and to reprisal after reprisal, without distinction and without mercy. We appeal to public opinion and to the Jewish leadership to take every possible step to prevent these vicious mob attacks.
>
> Let these recent regrettable incidents serve as a warning, not to let the mob rule us, not to destroy with our own hands the moral foundations of our life and our future.

Come February, Magnes mused to Buber that the current tragedy did not reside in "confusion and sorrow, the loss of precious, irretrievable human lives, struggles and more struggles whose end cannot be foreseen." It lay in the fact that, as in the days of the prophet Micah (3:9–10), "the rulers of the house of Jacob and the chiefs of the house of Israel . . . build Zion with blood." Throughout human history, states were almost invariably created with blood and injustice, he continued, and the terrible sufferings that the Jews have had to endure have been so unbearable "that they have deprived us the capacity to be patient. We have been incapable of contenting ourselves with daily creative work for a prolonged period of time, and we have fallen prey to the Fata Morgana of the state, as though it were a shield that could defend us against the enmity of the peoples." In Magnes's February 9 letter to the editor of the *New York Times*, he called for the UN Security Council to demand a truce and mediate between the two sides.²²

Across the Atlantic, Ernst Simon viewed the Palestine situation as dangerous not only for those living in Palestine but for the whole of world Jewry. He sought to form an informal group which would endorse the Magnes-Buber-Senator proclamation. In early March, he held almost daily conferences with a range of Jewish leaders—psychologist Erich Fromm, biochemist David Nachmansohn, Freeland League of the Jewish Territorial Organization founder Isaac. N. Steinberg, *Commentary* founder-editor Elliot E. Cohen, and political scientist Hannah Arendt—to produce a religious and moral statement signed by the spiritual leaders of American Jewry. Albert Einstein signed the draft, and prominent Holocaust survivor and theologian of Reform Judaism Leo Baeck agreed to join the group in a meeting at Fromm's home scheduled on March 24. Jewish Theological Seminary president Louis Finkelstein, while agreeing "emphatically" with the draft, did not feel that he could sign any pronouncements in view of his special position as head of the Conservative movement and his task in Jewish life. Leon Simon, chair of the Hebrew University's executive council, did not agree with the whole matter, however. He warned Magnes not to support the Committee for Justice and Peace in the Holy Land, founded in February by Kermit Roosevelt and former Barnard College dean Virginia Gildersleeve and was considered anti-Zionist and pro-Arab.²³

Prior to the meeting at Fromm's home, Ernst Simon sought Magnes's early reaction on March 17 to this joint endeavor. Simon explained that the same group, which was prepared to identify itself with Magnes's name on a more moral than political matter, might be ready to do so even on a political level if the time arose. The declaration would oppose methods adopted by groups in Palestine that threatened Jewish settlement and conflicted with the fundamental spiritual and moral principles of the Jewish heritage. Only methods which were defensible on moral grounds, his draft statement went on, could reinforce "the peaceful tendencies in the Arab population," and thus prepare the cooperation of the Jewish and Arab groups in Palestine—a necessary condition for a "peaceful and productive development of and for further large scale Jewish immigration into the Holy Land." Simon thoroughly opposed any political step, which might counteract the Jewish Agency's endeavors to secure an international police power for Palestine, yet he thought that the new group he assembled had to prepare the moment where partition and its international implementation failed. At that moment, he concluded, Magnes should be in America, if his state of health permitted it. Hexter had spoken with Magnes by telephone, expressing his hope that he would come to America to campaign for this end, and Simon continued to believe that was possible.[24]

Two days later, US Ambassador Warren Austin announced that the US delegation would retreat from partition in favor of a temporary Palestine trusteeship. This move shocked the Zionists and their supporters worldwide but found a few adherents. Loy Henderson, head of the State Department's Near East desk, urged the leaders of the American Council for Judaism to send a strong letter of support to Secretary of State George Marshall. The Council's president, Lessing Rosenwald, wrote to Austin; Lazaron spoke on radio across the country, and shared his views with the receptive *Samuel* McCrea *Cavert*, General Secretary of Federal Council of the Churches of Christ in America. The Committee for Justice and Peace in the Holy Land, which advocated the resettlement of Holocaust survivors in the United States and elsewhere, stepped up its lobbying against partition in the belief that it went against America's national interests and common justice. Jacob Rosenheim, president of the ultra-Orthodox Agudath Israel, urged his followers in Palestine not to participate in "an illegal Jewish government of an illegal state" opposed to religious tradition, and to favor trusteeship "without the frivolous game with statehood." Neither Robert Weltsch, former *Jüdische Rundschau* editor and ex-Agency executive member, nor Yale University law professor Eugene Rostow favored trusteeship, but they believed that the American switch necessitated a change to the Zionist helm: They advocated the return of Weizmann and his associates, who had been deposed at the December 1946 World Zionist Congress in place of the more militant Ben-Gurion and American Zionist Emergency Council chair Abba Hillel Silver.[25]

Magnes, for his part, wrote to Hans Kohn that the United States was finally "on the right track," and he urged Austin to "keep up your valiant efforts" in giving Arab and Jew the "great opportunity" for the first time of self-government. Magnes also cabled Hexter asking if Hexter could consult Alan Stroock, James Marshall, and other likeminded executives on the American Jewish Committee (AJC), who sought to have that body "shaking off shackles and seizing historic opportunity secure Jewish Arab acquiescence new American proposals including Trusteeship," a position which the Committee had always favored. To Truman, he sent a separate telegram: "Many thousands Jews Arabs Palestine and elsewhere pray you persist your humane wise effort behalf truce and understanding in Holy Land." Ichud released a statement as well welcoming the dramatic policy reversal, which the *New York Times* published in full on March 28.[26]

Thomas Mann, the German-born winner of the Nobel Prize for Literature, launched a public attack against the reversal of the US support for partition that particularly disturbed Magnes. For Mann, the switch represented "the most humiliating and revolting political event since the treachery against Czechoslovakia in 1938." He strongly defended a Nation Associates' pamphlet, which charged that the British armed forces could have prevented Arab attacks and that the Arabs themselves were incapable of sustaining a revolt against the UN partition vote. Further, the foundation of a Jewish State in partition's "extremely modest boundaries" could have been carried out with a minimum of conflict if that small area had not become "the vortex of the big power fight" involving oil and bases.[27]

Magnes, on the other hand, thought the US change of policy "the most humane and the wisest decision which American statesmanship could have taken." Humane, he wrote to Mann, because it called for a cessation of warfare and blood-letting, wise because it was a long-over-due attempt to meet the problem through conciliation and cooperation between Arabs and Jews. The "great god Propaganda" carried the partition resolution through the General Assembly on the mistaken assumption that the only alternative to partition was chaos and that the Arab threats of war were mere bluff, but partition had led and would lead to war and the destruction of peace between millions of Arabs and the Jews in Palestine. Power politics had lain behind the pro-partition UN decision; eastern Mediterranean oil was vital for the Marshall recovery program for war-torn Europe, intended against the spread of communism. Magnes concluded by stating that whatever the reasons for the America's new position, it stood for peace in

Palestine and for compromise and understanding, and he wished to help, if possible, "with my limited powers."[28]

On April 9, Henderson proposed to Undersecretary Robert Lovett, appointed by Marshall to oversee State's stance on Palestine, that "moderates and temperate" individuals like Magnes and Azzam Pasha be invited to the United States as soon as possible to possibly break "the present log jam" in the UN. Austin had called for a special General Assembly session to consider trusteeship and a truce under a Governor-General, and State awaited responses to the proposal which it circulated to that effect to European and Arab capitals. Henderson argued that the "extreme public positions" taken by the Jewish Agency and the Arab Higher Committee regarding sovereignty made it increasingly difficult for them to modify their positions sufficiently for arranging a UN truce and interim governmental machinery after May 15, the announced date of British withdrawal. Lovett approved Henderson's suggestion the next day. Telegrams to that effect were then dispatched to Jerusalem and Cairo. The message to Magnes included this assertion: "At no time has there been a greater need for courageously conciliatory attitude such as yours on part of Arabs and Jews. If such attitude is to prevail cooperation on part of moderate and conciliatory Arabs and Jews is essential."[29]

By then, Magnes had transmitted to US Consul Thomas C. Wasson in Jerusalem his thoughts about the Americans' fifteen-point "informal suggestions" for the proposed trusteeship over Palestine. It should be of indefinite duration; Arabs and Jews should from the first day have equal representation in government; a Governor-General should be appointed at once; and the cabinet should consist of an equal number of Jews and Arabs. In addition, there should be a democratically elected legislature where both "nationalities" were equal, regardless of who was in the majority or in the minority, as in the US Senate. Before the elections took place, however, they country should be "more or less" pacified, which might take six months or a year. The situation might be saved if the British troops stayed on until July 15, giving the Governor-General and his cabinet the opportunity of organizing the required forces. Finally, Jewish immigration should be permitted up to parity with the Arabs. Since "the reservoir" of possible Jewish immigrants had been "greatly depleted since the extermination of 6 million Jews in Europe during the war," he advised that the 100,000 Holocaust survivors on behalf of whom President Truman had made his plea to Churchill and then Attlee two years earlier be given priority. This would probably include the refugees now in Cyprus internment camps, held there for trying to run the British blockade against "illegal" Jewish immigration.[30]

As for the AJC's recent statement in support of partition—which reflected the overwhelmingly majority of American Jewry—Magnes wrote to Hexter that almost the entire *yishuv* was hoping and praying for a truce. The "realities of the situation, of political wisdom, and of human feeling" all ran counter to that declaration. Everywhere one went in Palestine the same story was heard: Food was scarce; the strategic position of the Jews was impossible; it was time to stop. Seeing that the American Jewish Committee had set itself up in opposition, this time, to US Government policy, it should be all the easier to form an ad hoc committee adopting the Ichud point of view, including that of a democracy based upon two equal peoples. A strong group of that nature "might make a great difference." Magnes would send copies of this letter to his son Jonathan, Marshall, and Simon, and he asked Hexter to share it with all individuals interested in his position.[31]

Encouraged by Henderson, a small group of these prominent supporters invited Magnes to come to America. Their hope was that his presence could help stop the deadly fighting in Palestine and check an expected invasion from the neighboring Arab armies immediately following the mandate's termination. The mounting violence in Palestine haunted Magnes, especially the Arab slaughter of a convoy heading to Hadassah Hospital and the Hebrew University on April 13, killing seventy-six workers and injuring another twenty while British forces nearby did not intervene for several hours. General Officer Commanding Gordon MacMillan's subsequent defense of the mandatory's armed response did not placate him. Three days later, Magnes consulted with his doctors on the advisability of a trip to the United States and wrote in his diary: "How can I not go and stand before the world and say: 'Friends, stop the bloodshed. Understanding is possible.' This is the moment I have been preparing for all these years." If the General Assembly vote on partition stood, he told Cairo Geniza scholar S. D. Goitein, there would not be peace between Jews and Arabs "even after two hundred years." Accompanied by his wife, Beatrice née Loewenstein, and personal physician Dr. Alexander Geiger, Magnes left for New York on April 21, his first return since 1946.[32]

Magnes's last personal mission for peace began on April 23, 1948, when he met with Austin to convey his anxiety that neighboring Arab armies would seek to cut across the Arab village triangle of Nablus-Tulkarm-Jenin in north-central Palestine, with its seventeen-kilometer-wide corridor separating the two parts of the projected Jewish State. Partition had united the Arab states and caused the present chaos today in the country. Magnes was convinced that a majority of Jews in Palestine wanted another twenty to twenty-five years of opportunity for constructive achievement and increased immigration, and he believed that war would risk everything that had been accomplished. A small "sincere and fanatic" group, supported by a considerable section of the *yishuv*'s youth and the Jewish terrorists—the latter whom Magnes acknowledged to be, for the most part, courageous, idealistic men—wished to fight it out. Moderates such as Musa Alami, who was afraid to return to Palestine now, should be encouraged, Magnes said, and Jews and Arabs together should administer the proposed trusteeship. The Jews had won Haifa and might be victorious in many other battles, he concluded to Austin, but they would lose a war.[33]

Magnes's innermost fears were shared with a small group of supporters who convened in the law offices of Edward Greenbaum on April 26 in New York City. Among the attendees were Hexter, Rosenwald, Judges Jerome Frank and Horace Stern, and James Marshall, who had in October 1947 had warned AJC executive chair Jacob Blaustein that a Jewish state would in the long run result in "the complete destruction of Palestinian Jewry." (The mandatory's Criminal Investigation Department had secured a copy of this letter at the time.) Magnes urged that only a truce and a commission sent to Jerusalem to set up a provisional government could safeguard that endangered city. The "great mass" of the Jewish populace would favor "*aliya* and *b'niya*" (immigration and upbuilding) to "*medina*" (statehood). Thirty additional years of fruitful progress were preferable to war, which the Jews would lose for four reasons: the world's Muslims numbered in the many millions; the Arabs had time—"the timelessness of the desert"; the Jews were in a hurry "because of our tragedy"; and, according to Magnes, the loss of an Arab life was "a relatively cheap sacrifice of lives as against the pitifully small remnant of world Jewry." The US Government could refuse to permit any monies to be sent abroad, while Arab oil was essential for the Marshall Plan's efforts to revive the struggling post-war economies of Europe. "Palestine can become OURS," he remained certain, not by force of arms, statehood, or conflict, but with Arab cooperation via a trusteeship in whose government both peoples took active part over the next thirty years.[34]

The same day, the General Assembly approved a resolution that the Trusteeship Council study "suitable measures" to protect besieged Jerusalem and its inhabitants, and submit proposals to that effect. An Australian amendment to refer action on Jerusalem to a General Assembly subcommittee rather than the Trusteeship Council was defeated (26 against, 20 in favor, and 7 abstaining), taken as an indication that the United States might find it impossible to reverse partition and have trusteeship adopted by the required two-thirds majority. AJC president Joseph Proskauer urged Shertok and Ben-Gurion to support the overall truce effort. He had been impressed by a letter to the *New York Times* by Einstein and Leo Baeck, former chief rabbi of Berlin and Theresienstadt Ghetto survivor, which endorsed Magnes's appeal for a truce call and called on Palestine's Jews not to "permit themselves to be driven into a mood of despair and false heroism which eventually results in suicidal measures."[35]

Realizing that the US Government's stance rested on the shoulders of Marshall and, especially, of Truman, Magnes drafted a lengthy and urgent memorandum to them. The first part stressed that, with the war in Jerusalem growing fiercer each day, only the United States taking the lead might the dire situation be saved. The Governor-General, representing the world's conscience, should be appointed immediately, then proceed to Jerusalem with, if necessary, a small staff and a comparatively small token force—not an army—to act as his guard. The 150,000 Jewish men, women, and children there continued to pray for this deliverance; the people of Jerusalem would join to bring about order, thereby obviating the need of a truce. Food should be distributed equitably among the population in accordance with individual needs. The UN could "conquer" Jerusalem by "imagination, moral force, and faith."

Magnes's memo went on: A truce for three months might then operate in all of Palestine, with a kind of central authority vested in the American, French, and Belgian consul committee in Jerusalem. It would assume the continuation of essential public services; a ceasefire; and no proclamation of a state or any other kind of sovereignty. What each side currently held would to be administered by its people as best as possible, and 12,000 Jewish immigrants would be permitted during that period. Should the question of Jewish immigration from Rumania and Bulgaria prove to be "a stumbling block"—an acknowledgment of fears in the Foreign Office and State Department that communist agents could arrive from these countries—priority could be given to the 35,000 Holocaust survivors in the Cyprus detention camps.

If a general truce could not be secured, then trusteeship had great merit. The United States should declare frankly that it erred in backing partition and was now proceeding in the constitutional way as laid down by the UN Charter, making a mandated territory into a trustee territory. This would allow the two rivals a chance to work and live together, seeking an agreement through conciliation and compromise, and the trusteeship period need not being "all too long." While it could take a federal form of government, giving areas a great degree of local or provincial autonomy, the Governor-General and the strong central government would control foreign policy, finance, and economic union. The country could be divided into zones or cantons, each having a separate legislative council, with a joint council of delegations established subsequently. The Anglo-American Committee of Inquiry had spoken of a binational state, and Switzerland offered a classic example of how this could function. Trusteeship, Magnes emphasized, near the closing of the memo, afforded the time and the opportunity for "working out this great problem in a peaceful way."[36]

On May 4 Magnes had a nearly hour-long interview with Marshall, which seemed promising. In the Secretary's opinion, the Jews had won the first battles, like the Germans in World War II, but they would ultimately lose the war. Consequently, "it would be well for them to make terms now." Besides, the economic cost of a war was very great, and the Palestinian Jewish economy was "largely artificial." Magnes agreed fully and suggested that the United States exercise financial sanctions equally on both sides as a last resort to stop the warfare, then outlined his thoughts on sending a special UN representative immediately to Jerusalem to arrange a truce plus trusteeship for the entire country "without prejudice to the eventual political settlement to be worked out by the Arabs and the Jews."

Responding that this was the first account of the Palestine question in which he could believe, Marshall instructed Robert McClintock,

Rusk's deputy, to arrange that Magnes see Truman. "You talk to the President just like you talked to me," he said. As for an imposed truce, Marshall confided that no government had yet come forward to accept the American proposal for participating in a military force for Palestine, and he did not think it advisable just then to have the United States "left in the middle to bear the whole brunt." Magnes went over the same ground immediately thereafter with Henderson, who remarked that it was "encouraging" to have him in the country just then. With the Jewish Agency's Nahum Goldmann having independently urged Rusk that the United States press for a truce and a trusteeship, State officials sensed some optimism at this critical stage.[37]

Magnes's off-the-record meeting with Truman in the Oval Office the next morning brought further hope. Expressing his deep concern for the whole Palestine problem, the President thought that no head of state felt so deeply and knew so much about the issue as he; it was a question that had to find an answer. Otherwise, "the peace of the world would be disturbed." After highly praising Marshall, Truman remarked that he knew the Anglo-American Committee of Inquiry document almost by heart and had reviewed it from time to time. "It was a thousand pities that that report had not been carried out," Truman declared: "We might have been spared much of this present misery."

Very disappointed that the Jews had refused his recent offer that the Arab and Jewish leaders fly aboard his *Sacred Cow* airplane to the much-contested area so that the opposing forces could continue their discussions of the Palestine dilemma, Truman revealed a personal dream that Jews, Moslems, and Christians, whose lives were based more or less upon the same moral code, might get to understand one another better. This, he added, might also help to "lift the world from the materialism which was holding the world down to the ground and might destroy it." Russia would then not have "a spiritual leg to stand on." Jews and Arabs were "spoiling things," however, not giving these three major religious communities a chance to have confidence in one another. "That is one of the reasons why I deplore so deeply this conflict in the Holy Land," Truman confided. Upon leaving the meeting Truman said rather emphatically: "Dr. Magnes, we won't give up! We shall hang on to this until we find a way. That is our duty."[38]

Reports still circulated at that moment in the State Department and the White House to the effect that Shertok had agreed to conditions for a military truce and "political standstill" in Palestine, forcing him to write to Marshall on May 7 in an effort to clear up this "persistent misunderstanding." He reminded the Secretary that his letter of April 29 had made it clear that the Americans' proposed truce deferred Jewish statehood and threatened to prolong British rule in Palestine. He also noted that private individuals (a hint to Magnes, Proskauer, and Goldmann) had differed with the Agency's line, but they did not represent the Jewish people of Palestine, bore no constitutional responsibility for its future, and were not in a position to give effect to the policy that they advocated. In response to an urgent call from the Jewish Agency Executive in Palestine, Shertok was about to return for consultation with colleagues, who alone would have to decide on the truce proposal as a whole. The Agency was still prepared to accept a ceasefire throughout Palestine, he concluded, provided the Arabs did as well. Rusk quickly observed to Marshall that Shertok's wish for an interview before his departure was of "considerable significance," As he saw it, the bitter debates between moderates—such as Goldmann, Epstein, and possibly Shertok himself, who favored a truce—and the "more extreme elements"—such as Silver and Ben-Gurion, who pressed for the immediate establishment of the Jewish state "by force if necessary" – made such a meeting important before Shertok arrived in Palestine and the decision would be finalized.[39]

Marshall warned Shertok on May 8 that a declaration of Jewish sovereignty now would lead to a war with bleak prospects against the Arab nations. Four days later, Marshall had a stormy confrontation with Truman's Special Counsel, Clark Clifford, who advocated for recognition of the Jewish state. Marshall remarked that should Truman take that step, Marshall would vote against the President in the next election Yet the forty-one-year-old Clifford was able to convince fellow Missourian Truman that political motivation, the national interests of the United States, and humanitarianism—the President's lodestar on this vexatious issue—did, indeed, coincide. Others in Truman's inner circle, including Samuel Rosenman, Marvin Lowenthal, David Niles, and Bartley Crum, endorsed Clifford's arguments. The personal interventions by Weizmann and Eddie Jacobson, Truman's former partner in the haberdashery business, coupled with his resentment of what he called the State Department's "striped-pants boys" who forgot who was the President of the United States, played an important role in Truman's thinking as well.

Another key factor was Truman's desire to strengthen the fledgling United Nations and to forestall the Soviets in recognizing a new state that had already proven itself on the battlefield. The devout Baptist also shared with Clifford a strong belief in biblical sources about the Lord's promise to give the Land of Canaan to Abraham and his descendants as "*an everlasting holding*" (*Genesis* 17:8), and in the prophecies of Isaiah, Jeremiah, Ezekiel, and Amos concerning the Jewish revival there. To the shock of the American delegation and others at the United Nations, Truman chose to recognize the State of Israel *de facto* eleven minutes after Ben-Gurion announced its independence on May 14, 1948. Although he personally preferred the Anglo-American Committee of Inquiry's recommendations, he thought, as he told a group of Kansas City businessmen who honored him in December 1961, that "the creation and recognition of the State of Israel was right."[40]

Magnes's personal diplomacy in the last year of his life, capped by the half-hour interview with Truman, had failed to alter the course of history. Now, the day after Israel's sovereign rebirth, he went to see Weizmann, the president-designate, at the Waldorf-Astoria, where the blue-and-white flag of the new state unfurled aloft for the first time above the hotel's Park Avenue entrance. Both men were in rather poor health, Beatrice Magnes recalled years later, as they discussed this historic denouement. "You know that I did not believe in an exclusive Jewish State," Magnes declared. "For a long time I was in favor of a bi-nationalist state. But now that there is a Jewish State, I will join in helping anyone to make the State a good state."[41]

Magnes found comfort in Arendt's essay that month in *Commentary*, which backed Magnes's trusteeship plan as the best temporary solution. She declared his version of a federated state resting on Jewish-Arab community councils to be realistic and the "natural stepping stone" for any later, greater federated structure in the region much more realistic. Her concern that the "victorious" *yishuv* would live surrounded by a hostile Arab population, forcing it to be absorbed with physical self-defense to such a degree that it would "submerge all other interests and activities," echoed his own deep fears. Historian Kohn blasted the Zionist-sounding call for Arab-Jewish cooperation by the AJC, which simultaneously endorsed Truman's recognition of the new commonwealth while stressing that American Jewry could have no political attachment to that government. He agreed with Arendt that the "pseudo messianic intoxication" for statehood that had seized the whole of Jewry for statehood would bring "a complete disaster" for the Jews.[42]

President Bayard Dodge of the American University of Beirut conveyed his sympathy to Magnes at a time when Magnes's beautiful university in Jerusalem was under fire, and all his dreams for a Holy Land of good will and cooperation seemed to be vanishing. In Dodge's view, Magnes resembled the prophet Jeremiah, who had warned his people of great danger and whose words were now spurned at a time when "rash propagandists" had plunged the land of Judah "into what may easily become another tragedy in its history." As he was about to return to Lebanon, Dodge conveyed to Magnes—"the wisest person to give advice about Palestine"—his deep appreciation "for your courageous work" and admiration "for your wisdom."[43]

Faced with a radically new reality, Magnes endeavored to find a modus vivendi that would allow for Jewish sovereignty, allay Arab fears, and create humane and peaceful ends for all. He pressed Edward Warburg, American Jewish Joint Distribution Committee (JDC) chair, to ensure that none of its philanthropic funds went to weapons for the Hagana. He also questioned Warburg as to why Ichud did not receive a grant on the grounds that (so Warburg declared) the JDC never funded organizations engaged in "essentially a political problem." The Ichud, Magnes insisted, was an educational body that never had participated in elections; its diverse membership was united in the conviction that force was not the way to preserve the *yishuv* from destruction and a belief in "the traditional Jewish idea of peace and reconciliation." He soon told Egypt's Mahmud Fawzi Bey that Lebanese delegate Charles Malik's speech on May 28 in the Security Council, which favored a four-week truce proposal, impressed him greatly. Given that possibility, he urged Israeli UN diplomat Mordekhai Eliash to have his associates consider some kind of federal solution to the whole problem. Eliash cautioned that it was doubtful that the Arabs would accept the truce. To Magnes's immediate offer to be of service, Eliash – a lawyer and soon-to-be the first Israeli minister to the United Kingdom—replied that he would pass on this offer of cooperation to his colleagues.[44]

On the morning of June 1, Magnes called the State Department's Henderson, who agreed that the proposed four-week armistice was "a

God-given opportunity" for bringing some kind of political settlement. If accepted by both states, Magnes said that he would wish to get in touch with various persons in the United States to suggest a federal solution. If the word "state" had to be retained, the whole structure might be called the United States of Palestine (the term suggested by McClintock during Magnes's meeting with Marshall). Henderson thought it would be most helpful if his visitor had preliminary conversations in this regard before determining whether or not Magnes should later return to Washington. Hearing that Magnes was torn between being in the United States or in Jerusalem, Henderson thought that if a truce came about, Magnes might find it advisable to be in Palestine to help Count Folke Bernadotte, the president of the Swedish Red Cross during World War II who had been appointed in May the UN Mediator for Palestine.[45]

A mild stroke on June 10 did not stop the driven man. The Ichud filed with the US Justice Department a few days earlier, while Arendt, sociologist David Reisman, *New York Times* correspondent Joseph Levy, and philanthropist Arthur Goldsmith had reviewed Magnes's memorandum "Political Union in Palestine." From his Hotel Mayflower suite, Magnes dispatched a letter on June 14 to McClintock, providing his detailed plan for a confederation of Arab and Jewish states closely linked in questions of defense and foreign policy, with Jerusalem as its capital. He had found interest in this when talking with the American UN delegate Philip Jessup, Fawzi Bey, Malik, and France's Alexandre Parodi. To Magnes's disappointment, an arrangement for the Arab Legion, then occupying Mt. Scopus, to safeguard the books, manuscripts, and scientific treasures in the university and Hadassah hospital had not worked out; it would help dissipate the all to prevalent notion that "our Semitic cousins" were nothing but marauders from the desert, in whose word no faith could be put. Some prominent Jews in New York City tried to organize a group to promote Jewish-Arab cooperation, and Magnes hoped that the substance of his program, along with the Mount Scopus situation, would be sent to Bernadotte at the earliest possible moment.[46]

In July Magnes mailed Bernadotte a copy of his confederation plan, offering a compromise between partitioning Palestine and maintaining its unity. He pointed out its similarity with Bernadotte's proposals except for Jerusalem, which Bernadotte had assigned to the Arab state. If that city could be internationalized and demilitarized, then made the capital of the Federal Union, Magnes wrote, a good chance existed that

Arab and Jew would agree. Additionally, this might succeed for the rest of Palestine. Bernadotte, while agreeing with the gist of the confederation plan, continued to disagree over Jerusalem. The Swedish emissary was skeptical about the efficacy of an international area existing within the boundaries of another state, and believed that the financial burden of maintaining an international organization was too heavy for a local population to bear. In mid-August, Magnes countered that world Jewry would pay the difference between what local taxes required and the amount needed to maintain the capital. He reported that a group of American Jews encouraging Jewish-Arab cooperation was making progress, and he and wife Beatrice hoped to get back to Jerusalem in the not-too-distant future. Upon his return, he hoped to "have the privilege of being able to help you in your devoted work." Bernadotte had "done more to advance the cause of peace and conciliation in Palestine than all other persons put together," Magnes asserted in a press statement on August 23, and he expressed the conviction that most of the UN Mediator's suggestions would continue to serve as a basis for all future discussions concerned with peace and reconciliation in the Holy Land.[47]

Magnes also sent a copy of his confederation plan to Silver, who was also serving as chair of the American Section of the Jewish Agency. This plan, Silver's response read, "advocated the restriction of Jewish sovereignty and the dilution of its independence." Further, the Agency deplored individual Jews' seeking the support of the US Government or the UN delegations "for policies which run counter to those which the government of Israel is striving so gallantly to defend." Silver enclosed a critique of Magnes's plan by Abba Eban, then serving as the new state's UN representative. Magnes wrote to Arendt that he found Eban's analysis, soon to be published in *Commentary*, "a well-reasoned, and perhaps helpful point of view, despite the several details of his article with which one must differ." He then wrote to Eban that the Jewish-Arab cooperation which they both desired could be achieved only by a "statutory confederation," and that "no looser form" such as Eban advocated would work.[48]

On August 18, Magnes released a press statement about his plan, printed in full by the *New York Times*, also citing Ben-Gurion's declared wish "to cooperate closely" with the Arabs of Palestine and the neighboring countries and urging that Jerusalem's character as "a spiritual center of world-wide importance" be preserved. Addressing the new

Israeli Prime Minister as a "dear and honored friend," he pointed out that the plan bore a "striking enough" resemblance to the public suggestions that Bernadotte had issued before seeing Magnes's proposal. He appealed to Ben-Gurion to settle the Arab refugee problem solely on "a human basis and not through political bargaining." Ben-Gurion's invitation to Arab countries for talks about to a peace settlement was welcome, but the proposal lacked details. Unfortunately, Magnes added, his "somewhat weak" health raised doubts about whether he would be permitted to return home soon: "I suffer from this thought."[49]

Magnes urged Warburg in September to have the JDC allocate funds for thousands of Arab refugees, which would "redound to the glory of the Jews throughout the world and not least in Palestine itself." Seeing no urgency within the JDC to address this problem, Magnes withdrew as long-time chairman of its Middle East Advisory Committee, stating his disappointment that the JDC had not "risen to this great opportunity" and that his own connection with the JDC, of which he was one of the founders, "should end so ingloriously." Warburg replied the following month that the JDC was seriously considering the issue, and glad that Magnes had decided to withhold his resignation. This is "one of my dramatic acts which make people take notice," Magnes wrote in a journal, even while mulling over the possibility of a Marshall Plan for the Middle East, contemplating that perhaps through economic aid some chance of peace would arise in place of "war and hatred for decades."[50]

Magnes thought James Marshall's idea for a kind of *Handbook on Confederation* was practical. He disliked, however, the idea that Rosenwald and others of that ilk should be excluded from the new group for Arab-Jewish conciliation to avoid appearing anti-Zionist—perhaps because he himself had been on too many proscribed lists. Magnes also noted to Marshall that Rosenwald was the one prominent Jew who had the courage to "buck the terror of the Zionist political machine." Using the JDC as an example, Magnes worried that this political machine would put "the Jewish vote in its pocket." He liked the suggestion by Marshall and Arendt that intellectuals and labor leaders who shared Magnes's views be formed to advance his program, and he proposed seeking the views of Kohn, Finkelstein, and Hebrew Union College president Nelson Glueck. In the meantime, his response to Eban's article in *Commentary* would be published there in October.[51]

Bernadotte's assassination in Jerusalem by the Stern group on September 14 had a seismic effect, as did his final proposals. The Swedish count's report, completed a few hours beforehand, had called for Jerusalem to be placed under the control of the United Nations; the Negev as well as the towns of Ramleh and Lydda (Lod) defined as Arab territory; the Galilee defined as Jewish territory; Haifa port declared a free port, with assurances of free access to interested Arab countries; the Arab airport of Lydda declared a free area with assurances of free access to Jerusalem and interested countries; and the establishment of a conciliation commission, which would answer to the United Nations. Marshall and Bevin endorsed it, with His Majesty's Government (HMG) particularly partial to Bernadotte's suggestion that "compelling reasons" existed for the Arab territory of Palestine to be merged with Transjordan. The USSR, however, declared that the General Assembly's vote for partition was endangered not only by certain states' proposals to revise that decision, but also by proposals to set up a trusteeship over Palestine and appoint a Mediator. The Israeli government took particular exception to the Negev's being defined as Arab territory in light of UNSCOP's recommendation that it go to the Jewish state, and the overall Arab reaction was negative. Malik remarked that the "chief bone of contention is the irrevocable views supported by the Bernadotte report and by the United States that a Jewish state was here to stay."[52]

Magnes issued a statement that Bernadotte had come closer than any other man to bringing the two warring peoples to an understanding, and that his murder was a tragedy of "historic importance" for both. This great task of peace-making was now deprived of Bernadotte's "integrity of heart and mind," as well as the "great store of insight" he had accumulated. Magnes went on to say that some responsibility for the Jewish terrorists rested with all—certainly with the US politicians, newspaper publishers, and the large number of Jews and others who supported terrorists morally and financially. A considerable measure of responsibility lay with those official circles in Israel who at one time or another had carried on joint activities with terrorist groups, he said, and a large share of the blame should be attributed to the "recklessness" of those who accused Bernadottee of acting as the prejudiced agent of HMG or of "British-American imperialism" or of "the oil interests." Magnes closed by saying that Dr. Ralph Bunche, now the Swede's successor, deserved the wholehearted support of all men of good will in carrying to completion Bernardotte's efforts at peace-making.⁵³

This rebuke appeared as a postscript to Magnes's lengthy essay in *Commentary* entitled "For a Jewish-Arab Confederation." While praising Eban's article—which called for a regional solution between Israel and the other Middle Eastern countries—he continued to defend Ichud's program. He pointed to the old Austrian-Hungarian empire as a precedent, since it allowed both countries to remain independent entities and with separate parliaments, yet topics such as foreign affairs, defense, and international loans were reserved for a council of delegations from the two parliaments. The US Articles of Confederation and Newfoundland's recent vote for confederation with Canada were other examples. For this Jewish-Arab confederation, Jerusalem would be the capital and seat of a joint economic board. A federal court, perhaps consisting of three Jews and three Arabs and a UN appointee chair, could also serve as the high court for the International City of Jerusalem. This proposed United States of Palestine was somewhat analogous to the American example, where sovereign states are nevertheless limited by their adherence to the federal union. Immigration regulations and land sales would be made by each state autonomously, one day to be taken up within the confederation framework. A statutory, binding political union would be mandated because the Jewish Agency had not made "one single sincere and systematic attempt" at conciliation, and the current "frightful, needless war with the legacies of hatred and ill-will on both sides" had intervened. He ended with an appeal for the Palestinian Arab refugees, many of whom had fled their homes for fear of a repetition of the Irgun-Stern atrocities at Deir Yassin.

Separately, Magnes expressed that he much appreciated Arendt's *New Leader* article on Bernardotte's mission, where she offered alternatives for another form of UN trusteeship. Feeling depressed about the murder of "a great and good man who started full of hope and ended almost in despair," Magnes considered either her alternatives or a continuation of the Jewish-Arab war "a grave choice, this way or that."⁵⁴

Early in his career, Magnes held the belief that voluntary consent between Arabs and Jews was essential to conciliation. During World War II, however, his article in *Foreign Affairs* asserted that London and Washington should, if necessary, impose a binationalist solution to the Arab-Jewish situation. His backing of the Anglo-American Committee of

Inquiry's recommendations in 1946 and then of the State Department's switch from partition to a UN trusteeship two years later reflected this belief. Yet by September 1948, his message at the opening of the Hebrew University's academic year sounded his former conviction: "In the eyes of many of us the chief value of an independent state is that we ourselves bear the responsibility for our own decisions and that we do not just have to accept the consequences of decisions made for us by others." At the same time, his plan did call for UN intervention in case of "irreconcilable conflict," which appeared most likely between the two opposing forces.[55]

Refusing as always to recognize the dichotomy between the moral and the real worlds, Magnes ended his *Commentary* essay with a striking sentence that Arendt, now chairing his nascent political committee, which she and Marshall advocated, had seen when editing the piece. Appealing for the Palestinian Arab refugees, he found it "unfortunate that the very men who could point to the tragedy of Jewish DPs [displaced persons] as the chief argument for mass immigration into Palestine should now be ready, as far as the world knows, to help create an additional category of DPs in the Holy Land." On October 26, he took a usual walk in New York City's Central Park, answered mail, and held meetings in his hotel suite with friends and family. That evening, Magnes typed a letter to Dr. E.M. Bluestone, director of the Hadassah Medical Organization, expressing his views on relocating the Hadassah Hospital in Jerusalem. He died of a heart attack the next morning.[56]

A simple ceremony marked the funeral service on the afternoon of October 28 at the Jewish Theological Seminary. No eulogies were delivered, in accordance with Magnes's wishes. Dr. Simon Greenberg, acting president of the Seminary, read selections from the *Psalms*. Dr. David de Sola Pool, long-time Orthodox rabbi of the Shearith Israel Congregation (Spanish-Portuguese synagogue) in New York City, officiated. In addition to the surviving members of Magnes's family, leaders from all walks of Jewish life, including Simon and other members of the Hebrew University faculty, attended the funeral. Consul-General Arthur Lourie represented the State of Israel. Burial took place at the Beth Olom cemetery in Ridgewood, Queens County, New York.[57]

Zionist spokesmen in the United States issued statements to mark Magnes's passing. Wise hailed him as "one of the most gallant figures in the history of world Jewry." Silver observed that the departed was an early champion of the Zionist movement in the United States, and emphasized that "his greatest achievement" was his leadership over many years of the Hebrew University. Pronouncements mourning Magnes's death were also issued by Dr. Emanuel Neumann, president of the Zionist Organization of America, and Judge Morris Rothenberg, president of the Jewish National Fund. A resolution from Hadassah, which expressed "deep sorrow" at the passing of "a distinguished colleague, a wise counselor, and a cherished friend," noted that, as chairman of its council in Palestine, he "selflessly and tirelessly" gave the benefit of his "profound wisdom and vast experience."[58]

Other American Jewish leaders offered their own tributes. Proskauer considered the death of Magnes, who was one of the AJC's Committee's founders, "a grievous loss to Jewry and to humanity." As president of Hebrew University, he "created a great instrument of education for the Middle East and for all the people thereof. His intellectual integrity and his uncompromising morality were such that he was held in the highest esteem even by those who differed from him in some of his objectives." Warburg, noting that the JDC had benefited continuously from his "leadership and insight" for over thirty years, viewed him thus: "As a Jew who thrilled to the spiritual heritage of his religion and to its ethical concepts, Dr. Magnes labored all his adult life in behalf of Jewish welfare, in the United States, in Europe and in Palestine." In special memorial services held a week later at Hebrew Union College, the Reform rabbinic seminary where Magnes had received ordination in 1900, Glueck declared that Magnes "had been a great leader and teacher, constantly battling for ideals which promised peace and occupation in Palestine and the world at large. He was always in the minority, and was forever respected by the majority."[59]

At a memorial meeting in Temple Emanu-El that December, to which Truman sent a message lauding his "vision and understanding," Kohn spoke of Magnes and Ahad Ha'Am, who was widely regarded as cultural Zionism's major ideologue, as his two great Zionist teachers—men who were much objected to in their times, who did not join in "emotional conformity" but "raised their warning though solitary voice against it." Both had sought to revive Judaism's prophetic ideals in the struggles of daily reality. In the 1920s, when Kohn lived in Palestine, Magnes had been "a great inspiration and a redeeming comfort." Like

Ahad Ha'Am and Buber, Magnes recognized the moral challenge that Palestine was a home of two peoples with deep roots in its past and its present. After the Arab riots of 1929, Magnes had written a pamphlet calling for binationalism, hoping that the Holy Land would pioneer in the future road to closer cooperation and inclusive federation of neighboring peoples. In his last years, Magnes, like Ahad Ha'Am, was faced with the spiritual and moral tragedy of terrorism, and almost his last utterance was a letter to the *New York Times* after Bernadotte's death, hailing Bernadotte's efforts to advance the cause of peace in Palestine. Magnes passed away soon thereafter, and no one could replace him. Yet his message, Kohn concluded, should inspire friends to try to follow where he had led, "a great American in the tradition of Western civilization and a great Zionist in the line of Jewish tradition."[60]

Arendt went even further, calling Magnes in 1951 "the conscience of the Jewish people." He had raised his voice primarily on moral grounds, and his authority was that "he was a citizen of Jerusalem, that their fate was his fate, and that therefore nothing he said could ever be blamed on ulterior motives." She thought him "a very practical and a very realistic man who passionately wanted to do the right thing," and who had "a healthy distrust of the wisdom of our *Realpolitiker*." Being a Jew and being a Zionist, Magnes was "simply ashamed" of what Jews and Zionists were doing. The last years of his life coincided with "a great change in the Jewish national character," by which Arendt meant the foundation of the State of Israel and the consequent flight of nearly 600,000 Arabs from Palestine. A people that for two thousand years had made justice the cornerstone of its spiritual and communal existence, she went on, "has become emphatically hostile" to all arguments of such a nature, as though these were necessarily the arguments of failure. "We all know," her encomium concluded, that "this change has come about since Auschwitz, but that is little consolation."[61]

Yet, seven decades after Magnes's death, a more balanced assessment is in order. Few doubted his integrity and his sincere wish to champion a Zionism sustained by what might be called prophetic humanism. It appears no coincidence that until his last days this outsider was working on a study of the Essenes, a monastic sect during the Second Temple period dedicated to piety, asceticism, charity, and an unshakeable belief that its members would change the course of history. His desire to build up a just society in Zion and for his beloved Hebrew University to take the lead as "a spiritual center for the Jewish people" remained constant and consistent. At the same time, even admirer Norman Bentwich, who authored Magnes's first biography, concluded that Magnes was "prone to oversimplify complex problems by concentrating on its ethical aspects and neglecting the state of facts; he could not adjust the order of thought to the order of things." Arthur A. Goren ended an introduction to his fine edition of Magnes's writings by noting that, when calling for a Zion redeemed in justice notwithstanding no positive response from the Arab side, he demanded from his people "perhaps more than the unfolding events of the years allowed."[62]

Scholem, who, like Ruppin, broke with Brit Shalom after the lethal 1929 Arab riots, saw Magnes as an incorrigible idealist of the nineteenth-century mold—"a free man" refusing to jettison Judaism's fundamental values when crisis shook the old, rational order. In the twentieth century, however, with nationalisms in conflict reaching fever pitch, the single-minded preacher's dream of peaceful coexistence appeared naïve and misguided to most. Shmuel Yosef (Shai) Agnon's posthumously published novel *Shirah*, taking place in the Hebrew University milieu of the 1930s, sharply critiqued Magnes (the unnamed *Nagid* who speaks in clichés about "everything human is Jewish and everything Jewish is human") and the faculty for being divorced from the real concerns of the Jewish community in Eretz Israel and elsewhere. The urgent needs of world Jewry after the Holocaust brought this disconnect more sharply into focus. In the end Magnes, the aloof man whom Eban recalled as having a "frigid temperament," failed to persuade, because Arab-Jewish cooperation remained further away than ever by the time of his death.[63]

Magnes did not doubt the rightness of his stand even while "skating on thin ice—very often" (his suggested title for an unwritten autobiography), but his political judgment must be deemed wanting. This honest maverick took seriously the assurances of adventurer H. St. John Philby after the 1929 riots to successfully engineer an Arab-Jewish understanding, only to discover that the Arabs, the British, and the Zionists did not. A murderous rivalry between the Nashashibi and Husseini clans for power in Palestine during the Arab Revolt, putting his life in possible danger, required the Magnes family to move in 1938 from their home on the top floor of an Arab house outside of Herod's Gate in the Old City to the Rehavya section in Jewish Jerusalem facing a children's playground that is now called Kikar Magnes. The few Arabs who agreed with him faced physical danger from their own people. Prominent attorney Omar Effendi escaped with a deep dent on the top of his head, but Darwish Husseini and some others, whose New Palestine Society draw up a protocol of agreement with the League for Jewish-Arab Cooperation in 1946, were soon murdered by loyalists of the former Grand Mufti Haj Amin al-Husseini. Eminent trade union leader Sami Taha, disagreeing with Haj Amin's intransigence, suffered the same fate the next year.[64]

Magnes failed to convince supposedly moderate Azzam Pasha that the Arab League's "constant negative was sterile." In September 1947 the League secretary told Eban and David Horowitz that the Arab peoples viewed Palestine Jewry as "an alien organism," whom the Arabs would eventually eject in the same manner as they had the European Crusaders after two hundred years of living uninvited in their midst. Azzam's "forcefulness and fanaticism" stirred his visitors, but left them depressed, realizing that with this encounter and his emphasis on a religious war (*jihad*) "vanished the last effort to bridge the gulf." In the end, Musa Alami also objected to further Jewish immigration, however much he admired the Hebrew University president. When James Marshall asked if Mount Scopus could be used as a university and hospital center for Arabs and Jews, Charles Malik replied that while this was the proper thing to do, "we Arabs do not compromise the way you Westerners do. We can't take one bite of the cherry, we have to have the whole cherry."[65]

The sad fact remained that scant hope existed for a peaceful resolution in Palestine, a small land so riven with strife, as the Arab world rejected the *yishuv*'s appeal for compromise and its claim to national sovereignty. Most of the UNSCOP members, García Granados recalled, agreed early on that binationalism had "all the inconvenience of partition without its finality" and would be rejected by both sides. Newspaperman Julian Meltzer may have seen Magnes as "the soul of rectitude and ethical rightness" in Jewish and Zionist affairs, but US representative Frank Buxton of the Anglo-American Committee of Inquiry on Palestine was closer to the mark, writing to a friend in January 1948 that "Magnes is a sweet soul and something in addition to that. But harsh realities do not seem to affect him at all." "Is he so prideful of opinion," Buxton, the *Boston Herald* editor and Pulitzer Prize winner, wondered, "that massacres of Jews do not sadden him but make him a trifle prouder of his judgment?" Concurrently, Richard Crossman of the

Anglo-American Committee's British delegation, observing to Lazaron that the American Council for Judaism ideologue's solution was completely unacceptable to either Jew or Arab, made a related point when declaring that "the Jewish community cannot escape from the nationalism of the world it lives in." "As a result," he added, "the Jewish State will be established in the worst possible way—by Jewish force."[66]

Arab rejection meant that Palestine was partitioned through war, five Arab state armies immediately invading the Jewish state, with a consequent, tragic harvest. Already in January 1946, Scholem had taken Arendt to task for championing what he termed "a patently anti-Zionist, warmed-over version of Communist criticism, infused with a vague *galut* [exile] nationalism." Her public call for universalism against "reactionary" Zionism and "something that is for the Jewish people of life or death importance," observed the pioneering scholar of Jewish mysticism, neglected what he termed the "eternity" of antisemitism, as well as the fact that the Arabs, refusing any plan that included Jewish immigration, were "primarily interested not in the morality of our political convictions but in whether or not we are here in Palestine at all." Arendt's views would not change.[67]

At the time of the partition vote, Mordecai Kaplan, one of Magnes's former associates in the New York City Kehilla and the later founder of Reconstructionist Judaism, reflected far more instinctively and accurately the feelings of American Jewry. "It is a long time, indeed, since we Jews have had occasion as we do tonight to sing '*LaYehudim Hai'ta Ora V'Sason V'Simcha Vi'Kar,*'" he wrote in a diary. Then, after adding the traditional *Sheh'Hecheyanu* prayer of thanks to the Creator, Kaplan noted the following:

> Considering the dreadful finality that an adverse vote might have had in that it would have put an end to all our hopes of resuming life as a nation in our homeland and would have rendered futile all efforts to keep Judaism alive in the diaspora, we should thank God with the benediction of "*HaTov V'HaMeitiv LaRa'im V'LaTovim Sheh'Gemalanu Kol Tov Selah.*"

And novelist Amos Oz vividly recalled that in northern Jerusalem, as elsewhere in the Jewish areas of Palestine, a "cataclysmic shout" was replaced by roars of joy and a medley of hoarse cries and "The Jewish People Lives" and somebody trying to sing "Hatikvah" and women shrieking and clapping and "Here in the Land our Fathers Loved", and the whole crowd started to revolve slowly around itself as though it was being stirred in a huge cement mixer, and there were no more restraints.[68]

Magnes's "religious eyes" (his own early characterization) failed to see this. Later champions have charged that he "yearned for a Great Community that would bond Jews and all mankind as they must be"; "founded the tradition of vigorous intellectual dissent which is such a crucial ingredient of Israeli political culture"; and understood that the peaceful coexistence with the nearby Arab countries was "a prerequisite" for the "guaranteed existence of a Jewish national home based on a strong moral, political, cultural, and social foundation." The fullest biography concludes that he was "the Zionist conscience." Yet the harsh, real—not ideal—world pressed forward with its own claims, directly challenging Magnes's credo, set down just before he left New York to live in Palestine, to call for a Judaism "which gives hope to redeem mankind by means of spirit rather than by brute force." Ethical visions, however lofty, cannot easily be reconciled with gritty and, at times, grim truths.[69]

Years after the Arab Revolt, Hexter conceded that there was "no likelihood" of a basis for compromise. Magnes had questioned Gandhi's advice, given in a letter to Magnes and Buber one day after *Kristallnacht*, that the Jews should practice passive resistance even unto death. Was it right, Magnes wondered, to sit quietly when children were being butchered? Magnes, the militant pacifist, also felt compelled to declare, although reluctantly, his support for the Allied war against Hitler. The bimillennial curse of Jewish powerlessness, culminating in the *Shoah* while the free world abdicated moral responsibility and stood by, convinced Jews and much of public opinion worldwide that only sovereignty in the land that had seen their birth as a people could put an end to their anguished wanderings across the globe.[70]

After Magnes's passing, a tumultuous future lay ahead for Arab and Jew. A recent scholarly article by Hedva Ben-Israel posits that the spirit and style of his "sermons" were so alien to most of the *yishuv* that they concealed from their eyes "the sober and realistic observation" which

Magnes kept repeating—"that without an agreement with the Arabs both nations would meet on a course of collisions for a long time." A second academic, Dmitry Shumsky, proposes that the Zionist political imagination, following in the spirit of a few of the movement's earlier ideologues, go today "beyond the nation-state."[71] Yet no resolution to the depth and obduracy of that conflict, even the possibility of a viable two-state solution in the distant future, is in prospect so long as the legitimate existence of the State of Israel is denied and demonized. Attempts at reconciliation appear to be a quixotic effort while Israel remains under attack both by the Palestinian Arabs' secular Fatah and fundamentalist Hamas leaderships and by surrounding Arab neighbors, particularly the Lebanese Shiite Hezbollah army, founded and funded by an Iranian government that threatens the Jewish commonwealth with obliteration. The State of Israel would offer sovereignty to the Palestinian Arab leadership in 1967, 2000, and 2008, only to be refused every time.

Not surprisingly, the overwhelming majority of Israel's Jewish citizens, witness to thousands of rockets, terrorism, and unceasing, murderous incitement after the Israeli withdrawals from Lebanon in 2000 and Gaza in 2005, are deeply committed to maintaining the territorial integrity of their ancestral homeland and to insuring the security of their families. In their view, for one people with a long, tormented history of exile and exclusion in a world without love or redemption, the new state born in war and beleaguered for decades by implacable enemies serves as a testament to Jewish resilience and faith in a better tomorrow. With that assessment, Magnes, "the agitator and troubler in Israel,"[72] would likely agree.

Endnotes

1. *New York Times*, October 28, 1948. For Magnes's pioneering activities to establish a comprehensive communal structure for New York City's Jewish community, see Arthur A. Goren, *New York Jews and The Quest for Community: The Kehillah Experiment, 1908–1922* (New York, 1970).
2. Monty Noam Penkower, *Palestine in Turmoil: The Struggle for Sovereignty, 1933–1939* (New York, 2014), vol. 1, *Prelude to Revolt, 1933–1936*, 250, 292, 304; vol. 2, *Retreat from the Mandate, 1937–1939*, 413, 418, 421, 438,

449–451. 455–460, 479–481, 490–491, 506, 535n31; Adi Gordon, ed., *Brit Shalom V'HaTsiyonut HaDu-Leumit: HaSh'eila HaAravit K'Sh'eila Yehudit* (Jerusalem, 2008); Dmitry Shumsky, *Bein Prague L'Yerushalayim: Tsiyonut Prague V'Ra'ayon HaMedina HaDu-Leumit B'Eretz Yisra'el* (Jerusalem, 2010). The eminent *yishuv* leaders who endorsed Magnes's June 1936 Jewish-Arab agreement included Judge Gad Frumkin; Palestine Electric Company founder Pinhas Rutenberg; Farmers' Federation head Moshe Smilansky; and Moshe Novomeysky, Palestine Potash Ltd. founder.

3. Magnes to Holmes, October 24, 1937, file SC-5164, American Jewish Archives (AJA), Cincinnati, OH; Susan Lee Hattis, *The Bi-National Idea in Palestine during Mandatory Times* (Haifa, 1970); Magnes to Norman, August 15, 1939, file P3/207, Central Archives of the History of the Jewish People, Jerusalem (CAHJP). For a broader, historical context of "transfer" solutions in the Middle East during the interwar period, see Laura Robson, *States of Separation: Transfer, Partition, and the Making of the Modern Middle East* (Oakland, 2017), particularly chap. 3.

4. Monty Noam Penkower, *Decision on Palestine Deferred: America, Britain and Wartime Diplomacy, 1939–1945* (London, 2002), 75, 85–86.

5. Ibid., 121–123, 153–156. 202, 367; Paul R. Mendes-Flohr, "The Appeal of the Incorrigible Idealist," in W. M. Brinner and M. Rischin, *Like All the Nations?, The Life and Legacy of Judah L. Magnes* (Syracuse, 1987), chap. 10; Judah Magnes, "Towards Peace in Palestine," *Foreign Affairs* 21 (1943): 239–249. Also see Yosef Heller, *MiBrit Shalom L'Ichud, Yehuda Leib Magnes V'HaMa'avak L'Medina Du-Le'umit* (Jerusalem, 2003).

6. Penkower, *Decision on Palestine Deferred*, 209, 367. The Balfour Declaration of November 2, 1917, pledged Great Britain to "facilitate the establishment of a Jewish National Home in Palestine."

7. Hooper to Byrnes, October 13, 1945, report XL 24351, RG 226, State Department files (SD), National Archives, Suitland, MD; Epstein to members, December 28, 1945, L35/98, Central Zionist Archives (CZA), Jerusalem. For Magnes's support of the Anglo-American Committee, see Magnes to Hinden, December 27, 1945, folder 221, Judah Magnes MSS., Hebrew University, Jerusalem; Epstein to Shertok, January 25, 1946, Z4/30969, CZA. For the Anglo-American Committee of Inquiry on Palestine, see Monty Noam Penkower, *Palestine to Israel: Mandate to State, 1945–1948* (New York, 2019), vol. 1, *Rebellion Launched, 1945–1946*, chaps. 2–3. The 1939 White Paper limited Jewish immigration to Palestine to 75,000 in the next five years, thereafter only with Arab consent. Fearing what it called a "flood" of Jewish

refugees, the Foreign Office doled out even these legal certificates, that number expiring in October 1945. Penkower, *Decision on Palestine Deferred*, passim.

8. Azriel Carlbach, *Va'adat HaHakira Ha'Anglo-Amerikanit L'Inyanei Eretz-Yisra'el*, vol. 1 (Tel-Aviv, 1946), 386–403; March 14–15, 1946, William Phillips Diary, Houghton Library, Harvard University, Cambridge, MA; Richard Crossman, *Palestine Mission: A Personal Record* (New York, 1947), 132–134. Mordekhai Ben-Tov, *Yamim Mesaprim, Zikhronot MeiHaMe'ia HaMakhra'at* (Tel Aviv, 1984), 86–87; Ben-Tov interview with the author, August 26, 1976. Hutcheson would repeat his appreciation of Magnes's views while criticizing "Russian influence" in the kibbutzim. Lefever report, March 30, 1946, C25/6522, CZA. For Arab views of Magnes, see Teller report, March 21, 1946, box 1534, Jewish Welfare Board Archives, New York City; "Arab Political Life" report, March 20, 1946, S25/22831, CZA.

9. Magnes to Hinden, May 1, 1946; Magnes to Cunningham, May 5, 1946; both in 249, Magnes MSS., CAHJP; *HaMashkif*, December 5, 1946; *Foreign Relations of the United States* (FRUS), *1947*, vol. 5 (Washington, DC,1971), 1126–1129; *Jewish Telegraphic Agency* (*JTA*), July 15, 1947; Magnes draft statement, n.d., 138, Magnes MSS., CAHJP.

10. Magnes to Simon, October 8, 1947, file 4-1751/K4, Ernst Simon MSS., National Library of Israel; Arthur Goren, ed., *Dissenter in Zion* (Cambridge, 1982), 451–456.

11. Magnes to Cunningham, October 10, 1947, file P3-2/18, CAHJP; Cable to Evatt, October 27, 1947, File 4-1751/K4, Simon MSS.

12. Magnes address, October 29, 1947, Lewis Strauss MSS., file P-632, box 1, American Jewish Historical Society, Center for Jewish History, New York City; *New York Times*, October 30, 1947.

13. Goren, *Dissenter in Zion*, 456–458. "For the sake of Zion" is taken from *Isaiah* (62:1). The phrase continues "I shall not be silent."

14. Magnes to Hexter, November 20, 1947, file 18/4, Jacob Billikopf MSS., AJA.

15. Magnes to Sulzberger, November 27 1947; Magnes to Hexter, December 1, 1947; both in file 11/12, Billikopf MSS., AJA.

16. Eliyahu Eilat, *HaMa'avak al HaMedina*, vol. 2 (Tel-Aviv, 1982), 449–452; Ruth Gruber, *Witness* (New York, 2007), 158.

17. Magnes to Ichud Political Committee, November 30, 1947, Ms.Var. 350/7, Martin Buber MSS., National Jewish Library, Jerusalem.

18. *JTA*, December 1, 1947.

19. Magnes to Hexter, December 1, 1947, Ms. Var. 350/7, Buber MSS.

20. Ibid.; Magnes to Simon, December 11, 1947, file 4-1751/K4, Simon MSS.

21. Simon to Magnes, March 17, 1948, file 4-1751/K5, Simon MSS. Vidkung Quisling was a Norwegian army officer whose collaboration with the Germans in their occupation of Norway during World War II established his name as a synonym for "traitor."
22. N. M. Glatzer and P. Mendes-Flohr, eds., *The Letters of Martin Buber, A Life of Dialogue*, trans. R. and C. Winston and H. Zohn (New York, 1991), 528; *New York Times*, February 9, 1948.
23. Simon to Finkelstein, March 10, 1948, file 4-1751/S1/A.F.; Finkelstein to Simon, March 22, 1948, file 4-1751/K5; both in Simon MSS.; Goren, *Dissenter in Zion*, 467–472.
24. Simon to Magnes, March 17, 1948, file 4-1751.S1/A,F, Simon MSS. Magnes had been suffering from a heart condition for the last two years.
25. Thomas A. Kolsky, *Jews against Zionism* (Philadelphia, 1990), 184; Rosenwald to Austin, March 23, 1948, file 124, American Council for Judaism (ACJ) MSS., University of Wisconsin Library, Madison; Lazaron address, March 31, 1948, RG18, 16/13, Presbyterian Historical Association; file 6044, Morris Lazaron MSS., AJA; Virginia Gildersleeve, *Many a Good Crusade* (N.Y., 1959), 409, 186; Gildersleeve to Taft, March 30, 1948, Virginia Gildersleeve MSS., Special Collections, Columbia University, New York City; Rosenheim to Va'ad HaPoel, March 22, 1948, Eretz Israel III, Jacob Rosenheim MSS., Agudas Israel of America Archives, New York City; Weltsch to Hexter, March 20, 1948, 4/1751/K5, Simon MSS.; Rostow to Frankfurter, March 22, 1948, box 99, Felix Frankfurter MSS., Library of Congress, Washington, DC.
26. Magnes to Kohn, March 31, 1948, box 38; Magnes to Austin, March 25, 1948, file 2/11; both in Robert Weltsch MSS., Leo Baeck Institute, Center for Jewish History, New York City; Ichud statement, March 28, 1948, file 999/28/20, Israel State Archives, Jerusalem; Magnes to Gildersleeve, March 8, 1948; Magnes to Hexter, March 22, 1948; Magnes to Truman, March 26, 1948; Simon draft, 1948?; all in file 4/1751, Ernst Simon MSS.; March 28, 1948, *New York Times*. Marshall's aunt was Magnes's wife.
27. Mann to Magnes, April 1, 1948, file 21/9, James Marshall MSS., AJA. The Nation Associates, spearheaded by *Nation* publisher Freda Kirchwey and director Lillie Schutz, was an organization created to advocate liberal causes worldwide and the creation of a Jewish state in Palestine.
28. Magnes to Mann, April 12, 1948l, file 21/9, Marshall MSS., AJA.
29. *FRUS, 1948*, 5:2, 804–807; Sack to Silver, April 8, 1948, box 3, Hyman A. Schulson MSS., Manuscripts and Archives Section, New York Public Library, New York City.

30. Goren, *Dissenter in Zion*, 475–477.
31. Ibid., 477–479.
32. Ibid., 481–482, 54. S. D. Goitein, "The School of Oriental Studies: A Memoir," in Brinner and Rischin, *Like All the Nations?*, 169. The assertion has been made that because of Magnes binationalist stance and criticism of Deir Yassin and other attacks on Arabs, as well as his defense of the mandatory government, he was discredited and "was in effect forced to quit his job," and that he left for the United States "ostensibly in search of funds for his beloved university." Benny Morris, *1948, A History of the first Arab-Israeli War* (New Haven, 2008), 129. No source is given for this claim, which bears no connection to his actual peace mission.
33. Magnes-Austin-Ross memo of conversation, April 23, 1948, file Rusk-2, Dean Rusk MSS., State Department (SD) records, National Archives, Suitland, MD.
34. Minutes of meeting, April 26, 1948, file M68-68, 1948, #4, ACJ; Marshall to Blaustein, September 1947, file 47/803, Hagana Archives, Tel-Aviv. Others present at this meeting included Mrs. Adle Levy, Alan Stroock, Harold Linder, Frank Altshul, and David Sher.
35. Creech Jones to Bevin, April 28, 1948, Foreign Office (FO) 371/68546, Public Record Office (PRO), Kew, England; *FRUS, 1948*, 5:2, 858–859, 864–868, 871, box 8, Joseph Proskauer MSS., American Jewish Committee archives, New York City; Rusk to Lovett, April 24, 1948, file Rusk-3, Rusk MSS.; Austin to Marshall, April 27, 1948, file McClintock-2, Robert McClintock MSS.; Garreau interview, April 26, 1948, file Rusk-3, Rusk MSS.; all in SD; *JTA*, April 19 and 27, 1948; Rusk remarks, April 26, 1948, file 7/1, Abba Hillel Silver MSS., The Temple, Cleveland, OH; Shertok to Ben-Gurion, April 29, 1948, S25/1558, CZA.
36. Magnes memorandum, April 29, 1948, file P3/162, CAHJP.
37. Goren, *Dissenter in Zion*, 488–493; *FRUS, 1948*, 5:2, 901–904, 917–923, 929.
38. Magnes to Mann, April 12, 1948, file 21/9, James Marshall MSS., AJA; Magnes memos, May 2, 1948, file P3/162, CAHJP; *Dissenter in Zion*, 494–497; C.L. Sulzberger memo, May 6, 1948, file Palestine and Zionism-2, Arthur Hays Sulzberger MSS., *New York Times* Archives, now in the New York Public Library, New York City.
39. *FRUS, 1948*, 5:2, 929–935.
40. Monty Noam Penkower, *Palestine to Israel: Mandate to State, 1945–1948*, vol. 2, *Into the International Arena, 1947–1948* (New York, 2019), chap. 10.
41. Beatrice Magnes, *My Four Lives* (1966), 119, 107.
42. Hannah Arendt, "To Save the Jewish Homeland: There is Still Time," *Commentary* 5 (May 1948): 398–406; American Jewish Committee statement,

May 17, 1948, file 5/5, Marshall MSS.; Kohn to Slawson, May 21, 1948, file 4-1751, Simon MSS.
43. Dodge to Magnes, May 21, 1945 (should be 1948), file 21/9, Marshall MSS. For a recent study comparing Magnes to Jeremiah, see David Barak-Gorodetski, *Yirmiyahu B'Tsiyon: Dat U'Politika B'Olamo Shel Yehuda Leib Magnes* (Ben-Gurion University, 2018).
44. Warburg to Magnes, May 19, 1948; Magnes to Warburg, May 25, 1945; both in file 21/9, Marshall MSS.; Goren, *Dissenter in Zion*, 498–499.
45. Goren, *Dissenter in Zion*, 497–498.
46. B. Magnes to Marshall, June 10, 1948, file 21/4; Magnes to McClintock, June 14, 1948, file 21/9; both in Marshall MSS.
47. Goren, *Dissenter in Zion*, 505n6, 506–507, 517–518.
48. Goren, *Dissenter in Zion*, 508–509; Aubrey S. Eban, "The Future of Arab-Jewish Relations," *Commentary* 6 (September 1948): 199–206.
49. Goren, *Dissenter in Zion*, 507–508.
50. Ibid., 519–520.
51. Ibid., 509–511.
52. Folke Bernadotte, *To Jerusalem* (New York, 1951); Kate Marton, *A Death in Jerusalem* (New York, 1994); Carry David Stanger, "A Haunting Legacy: The Assassination of Count Bernadotte," *Middle East Journal* 42:2 (Spring 1988): 260–272.
53. Cited in Goren, *Dissenter in Zion*, 517–518.
54. Judah Magnes, "For a Jewish-Arab Confederation," *Commentary* 6 (October 1948), 379–383. For the atrocities referred to by Magnes, see Eliezer Tauber, *Deir Yassin: Sof HaMitos* (Jerusalem, 2017).
55. Bernard Wasserstein, "The Arab-Jewish Dilemma," in Brinner and Rischin, *Like All the Nations?*, 194–196.
56. Gil Rubin, "From Federalism to Binationalism, Hannah Arendt's Shifting Zionism," *Contemporary European History*, 24:3 (August 2015): 393–414, and note 83; Goren, *Dissenter in Zion*, 517–519, 520n1; "The Mission of Bernadotte," in *The Jewish Writings, Hannah Arendt*, ed. J. Kohn and R. H. Feldman (New York, 2007), 408–416. The victorious Allied powers had officially termed Holocaust survivors "Displaced Persons" (DPs), thereby consciously masking their Jewish identity.
57. *JTA*, October 28, 1948.
58. *JTA*, October 28 and 29, 1948.
59. *JTA*, October 28 and November 5, 1948.

60. Hans Kohn, "In Memory of Two Great Teachers," file 26/13, Henry Hurwitz MSS.; AJA; *New York Times*, December 17, 1948. For Kohn's changing views, see Hagit Lavski, "Le'umiyut Bein Teioriya L'Politika: Hans Kohn V'HaTsiyonut," *Tsiyon* 67 (2002): 189–212; Adi Gordon, *Toward Nationalism's End: An Intellectual Biography of Huns Kohn* (Waltham, 2017). For Ahad Ha'Am (Asher Ginsberg), the major rival to political Zionism's founder, Theodore Herzl, see Monty Noam Penkower, *The Emergence of Zionist Thought* (Millwood, 1986), chap. 6.
61. Hannah Arendt, "Magnes. The Conscience of the Jewish People," *The Jewish Writings, Hannah Arendt*, 451–464: Efraim Karsh, *Palestine Betrayed* (New Haven, 2010), 264–267.
62. Norman Bentwich, *For the Sake of Zion* (New York, 1954), 303, 273; Magnes to Weizmann, May 25, 1923, cited in Brinner and Rischin, *Like all the Nations?*, 221n16; Arthur A. Goren, "Introduction," in Goren, *Dissenter in Zion*, 57.
63. Gershom Scholem, "A Free Man, On J. L. Magnes," in Gershom Sholem, *Devarim B'Go* (Tel Aviv, 1976), 208–210; Arnold J. Band, "Gown and Town," in Brinner and Rischin, *Like All the Nations?*, 159–163; Abba Eban, *An Autobiography* (New York, 1977), 57.
64. Bentwich, *For the Sake of Zion*, 313, 262; *The Magnes-Philby Negotiations*, ed. Menahem Kaufman, trans. Y. Goell (Jerusalem, 1998); Beatrice L. Magnes, *Episodes. A Memoir* (Berkeley, 1977), 93, 100; November 15, 1947 report, Mapai MSS., Beit Berl, Kfar Sabba, Israel; R. M. Graves, *Experiment in Anarchy* (London, 1949), 84.
65. Goren, *Dissenter in Zion*, 192; Eban report, Sept. 19, 1947, S25/2965, CZA; David Horowitz, *State in the Making* (New York, 1953), 234–235; James Marshall-Elliot Sanger interview, April 11, 1974, American Jewish Committee oral history program, New York City.
66. Jose García Granados, *The Birth of Israel, The Drama as I Saw It* (New York, 1948), 43–44; Meltzer to Montor, June 22, 1968, A371/40, CZA; Buxton to Ben-Horin, January 26, 1948, file 1660, Israel Goldstein MSS., Jerusalem; Buxton interview with the author, July 10, 1979; Crossman to Lazaron, December 3, 1947, box 4, Morris Lazaron MSS., AJA. Calling on the Council to follow Ichud's example in seeking peace between Jews and Arabs and criticizing the new government "severely" once the Israeli state was established, Lazaron acknowledged the Council's failures to convince the majority of American Jews that to follow Zionism would "isolate us from our fellow citizens" and to "stave the national influences which have slowly disintegrated

Judaism and transform all of its branches into a national religion for Jews only." *National Jewish Post and Opinion*, May 16, 1948.

67. Scholem to Arendt, January 28, 1946, in *Gershom Scholem, A Life in letters, 1914–1982*, ed. and trans. A. D. Skinner (Cambridge, 2002), 330–332.
68. November 29, 1947, Mordeccai Kaplan Diary, Jewish Theological Seminary archives, New York City; Amos Oz, *A Tale of Love and Darkness*, trans. N. de Lange (London, 2004), 343. The first quotation by Kaplan is "The Jews enjoyed light and gladness and honor" (*Esther* 8:16), and the second "He does good to the wicked and to the good / Who did all good to us *selah*" (Rosh HaShana prayer). The *Sheh'Hechehyanu* prayer expresses thanks to "the King of the Universe who has given us life, sustained us, and brought us to this time."
69. Bentwich, *For the Sake of Zion*, 38, 284; Moses Rischin, "Introduction," 15; Wasserstein, "The Arab-Jewish Dilemma," 197; Gavriel Stern, "He Looked Out on Zion from Atop Mt. Scopus," 184; all in Brinner and Rischin, *Like All the Nations?*; Goren, *Dissenter in Zion*, 357–365; Daniel P. Kotzkin, *Judah L. Magnes: An American Nonconformist* (Syracuse, 2010), chap. 8.
70. Hexter interview with the author, April 22, 1976; Gideon Shimoni, ed. *Gandhi, Satyagraha and the Jews: A Formative Factor in India's Policy towards Israel* (Jerusalem, 1977), 44; Monty Noam Penkower, *The Jews Were Expendable: Free World Diplomacy and the Holocaust* (Urbana, 1983). Also see Monty Noam Penkower, *The Holocaust and Israel Reborn: From Catastrophe to Sovereignty* (Urbana, 1994). Even after the Holocaust, which he called "the greatest crime of our time, Gandhi felt that the Jews should have "thrown themselves into the sea from cliffs. . . . It would have aroused the world and the people of Germany." Louis Fischer, *The Life of Mahatma Gandhi* (New York, 1950), 346–348. For Magnes's short-lived effort to create in the spring of 1939 a religious society carrying "a commitment to social action and practical political work," most of whose members would be drawn to the League for Jewish-Arab Rapprochement and Cooperation, see Paul Mendes-Flohr, *Divided Passions: Jewish Intellectuals and the Experience of Modernity* (Detroit, 1991), 344–350 and chap. 15.
71. Hedva Ben-Israel, "Bi-nationalism versus Nationalism: The case of Judah Magnes," *Israel Studies* 23:1 (2018): 102; Dmitry Shumsky, *Beyond the Nation-State: The Zionist Political Imagination from Pinsker to Ben-Gurion* (New Haven, 2018).
72. Goren, "Introduction," 57.

Index

A
"A Flag is Born," 231
AAUN. *See* American Association for the United Nations
'Abd al-Hadi, Auni Bey, 230
Abdullah, 88, 103, 200, 203, 205, 208, 210, 216, 222n60, 224n70
Abraham, viii, xiv, 159, 248
Academy for International Law, 72
Accinelli, Robert D., 126, 162n6, 163n7, 163n9
Advisory Committee on Post-War Foreign Policy, 126
Agnon, Shmuel, 258
Agudath Israel, 239
Agus, Jacob B., xviin5
Ahad Ha'Am, 15, 256–257, 268n60
Ahdut HaAvoda, 2, 8, 10, 19, 34n3
Akzin, Benjamin, 54, 77n22
Al Parashat Darkeinu, 228
Al-Alami, Musa, 228, 230
Albania, 136
Al-Haj Ibrahim, Rashid, 230
Al-Husseini, Abd al-Qadir, 101, 103
Al-Husseini, Fawzi Darwish, 230, 232
Al-Husseini, Haj Amin, 45, 76n19, 91–92, 122, 228, 259
Aliya bet, 16, 27–28
Aliya Hadasha, 2, 8, 19, 21, 35n14
Al-Kaukji, Fawzi, 101, 196
Al-Khalidi, Awni, 207
Al-Qastal, 103
Al-Quwatli, Shukri, 123
Altman, Aryeh, 10
Altschul, Frank, x
American Association for the United Nations, 123, 162n6, 211
American Council for Judaism, 108, 131, 139, 157, 160, 163n16, 167n63, 229, 239, 260, 265n25
American Federation of Labor, 138
American Friends of the Middle East, 160
American Jewish Archives, xiv, 74n6, 115n4, 163n16, 226n79, 263n3

American Jewish Committee, 95, 138, 142–143, 165n34, 166n49, 201, 218n18, 221n57, 240, 242, 266n35, 266n42, 268n65
American Jewish Conference, 7, 44, 74n7
American Jewish Congress, 42, 95, 229
American Jewish Joint Distribution Committee. See JDC
American League for a Free Palestine, 231
American Poale Zion, 7, 11
American Union for Concerted Peace Efforts, 126
American United Revisionists, 8
American University of Beirut, 165n47, 249
American Zionist Emergency Council, 54, 77n27, 190, 239
Amos, xiv, 248, 260
And the Crooked Shall Be Made Straight, 79n52
Anglo-American Committee of Inquiry on Palestine, xiii, 10, 158, 221n57, 230, 259
Anglo-Palestine Bank, 103
Anschluss, 54
antisemitism, 31–32, 48, 150, 167n60, 202, 210, 260
appeasement, 122, 164n23
Arab Charter for Palestine, 123
Arab federation, 227, 229
Arab Higher Committee, 52, 65, 76n19, 84, 102, 123, 128, 153, 169, 173, 180, 234, 236, 241
Arab infiltration, 128, 130, 133, 203
Arab Legion, 88, 101–102, 175, 183, 195, 198, 200–201, 206, 212, 216, 225n73, 250
Arab Liberation Army, 101, 133, 196
Arab refugees, 252, 254–255
Arab Revolt, 101, 133, 185, 228, 258, 261
Arab riots of 1929, 257
Arab Triangle in Palestine, 13, 243
Arab views of Magnes, 231, 264n8
Arabs invade Palestine, 104, 153
Arabs react to partition vote, 97, 122–123, 128, 130–131, 133–135, 143, 150, 171, 174, 193, 240, 260
Arafat, Yasser, 72
ARAMCO, 66, 78n41, 160, 167n64
Arazi, Tuvya, 86, 88, 90, 100

Arendt, Hannah, 79n52, 238, 248–252, 254–255, 257, 260, 266n42, 267n56, 268n61
arms embargo, 87, 100, 116n11, 128, 130–131, 135, 137, 142, 151–152, 158, 191–192, 204, 207, 220n38
Article 80, 41, 51, 56, 58, 193, 220n40
Arvey, Jacob, 212
Aryanization, 75n10
Atomic Energy Commission, 60
Attlee, Clement, xiii, xviii$n$12, 27, 51, 59, 107, 195, 203, 231, 241
Auschwitz, xix$n$13, 1, 32, 257
Auschwitz-Birkenau, 1, 32
Austin, Warren, 68, 102, 121–123, 137–140, 142–145, 147, 169–173, 177, 179, 185, 187–188, 192, 196–199, 204, 208, 213–215, 216n2, 218n18, 219n31, 220n43, 220n47, 221n56, 222n61, 239, 241, 243, 265n25–26, 266n33
Avriel, Ehud, 86, 110
Azcárate y Flores, Pablo, 171
Azzam Pasha, Abdul Raham, 123, 180–181, 206, 235, 241, 259

B

Backus, Dana, 149, 152, 155, 165n46, 166n56
Baeck, Leo, 238, 244
Baerwald, Paul, 95–96, 117n23
Baldwin, Stanley, ix
Balfour Declaration, x, 52–53, 55, 69, 76n20, 146, 153–154, 158, 214, 230–231, 263n6
Baltimore Hebrew Congregation, 131, 167n63, 229
Bar Kokhba Revolt, ix
Barnard College, 132, 218n18, 238
Bartoszewski, Wladyzlaw, 32
Basle, 1, 3, 12, 22–23, 25–26, 28, 33, 36n29
Battle of Dunkirk, 35n12
BBC, xv
Beeley, Harold, 93, 117n21, 176, 195, 215, 217n11, 220n43, 221n56, 224n68, 230
Begin, Menachem, xvi$n$4
Beit Sh'an Valley, 206
Belt, Guillermo, 208, 214
Belzec, 33
Ben Tov, Mordekhai, 10, 231, 264n8
Ben Yehuda Street. Bombing, 101
Ben-Gurion, David, xiii–xiv, xviii$n$12, xix$n$14, 2, 4–6, 8–9, 11–14, 16–23, 25–29, 33, 34n8, 41, 50, 58, 69–70, 79n47, 82, 86–90, 96, 100–101, 103–110, 122–123, 159, 175–176, 180, 184, 186, 190, 196–197, 202, 205, 213–215, 224n70, 231, 235, 239, 244, 247–248, 251–252

Ben-Gurion, Paula, 12
Ben-Israel, Hedva, 261, 269n71
Benny, Jack, 105
Bentwich, Norman, 228, 258, 268n62, 268n64, 269n69
Ben-Zvi, Yitshak, 36n26, 87, 176–177, 217n12
Berendsen, Carl, 197, 208
Bergen-Belsen, 31, 82
Bergman, Samuel Hugo, 227
Berkovitz, Eliezer, xvii$n$6
Berlin, Isaiah, 6
Berlin, Meir, 7
Bernadotte, Folke, 161, 212, 250–254, 257, 267n52
Bernheim Petition, 42
Bernstein, Peretz, 22
Bernstein, Philip, 28
Bevin, Ernest, 24, 27–28, 37n40, 51, 61, 94, 123, 146, 176, 178, 180, 194–195, 199, 202–203, 207–209, 212, 214, 220n47, 224n70, 230, 253
Bey Fawzi, Mahmound, 171
Beyth, Hans, 87
Bialik, Chaim Nahum, 37n40
Biblical sources, xiv, 159, 248
Bidault, Georges, 180
Biltmore Program, 5–6, 10–11, 13, 17, 19, 25, 229
bi-nationalism, 10, 269n71. *See also* Magnes, Judah
Bitburg military cemetery, 31
"Black Sabbath," 10, 15–16, 25, 85
Blaustein, Jacob, 166n49, 243, 266n34
Bluestone, E.M., 255
Blum, John M., 111–112
Blumovicz, Abrasha, 28
Board of Jewish Education, 227
Boettiger, Curtis Roosevelt, 106
book of *Job*, vii–viii
Borkenau, Franz, xvii$n$6
Boston Herald, 158, 259
Boukstein, Maurice, 106, 108
Bradbury, Ray, vii
Brest-Litovsk, xvi$n$4
Brewster, Owen, 134, 164n21
bricha, 4
Brisk, xvi$n$4
Brit Shalom, 227–228, 258
Britain turns to the UN, 10–11
British aid to Arabs, 91
British government *de facto* recognition of Israel, xviii$n$12
British mandate on Palestine, xviii$n$12

—272—

British Palestine quotas, 230
British Record on Partition, The, 156
British Royal Navy, 28, 208
British weapons to Arab states, 87, 94–95, 97, 101–102, 131, 135, 207
British Zionist Federation, 2
Brodetsky, Selig, 2, 11, 21–22, 223n67
Buber, Martin, 218n18, 227, 229–230, 232, 236–238, 257, 261
Bulgaria, 48, 136, 245
Bunche, Ralph, 171–172, 174, 182, 189, 192, 197, 199, 218n18, 219n31, 219n33, 220n40, 220n47, 253
Burganski, Bronia, 29
Burke, Edmund, 50
Burma Road, 107, 119n46
Buxton, Frank W., 158, 167n60, 259, 268n66
Byron, vii, 173
Bytom, 4

C

Cadogan, Alexander, 89, 178, 185, 187, 189, 195, 200, 202
Camp David Accords, xvin4
Campbell, Ronald, 181
cantonization plan, 7, 10, 59
Cantor, Eddie, 105
Caribbean, xiii, 65
Carlebach, Azriel, 17, 21
Carnegie Endowment for Peace, 152
Carter, Jimmy, 30
Casablanca, 161
Cavert, Samuel McCrea, 145, 239
Celler, Emanuel, 110, 138
Central Committee of Liberated Jews in the American zone of Germany, 3
Central Intelligence Agency, 139, 160, 169
Chamoun, Camille Bay, 123
Chatham House, 230
Chaucer, vii
Chautauqua System, 125
Chinov, 29
chol, vii–viii, xvin2–3
Christian Century, 139
Churchill, Winston, 83, 92, 107, 241
"Circle of Friends of Himmler," 75n10
Clark, Tom, 99
Clayton, I.N., 201
Clifford, Clark, 159, 166n58, 210–214, 222n60, 225n73–74, 226n80, 247–248
Coffin, Henry Sloane, 133
Cohen, Benjamin V., 143–145, 147, 151–152, 159, 165n37

Cohen, Elliot E., 238
Cohen, Michael, 26, 34n7, 36n17, 38n47
Cohen, Rachel, 103
Cold War, 71, 128, 160, 162n6, 212
Colonial Office, 38n44, 186
Comité des Délégations Juives, 42
Commentary, 37n41, 38n46, 238, 248, 251–252, 254–255, 266n42, 267n48, 267n54
Commission on Human Rights, 48, 71
Commission to Study the Organization of Peace, 126, 146, 160–161, 163n7
Committee for Concerted Peace Efforts, 126
Committee for Justice and Peace in the Holy Land, 141, 145, 160, 218n18, 238–239
Committee on International Relations, 146
Committee to Defend America by Aiding the Allies, 126
Confederation House, 30, 33, 39n58
confederation plan, 250–251
Conference on Jewish Material Claims against Germany, 72
Congregation B'nai Jeshurun, 227
Congress of Industrial Organizations, 138
Connelly, Mathew J., 211
convoys to Jerusalem, 103, 236
Coons, Isidor, 85, 102
Corcoran, Thomas, 143
Council of Foreign Ministers, 60
Council of Jewish Federations and Welfare Funds, 90, 116n17–18
Council on Foreign Relations, x, xviin7
Creech Jones, Arthur, 24–25, 38n43, 62, 68, 176, 199–200, 204, 207–209, 220n47, 222n61, 223n66, 224n68, 266n35
Crick, Wilfrid, 231
Criminal Investigation Department, 243
Crossman, Richard, xiii, xviiin12, 23, 231, 259, 268n66
Crum, Bartley, 159, 212, 247
Cunningham, Alan, 58, 70, 86, 116n11, 176, 189, 197, 204–205, 213, 218n20, 220n47, 222n61, 231–232, 236, 264n9, 264n11
Cyprus camps, xviii, 92, 135, 242, 245
Cyprus, 27, 54, 107–108, 174, 181, 184
Czech weapons to the Hagana, 103, 192
Czechoslovakia, 1, 44, 48–49, 103, 122, 124, 148, 182, 192, 216n2, 240

D

Dafna, 207
Dan, 207
Danzig, 29, 57
Davar, 17, 22, 26

Davis, Helen, 149, 151, 153, 155–156, 165n46, 166n51, 166n54, 166n56
Davis, Malcolm W., 152
Dayan, Moshe, 34n8
de Lima, Oscar A., 152
De Sola Pool, David, 255
Dead Sea, 13
death marches, 4, 29
Deir Yassin, 103, 254, 266n32
Der Tog, 8
Detroit Jewish News, 180
Deutsch, Monroe E., 156
Dewey, Thomas E., 108
Diaspora nationalism
Displaced Persons (DPs), 4, 9, 27, 51, 53, 56, 83, 134, 139–141, 151–152, 154, 157, 191, 223n64, 233, 255, 267n56
Dobkin, Eliyahu, 22, 87
Dodge, Bayard, 150, 165n47, 249, 267n43
Douglas, Lewis W., 194, 199, 202–203, 221n52, 222n59, 224n70
DP camps, 4, 9, 27–28, 83, 120n55, 223n65
Dresden, 4
Dubnow, Simon, 49
Dugdale, Blanche, 6–7, 11–12, 16
Dulles, John Foster, 129, 163n11
Dulzin, Aryeh, 29
Dumbarton Oaks, 127, 143
"Dunkerque spirit," 7

E
Eban, Abba, x–xi, 6, 15, 23, 37n40, 72, 79n53, 179–180, 190, 192–193, 205–206, 215, 220n40, 222n62, 251
Effendi, Omar, 259
Egypt, xv, xixn14, 31, 41, 58, 71, 89, 171, 202, 249
Eichelberger, Clark M., xiv, 123–132, 135–138, 140–144, 147–150, 152–153, 155–157, 159–161, 162n6, 163n7–11, 163n13–14, 164n17, 164n23–27, 165n31–32, 165n38, 165n42, 165n44–48, 166n50–51, 166n54–58, 167n65, 168n66–67
Eichmann Trial, 75n9, 79n52
Eichmann, Adolf, 45–46, 71, 114n1
ein breira, xiii, 90
Einstein, Albert, 238, 244
Eisenhower, Dwight D., 160, 192
El Nokrashy Pasha, Mahmound, 181
Elath, Eliyahu. *See* Epstein
Eliash, Mordekhai, 249
Eliot, George Fielding, 129, 180
El-Khouri, Faris, 65, 67, 78n42, 178, 185, 199, 201, 215

Elsey, George M.226n80
Elting, Victor, 152
Emerson, William, 145, 147–149, 151, 153, 155–156, 165n38, 165n44–46, 166n50, 166n55–56
Emile, xviiin10, 30
Encyclopedia Judaica, 72
Epstein, Eliyahu, 50, 100, 166n58, 171, 202, 210, 213–214, 218n20, 221n57, 225n72, 226n77, 230, 247, 263n7
Epstein, Judith, 8
Eshkol, Levi, 88, 112
Essenes, 257
Ethiopia, 136, 164n23
Etzion bloc, 91, 104
European Nationalities Congress, 41
European Recovery Program, 133, 162n6, 191
Evatt, Herbert V., 58, 188, 232, 264n11
Evian Conference on Refugees, 85
Exodus 1947, 28, 115n7
Export-Import Bank, 87
expulsion of Jews, xvin4, 41, 189
Eytan, Walter, 66, 78n40, 172, 174–175, 177, 182–183, 204, 217n8, 217n10, 217n13, 218n22, 222n61, 225n72
Ezekiel, ix
Ezekiel, xiv, 15, 248

F
Fabregat, Enrique R., 190
Fahy, Charles, 187, 195, 219n30, 220n44, 225n73
Farmer's Federation, 229
Fatah, 262
Federal Council of the Churches of Christ in America, 145, 239
Federal Union, 250, 254
federalization plan, 10
Federation of Jewish Philanthropies, 233–234
Federation of Polish Jews, 30
Feinberg, Abraham, 108–109, 119n49
Feisal, Prince, 206, 208, 223n64
Feller, Abe, 65
Fernandez, Gonzales, 178
"Final Solution of the Jewish Question," xi, 9, 45
Finanza Popolare, 112
Finkelstein, Louis, 238, 252, 265n23
First Crusade, xvin4
Fishman, Yehuda Leib, 5, 8, 22
Fletcher-Cooke, John, 89, 205, 219n31, 219n33
Flick Case, 75n10
"The Flying Caravans," 98
Flynn, Edward J., 212
"For a Jewish-Arab Confederation," 254, 267n54

Foreign Affairs, 229, 254
Foreign Office, ix, 24, 38n43, 66, 107, 114, 117n21, 123, 178, 185, 194, 215, 218n15, 220n42, 222n58, 222n60, 223n65, 224n69–70, 225n76, 226n80, 228, 245, 263n7, 266n35
Forrestal, James V., 146, 191, 223n65, 226n80
Fossil, ix, xi–xii
Frank, Jerome, 218n18, 243
Frankfurter, Felix, 23, 37n40, 265n25
Fraser, Peter, 41, 189
Freeland League, 238
Friedman, Herbert A., 84, 107, 109, 111–112, 115n6, 119n46, 119n49–51, 120n55
Friedman, Philip, 79n52
Fromm, Erich, 238
Frumkin, Gad, 262n2

G

Galilee, 92, 100, 161, 207, 253
Gandhi, 261, 269n70
Garcia-Granados, Jorge, 199
Gaza, 262
Geiger, Alexander, 242
Gelber, Lionel, 129, 163n12
General Assembly Political Committee, 17–18, 204–205, 207, 212, 224n69, 255
General Assembly, xiii, 31, 50, 53–54, 56–58, 61–63, 65, 67–69, 72, 84, 86, 88, 90, 96, 121–122, 128, 130, 132, 134, 140–141, 145, 147, 152, 159, 161, 162n2, 169, 185, 193, 196, 232–236, 240–242, 244, 253
General Principles, 177, 179, 182, 185, 187, 192–194, 217n14
General Zionist Council, 28
Genesis, xiv, 248
Gerstenfeld, Manfred, xixn13
Gesher, 206
Ghoury, Emil, 123
Gibson, Harvey, 104
Gildersleeve, Virginia C., 132, 139, 141, 144–145, 147–150, 153, 160, 164n17–18, 165n32–33, 165n38–39, 167n64, 218n18, 238, 265n25,
Giliwice, 4
Ginsberg, Asher, 15, 268n60
Ginsburg, David C., 213, 225n76, 226n77
Glueck, Nelson, 252, 256
Goitein, S.D., 242, 266n32
Goldenberg, Harry, 90, 98, 101
Goldman, Robert, 138
Goldmann, Nahum, 2, 4, 6, 8–10, 21–23, 35n13, 37n40, 50, 73, 76n12, 76n15, 80n54, 109, 129, 202, 205–206, 209–210, 222n62, 246–247

Goldsmith, Arthur, 250
Goldstein, Israel, 2, 29, 34n2, 99, 268n66
Goldwasser, I. Edwin, 96
Goren, Arthur A., 258, 262n1, 264n10, 264n13, 265n23, 266n30, 266n37, 267n44–45, 267n47–49, 267n53, 267n56, 268n62, 268n65, 269n69, 269n72
Governor-General for Palestine, 177, 182, 197, 241, 244–245
Graves, R.M., 205, 223n63, 268n64
Greece, 48, 67, 107, 124, 136, 142, 148, 202
Greenbaum, Edward, 243
Greenberg, Hayim, 11
Greenberg, Marian, 18, 22, 35n14, 36n29, 118n42
Greenberg, Simon, 255
Gromyko, Andrei, 57–58, 122, 171–172, 181, 185, 188–189, 194, 197, 207, 219n32
Grossman, Meir, 8
Gruenbaum, Yitshak, 2, 11, 22, 87
Guide to Jewish History under the Nazi Impact, 79n52
Gulf of Aqaba, 13
Gurney, Henry, 87, 89, 116n11, 196, 220n45

H

ha'apala, 16, 22
HaBoker, 22, 26
Hadassah Hospital convoy, 198
Hadassah, viii, 2, 8–9, 17–18, 22, 25, 29, 32, 95, 106, 113, 198, 229, 236, 242, 250, 255–256
Hagana, 4, 7, 15, 28, 82, 86, 88–90, 101–103, 109, 115n2, 116n15, 144, 149, 176, 186, 192, 195–196, 200, 206–207, 215, 217n10–11, 249
Hagglof, Gunner, 197
Haifa, 14, 28, 89, 103, 187, 195–196, 199–200, 208, 213, 220n43, 243, 253
Halprin, Rose, 2, 22, 106, 109
Hamas, 262
HaMashkif, 26, 264n9
HaMedina BaDerekh, xiii
Hammer, Gottlieb, 99, 103–104, 106, 108, 115n3, 117n32, 118n38, 118n40, 119n44, 119n48, 120n55
Handbook on Confederation, 252
HaNoar HaTsiyoni, 4
Hanukah, xvin4
HaPo'el HaMizrachi, 8
Har HaTsofim, 236
Harrison, Earl, 27, 83
HaShomer HaTsa'ir, 2, 8, 10, 17, 19, 21–22, 26, 34n3, 36n29, 37n34, 229–232, 235
HaTikva, xvin4, xviiin11, 19, 27, 261

Hausner, Gideon, 71, 79n52
HaVa'ad HaLeumi, 70
HaYotzek factory, 101
Hazan, Ya'akov, 8, 10, 17–18
Hebrew Union College, 252, 256
Hebrew University, xii, 131, 158, 180, 227, 233, 238, 242, 255–259, 263n7
Hecht, Ben, 231
Heliopolis, vii
Henderson, Loy, 139, 145–146, 180, 211, 223n65, 224n68, 239, 241–242, 246, 249–250
Herblock, 156, 166n58
Herod's Gate, 258
Herodotus, vii
Herzl Press, 29
Herzl Yearbook, 29
Herzl, Theodor, 1, 13, 33, 55, 112, 114, 268n60
Herzog, Vivian (Chaim), 180, 225n72
Herzog, Yaacov, xi–xii, xiv–xv, xixn14, 217n10, 225n72
Hexter, Maurice, 233, 235–236, 239–240, 242–243, 261, 264n14–15, 264n19, 265n25, 269n70
Hezbollah, 262
Hickerson, John, 219n32
Hilldring, John H., 84, 156, 166n58, 223n65
Hiss, Alger, 152
Histadrut Mapai, 85
Hitler, Adolf, ix, xiv, 41, 43, 81, 92, 107, 122, 203, 230, 261
Hitler's Ten Year War against the Jews, 43
HMS *Euryalus*, 213
Hofshi, Natan, 233
Hollande, Francois, xviiin10
Hollander, Sidney, 90
Holmes, John, 228, 263n3
Holocaust denial, xv, 167n60
Holocaust effect on Zionist enrollment, 2
Holocaust survivors, x, 16, 24, 31, 50, 71, 83, 113, 141, 159, 223n65, 230–231, 239, 241, 245, 267n56 numbers, 32, 53, to Palestine, 49, 51, 115n7
Holocaust, xi, xiii, xv, xvin4, xixn13, 1, 3, 10, 16, 24, 27, 30–33, 41, 43, 45–46. 49–51, 53, 70–72, 79n52, 82–83, 91, 112–113, 115n7, 141, 159, 167n60, 191, 223n65, 230–231, 234, 238–239, 241, 245, 258, 267n56, 269n70
Holocaust: The Nuremberg Evidence, The, 79n52
Holy Places, 52, 69, 70, 155, 175, 195
Holy Temples, destruction of, xvin4
Hood, John, 197–198
Hopkins, Garland Evans, 139
Horowitz, David, 206, 259, 268n65

Hoskins, Harold L., 133
Hullegeb theatre ensemble, 30
Human Rights and Fundamental Freedoms in the Charter of the United Nations, 47
Human rights, 33, 44, 47–48, 71, 75n9, 127, 141
Humphrey, John P., 48, 75n11
Husseini, Darwish, 232, 258–259
Husseini, Jamal, 65, 69, 76n19, 181, 183–184, 188, 194, 196, 201–202, 205, 207–208, 218n23, 219n25
Hutcheson, Joseph C., 231, 264n8

I

Ibn Saud, Abdul Aziz, 134, 208, 230
Ignatieff, Michael, 185
Ihud Association, 146
Ihud party, 4
Implementing a General Assembly recommendation, 88
India partition, 59
Institute of Jewish Affairs, 42, 47, 74n4, 74n7–8, 75n10
Internal Revenue Service, 108
International City of Jerusalem, 254
International Council of the Auschwitz Museum, 30
International Court of Justice, 54, 71, 132–133
International Federation of University Women, 132
International Military Tribunal, 45, 75n9
International Network of Children of Jewish Holocaust Survivors, 31
International Police Force, 128, 130, 136, 138, 182, 186, 197
International Refugee Organization, 56
Iran, 151, 160, 202
Iraq, 41, 58, 60, 89, 207, 228–229
Irgun Tsva'i Le'umi, 231
Isaiah, xiv, 6, 15, 248
Isaiah, 36n25, 264n13
Israel Bonds, 109–113, 119n51
Israel constitution, 64, 66
Israel Law Review, 46, 74n5, 75n9
Israeli Declaration of Independence, 79n47, 226n77
Israeli population, xi, 30, 107
Israeli withdrawals, 262
Istiqlal Party, 230
Italy, 4, 9, 48, 60, 76n20, 125, 136, 144, 164n23, 230
Izvestiia, 110

J

Jabotinsky, Vladimir Ze'ev, 3
Jackson, Robert, 45–47, 75n9–10
Jacobson, Eddie, 159, 192, 212, 247
Janner, Barnett, 2
Javits, Jacob K., 110, 131, 163n15
JDC, 81–82, 85, 90, 94–96, 99, 102, 105, 109, 114, 117n25, 249, 252, 256
Jebb, Gladwyn, 179
Jenin, 243
Jeremiah, xiv, 15, 248–249, 267n43
Jerusalem, viii, xv–xvi, 14, 20–21, 30, 33, 45, 50, 53, 57–58, 66, 70, 72, 81, 86–89, 92, 100–103, 105–107, 109, 112–114, 119n46, 131, 134, 139, 155, 172–177, 180–182, 185–186, 190, 193, 195–198, 200–201, 203–210, 213, 215, 217n11, 218n18, 221n57, 223n63, 224n69–70, 230, 233–234, 236, 241, 243–245, 249–251, 253–255, 257–258, 260
Jerusalem International Oud Festival, 30
Jessup, Philip, 192, 198, 205–206, 211–212, 214–215, 226n78, 250
Jewish Agency American Section, 224n69
Jewish Agency Committee on the Arab Question, 229
Jewish Agency for Palestine, xiii, 2, 4–5, 7, 21–22, 27–28, 41, 50–52, 54–63, 66, 76n17, 76n20, 81, 84, 93, 95, 99, 102–106, 108–109, 114n1, 115n2, 121–122, 129, 138, 144, 148, 152, 157, 159, 166n58, 169–170, 172–175, 179–181, 183–184, 187, 189–190, 192, 195, 198, 201–202, 204, 209, 211, 214, 218n23, 221n57, 222n60, 223n67, 224n69, 225n72, 225n74, 228–229, 231–232, 236, 239, 241, 246–247, 251, 254
Jewish Agency headquarters bombing, 101–102
Jewish Agency, Inc., The, 106
Jewish Frontier, 11
Jewish homelessness, 97
Jewish immigration to Palestine, x, 9, 56, 58, 60, 75n9, 76n16, 76n19, 77n25, 81, 140, 157–158, 170, 174–175, 180–181, 183–184, 188, 193, 199, 202, 206, 209, 219n25, 230–232, 234, 238, 241–242, 245, 259–260, 263n7
Jewish Social Services Quarterly, 74n7
Jewish Telegraphic Agency, xvin3, 12, 30, 76n13, 110, 113, 115n6, 217n8, 264n9
Jewish Territorial Organization, 238
Jewish Theological Seminary, 233, 238, 255, 269n68
Jewish War Veterans of America, 122, 225n76
Jews killed in Poland after WW II, 39n55
Jihad, 32, 216, 259
Johnson, Herschel V., 173
Joint Chiefs of Staff, 146, 191
Joseph, Bernard, 10
Jüdische Rundschau, 23

K

Kalvariski-Margalioth, Chaim, 228
Kaplan, Eliezer, 5, 17–18, 21–23, 73n3, 79n52, 81, 86–88, 90, 99, 105–106, 109–110, 114n1, 115n5, 116n10–11, 117n32, 118n43, 119n48, 216
Kaplan, Mordecai, 260
Kashmir, 196
Katamon, 207
Katowice, 4
Katz–Suchy, Julius, 208
Kaukji, Fawzi, 101, 133, 164n19, 196
Kedma Mizracha, 228
Kennan, George, 138
Kennedy, John F., 191
Keren Kayemet L'Yisrael, 86
Kfar Etzion, 89, 91, 212, 225n76
Kfar Szold, 207
Khalidi, Hussein, 176, 205
Khan, Zafrullah, 234
Khazars, 65
Khirbat Bayt, 107
kibbutz galuyot, 109
Kibbutz Merhavia, 85
Kibbutz Netiv HaLamed Heh, 116n15
Kibbutz Yehiam, 102, 149
Kielce pogrom, 32
Kielce, 4
Kikar Magnes, 258
Kirchwey, Freda, 138, 156–157, 159, 166n58, 220n41, 220n43, 265n27
Klein, Julius, 122, 213
Klotz, Henrietta, 83, 111–112, 119n54
Knudson, John I, 152
Kohanski, Alexander, 44, 74n7
Kohl, Helmut, 31
Kohn, Hans, 118n42, 145, 217n10, 219n34, 227, 239, 248, 252, 256–257, 265n26, 266n42, 267n54, 267n56, 268n60
Kohn, Leo, 182
Kopper, Samuel, 202, 206, 217n14, 221n56
Korea, 67, 124, 140
Kovno, 42, 80n54
Krakow, 4
Kristallnacht, 81, 114n1, 261

L

L'Behinat HaDerekh, 5, 34*n*8
Lamb, Harold, 133
Lamm, Maurice, xvi*n*4
Land of Canaan, xiv, 159, 248
Laski, Harold, 23, 37*n*40–41
Latin America, xiii, 65, 182, 215
Latrun prison, 11, 17, 36*n*18, 107
Lauterpacht, Hersch, 79*n*47
Lavon, Pinhas. *See* Lubianiker, Pinhas
Lawford, V.G., 178, 218*n*15
Lawrence, D.H., vii
Lazaron, Morris S., 131–132, 136, 140, 145, 149, 151, 153–158, 160, 162, 163*n*16, 165*n*30, 165*n*47, 166*n*54, 166*n*56, 167*n*59, 167*n*63, 229, 239, 260, 265*n*25, 268*n*66
League for Jewish-Arab Rapprochement and Cooperation, 228, 269*n*70
League of Nations Association, 125–127, 163*n*7
League of Nations Chronicle, 125
League of Nations Covenant, 69, 218*n*23
League of Nations, 41–42, 44, 55, 57–58, 69, 76*n*20, 77*n*27–28, 124–125, 127, 135, 142, 171, 183, 218*n*23
Lebanon, 123, 249, 262
Lehavot HaBashan, 207
Lehman, Herbert H., 97, 117*n*23, 117*n*27, 129, 151, 166*n*49, 212
Lerner, Max, 97
Levin, Aryeh, 116*n*15
Levin, Shmarya, 37*n*40
Levinthal, Louis E., 2
Levy, Joseph, 250
Lie, Trygve, 65, 68, 121, 169, 172, 183, 185, 189, 192, 197, 199, 216, 220*n*47
Linder, Harold, 96, 266*n*34
Lipchitz, Jacques, viii, xvi*n*3
Lippmann, Walter, 127
Lipsky, Louis, 2, 11
Lisicky, Karel, 182, 203, 218*n*20
Locker, Berl, 8, 22–23, 109
London Times, 26
London Conference, 6–7, 9–13, 16–20, 22–23, 25
López, Alfonso, 173, 183–184, 188, 194, 197–200, 218*n*23, 219*n*25–26
Lord Inverchapel, 146, 194, 209, 220*n*42
Lord Listowel, 199, 221*n*52
Lord Mountbatten, 59
Lourie, Arthur, 66, 78*n*41, 105, 118, 167*n*61, 204, 225*n*73, 255
Lovett, Robert A., 138–139, 142–143, 159, 163*n*34–36, 171, 180, 186, 191–192, 195, 201–202, 204–205, 209–215, 219*n*28, 219*n*32, 220*n*42, 221*n*49, 221*n*56–57, 241, 266*n*35
Lowenthal, Marvin, 247
Lowenthal, Max, 210
Lubianiker, Pinhas, 5
Ludlow amendment, 126
Lund, Roscher, 172, 183
Lurie, Harry, 90, 116*n*17
Lydda (Lod), 253

M

ma'apilim, 16, 27
Ma'ariv, 111, 119*n*54
ma'avak, 5, 16–17, 22
Macatee, Robert, 87
MacMillan, Gordon, 212, 242
"The Magellan," 108–109
Magnes, Beatrice, 248, 251, 266*n*41
Magnes, Judah Leib, xiv, 131, 144–145, 157–158, 160, 165*n*47, 167*n*63, 180, 209–210, 218*n*18, 224*n*71, 227–262, 262*n*2, 263*n*3, 263*n*7, 264*n*8, 264*n*10–12, 264*n*14–15, 264*n*17, 265*n*21, 265*n*24, 265*n*26–28, 266*n*32, 266*n*33, 266*n*38, 267*n*43, 267*n*54, 268*n*61, 269*n*70
Maimon, Yehuda. *See* Fishman, Yehuda Leib
Malik, Charles, 200, 215, 249–250, 253, 259
Malta, 54
Mankowitz, Zeev, 28, 34*n*4, 38*n*49
Mann, Thomas, 240
Mapai, 2, 5, 8, 11–12, 17–22, 25, 28, 34*n*8, 38*n*45, 38*n*49, 85, 103, 113, 118*n*39, 268*n*64
Marcus, Mickey, 119*n*46
Mark, Julius, 111
Marshall Plan, 148, 162*n*6, 191, 243, 252
Marshall, George C., 61, 66, 84, 100–101, 103, 123, 131, 136, 138–139, 143, 145–146, 148, 159–160, 163*n*15, 169–170, 173, 176, 186, 191, 204, 206, 209–215, 217*n*14, 219*n*31, 221*n*56, 222*n*60, 223*n*65, 239
Marshall, James, 240–247, 250, 252–253, 255, 259, 265*n*26–27, 266*n*38, 267*n*43, 268*n*65
Mass, Danny, 89
Massachusetts Institute of Technology, 145
Materials for Palestine, 82
McClintock, Robert, 178, 191–192, 210, 204, 211, 217*n*11, 218*n*16, 219*n*32, 220*n*43, 221*n*49, 221*n*56, 222*n*60, 245, 250, 266*n*35, 267*n*46
McCormick, Anne O'Hare, 40
McDonald, James G., 221*n*57, 231
McGill University, xi

McNaughton, A.G.L., 178, 218*n*20, 219*n*27, 226*n*80
Medieval blood libel, xv
"Medinat haYehudim," 23
Medinat Yisrael, 88, 103
Meinertzhagen, Richard, 26, 38*n*47
Meir, Golda. *See* Myerson, Goldie
Mekor Hayim, 206
Meltzer, Julian, 16, 115*n*5, 117*n*22, 120*n*57, 259, 268*n*66
Memel, 41
Memorial Foundation for Jewish Culture, 72
Metula, 30
Meyerhoff, Joseph, 109
Micah, 237
Middle East Advisory Committee, 252
Middle East Journal, 133, 164*n*19, 267*n*52
Middle East oil, 135, 160, 167*n*64
Midstream, 29, 31, 32, 38*n*50, 39*n*54–55
Miechow, 3
Military Staff Committee, 60
millet system, x, 230
Minhelet HaAm, 103, 213
Minorities Treaties, 44
Mishmar HaEmek, 103, 196
Mishmar, 21, 26
Mizrachi, 5, 12, 15, 18–19, 21–22, 24, 26, 34*n*3, 35*n*13, 36*n*22
Molotov, Vyacheslav, 188
Montor, Henry, 81–86, 90–91, 93–95, 98–99, 102, 104–106, 108–114, 114*n*1, 115*n*2–6, 116*n*8, 116*n*17, 117*n*20, 117*n*22, 117*n*24–25, 118*n*40, 119*n*48, 119*n*53–54, 120*n*57, 268*n*66
Moore, Hugh, 152
Morgan, Eduardo, 174
Morgenthau, Jr., Henry, 82–84, 94–99, 101, 104–108, 110–114, 115*n*7, 117*n*22, 118*n*43, 119*n*51, 119*n*53, 166*n*58
Morgenthau, Robert, 111
Morning Journal, 17
Morris, Benny, 266*n*32
Morrison-Grady plan, 36*n*17, 77*n*29, 214, 225*n*74
Morse, Wayne, 191
Mosaddegh, Mohammad, 160
Moslem Supreme Council, 102
Moynihan, Daniel Patrick, 79*n*53
Mt. Scopus, viii, 250, 269*n*69
Munich, 3, 122
Murray, Wallace, 229
Murrow, Edward R., xix*n*14
Mussolini, Benito, 164*n*23
Mustermesse hall, 1

My Day, 146
Myers, Stanley, 90–91, 97, 109
Myerson, Goldie, 5, 19, 22, 25, 50, 76*n*15, 81, 85–104, 113, 116*n*9, 116*n*11, 117*n*19, 117*n*21, 117*n*24, 117*n*33, 118*n*39, 173, 175, 184, 215, 217*n*14, 219*n*26

N

Nablus, 243
Nachmansohn, David, 238
Nahalal, 14, 233
Nahariya, 149
Nashashibi, 258
Natan, Marcie, 32
Nathan, Robert, 97, 109
Nation Associates, 156, 240, 265*n*27
Nation, 26, 138, 156, 222*n*58, 265*n*27
National Policy for the Oil Industry, The, 67
National Refugee Service, 81
Nazis, xi, xv, xix*n*13, 4, 9, 45–47, 55, 71
Near Eastern and African Affairs division, 87, 169, 180, 229
Negev, 14, 16, 87, 92, 100, 122, 161, 253
Nesbit, Edith, vii
Netanyahu, Binyamin, xviii*n*10
Neumann, Emanuel, 2, 4, 7, 9, 12, 13–15, 18, 22, 29, 34*n*6–7, 37*n*30, 134, 164*n*21, 256
Neutrality Act, 126, 164*n*23
Neveh Daniel, 149
Neveh Ya'akov, 198
"The new anti-Semitism," 32, 39*n*55, 39*n*58
New Deal, 143
New Encyclopedia of Zionism and Israel, 29
New Leader, 254
New Palestine Society, 259
New Palestine, 81
New York Herald Tribune, 62, 135, 141, 143, 145, 162*n*4, 164*n*22, 165*n*37
New York Kehillah, 262*n*1
New York Times, 16, 32, 36*n*26, 39*n*56, 40, 156*n*57, 121, 132, 155, 162*n*2, 167*n*63, 209, 218*n*18, 221*n*56, 227–228, 232–233, 238, 240, 244, 250–251, 257, 262*n*1, 264*n*12, 265*n*22, 265*n*26, 266*n*38, 268*n*60
"Next Year in Jerusalem!," 20
Nicholson, Harold, 23, 31*n*47
Niles, David, 166*n*58, 210–213, 247
Noel-Baker, Philip xviii*n*12
Norman, Edward, 228
Novomeysky, Moshe, 262*n*2
Nuremberg Trials, 167*n*60
Nuremberg U.S. Military Court, 75*n*10
Nuremberg War Crimes Tribunal, 45, 146

O

O.S.S., 133–134
Office of Special Political Affairs, 135
oil, 66–67, 122, 130, 133–135, 157, 169, 191, 196, 203, 218n16, 240, 243, 253
Old City, 30, 175, 177, 203, 258
On the Wings of the Raga Indian Music Days, 30
Operation Agatha, 85
Organizing for Peace, 160, 167n65, 168n66
Ostrowiec, 32
Ottoman Empire, x
Ovid, vii
Oz, Amos, 260, 269n68

P

Pacific islands, 68
Pahlavi, Mohammad Reza, 160
Palestine, x–xiv, xviii$n$12, 2–3, 5–15, 18, 20, 23–25, 27–28, 41–44, 48–63, 65–70, 72, 75n9, 76n16, 76n19–20, 81–83, 85–89, 91–94, 96–103, 114, 121–125, 128–159, 169–179, 181–216, 218n16, 218n23, 219n25, 220n40, 220n47, 221n56, 222n62, 223n64, 224n70, 225n74, 227–232, 234–236, 238–247, 249–261, 263n7
Palestine and the United Nations: Prelude to Solution, 61, 78n32
Palestine civil war, 65, 68, 86, 128, 132, 154, 181, 235
Palestine Commission, 65–68, 78n42, 100, 121, 128, 131, 134, 137–138, 140, 144, 152, 154, 171, 174, 176, 182, 187, 189, 196–197, 199, 203, 226n82
Palestine Currency Board, 203
Palestine Electric Company, 263n2
Palestine Land Development Company, 227, 262n2
Palestine Land Transfers Regulations 1940, 53
Palestine Liberation Organization, 72
Palestine Mandate (articles 4, 6, 11, 13, 14, and 28), 55, 69, 76n20, 141, 220n40
Palestine Mandate, 41, 44, 50–54, 57–58, 122, 124, 142, 146, 157, 193, 195
Palestine partition. *See* partition of Palestine
Palestine Pavilion, 82, 115n2
Palestine Post, 217n12, 219n33, 222n62, 226n82, 231, 236
Palestine Potash Ltd, 262n2
Palestine provisional governments. *See* provisional government for Palestine
Palestine sterling balances blocked, 189
Palestine Triangle, 13, 243
Palestinian Jews in the British Army, 134–135

"The Palestine Problem for Americans," 132
Paris meetings endorse partition, 11–12
Paris Peace Conference 1919, 143
Paris Peace Conference 1946, 49
Parodi, Alexandre, 178–180, 185, 192, 198, 203, 205, 208, 250
partition of Palestine, x, xii, 2, 5–11, 13–14, 16–18, 20, 22–23, 25–26, 29, 57, 59, 61, 63, 65, 68–69, 77n26, 86, 88, 95–97, 101–102, 121–123, 128, 129–159, 161, 162n2, 166n49, 166n58, 169–174, 176, 179–180, 182, 184–185, 188–190, 192–194, 196–202, 204, 208–211, 216n2, 217n10, 223n65, 224n68, 228, 230, 232–236, 239–240, 242–245, 250, 253, 255, 259–260
Patterson, Robert, 84
Paul, Randolph E., 108
Pazner, Chaim. *See* Posner, Chaim
Peace by Power, 163n12
Peace Planning Committee, 43
Pearl Harbor, 126, 230
Pearlstein, Harris, 94
Pearson, Lester B., xviii$n$12, 178
Peel Commission, 55, 77n23, 77n26, 193, 228
Peres, Shimon, 34n8
Perlman, Nathan, 44
Perlzweig, Maurice, 44
Permanent Court of International Justice, 42
Petain, Philippe, 17, 35n12
Petzold, Christian, xix$n$13
Philby, H. St. John, 258
Phoenicia, xv$n$1
phoenix, vii–viii, xiii, xv, xv$n$1, xvi$n$2–3
Phoenix film, xix$n$13
Piekarz, 28
Pinkerton, Lowell, 230
Pioneer Women, 85
Poale Zion, 7, 10–11, 19
Poland and restitution to survivors, 31, 39n53
Policy Planning Staff, 138, 169
Political Union in Palestine, 250
Pope Benedict XVI, 32
Pope Pius XII, 98, 221n57
Pope, James P., 147, 151, 155, 165n44, 166n56
Popular Front for the Liberation of Palestine, 72
Posner, Chaim, 103, 118n38
Potsdam Conference, 53, 83, 112, 144
Price, Byron, 173
Proskauer, Joseph M., 138, 142–143, 165n34–36, 166n49, 201–202, 204–205, 210, 221n56–57, 222n60, 222n62, 244, 247, 256, 266n35
Protocols of the Elders of Zion, xv, 167n60

provisional government for Palestine, 63, 68, 70, 103, 105, 118n39, 138, 148, 154, 194, 205, 208, 225n74, 243
Psalm 126, xvin4

Q
Quarantine speech, 126
Quisling, 265n21

R
Rabbi Binyamin, 229
Rabinowicz, Oskar K., xviin6
Radler-Feldman, Yehoshua. *See* Rabbi Binyamin
Rafael, Gideon. *See* Ruffer, Gideon
Rajistan, 59
Ramat Yohanan, 103
Ramleh, 107, 253
Rappard, William E., 56, 77n26
Rashi, viii
Reagan, Ronald, 31
Reconsiderations, xviin5
Rehavya, 258
Rehovot, 23, 37n40, 75n9
Reisman, David, 250
Remez, David, 20–21, 38n45, 216
Reparations Agreement, 71
reparations, 43
Resolution 181 (II), 138, 169, 174, 176, 185, 193, 198
Retter, Leon, 28
Revisionist Party, 3, 26
Revisionist Zionist, 232
Riftin, Yitshak, 10
Rise of Anglo-American Friendship, The, 163n12
Robert College, 134
Robinson, Jacob, xiv, 40–73, 73n3, 74n4–8, 75n9–11, 76n16–18, 77n23–29, 78n30–41, 79n47, 79n52, 80n54, 202, 218n23, 221n57
Robinson, Nehemiah, 43, 72, 73n3
Roman Legions, ix
Rome, xvin4, 112
Rommel, Edwin, 229
Roosevelt, Belle, 147, 149, 153, 155–156, 165n42
Roosevelt, Eleanor, 97, 100, 106–107, 111, 146, 151, 159–160, 166n58, 215, 231
Roosevelt, Franklin D., 82–83, 126, 129, 164n23
Roosevelt, Jr., Kermit, 133–134, 139–140, 143, 160, 164n19, 167n64, 238
Rosen, Pinhas. *See* Rosenbleuth, Felix
Rosenbleuth, Felix, 8
Rosenheim, Jacob, 239, 265n25
Rosenman, Samuel, 122, 170, 192, 198, 200, 247
Rosenne, Shabtai, 73, 74n5, 80n54

Rosensaft, Joseph, 82
Rosensaft, Menahem, 31
Rosenwald, Lessing, 139, 145, 158, 167n60, 239, 243, 252, 265n25
Rosenwald, William, 82, 94, 99, 111
Ross, John C., 192, 208
Rostow, Eugene V., 67, 239, 265n25
Rotenstreich, Natan, xviiin10
Rothberg, Sam, 82, 98–99, 109, 112, 115n3, 120n55
Rothenberg, Morris, 256
Rothschild, Edouard de, 192
Rousseau, Jean-Jacques, xviiin10
Rowling, J.K., vii
Royal Institute of International Affairs, 230
Rubashov, Zalman, 17
Rubinstein, Reubeen, 3
Ruffer, Gideon, 100, 117n33
Ruppin, Arthur, 227, 258
Rusk, Dean, 68, 135–136, 138, 159, 164n23, 164n27, 178–179, 186–187, 191, 201–209, 211, 214, 217n11, 217n14, 219n28–29, 220n42, 221n56, 222n58, 223n64, 224n70, 225n73, 246–247, 266n35
Rutenberg, Pinhas, 263n2

S
Sacks, Jonathan, xviin6
"Sacred Cow," 209, 246
Sadat, Anwar, xvin4
Samuel, Herbert, 228
Samuel, Maurice, xviin6, 37n40, 39n51
San Francisco, 40, 43–44, 50, 58, 61, 73n1, 127–128, 132, 141
San Remo Conference, 76n20
San Remo Declaration, 146
Sandler, Rickhard, 62
Sanhedrin, viii, xvin2
Sasson, Eliyahu, 201, 217n10, 218n19, 221n55
Satyagraha, 269n70
Saudi Arabia, 41, 78n41, 134, 167n64, 206, 208, 230
Sayre, Francis B., 198, 224n69
Schindler, Oskar, 4, 32
"Schindler's List," 32
Schneerson, Menachem Mendel, xvin3
Scholem, Gershom, 227, 258, 260, 268n63, 269n67
Schutz, Lillie, 265n27
Schwartz, Joseph J., 109, 111–112
Sears, Roebuck and Company, 139
Security Council, 60, 62–63, 67–68, 96, 100, 102, 121, 128–130, 133–134, 136, 138–139,

— 281 —

141, 143, 148, 151, 153–154, 169, 172–174, 178–179, 181, 183, 187–189, 193–196, 198–205, 207–208, 211, 216*n*1, 221*n*56, 222*n*62, 238, 249
Selassie, Haile, 164*n*23
self-determination, xiii, 41, 53–54, 77*n*21, 134
Senator, David W., 236, 238
Sh'eirit HaPleita, 3, 9, 27–29
Shakespeare, vii
Shapiro, Moshe, 8
Sharett, Moshe. *See* Shertok, Moshe
Shaw, George B., vii
Shazar, Zalman. *See* Rubashov, Zalman
Shearith Israel Congregation, 255
Shertok, Moshe, 5, 8, 10–11, 16–17, 19, 21–23, 25–26, 36*n*18, 50–51, 66, 68–69, 76*n*15, 78*n*40, 79*n*47, 82, 84–85, 93, 100–101, 103, 116*n*11, 129, 159, 163*n*12, 167*n*16, 170–175, 180–188, 190, 194, 196–197, 201–207, 209–210, 213, 216*n*3, 217*n*6-7, 217*n*10, 217*n*14, 218*n*19-20, 219*n*26, 220*n*40, 220*n*46, 221*n*55, 221*n*57, 222*n*58, 222*n*60-61, 223*n*63, 224*n*70, 225*n*73, 228, 230, 232, 244, 246–247, 263*n*7, 266*n*35
Shoah, xiii, 1, 20, 33, 72, 261
Shotwell, James T., 125, 127, 156
Shukairy, Ahmed, 216
Shumsky, Dmitry, 262, 262*n*2, 269*n*71
Silver, Abba Hillel, 2, 4–5, 7–8, 11–15, 18–27, 34*n*6-7, 38*n*42, 68, 77*n*29, 106, 187, 190, 199, 206, 214, 225*n*76, 239, 247, 251, 256, 266*n*35
Simchat Torah, 107
Simon, Ernst, 146, 218*n*18, 229, 232–233, 236, 238–239, 242, 264*n*10, 264*n*20, 265*n*21, 265*n*23-26
Sinai Campaign, xix*n*14, 110
Sinai Pact, 31
Six-Day War, xv, 167*n*63
Skolnik, Levi. *See* Eshkol
Slomovitz, Philip, 180
Smilansky, Moshe, 229, 232, 262*n*2
Smith, Gerald L.K., 158, 167*n*60, 185, 192
Smith, Trafford, 185, 192
Sneh, Moshe, 4, 8, 10–12, 15, 18–19, 21–22, 34*n*6-7, 37*n*32
Soloveitchik, Joseph B., ix, xvii*n*6
Sonneborn Institute, 82
South Tyrol, 54
Soviet government on Palestine, 110
Soviet Press on Zionism, 77*n*27
Soviet support for partition, 135

Special Committee to Investigate the National Defense Program, 210
Spielberg, Steven, 32
Sprinzak, Yosef, 5, 21
Standard Oil Company of New Jersey, 191
Standard Oil of California, 78*n*41, 167*n*64
State Department, 7, 35*n*10, 35*n*12, 38*n*47, 67–68, 82–84, 87, 115*n*7, 122, 125–126, 132, 135, 140, 143, 157, 159, 186, 190, 194, 200, 202, 205, 209–211, 215, 217*n*11, 217*n*14, 219*n*32, 221*n*52, 229, 239, 245–247, 249, 255, 263*n*7, 266*n*33
Statute of Jerusalem, 193
Stavropoulos, Constantin A., 65–66, 174
Steinberg, Isaac N., 238
Stern group, 10, 27, 233, 253
Stern, Edgar, 84
Stern, Gavriel, 229, 269*n*69
Stern, Horace, 243
Stroock, Alan, 240
Study of History, A, xvii*n*5
Stutthof, 29
Sudetenland, 54, 122
Suez Canal, 229
sultan of Morocco, 161
Sultanik family, 39*n*51
Sultanik, Kalman, 3–4, 28–33, 38*n*49-50, 39*n*51, 39*n*54-55, 39*n*58
Sulzberger, Arthur Hays, 162*n*2, 209–210, 218*n*18, 224*n*71, 228–229, 234, 264*n*15, 266*n*38
Syria, xv, 41, 61, 65, 107, 123, 178, 208
Szold, Henrietta, 229

T
t'chiyat hameitim, viii
Tabenkin, 2, 8
Taft, Robert, 145, 265*n*25
Tagore, Rabindranath, 77*n*29
Taha, Sami, 232, 259
Tal Shahar, 114
Talmon, Jacob L., xvii*n*6
Talmud burning, xvi*n*4
Talpiyot, 206
Taylor, Telford, 75*n*10
Tel Aviv, 14, 70, 85–89, 100, 102–104, 119*n*46, 122, 176, 195, 208, 213, 215, 220*n*43
Temple Emanu-El, 111, 227, 256
"Ten Days of Decision," 99
Tennessee Valley Authority, 147
tenuat hameri, 4
Texaco, 78*n*41, 167*n*64
Theodor Herzl Foundation, 29

Theresienstadt ghetto, 4, 244
Third Jewish Commonwealth, xv
Third Reich, 73n3, 114n1, 164n23
Thomas, Elbert D., 129
Thompson, Kenneth W., xviin6
Tiberias, 103, 200
Tish'a B'Av, xv, xvin4
Tito, Josip Broz, 65
Toff, Moshe, 65
Torczyner, Jacques, 4, 34n6–7
Tov, Moshe. *See* Toff, Moshe
Toynbee, Arnold J., ix–xii, xv, xviin5–6, xviin9
Trager, David, 3, 9, 27–28
transfer solutions, 263n3
Transjordan, 13, 69, 88, 161, 175, 183, 200–201, 253
Transylvania, 54
"Tree of Life," viiin3, xvin3
Trieste, 60, 124, 144
Troops to Palestine, 35n12, 170, 199, 202, 212, 216, 219n31
truce for Palestine, xiv, 17, 69, 103, 122, 152–154, 156–157, 169–176, 178, 180–192, 194–211, 218n18, 220n43, 221n56, 222n60, 222n62, 223n64, 224n69, 224n70, 225n73, 238, 240–247, 249–250
Truman Doctrine, 148
Truman, Harry S., xiv, 6–7, 27, 40, 45, 49, 51, 68, 83–84, 99, 104–105, 108–110, 112, 115n7, 118n43, 119n54, 122, 124–125, 131, 146, 148, 156–157, 159–161, 162n6, 166n58, 170, 180, 186, 190–192, 196, 198, 200, 206, 209–215, 216n2, 223n65, 225n74, 226n79–80, 240–241, 244, 246–248, 256
Trusteeship Committee, 198
Trusteeship Council, 57, 60, 62, 121, 134, 179, 198, 203, 205, 207–208, 217n7, 236, 244
Trusteeship for Palestine, xiv, 68, 78n30, 121, 145, 169–216, 239
Trusteeship, 24, 41, 56–57, 59–60, 68–69, 102, 122–124, 127, 131, 139, 146, 150–152, 154, 170–183, 185–187, 190, 192–195, 197–201, 203, 205–209, 211–213, 215, 218n18, 220n40, 222n62, 224n68–69, 230, 239–241, 243–246, 248, 253–255
Tsarapkin, Semyon K., 65, 208
Tsiang, Tingfu, 178, 208
Tuck, Pinkney, 181, 221n55
Tulkarm, 243
Turkey, 107, 148, 151, 202
Tyre, xvin1

U
Udell, Mrs. Jerome I., 97
Ueberall, Ehud. *See* Avriel
Ulloa, Alberto, 62
UN Charter (Articles 2, 10, 11, 14, 24, 37, 39, 40, 52, 76, 79, 80, 81), 41, 51, 53, 58–59, 62, 128, 136, 141, 150, 169, 178
UN Charter, 40, 44, 52, 55, 57, 70, 124–125, 131, 140, 143, 145, 149, 184, 193, 236, 245
UN Conference on International Organization, 127
UN created in San Francisco, 40
UN Economic and Social Council, 148
UN Human Rights Commission, 146, 160
"The U.N. is My Beat," 128
UN Mediator, 161, 212, 214–215, 250–251
UN resolution on Zionism and racism, 79n53, 174
Union of Hebrew Congregations, 138
United Israel Appeal, 30, 106
United Jewish Appeal, 49, 81, 85–86, 94, 166n49
United Nations Association of the U.S.A., 161
United Nations Special Committee on Palestine (UNSCOP), 28, 51, 53–54, 56–57, 60–62, 64, 67, 76n19, 171–172, 190, 193, 199, 231–232, 234, 253, 259
United Palestine Appeal, 81
United States Holocaust Memorial Council, 30
United States of Palestine, 250, 254
United Zionist Federation of Germany, 3
Universal Jewish Encyclopedia, 74n7
University of Chicago, 133, 146
UNSCOP. *See* United Nations Special Committee on Palestine (UNSCOP)
Unzer Veg, 3
Upper Galilee, 100, 207
Upper Silesia, 42, 73n3
US Articles of Confederation, 254
US election platforms on Palestine – 1944, 7
US Holocaust Memorial Museum, 31, 34n5, 74n4
US Selective Service recruitment law, 216n2
US state legislatures pro-Zionism, 7
Ussishkin, Menahem, 37n40

V
Va'ad HaLeumi, 103, 176
Va'ad HaPoel HaTsiyoni, 265n25
Valero, A., 229
Vandenberg, Arthur, 180
Vichy, 7, 35n12

Vilfan, Joza, 65
Vilna, 42, 116n15

W

Wadsworth, George, 123
Wagner, Robert F., 129
Walesa, Lech, 30
War Department, 66, 87, 169
War Emergency Conference, 43
War Refugee Board, 83
Warburg, Edward, 95, 99, 104, 249, 252, 256, 267n44
Warburg, Felix, 228
Washington Post, 71, 79n51, 156, 159, 166n58
Wasson, Thomas C., 209, 218n18, 241
Wehrmacht, 35n12, 228
Weisgal, Meyer, 17–18, 36n26, 81–83, 226n81
Weizmann, Chaim, 2, 4–6, 8–12, 14–26, 33, 36n25, 37n40–41, 46, 75n9, 82–83, 94, 109, 112, 122, 159, 166n58, 170, 190–192, 198, 200, 213–214, 216, 219n36, 222n60, 226n81, 231, 239, 247–248, 268n62
Welles, Sumner, 62, 126–127, 129, 135, 147, 150–151, 164n22, 165n44, 225n74
Weltsch, Robert, 23, 37n41, 239, 265n25
Welty, Eudora, vii
Western Wall, xv
White Paper, 1939, 6, 16, 18, 27, 51, 59, 75n9, 76n16, 179, 184, 199, 202, 219n25, 230, 263n7
Wiesel, Elie, 31, 39n54
Wilkins, Fraser, 211, 226n78
Wilson, John A., 133
Wilson, Mrs. Woodrow, 214
Wilson, Woodrow, 127, 192
Wise, Stephen, 2, 13, 20, 22–23, 36n23, 37n40–41, 229, 255
Wisliceny, Dieter, 46
World Confederation of General Zionists, 2, 29
World Federation of the United Nations Association, 128
World Jewish Congress, 30, 32, 41–42, 74n6
World Zionist Congress, 1946, xiv, 1, 3–4, 11, 20, 28–29, 33, 239
World Zionist meeting 1945, 13
World Zionist Organization, 2, 38n50, 55, 82, 85, 122, 170, 231
World's Fair, 82, 115n2
Wright, Quincy, 146–147, 149–153, 164n20, 165n42, 165n48, 166n50–51
Wright, Walter L., 133–134

Y

Yad Vashem, 71, 79n52
Yaffe, 28
Yalta Conference, 53
Yediot Acharonot, 17, 21, 36n29
Yehiam, 89, 102, 149
Yeshiva University, x
yishuv, xiii, 2, 4, 6–8, 10–14, 16–17, 20, 22, 25–28, 41, 50, 68, 81–82, 85–88, 90–95, 98–102, 105, 113, 115n2, 118n42, 123, 128, 130, 137, 171, 174–176, 180–181, 183, 189–190, 192, 194, 196–197, 202, 205, 228–229, 231–232, 242–243, 248–249, 259, 261, 262n2
Yitshak Tabenkin, 2
YIVO Institute for Jewish Research, 72
Yosef, Dov, 10
Youth Aliya, 55, 87, 161
Yugoslavia, 42, 44, 48–49, 60, 65, 136, 144

Z

Zabrze, 4
Zeilsheim, 27
Zeitlin, Solomon, xviin6
Zerubavel, Ya'akov, 10
Ziff, William, 12
"Zionism is a form of racism and racial discrimination," 72
Zionist General Council, 29, 69
Zionist Organization of America, 2, 4, 13, 18, 24, 35n13, 36n22, 95, 106, 110
Zionist thesis, xiii
Zisling, Aharon, 10
ZOA. *See* Zionist Organization of America

www.ingramcontent.com/pod-product-compliance
Lightning Source LLC
Chambersburg PA
CBHW051111230426
43667CB00014B/2528